A Miscellany of
American Christianity

Barber, *Hendersonville*

A Miscellany of
American Christianity

ESSAYS IN HONOR OF
H. SHELTON SMITH

edited by

STUART C. HENRY

DUKE UNIVERSITY PRESS
Durham, North Carolina
1963

© 1963, Duke University Press

Library of Congress Catalogue Card number 63–14288

Cambridge University Press, London N.W.1, England

Printed in the United States of America
by Kingsport Press, Inc., Kingsport, Tenn.

Preface

Included here are essays by present and former colleagues of Professor Smith, and by students whose research he directed or whose progress he guided while he was Director of Graduate Studies in Religion at Duke University. In every case the choice of essay represents a special connection with the study of American Christianity at Duke University, and H. Shelton Smith's identification with this discipline.

The immediate reaction of those asked to contribute to this volume was uniformly twofold: all were enthusiastic to have a part in an endeavor which seemed eminently worthy, and each was hesitant to offer an essay as adequate for the projected work. All the writers know Professor Smith well and hold him in such warm regard that the desire to honor him overcame resistance.

The preparation and publication of this volume would not have been possible without encouragement and help from more sources than, regretfully, can here be designated. Specific mention, however, is made of those to whom special thanks are due. Professor Robert E. Cushman, Dean of the Divinity School of Duke University, and Professor Waldo Beach, Director of Graduate Studies in Religion, provided guidance and endorsement when the project was initiated. Publication was assured through support and subsidy of the Gurney Harriss Kearns Foundation and the Duke University Press.

At every stage of endeavor the staff of the Duke University Press has given imaginative co-operation, and gracious assistance beyond any that contributors or editor would have expected. Mr. Ashbel G. Brice, Director, and Mr. John Menapace, Production Manager, have—from the first—been unfailingly helpful, anticipating necessity, and meeting every need. Mr. Robert Mirandon, assistant editor, rendered vital service at a crucial time. The late William Owens granted special consideration. Mr. Larry McMullen contributed ability and fidelity in bringing the volume to press. Mr. Timothy Goodman assisted in reading proof.

In their several ways Mesdames Janice H. Choate, Lessie L. Detwiler, Joyce Lockhart Farris, and Mary M. Salter made it possible to meet deadlines with manuscript copy. Particular appreciation must go to Mrs. Anne Moorman Bell, who worked with cheerful and efficient diligence in typing most of these essays in the form they here present.

Finally, sincere gratitude is expressed to Professor Donn Michael Farris, Librarian, Divinity School, Duke University, who gave characteristically sage counsel, and to Professors Barney L. Jones and McMurry S. Richey of Duke University, and Professor H. Burnell Pannill of Randolph-Macon College, members of a special committee who worked gladly when they were asked, and stood ever ready to do more.

Appreciation for all here mentioned, and for many whom circumstance does not allow to signify by name, is sincere and deep.

S. C. H.

Contents

A Miscellany of
Amerian Christianity

H. Shelton Smith: An Appreciative Memoir

ALBERT C. OUTLER

"Greatness," as Phillips Brooks once said, "in spite of its name, appears not so much a certain size as a certain quality in human lives." This quality, where we can recognize it, is a function of a man's actualization of truly significant goals. High aspirations do not suffice for greatness, nor does the achievement of the commonplace. Those only are great who put their talent to its fullest use. Ability is prerequisite and vision is necessary, but it is a man's total, cumulative impact that counts at the end of the day.

It is only now, when Shelton Smith has lived to see at least three of his main goals achieved, that the rest of us may fully recognize in retrospect the quality of greatness in his life. It was not always so apparent, as his older friends can testify. All of us have memories of hazardous passages in his career when his ventures seemed in jeopardy, when clearer heads than his could calculate the odds against his hopes and come up with the reluctant judgment that what he was attempting was most unlikely.

Take, for example, the goal which he set for himself a full generation ago: of developing a truly respectable doctoral program in religion in a Southern university, where none was nor ever had been. He managed to bring that off, as everyone now knows. But what many may not know is how nearly impossible it seemed *in prospect*—against opposition in the university, indifference in the region, and something less than enthusiastic support from some of his colleagues.

Or, again, it is worth trying to imagine what it was like, three decades ago, to work at the beginnings of an effective program of ecumenical study and action in an environment where militant denominationalism was thought to stand in the course of nature. Today, the ecumenical outlook is nearly normal in North Carolina, but the veterans of the Council of Churches there will tell you of Shelton Smith's services as its architect and engineer in its formative years. *Mutatis mutandis,* the academic study of religion at Duke is now no more denominational than is the study of economics or political theory—and this in a university nominally related to the Methodist Church. Shelton Smith was determined that it should be so and would not rest until it was.

His third great undertaking, as I have come to reckon his purposes in life, was to establish the study of American Christianity as a major academic field in its own right—freed from its satellite status in relation to European church history and ballasted with the appropriate concerns of both historiography and theology. He began his work on this project in a day when such an aspiration was a rarity and when the primary sources for such a study were neither organized nor accessible for scholarly use. Now, thirty years later, we can recognize the central place which American church history has had in the curriculum at Duke—and we can cite the publication of *American Christianity* (a unique source book which Prof. Smith has edited, in collaboration with Profs. Robert T. Handy and Lefferts A. Loetscher). But the most impressive evidence of how nearly he achieved his aspirations in this field comes from the score of able young protégés of his who are now teaching and studying in colleges and universities over the country.

Thus, in his lifetime, Shelton Smith has seen at least some of his dreams come true before his eyes and under his hands. He would be the first to reproach me for implying that he was altogether unique in these concerns—and I make no such suggestion. But two things I do remember: he was dreaming while many another was deep asleep; and he persisted when

many another faltered or turned aside. It has not been given
to many men whom I have known to come as near as he has to
the sight of what he dreamed might be.

Looking backwards, I can now recall that my first encounter
with him was a typical example of his way with students and
colleagues—for I was subsequently to discover that it was his
way to treat his students as colleagues. Our first meeting was
at a Methodist Pastors' School in Macon, Georgia, in the grim
depression summer of 1934. Dr. Smith was one of the instruc-
tors in the school—come lately to Duke from Yale and still
trailing some of the splendor I then ascribed to faraway places.
I was a young circuit rider out in the hill country from Macon,
with a freshly minted seminary degree from Emory, still
eager for theological fireworks. By the canons of expectation in
such groups, a good lecturer was supposed to be eloquent or inspiring. Professor Smith's lectures were articulate enough but
they were not really "eloquent"; and he seemed almost de-
liberately to stifle emotional response. If I had known more of
his background at the time, I might have realized that his recent studies in the phenomena of American revivalism had
given him so unfavorable a view of its latter-day degeneration
into emotionalism that he was wary of all pietists and their
spiritual offspring.

Nevertheless, his class sessions were curiously exciting—intense, provocative, occasionally outrageous. Indeed, he had a
reckless way of flouting the commonplace that finally overcame
my sense of academic propriety (as defined in the code of
manners I had been bred to). To my own surprise—and the
disapproval of my elders—I found myself *arguing with the
professor in class.* As all good Southerners of that vintage know,
it was standard procedure to attack one's professors in private,
but good form demanded that one keep the peace in public. It
might well be that this lapse in academic etiquette played a
decisive part in the shifting of my career from its well-
charted course in the pastoral ministry over to the doubtful
fortunes of my work as a scholar-teacher. For, instead of repelling my upstart comments, Professor Smith seemed delighted

to have provoked a critical reaction. What was even more amazing, he proceeded to make sense out of what I said and to deal with it seriously. Afterwards, he looked me up, drew me out, told me of his vision of a graduate program at Duke, and managed to lodge in my head the preposterous notion that I had the makings of a scholar.

The following summer he came back to the same school and the same sort of intellectual ferment began to stir again. Here was a man—the first I had known quite like him—whose chief business in life was to barter ideas. He was always at it, too: at table, on the golf course, in the swimming pool—anywhere. His mind was as lanky and as tireless as his body, and this made theological discussion with him strenuous and demanding. In all these different ways he made theology seem to be the proper business of every thoughtful Christian and he made me feel that I was a full partner in the dialogue. These experiences were enough to overcome my hesitation and self-doubt; from them came the courage to weigh anchor and set sail for graduate school.

Wisely or unwisely, I chose to go to Yale instead of Duke and to major in patristics instead of American church history. No matter; Professor Smith continued to be as interested in my career as he was in those of his students at Duke. Whenever we met, I had to give him an accounting of my academic stewardship; and he would always prod me with a question that probed the weakest spot in any thesis I might be propounding. In the spring of my dissertation-year at Yale, I was appointed to the Duke faculty as instructor in historical theology. I have always supposed that this was largely Shelton Smith's doing (although he would never assume either credit or blame for it). At any rate, it was under these circumstances that I had the privilege of serving as his colleague for seven years.

Working with Shelton Smith, as others also will testify, was something like enjoying the best features of the life of a graduate student plus the satisfactions and responsibilities of the professional educator. His daily meat and drink was hard study and good talk. Wherever he was and whoever was about, this is what he would be doing—unless some ceremony enjoined silence. Even then you could suspect that he was ransoming the time with his own ruminations. He had little time for small talk and no time at all for clichés. The wonder of it was that this sort of thing went on without his dominating the group. Brilliant conversationalists are rare and valuable birds. But there is an even rarer sub-species:—the brilliant *listener,* who challenges another's mind by hearing him and asking the right questions.

> Yet he was kind; and if severe in aught,
> The love he bore to learning was at fault.

Professor Smith was born to teach. His mind has a sort of inexhaustible vitality, and I have never seen it unemployed. For example, he liked to bowl at duckpins, and we tried to manage a weekly session. Even after twenty years, I have vivid memories of his arching the ball and then being seized in mid-air by a comment. He would stop, swing round and deliver himself—with the poor pin-boy at the other end of the alley still waiting in baffled wonder. Our wives encouraged us to play golf —whether for our good or theirs they would not say. It was not a game worth watching, but it might have been interesting to overhear. I have seen him halt a backswing—his or mine— when a fascinating notion had occurred to him. He and Harvie Branscomb and I used to bring our lunches to eat together under the pines behind the Chapel. Those sandwiches, plus the talk that flowed, made far richer fare than any banquet. Professor Smith organized a group of ministers and faculty members into a weekly luncheon group that was promptly dubbed "The Wranglers." It was the only group of its kind I have ever known in which serious theological discussion consistently pushed clerical jokes and gossip into the background. Even his "evenings at home," though wonderfully hospitable and pleasant, were still strenuous. The wonder to me was that a man could be so constantly in dead earnest and yet never deadly, so relentless in critical inquiry and yet so richly human and helpful. It was nothing that I could imitate myself—but from it I learned more about inquiry as "a way of life" than I had ever known before.

This wonderful talker and listener was also a man of shrewd and effective action. I have already mentioned that his fondest dream was to have a graduate department of religion at Duke equal to the best in the country. The obstacles to any such development were, in my judgment, insuperable. They ranged the gamut from insufficient funds, through the tangled thicket of political tensions in the university, to the ill-concealed prejudice in some quarters that religion was not a respectable academic discipline. Shelton had itemized these difficulties as realistically as any of the rest of us, but he seemed to weigh them in a different scale. He was as tough-minded in practical affairs as he was lavish with his ideas. He would not be discouraged; he would not retreat; and he has never really changed his basic aims in all the thirty years that I have known him. It would be a story well worth telling how, almost singlehanded, he found and cultivated the resources which, as they have now accumulated, make the present graduate department of religion at Duke one of the country's best endowed. The most exciting chapter of the story would be the development of the Gurney Harriss Kearns Foundation. Yet another chapter would interpret the ways in which he resolved and reconciled the complex relationships between the department of religion in the Graduate School, the undergraduate department of religion in Trinity College, and the Divinity School. Still another chapter would tell how he attracted top-flight students, how he guided their work, helped them in job hunting, and continued to follow them as they put their training to the service of sound learning in American higher education.

Seven years at Duke with Shelton Smith also gave me my first really significant orientation in the ecumenical movement. I had known about it, of course, but I had never really seen it in action at close range. The Protestant churches of North Carolina were then in the early stages of their first serious experiments in interdenominational co-operation—although, naturally enough, they preferred to conceive this in terms of "life and work" rather than risk the painful struggles that accompany the issues of "faith and order." Smith was a member of the Executive Committee of the State Council and presently enlisted me in the program. It was in this connection that I came to know him as a churchman, and, as usual, this experience with him forced upon me a critical revision of some of my preconceived notions. By title, he was a Congregationalist; but presently I learned that his remoter background lay in the tradition of those O'Kelly-ite "Christians," in Virginia and North Carolina, who traced their origins back to James O'Kelly in his revolt against the monarchical policies of Francis Asbury and the "clericalism" of the Methodist Episcopal Church. As a dutiful son of Episcopal Methodism, I had been taught that the O'Kelly-ites and their like were ructious schismatics. Smith had actually gone to their college: Elon, B.A., 1917. What I had never realized before was how deeply the democratic, laic temper of American free church Protestantism (Smith's tradition) had been in conflict with the organic polities of episcopal or synodical church government (such as mine). We had many a rousing argument about the respective claims of freedom and authority in the Christian community. I have sometimes feared that Professor Smith will never in this life learn the real meaning of organic unity or catholicity—but, even so, he has already put many of us in his debt by depriving us of the easy alternative of confusing the meaning of Christian unity with any notion of a linear evolution of the historically established churches toward oneness. Thus, gradually, I came to be able to understand his ecumenical perspective: Christians must seek real unity in worship and work, but, since ecclesiastical power corrupts as surely as any other, it must be dispersed and balanced if it is to be bearable.

In the decade of the thirties it was difficult even for those of us who knew him to get a clear view of Professor Smith's theological position. Not everyone now remembers that he was then a professor of religious education. This had been the field of his Yale doctorate (1923). He had begun his intellectual majority as a disciple of John Dewey, George Albert Coe, and Luther A. Weigle. He had served a stint as director of Leadership Education in the International Council of Religious Education (1923–1928); he had taught at Teachers' College (1928–1929); he had moved from Columbia to Yale for two years before coming to Duke in 1931. In the course of these shifts he had published very little. The first thing of his I can recall reading was an admonition to religious educators that they should forthwith begin to reckon with the new theology of Karl Barth and its growing influence in America—this in 1934. What actually was happening was that he was deep in a thoroughgoing examination of the premises and presuppositions of the religious education movement in America. This movement, as everyone now knows, having dominated the American theological scene in the twenties, had begun to falter in the thirties, and would stumble before the shocks and disenchantment of the forties.

The first reaction of many of its spokesmen was defensive and refluent. But Smith was still enough of a disciple of John Dewey to raise the pragmatic question as to why the program was not working its magic as before. His efforts to answer this question led him in two new directions at once. One of them was a canvass of the theological criticisms then being leveled at liberal theology—criticisms then conveniently lumped together under the single, misleading label, "neo-orthodoxy." The other direction of his inquiry led him back into the history of Christianity in America. Religious education was a uniquely American phenomenon, and if it was to be rightly judged, this had to be done from within the American perspective—rather than in the terms of the incommensurable dimensions of European and American church life. It was his interest in making this kind of valid judgment that led him to take up the history of American religious thought as a professional enterprise. There was one time when Professor Smith was teaching courses in religious education, in Christian ethics, and in American religious thought, all in the same curriculum—"a farm rather than a field," as he commented. There were those who supposed that this shifting of fields meant an abandoning of his original discipline. Actually, it was rather more of a drastic rearrangement of the original co-ordinates of his theological concern. Religious education, he had become convinced, needed a basic critique. It also deserved an ampler setting in the context of American church history. The first was called for by the rising storm of criticism directed against Enlightenment theology and all its works—with religious education being its most conspicuous "work" in America. The second project, however, opened the door into what has turned out to be his major scholarly service: the reconstruction of American *church* history.

Faith and Nurture (1941) represented the confluence of these two projects: theological criticism *and* historical reconstruction. On the one hand, it was a critical survey of the then current theologies, with special references to the problems of religious education. On the other hand, the footnotes record his new insights into the American past. It was a real dialogue between historical and contemporary theology. His first conclusion was:

> . . . that the thought-patterns of modern liberal religious nurture have largely exhausted their vitality, and that failure to reconstruct them in terms of a more adequate faith will ultimately result in the collapse, or at least the slow death, of the twentieth-century movement of religious education. (p. vii)

His positive purpose was:

> . . . to raise into sharp relief certain basic aspects of Christian faith which seem either to be ignored or else inadequately incorporated in the modern theory of liberal religious nurture. The central emphases of liberal faith are considered in their broad cultural contexts, and in terms of their long-time historic trends. Only from this perspective, it is believed, may one adequately comprehend the wider significance of the contemporary faith of Protestant nurture. (p. viii)

I have always been proud that my name appears in the preface to *Faith and Nurture*. It was Smith's first book—and my first preface. It signified my first close contact with a scholar whose working slogan seemed to be: "He who writes and throws away may live to be read another day." My memory is blurred as to how many drafts and versions of various parts of that manuscript I read. But I do recall my heady amazement at how seriously the older scholar would take the criticisms and suggestions offered by a younger one.

The book raised a considerable hue and cry in theological circles generally, but particularly amongst the partisans on the two extremes. There were liberals and fundamentalists alike who saw in it a repudiation of the religious education movement in general. The liberals deplored what they could only construe as apostasy; the fundamentalists took the "elder brother's" attitude toward a penitent prodigal. The majority verdict on the book, naturally enough, ran to the effect that it was a timely and significant reappraisal of the religious education movement, in the light of the newer emphases in the then contemporary theologies. Most reviewers agreed, however, that a final verdict should be withheld until Smith produced a "sequel" —that is, his own alternative, constructive theory of Christian nurture.

It was generally agreed that a radically new beginning in the field of pedagogic theory was long overdue, and there was now a lively hope in some quarters that Professor Smith was the man who could get this started. It took a while, therefore, for some of us to realize that the experience of writing *Faith and Nurture* had effected a decisive redirection of his scholarly interests and, consequently, his future academic program. When he had begun the book some years before, he had had no more than an amateur's interest in the experience of Christianity in American life. As his study proceeded, however, he had turned almost instinctively to the sources of American Christianity as background for his contemporary evaluations. In these sources he had found a bill of indictment against religious education on its own terms—that is to say, in its doctrines of anthropology and social ethics. He had discovered that, in its beginnings, the "social gospel" had emerged from the evangelical, christocentric tradition of American Protestantism. This gave him a new perspective on the modernist-fundamentalist controversy—in which he could criticize both parties in good conscience, as aberrations of their respective prototypes in American Christianity.

In the course of this review, he came to be more and more dismayed by the mounting evidence that American *church* history was something of an academic orphan. The vast majority of the students of "general" American history were happily incompetent in matters theological. At the same time, however, it became plain that most American church historians were either denominational partisans, or else bland neutralists. It was not surprising, therefore, that the familiar stereotypes in the so-called textbooks did not square with the primary sources to which they occasionally referred. This realization reinforced Smith's determination to get back to the texts themselves—and to make them readily accessible to students. There followed many a tedious hour in many a neglected volume; and many a substantial accession to the Americana section of the Duke library. I remember thinking that he found in the Niebuhrs and Tillich (not yet "famous" then) a sort of dramatic relief from the drudgery involved in his patient dissections of such stolid worthies as John Cotton, Samuel Hopkins, and Edwards A. Park. Even before the publication of *Faith and Nurture,* he had begun to work up the copious notes he had taken into a course on "Religion in the Rise of American Culture." This became his most popular and influential offering to the students.

Whatever the rest of us might have expected or desired, *Faith and Nurture* has had no sequel. Christian nurture still awaits its still needed theoretical re-evaluation. Smith might have contributed to this; I have a feeling that he had more than one occasional impulse to attempt it. What is certain is that he maintained his competence in the field together with an unwavering conviction that any theory of Christian nurture must be constructed within the compass of an adequate doctrine of the Christian church. But now, however, because he had come upon so vast and undeveloped a territory in American church history, so directly relevant to the needs of contemporary theology, it turned out that his first book in his first field was his last. *Faith and Nurture* must be set down as an official announcement of the close of the heyday of conventional religious education—plus an explanation of how it had come to be and why it was passing away.

As Shelton Smith began to concentrate on American Christianity, he found himself more and more engaged in editorial and exegetical reconstruction. He undertook to carry this enterprise forward—knowing full well how massive and complex a task it was. He enlisted a majority of his talented students in the business of quarrying out the building blocks of basic research in the field. For himself, he undertook to thread the maze of one of the most interesting puzzles in American Christianity—the history of the doctrine of original sin. Here, again, he had found a pivotal issue, a bone of contention between Enlightenment Christianity and classical Protestantism. Reflection upon the nature of human nature has been a perennial preoccupation with American theologians—and all their theories have had some measure of recognition of life's pathos and dark shadow. In the past two centuries, the prevailing views of man in America have shifted from the scholastic orthodoxies of the eighteenth century, through the Enlightenment enchantment with man's perfectibility, to an equal and opposite disenchantment proclaimed in the various versions of "neo-orthodoxy." It is not mere coincidence that Shelton Smith had recapitulated the successive stages of this doctrinal evolution in his own theological progress from youth to maturity. Thus he was working with familiar issues but not always in familiar material. Nevertheless, it took him nearly fifteen years to complete his study and publish the results: *Changing Conceptions of Original Sin; A Study in American Theology Since 1750* (1955).

There was a bit of by-play in connection with this book that throws further light on Shelton Smith's disinterested realism as a scholar. It is, of course, a natural impulse to conclude a historical survey with a constructive statement by the surveyor which purports to garner up the wisdom gained in the process. Several of us who saw the expository chapters of *Original Sin* strongly urged that they should have some such conclusion. Professor Smith quietly ignored us and published his book without a peroration. Afterwards, he explained that he had noticed that a historian's "conclusions" were often the first part of his work that became dated or even outdated. Here, again, he was right.

Meanwhile, he kept his students at work in various sectors of the field, aiding and supporting the renaissance of American church history. In the process, it became more obvious than ever that what now was needed, by students and teachers alike, was an adequate collection of source materials, properly edited. How can a teacher teach or students learn if all they have at hand are secondary sources, or partial selections from primary texts, arbitrarily selected? This is a problem in all historical studies but it was more acute in American church history because of the carry-over in it of those methodological premises which have dominated the study of European church history and the history of dogma. In this approach American Christianity has consistently gotten short shrift, as the tail end of the longer parade of ancient and European history. Moreover, it is consistently misleading to apply the interpretive patterns appropriate to the development of European Christianity to the American scene without due modification.

It was a milestone in his career when Professor Smith came at last to the point where he began to feel some confidence in his mapping of the field of American Christianity and began to plan the form and substance of his source book. This was, in many ways, his most formidable undertaking— more so than non-experts can imagine, or even some "experts." In it, he was fortunate to have the able assistance of Professor Robert T. Handy of Union and Professor Lefferts A. Loetscher of Princeton Seminary. Their work together turned out to be one of those germinal exercises in which the partners both learned from and taught each other. The end-product was incalculably better than if it had been done *solo,* or in the haste that was urged upon the trio by their well-meaning friends.

The first volume of *American Christianity: An Historical Interpretation with Representative Documents* appeared in 1960; the second in 1963. These volumes have, as the editors point out,

a two-fold aim. . . . First, they interpret in historical perspective the major movements, both Catholic and Protestant, which emerged in American Christianity. . . . Second, they correlate with this interpretive narrative a body of representative primary documents. Thus the reader is supplied with both interpretive exposition and illustrative documents. Roughly one-third of the text is interpretive, and the remainder is composed of documents.

The simplest and sincerest thing to say about this book is that it matches the best source books we have in any part of the field of church history and surpasses all its predecessors in the American field.

One of the provocative notions that Shelton Smith had flung out in that first Pastors' School in 1934 was his opinion that Horace Bushnell (patron saint of all religious educators, then, at least) had actually been much more definitely an evangelical liberal Christian than a disciple of the Enlightenment; further, that *Christian Nurture* was not Bushnell's most characteristic or creative book. I recall my feeling of amazement that an eminent scholar could be so badly misinformed. I knew better—from my seminary lectures, of course. Why shouldn't he? His reaction to my corrective comments took the form of a series of questions—the Socratic ploy, that most effective weapon of the skilful teacher. "What have you read of Bushnell?" "What *else* does Bushnell say in *Christian Nurture,* besides his slogan that a child should grow up as a Christian without ever knowing himself to be otherwise?" "Have you thought much about Bushnell's theory of language and his Christology in *Nature and the Supernatural?*" Such queries had the intended effect: a visit to the library and the embarrassing discovery that I had been trusting my unexamined stereotypes—and if in the case of Bushnell, then how many others besides? Ever since, I have been hoping for a book on Bushnell by Shelton Smith—the more especially since I knew that here was one of his lodestones. When, therefore, the prospectus for

A Library of Protestant Thought was drawn up, there was ready agreement in the editorial board that Smith should edit the Bushnell volume.

Another of my debts to Professor Smith was the help he gave me in learning how to teach. As an experiment, we worked up a joint seminar in "Religious Thought in the Nineteenth Century," in which I covered the European and he the American developments. Watching him in a class was a most rewarding experience. What came through to me—and his other students —was that he was concerned, above all, with two things: intellectual venturesomeness and intellectual integrity. Woe betide the student who turned up with threadbare commonplaces. Yet an even sterner judgment was in store for the man who dared to argue without evidence, or who skewed his evidence to support a shaky case. Smith understood very well that a preoccupation with history can lead to a sterile historicism unless it is offset by vigorous dialogue with constructive theology, ethics, and philosophy. At the same time, however, he had great faith in the power of critical history to provide *perspective*. He was, therefore, determined to bring dogmatics—and dogmaticians—before the bar of historical judgment. In all of this, his manifold interests were organized by a common purpose that looked beyond methodology. What he was after was a new theological climate, better suited to the swirl and convulsions of the modern world—in which new insights might emerge and be developed in the light of the longer and deeper experiences of the Christian community in space and time. It would be altogether fitting if the "sequel" to *Faith and Nurture* should be produced by one of its author's students.

What I have tried to suggest is that Shelton Smith's career is best understood in the context of the three decades of his single-minded, constant devotion to his job at Duke, in the cumulative impact of his work with students, colleagues, and constituency. This has meant a careful rationing of the time and energy he could spare for extramural engagements—a rationing that has sometimes seemed scanty in the face of the unusual opportunities and demands with which he has been besieged.

Within the margin of his calendar, however, he has been involved in many significant projects. For example, he has been in one office or another in the American Society of Church History for the past twenty years—as president in 1957. He has also been a long-time member of the American Theological Society—president in 1958–1959. He has done the major lecture series at Pacific School of Religion, Eden Theological Seminary, Hebrew Union College, Austin Presbyterian Seminary, and Princeton Theological Seminary. Along the way, he has garnered two well-deserved honorary hoods (Defiance, D.D., 1926, and Elon, Litt. D., 1940).

Of all the scholar-teachers I have known, Shelton Smith has been one of the wisest and most practical operators in the strange and chancy world of university affairs. I could never quite tell how he managed it, but he always knew what was going on, and he seemed always to know when and how to move, when to stand his ground. He was realistic enough (the import of his doctrine of original sin) not to be taken in by the schemers but was saved from cynicism by a curious charisma of grace and optimism. I never saw him lose his head, or even his temper (except on purpose), and I never saw him do a cruel or vindictive thing.

In this rehearsal of his career, one is impressed above all with the "efficiency" in it all—the near total concentration of the man's time, energy, and talent on worthwhile projects of his own choosing. He has had, of course, his share of the slings and arrows of academic fortune, but in them there has been a near minimum of those distractions and detours which often stultify a scholar's productivity. It should come as no surprise that this has been made possible by a remarkable system of domestic logistics, directed by a knowledgeable and efficient chief of di-staff. Alma Bowden Smith will hardly reach to an even five feet, alongside Shelton's six foot one; but her swift intuition and talent for order have made her the fully equal partner in what has, in fact, been a joint career. It is notoriously difficult for wives of academic men to manage the working situations *of* their husbands without trying to manage the man *in* those situations. Somehow Alma Smith has found the formula for this distinction but she never bothered to publish it. One has the suspicion that Shelton would be unable to give a fully satisfactory account of the process which has afforded him more comfort and unobtrusive help in his work than most men get—and this in a gracious family setting happily free from the usual signs of competition or possessiveness.

But even the scholar, if he is sensitive and conscientious, is drawn into the convulsions of the world in which he lives— and Professor Smith has been more deeply involved than most in the tragic strains and stresses of modern life, particularly as they have shown up in the characteristic tensions of his own region. His primary interest in the Christian faith has always been practical: Christianity active in the present and open toward the future. This interest has never waned nor been eroded by the disappointments that every hopeful man has suffered in this century. With all his passion for analysis, Smith is a minor prophet—moralist, gadfly, reformer. Friends and foes alike have grown accustomed to his being out ahead of them in his diagnoses of the major social crises that have swept our modern world in series, like line storms across the prairie.

For example, I remember being puzzled, very early in our acquaintance, over his apparent lack of certain of the traits and prejudices typical of Southerners in his generation—even the "emancipated" ones. It took a while to discover that this man had a different legacy, bequeathed him by a different tradition and history. He was a descendant of that small but very significant minority of upland freeholders in the old South who had never been bewitched by the plantation mythology and the ghosts of the magnolia jungle. These people had been anti-slavery long before the Civil War; they had been anti-secessionist, but also anti-carpetbagger. Thus, Smith's convictions about "the American dilemma" had never been befuddled by the peculiar mixture of good and bad conscience that drives some Southerners into diehard barbarism and others into a self-conscious liberalism which still fails to liberate. In the agony of the race relations issue in the South, Smith has been less a prisoner of history than the vast majority of us, white *and* Negro. Consequently, he has been both more resolute and more rational than many in his consistent demands for social justice, civil liberties, and political responsibility on both sides. In 1956 he wrote:

> Thousands of white Southerners, including especially youth, can no longer morally justify the principle of racial segregation. . . . Where there is true faith in one God there is no color bar.
>
> Is it not clear, then, why we white churchmen are conscience stricken? We do not presume to be better than our worthy forefathers, yet we do believe, as most of them apparently did not, that a racially segregated church is a tragic denial of that community which is inherent in one Lord, one faith, one baptism. Since God is one, we are members one of another—equally subject to His judgment and mercy; equally accountable to Him; equally valuable in His sight. Hence, to discriminate against a single one of His children on the ground of race is to impugn the moral character of God.

For forty years he has striven to implement this faith. If there are those who have wrought or suffered more than he, they only are entitled to throw the stones of impatience.

Along with his involvement in affairs close by, Professor Smith has never flagged in his concern for justice and humanity in the wider order of national and international relations. Over the years I have been impressed by the detail and acumen of his understanding of American politics and foreign affairs. It is interesting to see how little he is bound to a party line; how rarely he waits for the experts to agree before he forms his own judgment, shaped by his historical perspective and his deep antipathy to inhumanity in every form. He was a chaplain in World War I and yet also consistently anti-militarist. He was one of the first men I knew to take the full measure of the dangers of totalitarianism long before the rest of us recognized or were alarmed by them. On the other hand, he never was a dupe for the "popular fronts" of the thirties and never did he exalt sentimentality to the level of a political principle. The proof of learning, for him, is in its yield of wisdom and the proof of wisdom in its service to the common good.

Festschriften are offertories and exhibitions—samples of their work presented by grateful disciples in honor of a great teacher. These essays must, of course, be judged on their merits, for this is the first rule Shelton Smith tried to teach his students. But this volume is also something of a mirror in which the reader may discern the basic shape and coloration of a unique career. The contributors are the first fruits of a graduate program that counts its history in terms of a single score of years and a single director—until four years ago. They are concentrated in a field of inquiry which has an important future, partially gained for it by the endeavors of their teacher. They can be counted on to multiply his sowing thirty, sixty, and a hundred fold—and no one will be more gratified than he with their successes. In this way, they will bear testimony to that quality of greatness they have seen in him. Is there a better advertisement for the good life in *Academia*?

Bishop Francis J. McConnell
and the Great Steel
Strike of 1919-1920

WALTER W. BENJAMIN

Long-haired preachers come out every night,
Try to tell you what's wrong and what's right;
But when asked 'bout something to eat
They will answer with voices so sweet:

CHORUS
You will eat, bye and bye;
In that glorious land above the sky;
Work and pray, live on hay,
You'll get pie in the sky when you die.

About the year 1880 an Ohio country lad came into local prominence as a long-distance runner. Two men had laid a five dollar wager on whether a preacher's kid named Frank McConnell could catch a wayward calf. The barefoot boy started out in pursuit of the calf in an extremely unorthodox and an unboyish manner. A brilliant and blood-stirring hundred-yard dash, which would have won the plaudits of the man who had put five dollars on his nose, was not for him. He caught the calf by jogging along after the animal with a steady and consistent stride until the puzzled bovine finally lay down as if to say, "This thing has gone far enough." [1] Although it took him all afternoon to catch the calf, there was nothing in the wager about a time limit; the point that was specified was met—he corralled the calf by jogging on to the end of the day. In a

1. "A Statesman Can Be A Prophet," *The World Tomorrow*, XIV (Feb., 1931), 40.

very real sense this boyhood episode proved typical of the later life and attitude of the man for, without playing to the crowd, Francis J. McConnell accomplished by ceaseless and irresistible pressure and pursuit whatever goal he set his mind to attain.

For thousands of Protestants during the era of the Social Gospel, Francis J. McConnell was "The Bishop" in a sense in which the term applied to no other American clergyman. His life revealed a leadership and left a legacy which bore the marks of an apostolic authority surpassing any conferred by ritual.[2] His active ministerial career of fifty years—from 1894 to 1944—touched almost every conceivable facet of human life with a redeeming impulse. He was concerned with the widest possible extension of the Christian ethic, and it was his driving passion to transform Christian ideals into practicable realities. As such, his life was in marked contrast to the sarcastic refrain that scored the traditional archconservatism of high ecclesiastics:

> Our Fathers have been churchmen,
> Nineteen hundred years or so,
> And to every new proposal,
> They have always answered, No.

This essay will investigate one of the high moments in the career of Bishop McConnell—the Great Steel Strike of 1919–1920 —wherein he answered the working men of America with a resounding "Yes." With the Social Gospel today in disrepute it might prove instructive to turn to a specific case history as illustrative that, in spite of the Neo-Orthodox critics, there were indeed "giants on the earth in those days."

The Great Steel Strike took place during the widespread economic and social dislocation that followed the "Great Crusade," the battle to "make the world safe for democracy." Most Americans regarded World War I as but a four-year period of delay in the pilgrimage toward the eventual conquest of eternal peace, progress, and prosperity. The real horrors of the fight against the Hun only superficially affected the sanguine disposition of the average American, who, as Uncle Sam wel-

2. "The Bishop," *Christian Century,* LXX (Sept. 2, 1953) , 983.

comed Johnny Doughboy home with ticker-tape and confetti, turned his back on the rest of the world and with rosy optimism set to work toward the completion of the American Dream.

But the social millennium was not immediately ushered in. The drums of war were hardly silenced and the "return to normalcy" scarcely begun before a dark and irrational specter took possession of the collective spirit of America. For, although America had her back turned to the world, every man who owned a garden, Liberty bond, and Sunday suit of clothes, was neurotically conscious of what was happening in Leninized Russia. America was "hagridden" by the bogey of bomb-carrying, bristly-bearded Bolsheviks.[3] Politicians were parroting the suggestion of Guy Empey that the proper implements for dealing with the "army" of American Reds—some estimated their number "conservatively" at 600,000—could be "found in any hardware store." Some patriots were proclaiming, "My motto for the Reds is S.O.S.—ship or shoot. I believe we should place them all on a ship of stone, with sails of lead, and that their first stopping place should be hell." [4] Confronted by an era which called for a departure from the status quo and the adoption of novel social and economic policy, the American citizenry became afraid, suspicious, and intolerant. In spite of the fact that over seventy bills against Bolshevism and Anarchism were introduced in Congress, many newspapers were up in arms because all too few Reds were being deported.[5] "Patriotic" organizations sprouted by the hundreds giving big-navy men, drys, anti-cigarette campaigners, anti-evolution fundamentalists, book censors, Jew-baiters, Negro-haters, landlords, and capitalists the opportunity to wrap themselves in Old Glory, make the eagle scream, and daub any Liberal cause with the Bolshevist brush.

3. Preston William Slosson, *The Great Crusade and After,* "A History of American Life Series," XII (New York, 1939) , 79.

4. Frederick Lewis Allen, *Only Yesterday* (New York, 1931) , p. 58. For an excellent treatment of the post-World War I fear of Bolshevism, see Robert K. Murray. *Red Scare: A Study in National Hysteria, 1919–1920* (Minneapolis, 1955).

5. "Congress Grapples With the Question of Bolshevism and Anarchism," *Current Opinion,* LXVIII (Jan., 1920) , 9.

Throughout 1919, we were afraid of the dark. Bolshevism was no mere word, but a gargantuan bogey to gobble us all up. Glance over a few headlines for that year: "Senate Orders Nationwide Probe of Bolshevism," "14 Spanish Radicals Jailed; Plot to Assassinate Wilson Bared," "53 Reds sent East for Deportation." . . . Reds, who, as President Wilson warned, advocated the overthrow of the government by force for the big lead; and labor for the little.[6]

Nevertheless, there was visible proof at every hand that there was a radical distortion of the American social fabric in 1919, whether Red-inspired or not. In that year over four million men went out in 3,253 strikes and lockouts in the United States. Many basic industries—coal, steel, railways, textiles—suffered in turn from the struggles of the workers to make their wages meet the postwar inflated price levels. The nation was particularly horrified at the Boston Police Strike (completely overlooking the just grievances of the police), which raised the classical question, "Who shall guard our guardians?" but Americans wholeheartedly agreed with Governor Calvin Coolidge that "there is no right to strike against the public safety by anybody, anywhere, anytime." [7] By all odds, however, the greatest industrial dislocation of the year, perhaps in the century to that time, was the Great Steel Strike, in the settlement and evaluation of which Bishop McConnell played such a vital role.

Bishop McConnell conducted the investigation of the strike as a member of the special Commission of Inquiry of the Interchurch World Movement. The Interchurch World Movement was an ecumenical missionary, if visionary, venture, of a year and one-half duration, which wanted to harness the moral and financial resources of the country toward ends more worthwhile than war. With a financial goal it hoped would ultimately reach $336,777,572, and in spite of generous contributions by men of the caliber of John D. Rockefeller, Jr., the movement was almost stillborn because of its inability to overcome the antipathy that wartime drives had left upon the pub-

6. Laurence Greene, *The Era of Wonderful Nonsense* (New York, 1939), p. 30.
7. Slosson, *op. cit.,* p. 82.

lic.[8] Nevertheless, the Interchurch Movement's swan song was an utterance the nation would not soon forget. For those who were to look upon its skeletal remains years hence would remember it, not for what it failed to do, but for the one very necessary earthly job it did exceedingly well. Under the direction of Bishop McConnell a group of churchmen vacated pulpit and study to conduct an investigation and write a report on the titan of American industry—an investigation the ultimate significance of which was to affect the American economy from life within the inner portals of Wall Street to the working conditions and pay check of the poorest immigrant steel worker.

The first warnings that foretold the possibility of a capital-labor war on the battlefield of steel occurred on August 1, 1918, when the representatives of twenty-four American Federation of Labor trade unions met in Chicago to establish a National Committee for Organizing Iron and Steel Workers. The steel combine was the last industrial bastion of the twentieth century operating upon a nineteenth-century philosophy of the "divine right of capital," autocratic control, and a "no-conference, no-union" policy. As such, it had always been a thorn in the flesh of organized labor and, as a consequence of the 1892 and 1909 steel strikes, the industry had wiped out "every trace of unionism" from its plants.[9] Nevertheless, because of the war, the abominable working conditions, the demand for steel, the scarcity of labor, and the pro-labor Wilsonian administration, the AF of L believed that 1918 presented an unparalleled opportunity to unionize this basic industry. Thus, from August, 1918, to June, 1919, steel organizers, although beaten, kidnaped, and run out of the mills countless times, had enlisted over 100,000 workers, and Foster could boast that there was a strong union in every mill town.[10]

Because the membership drive succeeded beyond all expectation, Samuel Gompers on June 20, 1919, asked Judge Elbert H.

8. "Why the Interchurch Movement Failed," *The Literary Digest,* LXVI (Aug. 7, 1920) , 42. For McConnell's evaluation of the failure, see Francis J. McConnell, *By the Way* (New York, 1952) , p. 219.

9. William Z. Foster, *The Great Steel Strike and Its Lessons* (New York, 1920) , p. 13.

10. *Ibid.,* p. 49.

Gary, Chairman of the United States Steel's Board of Directors, for a conference to discuss conditions in the steel industry and possible improvement of the workers' position. "To Mr. Gompers' courteous letter Czar Gary did not deign to reply." [11] After drawing up a list of general demands that included the right of collective bargaining; one day's rest in seven; double rates of pay for overtime, holiday, and Sunday work; the principle of seniority in hiring, firing, and advancement; the abolition of company unions; etc., the National Committee felt it had no other alternative except to circulate a strike ballot among the local steel unions. By the end of August, with 98 per cent of the union membership in favor of a strike, Judge Gary was asked again to accede to an arbitration conference. His reply on August 27 set forth the open-shop policy of United States Steel: "The officers of the corporation respectfully decline to discuss with you, as representatives of a labor union, any matters relating to employees." [12] In spite of President Wilson's last-ditch attempt in the role of pacifier, capital and labor were at an impasse. Under tremendous pressure from its locals because all known union members were being purged from their jobs, the National Committee was powerless either to abolish or postpone the groundswell of strike sentiment.[13] Thus the strike call, printed in two hundred thousand copies and in seven languages, was broadcast across the entire steel industry:

STRIKE SEPTEMBER 22, 1919. The Workers in the iron and steel mills and blast furnaces . . . are requested not to go to work on September 22, and to refuse to resume their employment until such time as the demands of the organizations have been conceded. . . . And in our stoppage of work let there be no violence. The American Federation of Labor has won all its great progress by peaceful and legal methods.[14]

The Great Steel Strike thus began with 365,000 men quitting their jobs, and was not to end until 109 days later, on January 8, 1920, when the National Committee voted to permit the 100,-

11. *Ibid.*, p. 76.
12. Murray, *op. cit.*, p. 137.
13. John A. Fitch, "The Closed Shop," *Survey*, XLIII (Nov. 8, 1919), 56.
14. Foster, *op. cit.*, pp. 94–95.

ooo men still on strike to return to work upon the best terms they could secure. Although the strike initially was 90 per cent effective, it ended with steel production 70 per cent of normal. The workers had gained not a solitary concession, over twenty lives had been sacrificed, hundreds had been injured, and over $112,000,000 had been lost in wages.[15] Although the tremendous loss to the steel companies could not be calculated, they evidently considered the expense worthwhile in the titanic struggle to smash trade unionism.

The first indication that the year-old Interchurch World Movement was interested in the basic issues of the strike came as the result of a meeting of one hundred clergymen in the Pennsylvania Hotel in New York a week and a half after the onset of the strike. Bishop McConnell, as chairman of the group, recalled that a unanimous vote was taken to ask the Industrial Relations Department of the Movement to conduct an investigation of the strike.[16] Immediate difficulty was encountered, however, because some "prominent churchmen" declined to serve on the special committee of inquiry. As Bishop McConnell reported it, "Two very prominent progressives whose names, even if the men did not work, would have added weight to the task, declined, for no important reasons that I could see." [17] Evidently some of the ecclesiastical "heavyweights" were extremely fond of the Sabbath sport of jabbing the captains of industry while they were pinned to their pews, but were extremely reluctant to engage them in a rolled-up-sleeve, Monday-through-Saturday brawl in which telling blows could be landed. In this situation where everyone wanted the job done, but no one was willing to expose himself to danger, McConnell was chosen, as he believed, as "the last resort." Eight other members were selected to serve with McConnell on the Commission of Inquiry and, although they hired a bureau of industrial research to handle the statistical and technical data, most of the personal interviews among management and

15. Murray, *op. cit.*, p. 152.
16. *By the Way*, p. 214.
17. *Ibid.*

the steel workers were garnered by the members of the Commission.

The initial obstacle McConnell encountered was the refusal of the steel management to take the investigation seriously. "As far as I could see," wrote the Bishop, "the feeling of the steel leaders was at first somewhat of amusement, changing to surprise that the Committee should think itself qualified to ask any questions, and at last pain at being questioned." [18] Difficulties in securing pertinent data exceeded all expectations. McConnell was accused of being a "Bolshevist" and an "Anarchist"; other clergymen were condemned as "Reds" and one even arrested. A threat of legal action against a large organization was necessary to force it to stop such rumors and submit a full retraction. After the Committee's expenditure of $12,000 and the fight against conservative clerical and economic sentiment, there was a "leak" that the findings were decidedly hostile to the steel combine, and "outside pressure" not to publish the *Report* became almost intolerable. McConnell, in session at the Methodist General Conference at Des Moines, Iowa, took the first train to Cleveland to strengthen the wavering Committee, and the "report was soon adopted and published." [19]

The Commission found that the cause of the strike "lay in hours, wages, and conditions of labor," which were "arbitrarily" fixed by the directors of the United States Steel Corporation.[20] By carefully collecting and analyzing five hundred statements and affidavits from strikers and non-strikers, the clergymen were convinced that the very attitude and arbitrary treatment of management engendered the "strike spirit" within the worker. "The frame of mind of the steel workers . . . grew

18. *Ibid.,* p. 215.
19. *Ibid.,* p. 219. The Commission of Inquiry, the Interchurch World Movement, *Report on the Steel Strike of 1919* (New York, 1920). Cited hereinafter as *Report.* It should be noted, that inasmuch as this is a committee report, there is no possible way by which to ascertain which portions come directly from the pen of Bishop McConnell. Those who attempted to discredit the *Report* affirmed that the Bishop and his Committee had little or nothing to do with its authorship. However, this essay is based on the premise that, in view of McConnell's endorsement, support, and battle for the publication of the *Report,* it fundamentally represented his conviction with respect to the strike.
20. *Report,* p. 4.

out of the conditions of labor," circumstances with which Mr. Gompers, and the other so-called "radicals," "agitators," and strike organizers had little to do.[21] The workers had been in a chronic state of rebellion for years as the result of physical exhaustion and deprivation. The extraordinary labor turnover— in one plant 575 workers quit every month out of a total labor force of 11,500—indicated that thousands of workers had been going on "individual strikes" for years.[22] The workers were not, as critics of McConnell affirmed, striking for a "sovietized America" or a "classless state."[23] "Of the hundreds of strikers and non-strikers interviewed . . . few could put together two sentences on 'soviets' but almost all discoursed on or, more accurately, cursed 'long hours.' "[24] Many were foreign-born, unable to read or write, and ignorant of all ideology except that immediately concerned with pay check, bread, clothes, and rent. McConnell was convinced that the strike occurred because basic human rights were being denied:

In the course of our investigations, one man was asked why he was striking. He said the trouble was in the twelve-hour day and the double shift. When asked just where the pinch came, he answered: "From the mere length of time away from home. Last Sunday I buried my daughter twelve years of age, and as I stood by her grave I thought: 'I have never had a chance to know this child. I was too tired when I got home from work, or she was already in bed, and I am burying my own flesh and blood, and yet a stranger to me.' I have another child, and I am striking for a chance to get acquainted with my own child."[25]

21. *Ibid.*, p. 147.
22. *Ibid.*, p. 148.
23. The "steel answer" was drawn up by Marshall Olds in *Analysis of the Interchurch World Movement Report on the Steel Strike* (New York, 1922). Cited hereinafter as *Analysis*. Olds blamed the strike almost entirely on "outside professional labor leaders who, uninvited and undesired by any considerable proportion of the steel workers, began a campaign of agitation, including radical agitation, chiefly among the unskilled foreign workers, and by appealing to their ignorance and class prejudices, formed a strike nucleus, and then by skilful manipulation of mass psychology, coupled with intimidations, succeeded in getting only a minority of the workers to stop work and that even this minority rapidly dwindled as soon as protection against intimidation was assured." *Analysis*, pp. 178–179. Members of the Commission such as Dr. Alva W. Taylor and F. Ernest Johnson, however, found the book "teeming with mutilated quotations, garbled statistics, misleading statements, and factual errors." Robert Moats Miller, *American Protestantism and Social Issues, 1919–1939* (Chapel Hill, 1958), p. 212.
24. *Report*, p. 54.
25. Francis J. McConnell, "Spirit of Social Service," *National Conference of Social Work* (1920), p. 39.

In contrast to the illusion that steel was a "high wage" industry, McConnell found that the annual earnings of over one-third of all workers was below the level set by government statisticians as the minimum or "subsistence standard" for families of five. Seventy-two per cent were not able to earn enough to attain the "minimum of comfort level," thus forcing other members of steel families into outside work with consequent harmful effects. The steel interests, moreover, were rather slippery with wage statistics in trying to convey the notion that the workers were rolling in wealth by making an average of $6.23 a day. This figure was arrived at by lumping together the salaries of all administration and selling-force personnel. Concerning such a procedure, a labor sympathizer retorted: "One might as well say that the average wage of the scrub woman at ten dollars a week and of the President of the United States at $1442 a week is $726.00." [26]

More serious than the low-wage policy, however, was the twelve-hour day, seven-day week. The Commission discovered that one-half (52.4 per cent) of all workers were subjected to the twelve-hour day, and that one-half of these, in turn, were forced to work a seven-day week. There was nothing "voluntary" about this arrangement of which the Commission said at the time that the "twelve-hour day workman cannot knock off at the end of eight hours. . . . He can 'take it or leave it' but he cannot bargain over his job's hours." [27] The average time of work for all employees was 68.7 hours per week, or over 11 and 2/5 hours per day on a six-day mathematical average. These figures stood in stark contrast to those of the English steel industry, where the twelve-hour day had been abolished before 1915 and the average employee was on a 47–48 hour week.[28]

Thrown on the defensive, the steel companies attempted to justify the twelve-hour day by appealing to foreign competition, metallurgical necessity, a shortage of labor, the avowal

---

26. "The Steel Strike," *The New Republic*, XX (Oct. 1, 1919), 245.
27. *Report*, p. 45.
28. *Ibid.*, p. 56.

that "the men wanted it," and the insistence it was "good for them." Many company presidents fondly recalled the happy days of their youth "on the farm" where they worked from 5 A.M. to 10 P.M. and enjoyed "every moment of it." If, however, the steel magnates actually believed their workers accepted the virtuous words they parroted about the twelve-hour day, they were living in a world of fantasy. If the executives had but vacated their walnut-paneled offices and spent less time socializing with the country-club set, they might have renounced the illusions formed from their company-faithful foremen and spy reports. As it was, Bishop McConnell, by rubbing shoulders with the strikers, came to a most poignant awareness of the misery and suffering in their work-a-day world. McConnell found the twelve-hour day a cancer that destroyed the very tissue of individual, family, and community life. If life was but an inhuman round of eating, sleeping, and working, all attempts to "Americanize" the "Hunky"—the slang term for the foreign-born worker—through night schools, Carnegie libraries, and self-improvement opportunities went for naught. Worker hostility was typified by a Pole's first public speech in English at a striker's meeting:

Mr. Chairman—just like horse and wagon. Put horse in wagon, work all day. Take horse out of wagon—put in stable. Take horse out of stable, put in wagon. Same way like mills. Work all day. Come home—go sleep. Get up—go work in mills—come home. Wife say, "John, children sick. You help with children." You say, "Oh, go to hell"—go sleep. Wife say, "John, you go town." You say, "No"—go sleep. No know what the hell you do. For why this war? For why we buy Liberty bonds? For mills? No, for freedom and America—for everybody. No more horse and wagon. For eight-hour day.[29]

The real tragedy of the "horse and wagon" twelve-hour day was that it tended to destroy that which was distinctively human in man. By treating men as twelve-hour automatons, impersonal entities, as factors in production, it slowly but inexorably brutalized them. And McConnell knew that all appeals to profit margins, metallurgical necessities, rights of

29. John A. Fitch, "The Closed Shop," *Survey,* XLIII (Nov. 8, 1919), 91.

property and management could not expurgate the evil from the barbarous system.

McConnell readily admitted that concerning "some broad questions of human welfare the steel interests were beyond criticism." [30] The old adage of his youth—"there are too many one-legged men around a steel mill"—was no longer valid at the time of the inquiry. The severest critic interviewed could find no fault with the safety equipment in the mills. Nevertheless, the clergymen perceived that charity loomed larger than justice, philanthrophy larger than equity in corporation policy. Shower baths, baseball fields, and housekeeping centers were nice, but they could not atone for the sins connected with arbitrary management and control. Corporation policy was still in the state of "detectives and toilets"—that is, the employees were alternately confused by charity and injustice, clean comfort stations and industrial espionage. "The Corporation's executives . . . are forced to grind the faces of the 'hunkies' and to trust to 'welfare' to salve the exacerbations." [31]

Although the cause of economic justice was with labor, the steel combine was too large and powerful to be defeated by 365,000 striking workmen. The facts of the situation were that it had an enormous cash surplus, allies among other businesses, strong influence in almost every social institution, and within its own walls an absolute centralized control. It was, accordingly, almost impregnable. Nevertheless, the steel combine eroded the initial public sentiment for the striker by freely utilizing such emotionally laden words as "Bolshevism," "sovietism," "plot," "conspiracy," "revolution," "Syndicalism," and "radicalism," and successfully promoted an irrational antipathy to the strike rather than a logical evaluation of it. In spite of the capitalist cry, "red wolf," and although hundreds of strikers were arrested as "radicals," the only "evidence" steel interests could produce of "sovietism" was a poster signed by AF of L officials which was headlined, "Abolish Garyism." [32]

30. *By the Way*, p. 216.
31. *Report*, p. 127.
32. *Ibid.*, pp. 32–33.

William Z. Foster, at that time a trade unionist and the moving force behind the unionization of the industry, was an especial point of attack. Steel magnates frantically pointed out that he was a "notorious syndicalist" and a "borer from within" —that is, a "red wolf" in trade unionist sheep's clothing. The AF of L acknowledged that it was aware of the unorthodox aims of Foster but that it could control him, and pointed out that however much his "boring might be through the unions, it was certainly against the anti-union employers." [33] Foster's book *Syndicalism,* which had been out of print for years, was reprinted and distributed widely by the steel interests to clergymen, educators, and newspaper editors, even though it was not found in the possession of a single strike leader or organizer. Newspapers in New York and Boston, far from the strike areas, carried extracts "as the principal news of the beginning of the strike. The book's relation to the strike, therefore, was in no sense causative; it was injected as a means of breaking the strike." [34]

McConnell's Commission held that there was no substance to the steel "Bolshevik" propaganda; a strike "movement of 300,000 men in a dozen states is about as secret as a presidential campaign." Many reputable journals and newspapers made little attempt to get the facts; more often than not they published the press releases of the steel industry with no investigation of their authenticity.[35] Newspapers reported that workers who made $70 a day took the strike as the occasion to take a vacation and spend their "high wages" in the more luxurious New York hotels. Moreover, at the time the AF of L estimated the strike 90 per cent effective, the press printed such strike-breaking, propaganda headlines as: "CONDITIONS ALMOST NORMAL IN ALL STEEL PLANTS," "WORKERS FLOCK BACK TO JOBS," and "STRIKE CRUMBLING." [36]

33. *Ibid.,* p. 156.
34. *Ibid.,* pp. 34–35.
35. "Speaking of the 'Poor' Steel Workers Who Get From $4 to $70 a Day," *Current Opinion,* LXVIII (Jan., 1920) , 122–123.
36. Murray, *op. cit.,* p. 143.

Though in times past the press had prophetically and fear-lessly attacked the "menacing steel trust," now it was almost completely subservient to it because of the enormous social in-fluence which radiated from steels' all-embracing activities. Steel "tentacles" extended into railroads, mines, coal fields, shipyards, general industries, and banks. It owned entire cities, and in many localities the existence of churches, schools, and newspapers was dependent upon "staying right" with steel. Thus, it seemed to be a matter of he who pays the piper being able to call the tune. Nevertheless, the workers were of the opinion that the press was but a strike-breaking instrument, that it suppressed and colored the facts and denounced them without cause. McConnell recommended that the press free itself from an anti-labor, pro-capital bias and publish industrial facts and questions without "fear or favor." [37]

McConnell also discovered that the steel companies ex-ploited the latent racial antipathy between the native and foreign-born workers to break the strike. The steel trust's un-ceasing refrain affirmed that the strike was solely a "Hunkie"-inspired movement and that native-born Americans, for patri-otic reasons, were not participating in it. Handbills were dis-tributed stating: "Don't Let the 'Hunkies' Rule the Mill," and "Don't Let the Foreigners Take American Jobs." [38] Moreover, Negroes became willing pawns in the strategy of strike-break-ing. Possessing little or no understanding of trade-union ide-ology, most were quite willing to play the role of the "scab." [39] The AF of L estimated that the companies recruited and shipped in from 30,000 to 40,000 Negroes, most of them from the South, to convey the impression that the mills would run with or without white workers.[40] Promised four dollars a day with one dollar taken out for food, they were shipped into Youngstown and Pittsburgh at night in locked boxcars. Bands of Negroes were shifted from plant to plant conveying the

37. *Report,* p. 250.
38. *Ibid.,* p. 199.
39. Foster, *op. cit.,* pp. 205–208.
40. *Ibid.,* p. 207.

impression that the mills were in full operation, and in Gary they were ostentatiously marched through the streets.[41] The clergymen and Foster, however, were highly critical of the racial policies of both the AF of L and steel. The disposition of the Negro toward strike-breaking, while abetted by steel tactics, was in no small measure due to the color-line and Jim Crowism within the Union itself.

The Commission discovered that police aggression and the denial of civil liberties to the strikers contributed to the failure of the strike.[42] Another observer was shocked at his findings:

There have been few strikes where the policing authorities so completely ranged themselves on the side of the employing companies as did the local police and the State Constabulary of Pennsylvania. . . . strikers were harassed and interfered with constantly. . . . Evidence of the most unquestioned sort exists showing that strikers were beaten on the street, in public buildings, and even in their homes, by police officials.[43]

Pittsburgh city police were difficult to distinguish in behavior from the "Pinkerton men" or "mill police" and eagerly tried to outdo each other in breaking up union meetings and peaceful picket lines. In Sharon and Farrell seven thousand workers, denied the right of assembly in the streets or union halls, marched weekly across the state line into Ohio to hold mass meetings.[44] There are several photographs extant showing mounted troopers "riding over" pedestrians on the sidewalks and even entering places of business.[45] Civil liberty became such a dead letter in Duquesne that, in denying permits of assembly to strikers, Mayor Crawford boasted, "Jesus Christ himself couldn't hold a meeting in Duquesne!" [46] At the end of the strike one steel company gave $150.00 to every policeman who had patrolled its district.[47]

41. *Report,* pp. 177–178.
42. *Ibid.,* p. 15.
43. John A. Fitch, *The Causes of Industrial Unrest* (New York, 1924), pp. 250–251.
44. S. Adele Shaw, "Closed Towns," *Survey,* XLIII (Nov. 8, 1919), 61.
45. *The Great Steel Strike,* frontispiece and opposite p. 122.
46. Shaw, *op. cit.,* p. 62.
47. Fitch, *op. cit.,* p. 246.

Public officials in mill towns asserted that the restriction of civil liberties was necessary to prevent violence. Nevertheless, because of the correlation between civil and steel office-holding and a type of industrial-civil nepotism, "steel justice," rather than impartial justice, became the order of the day. When a striker was taken before these combination mill-public officials he had considerable grounds to infer that his fate was directly tied to the desires of the steel combine. When he read the proclamations of public officials denying him and the union the necessary and legal action for the strike and saw that the persons issuing the orders were officials of the companies against which he was striking, he was convinced that they were but masquerading in the guise of impartial administrators of the law. The striker believed that democratic government was the private property of his employer. "The steel strike made tens of thousands of citizens believe that our American institutions are not democratic or not democratically administered." [48]

McConnell was especially shocked in his investigations to discover a vast spy system or network which ran through the warp and woof of the steel industry.

We have just now in American industry a spy system—hired tattlers reporting to their employers what their fellow workers are saying. I have sat at a table opposite a Christian business man who admitted to me that he employed such spies, who frankly declared that he could not understand what I was talking about when I called spying the devil's own method. . . . this diabolical *spying is in large part the cause of that distrust and fear which eats the heart out of industrial morale.* . . . if industry has to advance by such methods as this, better let industry lag behind.[49]

Industrial espionage necessitated undercover men both from within the ranks of steel and from "labor-detective" agencies. A manager from one of the latter agencies affirmed that he had over five hundred operatives in the "field." The spies were of two kinds: "spies pure and simple who merely furnished information; and spies who also acted as propagandist strike breakers, mingling with the strikers and whispering that the

48. *Report,* p. 239.
49. "The Lesson Exposition," *The Sunday School Journal,* LVI (July 27, 1924) , 444.

strike was failing, that the men in other towns had gone back, that the union leaders were crooks. . . ." [50] The reports from the labor "fifth-column" ran from "illiterate scribblings" to the "most accurate transcriptions of union locals' secret meetings." [51] Because they usually contained what the company wanted to believe about labor, their contents were regarded as inviolable and were treated with great dignity. They engendered a great deal of terror and suspicion within the ranks of labor and the *esprit de corps* of the strike suffered, with workers afraid to communicate with one another for fear that one of them might turn out to be a stool pigeon. McConnell's report stated, however, that as long as the "no-conference" industry turned a deaf ear to the duly elected officials of the labor organization and accepted spy reports as sacrosanct, so long would industrial warfare continue.

An evil outgrowth of the espionage system was the practice of "blacklisting." The companies diligently kept common "labor files" containing names of men considered "unfit" (i.e., union members) for employment. Although Judge Gary explicitly denied that discrimination existed against union labor, the Commission gathered hundreds of affidavits proving that men had been discharged from work solely because they held a union card.[52] Additional light, however, was thrown on the Gary statement when one of his subordinates explained: "We don't discharge a man for belonging to a union, but of course we discharge men for agitating in the mills." [53] So efficient was the hated blacklist that many fired union workers felt it necessary to change their names when applying for work at another mill.

In January, 1920, the workers, "sullen, gutted, without hope, were dragging their broken-spirited bodies to the furnaces," again submitting to the twelve-hour day with earnings under a living wage. Those who were able to evade the blacklist were compelled to surrender their union cards and bow unconditionally to arbitrary control. The strike had "bled to death like

50. *Report,* p. 221.
51. *Ibid.,* p. 225.
52. *Ibid.,* pp. 213–214.
53. *Ibid.,* p. 210.

a living thing." [54] McConnell's report concluded with these disquieting words as to the worker's state of mind concerning his industrial peonage:

For escape he had turned to the A. F. of L. and in 1920 the A. F. of L. was not succeeding in freeing him. He hesitated to turn to the I.W.W., for the I.W.W. was "outlawed." He could not turn to the Steel Corporation. . . . He did not turn to the press. Among American democratic institutions he found none to fit his need . . . no one was reaching out to learn his grievances. The beaten steel worker displayed little interest in governmental institutions; instead he had acquired a rather active distrust of them. While many of the "foreigners" began piling up money to get themselves out of America the great majority began waiting for "the next strike." That was the only resource thoughtfully provided for them among the democratic American institutions.[55]

There can be little doubt that Bishop McConnell deplored the ostrich-like role played by the majority of the clergy in America during the struggle, and he affirmed that "a fair and comprehensive history of the strike would not require mention of either the Protestant Church or Catholic Church." [56] Hundreds of thousands of workers struggled in a nether world of industrial barbarism that most clergy neither knew of nor cared about as they toiled up the rungs of the ladder of ecclesiastical preferment. Many were suspicious of the newspaper version of the strike but were "ineffective for organizing concerted action, even for purposes of self-information." [57] Most steel workers assumed that whenever a minister preached against the strike or graciously accepted a large gift from a steel official, the church was just another enemy of the union and the working class. On one occasion steel interests imported and "used" a New England divine, who is reported to have pleaded: "We are, I wish to emphasize it, a God-fearing country. . . . The only place where your wages can be raised is the mill. Go back to the mill with a heart full of love for your foreman." An observer remarked that, "The workers' laughter that followed, the quality of it, the toothed edge of it, was plentifully

54. Miller, *op. cit.*, p. 210.
55. *Report*, p. 244.
56. *Ibid.*, p. 243.
57. *Ibid.*

instructive." [58] The apparent hand-in-glove operation by church and industry prompted a discerning old worker to comment, "The preacher points your eyes to heaven, and then the boss picks your pocket." A candid union president commented: "You want to know what labor thinks of the church. I tell you, very frankly, that labor does not think very much of the church, because the church does not think very much of labor." [59] "The great mass of steel workers paid no heed to the church as a social institution." [60]

With the publication of the *Report* in the summer of 1920 there was a strong blast from pietist and conservative Protestants against McConnell and the Commission. In the van was *The Presbyterian,* which held that the Commission had "neither spiritual, civil, nor any legal right" to engage in such mundane matters as workers' wages, hours, and conditions. The Church should live within her "spiritual" domain, "adhere to her own work of saving and making men good, and leave the adjustment of civil rights to properly constituted authority." [61] Many liberal Protestant journals, however, launched a vigorous counterattack and came to McConnell's defense. The *Churchman* (Episcopal) stated: "Missionaries are permitted to denounce the Chinese custom of foot-binding. Is it stretching a Christian point for the Churches in America . . . to denounce, wherever they may find it, soul-binding? A twelve-hour day, seven days a week, is, we think, a soul-binding process." [62] Gerald G. Treacy, writing in *America* (Catholic), held that the steel strike was an American fight for justice, and that the striker was "now vindicated by a report that . . . was impartial, sincere and honest." The *New York Christian Advocate* (Methodist) advised the industry to face up seriously to the *Report* and not to assassinate the character of the members of the Commission.[63]

58. "After the Strike," *New Republic,* XXI (Jan. 28, 1920) , 261–262.
59. Miller, *op. cit.,* p. 204.
60. *Report,* p. 243.
61. "The Church as a Critic of Industry," *Literary Digest,* LXVI (Sept. 4, 1920) , 41.
62. *Ibid.*
63. *Ibid.*

The forces of economic conservatism, however, refused to take such sage advice and preferred to disparage the personalities connected with the *Report* rather than look for flaws in its findings. Manufacturer's associations, chambers of commerce, Rotary clubs, and other such groups automatically assumed that such insidious revelations were the result of "labor spies" and a "nest of radicals" within the Interchurch agency.[64] Conservatives noted with glee that Mr. Heber Blankenhorn, secretary to the Commission, had been a captain in military intelligence and propaganda in World War I, and inferred that he had used his talents well in contributing to the masterful smear of the beneficent steel colossus. A careful investigation was made of the social and economic philosophy of Mr. Blankenhorn and his "technical assistants" and, inasmuch as he and his assistants were typed as "quite unorthodox," the investigation opened the way for a detour around the cold, hard facts of the *Report*.[65] To be sure, the economic ideology of Bishop McConnell and the other eight members of the Commission was scrutinized, but here incriminating evidence was rather meager—McConnell could be typed as only a "near socialist." [66] Hence, the steel interests concluded that the Commission's only function had been to give its imprimatur to the infamous document.

In truth, it is impossible to determine whether Blankenhorn and his investigators wrote all, part, or none of the *Report*. McConnell stated that only the "actual investigation of technical matters" was intrusted to "expert social workers," and that the secretary was concerned "for facts and facts only." "The report never could have made the impression upon the public that it did if the committee had not had the mass of information that Blankenhorn secured." [67] Moreover, the steel interests were deluded in assuming that because McConnell's Commission was largely composed of members of the cloth, it was "lost in the woods" when it came to economic theory, profit margins,

64. *Survey,* XLV (Feb. 5, 1921) , 671.
65. *Analysis,* pp. 426–431.
66. *Ibid.,* pp. 408–416; 465–466. *Current Opinion,* LXIX (Sept., 1920) , 362.
67. *By the Way,* p. 215.

and labor problems and grievances. More than once a capitalist titan was put to shame when faced by the Bishop's mastery and comprehension of intricate economic data. The following story is enlightening:

In one city in Pennsylvania the president of a steel company asked to see me when I was there on church business. I told him I should be glad to see him. When he arrived at the hotel, he had two assistants with him. In a polite way he said he had come to tell me what a dreadful mistake I had made in getting mixed up in the steel investigation. He conceded that I was a good enough fellow as long as I stuck to my own field, but that in dealing with wage scales and similar matters I could not possibly know what I was talking about. Then he told me about the generosity of the wages in a certain department of his mill. Finally I said, "Mr. So-and-so, I want you to get full credit for your wage scale. In fact the hourly wage in that department is ten cents higher than you have said." He replied, "I have the wage scale right here, and I'll show you." One of the men with him handed him a sheet, and I was right. . . . Inasmuch as his whole argument was based on the assumption that I didn't know anything, there wasn't much use in prolonging the conversation. That steel man was a good sport; when he left, he expressed appreciation of the sermon he had heard me preach the day before.[68]

Judge Gary played a leading role in attacking the *Report* by printing and distributing a million and a half copies of an address by the Reverend E. Bigelow entitled *Mistakes of the Interchurch Steel Report.* One of the many blunders made by the Commission, Bigelow discovered, was its condemnation of the twelve-hour day. "It may be that eight hours is a good standard day for reckoning a unit of toil," pontificated this toiler in the Lord's vineyard, "but this world would have many empty larders and raw comforts if men didn't work more than eight hours in twenty-four. Nature is so obdurate and man's needs are so many that it is physically impossible to produce what we need in those hours." [69]

Although blast and counterblast continued to reverberate for years over the authorship and authenticity of the *Report,* its effect for good was almost instantaneous. Before the end of 1920 the steel companies had completely abolished the seven-

68. *Ibid.,* pp. 214–215.
69. Cited by Miller, *op. cit.,* p. 212.

day week and were in the process of switching to an eight-hour day. The twelve-hour shift which had been believed as necessary in the production of steel as the sun to our solar system was never again a part of the American industrial scene. One steel official stated: "After the men have once got used to the three-shift system, you could not pull it away from them with tongs," and another added, "It didn't cost us any more to be human." [70] What had been dreadfully feared seemed to benefit everyone. There was an increase in production, the worker's *esprit de corps* was markedly better, the foremen were "glad they made the change," and there was little absenteeism.

There can be little question that the *Report* signaled the death knell for "Garyism" in the steel industry. Although steel could claim a tactical win because the strike failed, its advantage proved to be fleeting, for the just cause of labor could not be denied. As the twentieth century progressed, "divine right of management" would lose some of its prerogatives, and there would be increasingly less antagonism to and more partnership with organized labor. The tragedy of "Garyism," of course, was its absolutism and lack of vision. The steel hierarchy stood so close to the colossus it had created that it could not comprehend or understand some of the broad and progressive social movements of its day. Whereas it employed the most up-to-date and advanced scientific techniques in the making of steel, it relied upon a brutal, feudal, and antiquated ideology of personal relations in the conduct of its mills. "Garyism" saw no difference between a Gompers and a "red," the AF of L and the IWW, craft and industrial unionism, collective bargaining and sovietism. Not cognizant of the social and industrial *Zeitgeist* in which it lived, it attempted to remain immovable and impervious to all the changing wind of doctrine without.

McConnell, too, was close to the steel industry, but unlike many steel magnates, he saw both "trees and forest." He asked what profit it was to this basic industry if, in building its fabulous wealth and production, it destroyed the very souls of men in the process. And McConnell knew of that about which he

70. "Three Shifts in Steel," *Survey,* XLV (Dec. 11, 1920) , 387.

spoke, for, in trudging the picket lines and wandering the dirty mill-town streets, he had seen the brutalizing mode of existence of the steel worker. The smug assumption that McConnell was a harebrained preacher lost in an unfamiliar field was soon dissipated when it was discovered that the bishop had a more existential knowledge of what was happening in the mills than Mr. Gary himself. While Judge Gary had read company spy reports, McConnell had rubbed shoulders with workers. Gary was interested in profit margins and dividends to stockholders; McConnell was concerned about the food, clothing, and shelter of workers. Gary looked down upon the strike from a board of directors' "balcony" perspective; McConnell viewed the strike from the "road" of the picket line.

Although McConnell necessarily fell heir to some of the theological naïveté that was characteristic of the social gospel liberalism of his era, it seldom affected his practical consideration because of his wide experience with all kinds of individuals and with almost every facet of life. Indeed, he possessed a far greater degree of realism in his practical ethics than did most liberals who now serve as the theological whipping boys of the Neo-Protestant theologians. To be sure, he was a solid member of the liberal school, but his liberalism was qualified by many "realistic" insights into social ethics before "Christian realism" became the dominant theological motif in American Protestantism. For a man who believed in the reasonableness and basic altruistic nature of man, McConnell possessed "the wisdom of the serpent" when it came to confronting social injustice, economic contention, and power-politics. As has been indicated, when the steel trust was torturing the souls of the "Hunkies" before the steel hearths with the twelve-hour day, the Bishop did not piously ask Gary to recognize that even his Croats, Poles, and Serbs possessed infinitely sacred personalities. Not content to trust the leaven of moral suasion peacefully to persuade steel management to do justice, he took his case before the bar of public opinion, where reaction was immediate. Moreover, his fight for the establishment of the closed shop came at a time when such action was regarded as revolutionary.

Although one of his wealthy parishioners called him, half in earnest and half in jest, an "old Bolshevik," McConnell was as far removed from the fanatical "left" as he was from the chimerical. He was more concerned about meeting concrete social conditions than in blue-printing a new heaven and a new earth. Not for him were the "never-never land" utopias such as Brook Farm, New Harmony, and Oneida. He held that such Christian-Communist social experiments were actually motivated by escapism and that they were so small and of such short duration as to provide little help for modern society. McConnell's feet, which suited "his two-hundred-pound-body," were always planted squarely on the ground, "and his good-sized head" was never at home "in the clouds or in the rarefied air of speculative controversy."

The crowning greatness, however, of Bishop McConnell was his courage. To investigate the herculean steel interests was ticklish business at best. Like many others he could have rationalized: "I would like nothing better personally than to do this, but because of my position . . . the demands upon my time . . . I find it quite impossible." H. G. Wells' sarcastic barb at Anglican bishops—that they were "socially much in evidence but intellectually in hiding"—certainly did not pertain to the Bishop; neither mental frugality nor hiding was characteristic of him. Both Clarence Darrow and Harry Elmer Barnes, in their public debates with him, found that his was an intellect which easily demolished the stock arguments of the village atheist.[71] Unlike many liberals who aimed sharp verbal barbs against the satanic capitalist economy but went into hibernation when a practical task needed to be done, McConnell was not known for running away from a fight. He never learned the crab sidestep. Christianity had something to say about the hell of steel hearths as well as about a heavenly beatitude, and

71. "A Statesman Can Be A Prophet," *The World Tomorrow*, XIV (Feb., 1931), 43.

he would say it whatever the consequences. He took satisfaction in the fact that the Pittsburgh Annual Conference supported the *Report* and was not influenced by the steel trust.

The Pittsburgh laymen were very kindly. One of them asked if he was not going to leave the church rather than put up with me. "Oh, no!" he answered, "I'm not going to lose my religion because we have a fool for a bishop, and more than that I do like to hear the old bolshevik talk." [72]

Nevertheless, McConnell was subjected to a great deal of abuse and vilification, for "anyone who gets into an attack on a widespread industry may have to pay a price which now and again may be heavy." [73] Detectives shadowed everyone connected with the inquiry, and a spy ransacked the files of the Movement's Industrial Relations Department in an attempt to find incriminating data. There were protests against his appearing for speaking engagements on college campuses. At various times he was threatened and heckled; however, he believed that he never had to "take disagreeable consequences, beyond what was to be expected," because of the causes he espoused.[74] Although a number of trustees of various institutions tried to deny him honorary degrees because of the strike report, the University of Colorado conferred the LL.D. degree on him because of his role in that investigation.

By his personal behavior McConnell gave the lie to the claim of the Marxist that the Church is an instrument of class. In an era in which the Church was rapidly losing the potency of its influence upon society, McConnell was known as a churchman of vigor. The economic and socially dispossessed looked upon him as their ecclesiastical champion, and the role of the Church and the Christian faith took on a new significance in their eyes as a result of his activity. He had no such dignity of office nor pride of intellect to prevent his associating publicly with discontented laborers and radicals whom most of the well-to-do considered dangerous. He never revealed any great enthusiasm

72. "Some Attempts to Improve Me," *Christian Century,* LXVII (Jan. 18, 1950) , 77.
73. *By the Way,* p. 221.
74. *Ibid.,* p. 222.

for the scriptural injunction about putting up with fools, nor any propensity to accept ecclesiastical stuffed shirts at their own valuation. A noted Jewish rabbi said that he and his people looked upon McConnell as "their Bishop," while striking workers, who had retorted that preachers were "but a damn bunch," upon meeting him, referred to him warmly if irreverently as "the Bish."

McConnell was a great bishop because he never lost the human touch. The importance and prestige of his high ecclesiastical office had no effect upon his self-evaluation. In his case, the man affected the office; not the office the man. His life broke for millions the stereotype associated with both the office and the term "bishop." For McConnell was not content to be a desk administrator, give humorous after-dinner speeches, lay church cornerstones, or intone somber invocations at gala social affairs. Nor did he spend his time fawning before Methodist economic royalists with hat in hand, bartering his liberal birthright in exchange for a generous contribution to a pet ecclesiastical project. McConnell's prophetic tongue was above price. He proved that a statesman could be a prophet; that a man who stood at the very center of the ecclesiastical machinery need not be enslaved or crushed by it, but could utilize it to carry into the complex welter of modern life the spiritual and ethical implications of the Christian gospel.

The Communitarian Quest
for Perfection

JOHN W. CHANDLER

As much as he has tasted of global war, the bitterest fruit of modern technology, modern man continues to dwell on the possibility that the tree of scientific knowledge may be so grafted and pruned that it will bear only sweet fruit. After long preoccupation with the theme of social disintegration, social anthropology has recently taken a turn toward utopian thinking, toward the definition of social goals which can be served by, and give significant direction to, our vast technological resources.[1]

An early indication of this trend came in the significant study of the value structure of American society, *The Lonely Crowd*, first published in 1950. In the concluding chapter of that study, entitled "Autonomy and Utopia," there is held out the prospect that if America can get political leaders who will dare to think in utopian terms, "people may some day learn to buy not only packages of groceries or books but the 'larger package' of a neighborhood, a society, and a way of life." [2]

With the current growing emphasis on the social importance and necessity of utopian reflection, perhaps Americans are now in a better mood than they have been for many decades to appreciate that era in their history in which utopian reflections and experimentation reached their zenith.

Since the latter half of the seventeenth century, North America has been the scene of hundreds of efforts to establish small

---

1. Paul Goodman, "Utopian Thinking," *Commentary*, XXXII, No. 1 (July, 1961), 19.
2. David Riesman, *et al.*, *The Lonely Crowd: A Study of the Changing American Character* (abridged ed.; New York, 1956), p. 349.

utopian societies. During the second third of the nineteenth century the number of these efforts reached such torrential proportions as to turn this continent into a vast social laboratory. Emerson, who was related to the Brook Farm utopian venture, wrote to Carlyle in 1840: "We are all a little wild here with numberless projects of social reform. Not a reading man but has a draft of a new community in his waist coat pocket. One man renounces the use of animal food; and another of coin; and another of domestic hired service; and another of the State. . . ." [3]

The utopian experiments usually took the form of communities made up of from fifteen to six hundred persons. Ordinarily a community had a constitution or some other form of regulations, a set of religious or philosophical principles to which all were expected to subscribe, common ownership of property, and some modification of the institution of monogamous marriage so as to facilitate a communal rather than a family style of living.

The Secular Communitarians

American communitarianism had both its secular and religious expressions. Although our primary concern is to examine the religious movement, the secular movement was so related to it in character as to warrant brief attention.

The secular movement occurred in two phases, each associated with a prominent European thinker. Robert Owen (1771–1858), a wealthy Scottish industrialist and reformer, arrived in the United States in April, 1825, announcing with persuasive exuberance that he was ready to introduce a system of society which would gradually harmonize all interests and remove all causes of rivalry and envy among individuals. To the attentive ears of President John Quincy Adams, of former President James Monroe, and of other eminent Americans, he explained his proposal for modifying the human environment so as to

3. Quoted in Mark Holloway, *Heavens on Earth; Utopian Communities in America, 1680–1880* (New York, 1951) , p. 19.

produce a set of ideal human relations. In his talks he exhibited models of the buildings which, he claimed, would radically transform their inhabitants. The first Owenite community began, however, not with a newly constructed village, but the buildings of the old Rappite settlement at New Harmony, Indiana, in May, 1825. Owen and his American followers established nineteen communities between May, 1825, and 1830. Personally hostile to the tenets of Christianity, Owen required no religious or other ideological membership tests for his communitarians.[4]

The Owenite communities were of short duration, but their end meant no abatement of the public excitement over Owen's ideas. Indeed, public interest became more intense, largely because of the writings and speeches of his son, Robert Dale Owen, and Francis Wright.

The Owenite excitement prepared the way for Fourierism, the second phase of nineteenth-century secular communitarianism. "The same men, or at least the same sort of men that took part in the Owen movement were afterward carried away by the Fourier enthusiasm. The two movements may therefore be regarded as one; and in that view the period of the great American socialistic revival extends from 1824, through the final overwhelming excitement of 1843, to the collapse of Fourierism after 1846."[5]

Fourierism was promoted in the United States, not by Charles Fourier, a Frenchman who died in 1837, but principally by Albert Brisbane and Horace Greeley. In 1840 there appeared Brisbane's *Social Destiny of Man,* a simplified version of Fourierist thought. Greeley's conversion came about through Brisbane's book. As editor of the *New Yorker,* and later of the *New York Tribune,* Greeley took advantage of these positions to promote the Fourierist cause.

The arrangement of Fourier's "Phalanx," or ideal community, was designed to exhibit the divine harmony by which God

---

4. *Ibid.,* pp. 104 ff.
5. John Humphrey Noyes, *History of American Socialisms* (Philadelphia, 1870), p. 24.

intended to order the relations of men. The main area of the phalanx, which embraced a territory of about three square miles, was to be covered by orchards, gardens, and fields. A huge building known as the "phalanstery" was designed to provide the members with living and dining quarters, ballrooms, workshops, recreation rooms, and so on.

Of the more than forty Fourierist communities which were established in the United States, not one was able to afford the magnificent facilities prescribed by Fourier. "Instead of living in palatial Phalansteries, they huddled together in miserable log huts; and far from raising abundant crops and orchards of luscious fruit, they often starved. . . ." [6] Only a half dozen of the Fourierist communities lasted longer than fifteen months, and only three survived longer than two years.[7]

There were, of course, many similarities between the secular and the religious communitarian ventures, and more than coincidence was involved in the simultaneity of their prominence. Public knowledge of and interest in the Shakers and other religious communitarians had undoubtedly helped to prepare the way for the secular communitarian movements.

The Religious Communitarians: A Historical Sketch

This paper will treat two of the religious communitarian groups, the Shakers, who were officially known as the United Society of Believers in Christ's Second Coming, and the Oneida Perfectionists. These two movements are selected because they proved to be among the most durable of the communitarian ventures, and because they exhibit basic similarities beneath surface differences which seem at first glance to be vast.

Communitarianism appears on the surface to exhibit a wildly aberrant mood of the American religious mentality, and this fact has invited treatments which concentrate excessively upon the more fascinating eccentricities of the communitarians. It

6. Holloway, *op. cit.*, pp. 142 f.
7. For a complete list of Fourierist phalanxes, see Arthur E. Bestor, Jr., *Backwoods Utopias: The Sectarian and Owenite Phases of Communitarian Socialism in America: 1663–1829* (Philadelphia, 1950) , pp. 238–240.

will be the purpose of this study to demonstrate the extent to which and the main points at which the communitarian tributaries were joined to the main stream of American religious life and thought in the nineteenth century.

Shaker origins had their roots in a period of religious excitement in southeastern France late in the seventeenth century. Attended by remarkable bodily manifestations and by prophetic proclamations of the impending millennial reign of Christ, this movement spread to England in the first decade of the eighteenth century when some of its adherents went there to warn of the imminent second coming of Christ. The movement was unorganized and appeared to be dying out when, about the year 1747, James and Jane Wardley organized a religious society near Manchester. The little group operated much in the fashion of the Quakers, and, indeed, came to be known as the "Shaking Quakers." They had no set forms of worship and no formal rule of faith.

Sometimes, after sitting awhile in silent meditation, they were seized with a mighty trembling, under which they would often express the indignation of God against all sin. At other times they were exercised with singing, shouting and leaping for joy at the near prospect of salvation. They were often exercised with great agitations of body and limbs, shaking, running and walking the floor, with a variety of signs and operations, and swiftly passing and repassing each other, like clouds agitated with a mighty wind. . . . From these exercises, so strange in the eyes of mankind, they received the appellation of *Shakers.*[8]

The leadership of the group passed gradually to Ann Lee. Born in Manchester on February 29, 1736, this illiterate but highly intelligent young woman sought consolation in the faith and company of the Shakers. Dragooned by parental persuasion into an unhappy marriage with a blacksmith, Abraham Stanley, she passed from deep unhappiness into almost continuous grief as she observed each of her four children die in infancy.

Having joined the Shakers in 1758, she became the recog-

8. Calvin Green and Seth Y. Wells, *A Summary View of the Millennial Church, or United Society of Believers, Commonly Called Shakers* (2nd ed., revised; Albany, 1848), p. 11.

nized leader of the group in 1770 as a result of a remarkable series of visions which she reported while in prison, to which she had been committed for "profanation of the Sabbath." One of the visions revealed to her was that the sin of Adam and Eve was sexual intercourse. This revelation became the basis of Shaker celibacy. It was also crucial in the Shaker conviction, which became a central tenet of their faith, that Ann Lee was the female incarnation of Christ, just as Jesus of Nazareth had been the male incarnation.

"Mother Ann," as she now came to be called, reported another vision which directed her and her most ardent followers to America. Emigrating to New York, they bought some land in Watervliet, near Albany. The ranks of the group gradually grew as the Shakers capitalized upon outbreaks of revivalist fervor at various places near Albany and in Massachusetts.

Mother Ann died in September, 1784, three years before the Shakers decided to adopt a communitarian and communist mode of life. The center of the movement shifted away from Watervliet, New York, to near-by New Lebanon. In September, 1787, the Shakers began to organize the New Lebanon community. Elders (both male and female) were appointed to guide in both temporal and religious matters, regulations were drawn up, buildings were constructed, "so that in the year 1792, the church was considered as established in the principles of her present order and spirit." [9]

The New Lebanon settlement served as the mother church and provided the model for subsequent Shaker communities. The "ministries" (composed of the elders) of the various communities deferred to the authority of the New Lebanon ministry. Shortly after the founding of the New Lebanon community the Watervliet Shakers organized themselves for communal living. By 1826 there were nineteen communities, each containing from one hundred to six hundred members. The movement reached its peak strength in the East about the middle of the nineteenth century, and probably somewhat earlier in the

9. *Ibid.*, p. 59.

West.[10] Although the Shakers remained concentrated in New England and New York, some communities were established as far west as Ohio and Indiana, and still others as far south as Kentucky. Two short-lived communities were founded in the deep South, one at White Oaks, Georgia, and the other at Narcoossee, Florida. The approximately two dozen Shakers alive today reside at the communities at Canterbury, New Hampshire, and Sabbathday Lake, Maine.[11]

The history of the Oneida Perfectionist movement is intimately associated with the biography of John Humphrey Noyes, who led the movement from its inception in Putney, Vermont, in 1836 until the Oneida Community became a joint stock corporation in 1881.

Born into a prominent family in Brattleboro, Vermont, in 1811, Noyes planned to follow a legal career after his graduation from Dartmouth in 1820. He was converted during the great revival of 1831, and immediately abandoned his law studies in order to enter Andover Theological Seminary. He found the religious indifference of Andover depressing to his new zeal, and transferred to the theological seminary at Yale the next year (1832). Here he discovered little more inspiration than at Andover, but the relaxed academic demands of Yale gave him bountiful opportunity for cultivation of his own preferred brand of piety, for study of the Scriptures, and for revival work in the city of New Haven. Partly through his own study of the New Testament, and partly through the influence of the dozen or so revivalists with whom he became associated, Noyes veered increasingly toward a doctrine of perfection. On February 20, 1834, he declared himself free of all sin. This bold declaration led to his expulsion from Yale and to the suspension of his Congregational preacher's license.[12]

Returning to Putney, Vermont, now his family's home, Noyes faced the task of completing the delineation of his theology

10. For the best available summary of statistical data on Shaker membership, see Edward D. Andrews, *The People Called Shakers: A Search for the Perfect Society* (New York, 1953), pp. 290–292.

11. *Time*, LXXVIII, No. 4 (July 28, 1961), 53.

12. William A. Hinds, *American Communities* (rev. ed.; Chicago, 1902), pp. 144–153.

and of clarifying his relationship to the various persons and parties involved in the general perfectionist movement which was then powerful in New York and New England. Repudiating those libertine perfectionists who were guilty of scandalous sexual misbehavior, Noyes decided to gather his own band of disciples and build his own perfectionist movement.[13]

In the winter of 1836–1837 he began at Putney his "Bible School." Starting out with a nucleus consisting mainly of the leader's close relatives (his mother, two sisters, and a brother), the Bible school grew slowly, being augmented in 1838 by Harriet Holton, Noyes' bride. John Langdon Skinner joined the group in the autumn of 1839. He married one of the Noyes sisters, Harriett, and proved useful in the editorial management of *The Witness* and its successor, *The Perfectionist,* journals published by Noyes and his group.[14]

What began as essentially a Bible study group gradually evolved into a communist society, going through the intermediate stages of "The Society of Inquiry," "Contract of Partnership," and "The Putney Corporation." Finally, in 1846 the steady advance toward a full communism was culminated with the introduction of the novel institution of "complex marriage," whereby the exclusiveness of monogamous marriage was rejected in favor of an arrangement by which each woman was considered to be the wife of each man and each man the husband of each woman.[15]

The outraged monogamists of Putney moved quickly to crush the radical social innovation of complex marriage. William A. Hinds, who was a member of Noyes' community at Putney, reports that "indignation meetings were held in which the doctrine and practices of Mr. Noyes and his followers were denounced, the immediate suppression of their paper demanded, and legal proceedings threatened." [16] Legal proceedings were, indeed, instituted.

As early as July, 1847, Noyes was beginning to look for a new

13. Benjamin B. Warfield, *Perfectionism,* II (New York, 1931), pp. 271–275.
14. Hinds, *op. cit.,* p. 157.
15. Warfield, *op. cit.,* p. 276.
16. Hinds, *op. cit.,* p. 171.

location for his Putney experiment. At two conventions of perfectionists held in September, 1847, in central New York, Noyes explained the Putney tenets and tried to interest the New York perfectionists in beginning a communitarian venture. Out of the interest stirred up at these meetings there began, in February, 1848, a community at Oneida, New York. Noyes, who had fled bail and left Putney for New York City the previous November, joined the Oneida founders almost immediately and became leader and president of the new organization. Within a few months most of the approximately forty Perfectionists of Putney had joined the group at Oneida. New members came in from various parts of New York, New Jersey, and New England, so that the membership on the first day of January, 1849, was eighty-seven. By February 20, 1851, there were 205 members, and by 1878 there were 306.[17]

A small branch community was established in 1849 at Brooklyn, New York, and other branch societies grew up shortly thereafter in Wallingford, Connecticut; Newark, New Jersey; Putney and Cambridge in Vermont; and Manlius, New York. In 1873 the Perfectionists decided to operate only the communities at Oneida and Wallingford and to limit the membership to very slow increase.[18] Charles Nordhoff reported in 1873 that although the Perfectionists received over one hundred membership applications by letter and a nearly equal number in person, their policy was to admit no new members.[19] William H. Dixon had reported earlier that when he was visiting Oneida in 1866 the applicants were numerous but that few members were being received.[20]

Getting off to a shaky economic start, the Oneida Perfectionists prospered from 1855 on, largely because of their good judgment in trying to achieve a balance between agriculture and

17. *Ibid.,* p. 175.
18. *Ibid.*
19. *The Communist Societies of the United States; from Personal Visit and Observation: Including detailed Accounts of the Economists, Zoarites, Shakers, the Amana, Oneida, Bethel, Aurora, Icarian, and Other Existing Societies, Their Religious Creeds, Social Practices, Numbers, Industries, and Present Condition* (New York, 1875) , p. 264.
20. *New America* (3rd ed.; Philadelphia, 1867) , p. 423.

industry, and through their good fortune in attracting to membership Sewell Newhouse, inventor of a remarkable steel trap. Mass production of the trap started at Oneida in 1855, and the trap became the standard in America and was widely used throughout the world.[21]

The Oneida venture met shipwreck—just as Putney had—on the issue of complex marriage. Resistance to the practice arose both inside and outside the community, and the combination of pressures finally led to disintegration of the movement. The external opposition was organized mainly by Professor John W. Mears of Hamilton College, a Presbyterian leader. In 1873 the Presbyterian Synod of Central New York appointed a committee of seven to confer with other religious bodies on the question of possible action against the Oneida Community. This move led to a series of actions and eventuated in Noyes' resigning as head of the community in May, 1877, and turning its management over to his son, Theodore Noyes. Theodore was an agnostic, a circumstance which made it difficult for the older members of the community to accept his leadership. Another source of internal dissension was James William Towner, who joined the Oneida group in 1874. A former clergyman and lawyer, Towner became the confidant of disaffected members of the community just when Noyes' leadership capacities were being curtailed by deafness and a speech difficulty. In June, 1879, the elder Noyes slipped away from Oneida in the middle of the night and went into exile in Ontario. On August 20, 1879, the Perfectionists at Oneida received from Noyes a series of recommendations designed to placate both the outside critics and the dissident (mostly younger) members within. The most drastic recommendations proposed the abandonment of complex marriage and the encouragement of celibacy, with monogamous marriage to be permitted. The other primary features of the community—joint ownership of property, common living and eating quarters, children's department, daily evening meetings—would be retained. These recommendations,

---

21. Pierrepont Noyes, *My Father's House: An Oneida Boyhood* (New York, 1937) , pp. 14–15. See also Dixon, *op. cit.,* p. 414.

which were adopted on August 26, did not have the desired effect. Monogamous marriage proved a much more popular option than celibacy, and the arrangements at Oneida obviously could not tolerate monogamous marriage as the norm. By the end of 1880 all of the communistic features of the community were gone, and on January 1, 1881, it became an ordinary joint stock company.[22] Today Oneida, Limited, is a vigorous and successful corporation specializing in the manufacture of silverware. An unusual profit-sharing plan and the presence of many descendants of the Perfectionists among its employees attest to its origins.

Communitarianism, Revivalism, and Perfectionism

There can be no understanding of American religious communitarianism apart from an understanding of revivalism, for it was the revivalistic idea of perfect sanctification which led to widespread interest in communitarian living as providing the only conditions under which santification could be achieved. The undulating fortunes of Shakerism illustrate well the dependence of communitarianism upon revivalism.

The Shakers got their start in America just prior to what was perhaps the most irreligious period in American history, that from the end of the Revolution (1783) until the end of the century.[23] Building up a small membership by capitalizing upon revivalistic fervor in a few areas of eastern New York and Massachusetts,[24] the Shakers then began a quiescent period as Deism and irreligion became more rampant. The interim of general indifference was used by the Shakers as an opportunity

22. Robert A. Parker, *Yankee Saint: John Humphrey Noyes and the Oneida Community* (New York, 1935), pp. 204–206.

23. For a lucid summary of religious conditions during the Revolutionary era, see Frank G. Beardsley, *A History of American Revivals* (New York, 1904), chap. iv. For a more detailed study, see Gustav A. Koch, *Republican Religion: The American Revolution and the Cult of Reason* (New York, 1933).

24. Frederick W. Evans, *Ann Lee (The Founder of the Shakers)*; a Biography, with Memoirs of William Lee, James Whittaker, J. Hocknell, J. Meacham, and Lucy Wright; also a Compendium of the Origin, History, Principles, Rules and Regulations, Government, and Doctrines of the United Society of Believers in Christ's Second Appearing (4th ed.; London, 1858), pp. 26 ff.

for deepening and stabilizing the life of their societies.[25] But once the Second Great Awakening had broken the Deistic spell, then the Shakers emerged from their seclusion in order to make known the Shaker way to the excited and questing throngs who flocked to hear evangelists. In 1802 the Shakers dispatched two missionaries, Elder Benjamin Seth Youngs and Issachar Bates, to take the Shaker message to New England areas affected by revivalistic ferment. Within a year the Shakers had garnered a harvest of over sixteen hundred new converts, and other harvests were ahead in the West, as yet untouched by Shaker fervor.[26]

At three o'clock in the morning of the first day of January, 1805, Bates, Youngs, and John Meacham set out from New Lebanon in order to take this Shaker witness to the frontier throngs who were responding sensationally to the preaching of Methodist, Baptist, and Presbyterian revivalists. Among the first converts of the new frontier missionaries was Richard Mc-Nemar, along with his wife and children. McNemar was pastor of the largest Presbyterian church in southern Ohio, Turtle Creek. He was prominent among the "New Lights," a sect which originated when some Presbyterians withdrew from the Synod of Kentucky in September, 1803, in order to escape ecclesiastical discipline and thus be free to follow the Bible as the sole rule of faith and practice. The New Light Presbyterians were in full sympathy with revivalism, and they modified their worship procedures to incorporate some of the vivid gestures which emerged out of the revival. In one of the classic reports on the Kentucky revival, McNemar describes New Light worship:

Hence by giving the right hand of fellowship to those who were admitted into the community, and finding that it tended to encrease [sic] the inward workings of the spirit; it was gradually introduced as a common act of worship, in concert with singing hymns and spiritual songs. The whole society, old and young, male and female, would commonly unite in this mode of worship; and taking each other by the hand, would shake not only their hands, but their whole bodies, like one churning; with such violence that

25. Green and Wells, *op. cit.*, p. 77.
26. Andrews, *op. cit.*, p. 71.

the place would seem to quiver under them. This they called rejoicing. . . .[27]

Out of these religious exercises there evolved religious dancing as a form of praise to God.[28] Thus the New Lights prepared the way for the Shakers, whose principal service of worship was a rapid dance performed in unison by rows of "brothers and sisters."

The Shaker doctrine of celibacy aroused bitter opposition, so that it was often impossible for Shaker evangelists to get a public hearing at camp and church meetings. Accordingly, the Shakers quietly sought out interested individuals among the revival crowds and gradually won converts. Meeting mainly at first in the homes of leading spirits, the Shakers were able to gather their new converts into communities as they began to receive bequests of land. The first formally organized Western Shaker community, made up of eleven brothers and eight sisters, moved into its new buildings at Lebanon, Miami County, Ohio, on October 22, 1806. On January 15, 1812, the community was renamed "Union Village." Union Village served as the mother community for subsequent Western settlements, playing for Western Shakerism much the same role which New Lebanon played in the East. After Mount Union, the Western movement continued with the establishment of communities at Watervliet, Ohio (1806), Pleasant Hill, Kentucky (1807–1810), West Union, Indiana (1810–1811), North Union, Ohio (1822), Whitewater, Ohio (1824–1825), and Sodus Bay and Groveland, New York (1826). By 1823 there were approximately 1700 Shakers in the Western communities.[29]

Western Shakerism was built on the revivalistic foundations

---

27. *The Kentucky Revival; or, A Short History of the Late Extraordinary Outpouring of the Spirit of God, in the Western States of America, Agreeably to Scripture Promises and Prophecies, Concerning the Latter Day: With a Brief Account of the Entrance and Progress of What the World Call Shakerism, Among the Subjects of the late Revival in Ohio and Kentucky* (Cincinnati, 1807), p. 69.

28. *Ibid.*, p. 71.

29. For details of the relationship of Shakerism to early nineteenth-century frontier revivalism, see Andrews, *op. cit.*, chap. v, and Julia Neal, *By Their Fruits: The Story of Shakerism in South Union Kentucky* (Chapel Hill, 1947), chaps. ii-v.

prepared by the labors of evangelists of established faiths. With each denomination proclaming itself to be the one true church, the Shakers—like the Mormons a little later—were able to buttress their claim by presenting a set of theological tenets and a mode of life which contrasted markedly with the faith and practices of the main line denominations. The opposition and persecution which they met simply served to unify them, to increase their separation from the world, and to lend added credence to their claims of being a peculiarly holy people.

Revivalism was no less important in the history of the Oneida Perfectionists than it was in the history of Shakerism. Noyes' comments on nineteenth-century American social thought are informed by unusual perception, and some of his most acute comments concern the dependence of communitarianism upon revivalism. Converted himself in the great revival of 1831, his earliest conception of his religious vocation was that of an evangelist. He was a member of an evangelistic clique in New Haven. He points out that his original group at Putney were simply revivalists. They were not socialists in either form or theory.[30]

Noyes discerned that in the case both of his movement and the Shakers the communal mode of existence was a device for surrounding the members with a continuous atmosphere of revivalist zeal. The expedient of protracted meetings, relied upon by the main line denominations, failed to transform the churches into familial brotherhoods, so that the world constantly reabsorbed the converts of such meetings.[31] Noyes was convinced that his movement was a repristination of the primitive Christian church, in which those who were filled with the Holy Spirit at Pentecost "were of one heart and soul, and no one said that any of the things which he possessed was his own, but they had everything in common" (Acts 4:32, RSV).

Christian perfection was the chief theme of the frontier revivalist preachers of the middle third of the nineteenth century, an emphasis which contrasts sharply with the theological

30. *Op. cit.*, p. 615.
31. *Ibid.*, p. 27.

tenor of seventeenth- and early eighteenth-century Protestantism. The beginning of Protestant experience in America reflects the anti-utopian element in the thought of Luther and Calvin, the conviction that man's hope lies in trust in the perfect goodness of God rather than in the prospect of achieving moral perfection of his own. In his classic study of American religious thought, Richard Niebuhr comments:

> Seventeenth century Protestants could not be utopians or idealists in the popular sense of the words, for they did not share the fundamental presuppositions of utopianism—the beliefs that human ills are due to bad institutions, that a fresh start with good institutions will result in a perfect commonwealth, and that human reason is sufficiently wise, or human will sufficiently selfless, to make the erection of a perfect society possible. They were for the most part thoroughly convinced that mankind had somehow been corrupted; they knew that the order of glory had not yet been established; they were pilgrims all who did not expect to be satisfied in the time of their pilgrimage.[32]

As Niebuhr convincingly argues, the idea of the Kingdom of God was gradually transformed in American religious thought from the conception of the sovereign rule of transcendent God over the processes of history to the idea of the direct rule of the Spirit of Christ in the lives of men. From the period of the Great Awakening in the 1740's and continuing through the great revivals of the nineteenth century, American Protestantism was largely controlled by the conception of God, not as sovereign bound to his people by covenantal terms spelled out in the Bible, but as Father exhibiting his compassion through his Son, Jesus Christ. The perfect love of God as exhibited in Christ became the model for ordering the moral life of the Christian.

Revivalistic perfectionism was not confined to America, and one of its important roots extended back into eighteenth-century English Methodism. John Wesley's "Plain Account of Christian Perfection" was widely known in America. Still, American perfectionism reflected primarily the American milieu. The doctrine was in large part the religious idiom for

---

32. *The Kingdom of God in America* (New York, 1937), p. 49.

expressing the buoyant confidence of a new nation with vast economic resources, a much admired political system, and a proud history.

Charles G. Finney (1792–1875), one of the great revivalists of all times, showed his confidence in the future of Christianity and of America when he declared in the early 1830's: "If the church will do all her duty, the millennium will come in this country in three years." [33] The substance of Finney's preaching and writing was that personal regeneration would result in a regenerated social order. He called for "entire consecration" or "sanctification," and this strand in his preaching became dominant to the point that his theology came to be known as "Oberlin Perfectionism" after he moved to Oberlin, Ohio, and became associated with Oberlin College. Assessing the importance of Finney in the American religious scene of the second third of the nineteenth century, Timothy L. Smith concludes:

The revivals of the Jacksonian era produced in Charles G. Finney a perfectionism quite as radical as any that John Wesley's followers ever taught. Since the Oberlin doctrine did not look back to an eighteenth century prophet, but rather grew out of the religious climate of the age, its history serves well to introduce the current which swept across American Protestantism between 1835 and the end of the Civil War.[34]

Finney grew up in Oneida County, in western New York, and he won initial fame as an evangelist from his sensational revivals in western New York in 1824. By the time his perfectionism had become fully explicit in the late 1830's he was the most influential religious figure in America, and perfectionism had become a widespread movement.[35] It was a source of painful irritation to Finney that his name was connected indiscriminately with various forms of perfectionism. He repudiated antinomian forms of perfectionism and took pains to make clear

33. *Lectures on Revivals of Religion,* ed. William G. McLoughlin (Cambridge, Mass., 1960), p. 306.
34. *Revivalism and Social Reform in Mid-Nineteenth-Century America* (New York, 1957), p. 103.
35. Warfield's study (*op. cit.*) extensively documents the connection between perfectionism and the Finney revivals. For a more recent study which emphasizes this connection, see Whitney R. Cross, *The Burned-Over District: The Social and Intellectual History of Enthusiastic Religion in Western New York, 1800–1850* (Ithaca, New York, 1950).

that his perfectionism required rigorous obedience to a strict code of behavior.[36] Finney classified Noyes as an antinomian, and he looked with abhorrence upon complex marriage.

The perfectionist motif in separatist Protestantism found favorable soil and broke forth into luxuriant and profuse growth in central and western New York in the late twenties and early thirties of the nineteenth century. Oneida Perfectionism is to be viewed—along with Mormonism, the Millerites, and numerous other sectarian movements—as a product of the waves of religious excitement which swept and reswept through that region.[37] Proceeding out of New York, perfectionist zeal found "its way in the early thirties into New England and thence over the world."[38]

The perfectionist movement in New York and New England in the 1820's and 1830's was extremely complex. All of the established denominations had perfectionist factions, and there were some attempts (such as conventions) at organization; but the perfectionist movement never became a distinct sect or denomination. Perfectionism generally remained within the framework of the denominations, where it was a divisive and disruptive force.

Public antipathy and suspicion toward the Oneida community were stirred up among those who associated Noyes' movement with the antinomian perfectionists whose declaration of freedom from sin led them to abandon the traditional code of sexual behavior. Some of the antinomians interpreted this freedom as a license for sexual promiscuity, while to others it simply meant that the usual cautions against sexual temptation might be disregarded by one whose sanctification had made him impervious to temptation.[39] This latter interpretation led to the reinstitution of the "spiritual wives" (the *agapetae* or *virgines subintroductae*) of the early church.

---

36. *Lectures on Systematic Theology, Embracing Ability, (natural, moral and gracious,) Repentance, Impenitence, Faith and Unbelief, Justification, Sanctification, Election, Reprobation, Divine Purposes, Divine Sovereignty, and Perseverance* (Oberlin, Ohio, 1847) , Lecture LX.
37. See Whitney R. Cross, *op. cit.*
38. Warfield, *op. cit.*, p. 222.
39. *Ibid.*, pp. 242–245.

Needless to say, some of these spiritual companions became mistresses.[40]

Noyes was not averse to radical social innovations, but he was repelled by the devotion of the antinomian perfectionists to what he called the principle of "disunity," [41] a principle which rejected any form of order or organization as evil. It was on this issue that Noyes broke with James Boyle and Theophilus R. Gates, who had influenced him toward perfectionism during his New Haven days, and founded his own perfectionist cult. William A. Hinds, who was a disciple of Noyes both at Putney and at Oneida, quotes James Boyle as having said: "Perfectionists stand as independent of each other as they do of any anti-Christian churches—they will not be taught of each other, as they are all taught of God, nor will they acknowledge any man as a leader or chief or anything of the kind." [42] Obviously such extreme individualism would make communitarian existence impossible. Noyes enforced a rigid discipline both at Putney and Oneida. Complex marriage was carefully regulated, and those—such as Benjamin Warfield and Everett Webber [43]—who treat it as an example of perfectionist libertinism, misrepresent it.

Central to Noyes' doctrine of perfection was his theory of conversion as involving two distinct stages. By the first stage one becomes the servant of God and by the second he becomes the son of God. The servant of God is concerned primarily with duty. The second conversion, which Noyes and many of his followers claimed for themselves, brought perfect holiness and a sense of absolute security against sin.[44] Ingredient to the experience of perfect sanctification was the awareness that the second coming of Christ has already occurred, that it occurred, indeed, in A.D. 70. The second appearance was a spiritual one, but also

40. The most famous account of this weird phenomenon is to be found in W. H. Dixon, *Spiritual Wives*, (2nd ed.; Philadelphia, 1868) .

41. *The Berean: A Manual for the Help of Those Who Seek the Faith of the Primitive Church* (Putney, Vt., 1847) , p. 68.

42. *Op. cit.*, pp. 158–159.

43. Everett Webber, *Escape to Utopia: The Communal Movement in America* (New York, 1959) , chap. xix.

44. *The Berean*, p. 153.

a bodily one, and the Spirit of Christ makes possible holiness of life and perfect community. These conclusions, it is important to note, were buttressed by Noyes' exegetical studies of the Bible. Among the passages which he cites in support of the argument for perfect holiness are I John 3:2–10; 4:17; 5:18. The crucial scriptural foundation for his argument that the second coming of Christ had occurred within one generation of his death and resurrection was Jesus' statement, regarding the disciple John: "If it is my will that he remain until I come, what is that to you?" (John 21:22, RSV).

The Shaker practice of grading the spirituality of their members according to orders suggests at least an implicit agreement with Noyes' "two conversion" theory. Shaker communities ordinarily had three orders: the children's order, the novitiate, and the church order. Novices might be newcomers, but many of them were Shakers of long standing who had never achieved the degree of spirituality necessary to advance to the church order. Not all of the members of the church order claimed to have attained perfection, but such claims were not uncommon. Nordhoff reports: "In their daily lives many profess to have attained perfection: these are the older people. . . . One of the older Shakers, a man of seventy-two years . . . said to me . . . that he had lived for years a sinless life." [45]

Neither the Shakers nor the Oneida Perfectionists conceived of perfection as a static mode of experience. The Shakers in particular emphasized spiritual growth.

Therefore, tho' a soul in the progress of faithful obedience to the increasing light and work of God, may become divested of all sinful desire and propensities; yet his life and happiness must and will consist in a further and progressive growth in the knowledge and nature of God, to the endless ages of eternity. And yet a soul who is perfectly obedient to the revealed will of God, is equally perfect before God, in every step of his travel, according to his capacity and God's requirements. [46]

The vision of perfection held by the Shakers and Perfectionists, though ostensibly inspired by the New Testament, was, in

45. *Op. cit.,* p. 163.
46. Green and Wells, *op. cit.,* p. 373.

large part, simply another expression of the confidence in human progress which became in the eighteenth century the chief tenet in the *credo* of the Western World.[47] The general confidence in progress became an almost feverish mood of expectancy in America in the 1830's. Speaking of this period, Warfield writes: "Men stood in a condition of permanent astonishment. Everything seemed possible. They did not know what would come next. . . . They lived on perpetual tiptoe." [48] Illustrating precisely this mood, Noyes wrote: "The whole world seems to be looking for a Revolution. Some expect an orthodox Millennium; others a golden age of phrenology; others still, a physiological regeneration of the human race; and not a few are awaiting, in anxious or hopeful suspense, the trump of the Second Advent, and the day of judgment." [49]

Noyes states his own philosophy of history in terms of progress delineated in the form of four dispensations: 1. The age from Adam to Moses witnessed man's physical development. 2. The era from Moses to Christ was one of human moral development. 3. From the time of Christ to the present has been the age of intellectual development. 4. The impending period will be one of spiritual development. Such movements as Swedenborgianism, mesmerism, and Shakerism are all portents of the coming age.[50] Not evident in this sketch is Noyes' belief that spiritual progress proceeds in undulating and slow fashion. He regarded the primitive Christian movement as having had a brief period of vitality followed by a lengthy period in which its genius was buried beneath the distortions and perversions which eventuated in Roman Catholic Christianity. The primitive movement lay quietly buried as a seed and began to break forth into bloom again in the form of Perfectionism.[51]

Writing in 1900, Allan Estlake, who had been a member of the Oneida Community, was able to look back upon the col-

47. See John B. Bury, *The Idea of Progress; An Inquiry into its Origin and Growth* (London, 1920).
48. *Op. cit.*, p. 227.
49. *The Berean*, p. 52.
50. *Ibid.*, p. 54.
51. *Ibid.*, p. 297.

lapse of Oneida as but the beginning of another period of dormancy for the pure spirit of Christianity. He wrote:

Disintegration of old organizations with integration of new sects has been the experience of Christendom from the Romish Church to the Salvation Army. In its appointed place came the Oneida Community; it also disintegrated as did the primitive Church, which was its prototype, and then commenced the integration of numerous phases of communism, socialism, populism, and the numerous isms of that genus in which the unrestful spirit of America is seeking some refuge from the growing selfishness of the age. They will all disintegrate, to be succeeded by something only a little in advance, and this routine must continue until in processes of evolution will be reached the universal dissemination of the brotherly love of which Christ was a prophecy, and of which the Oneida community was an exemplar and object lesson.[52]

Passing on from the question of the historical nature of the Christian movement, Estlake expands his treatment into a general theory of progress. The progress of mankind depends, he argues, upon the twin forces of education and religious regeneration. The educated mind undirected by a regenerated heart tends to turn to acquisitiveness. The educated mind directed by a regenerated heart seeks perfection within community. Communist communitarianism is the end product of education and regeneration.[53]

Estlake's analysis of the history of Christianity in terms of undulating processes of integration and disintegration would be, if stripped of the contention that succeeding processes of integration always represent advances, a close parallel of Ernst Troeltsch's distinction between church-type and sect-type Christian movements,[54] and an even closer parallel of H. Richard Niebuhr's refinement of Troeltsch's teaching.[55] Troeltsch's list of the chief characteristics of sect-type groups clearly fits the Oneida Perfectionists and the Shakers:

52. Allan Estlake, *The Oneida Community: A Record of an Attempt to Carry Out the Principles of Christian Unselfishness and Scientific Race-Improvement* (London, 1900), pp. 138–139.
53. *Ibid.,* pp. 139–158.
54. *The Social Teaching of the Christian Churches,* trans. Olive Wyon (New York, 1960), I, 331 ff.
55. *The Social Sources of Denominationalism* (Hamden, Conn., 1954), pp. 17–21.

lay Christianity, personal achievement in ethics and in religion, the radical fellowship of love, religious equality and brotherly love, indifference towards the authority of the State and the ruling classes. . . . the separation of the religious life from the economic struggle by means of the ideal of poverty and frugality, or occasionally in a charity which becomes communism, . . . the appeal to the New Testament and to the Primitive Church.[56]

Whereas Troeltsch emphasizes that both sect-type and church-type traits are rooted in the Christian movement, Niebuhr seems definitely to believe that sect-type groups are nearer to the genius of Christianity, and he represents church-type traits as developing mainly out of sects in process of disintegration. Estlake's thought conforms more nearly to that of Niebuhr, but here again the crucial difference is that Estlake subscribed to the notion that the successive sectarian expressions of the primitive Christian genius represented progress both in the purity of their truth and in the extent of their influence.

It is a little surprising to find the Shakers advocates of the doctrine of progress, since the degree of their alienation from the prevailing culture was greater than that of the Oneida Perfectionists. And yet, Shaker literature abounds with exclamations of this sort:

The present age is an age of wonders. . . . It appears to be the prevailing sentiment and expectation among nearly all ranks and orders of people, that something wonderful is about to take place; that there will be such a revolution of public sentiment, and such a reformation will be effected in the various branches of human economy as never has been exhibited in the world since the creation of man.[57]

The Shakers viewed the date 1747, in which year James and Jane Wardley began their society, as being the beginning of a new dispensation. Like the Oneida Perfectionists, they, too, believed that the second coming of Christ had already occurred: Ann Lee was the second incarnation of Christ on earth. Shaker theologians worked assiduously trying to square biblical

56. *Op. cit.,* p. 337.
57. Green and Wells, *op. cit.,* p. 1.

eschatological passages with their notion of an endless perfect social order on earth. In a typical Shaker theological exercise, John Dunlavy, a former New Light Presbyterian, argues that the account in Revelation 20:1–6 of the thousand-year-reign of Christ and his saints "is by no means inconsistent with the continuance of the kingdom forever." [58] The millennium, he affirms, is already under way, with the second appearance of Christ having occurred in Ann Lee. The last judgment is not a "day," but rather, a progressive process, already going on, "in which all mankind are to be called into a deeper work, and a more consummate trial of their true state and character, . . . and their final character and condition to be unalterably decided according to their works." [59]

We have seen, then, that Shakerism and the Noyesian Perfectionism were essentially expressions of revivalism, and that their emphasis on perfect personal holiness was also the central doctrinal emphasis of revivalist preaching. But their understanding of perfection was a curiously compounded blend of New Testament eschatological and ethical thought, on the one hand, and, on the other hand, Enlightenment confidence in history as an ameliorative process which will witness increasing wisdom, brotherhood, and happiness in the affairs of man. The communitarian pattern of social organization, to which we now turn, was designed to insure optimum conditions for the achievement and continuation of revivalist fervor and personal sanctification.

Social Organization

There is no intention here to present a full and detailed account of the social organization of the Shakers and the Oneida Perfectionists, since many such accounts are available elsewhere. What I wish to do is to make clear how the communitarians implemented practically their conviction that the

58. *The Manifesto, or a Declaration of the Doctrine and Practice of the Church of Christ* (New York: reprinted by Edward O. Jenkins, 1847), p. 384.
59. *Ibid.*, p. 398.

holy community (the *koinonia,* the church) ought to provide optimum conditions for producing personal sanctification.

PROPERTY. The problems associated with property and with the relations between the sexes undoubtedly account for a large proportion of human misery, and most utopian reflection and experimentation propose radical reforms in these areas.

Says Reinhold Niebuhr: "Every relation between persons ultimately involves the question of possessions. The 'I' is so intimately related to the 'mine' and the 'thine' that relations of accord or conflict between individuals usually imply questions of property." [60] Both the Shakers and the Oneida Perfectionists came to the conclusion that the economic system based upon private ownership of property set definite and undesirable limits upon the degree of cohesiveness possible within their respective fellowships. Neither movement began as communist, but both arrived at communism as an economic arrangement which, they believed, would provide optimum conditions for cultivating and maintaining community cohesiveness. Each movement cited, of course, the communism of property of the primitive church, but the scriptural warrant provided them rather with an ex post facto sanction than with an original inspiration.

The Shakers required new members to be free of debt, and to be a member of the church order one had to be entirely free of economic entanglements with the outside world. An individual Shaker had no need of money, for the fields and shops of the community provided him with almost anything he might need. Each man had assigned to him a sister who saw to it that his clothes were clean and in proper repair and who advised when new clothes were needed. The Shaker communities naturally needed cash in order to transact business with the capitalist world outside. They managed to keep a sufficient supply of cash by marketing surplus commodities. There was a large demand for their garden seeds, and their apothecary

60. *The Children of Light and the Children of Darkness: A Vindication of Democracy and a Critique of Its Traditional Defense* (New York, 1944), p. 86.

shops produced drugs of famed quality. They were ingenious inventors, and some of their labor-saving devices were marketed with signal success.[61] The separate "families" within a Shaker community operated as virtually autonomous economic units. Since a family generally consisted of from thirty to ninety persons, it was easy for individuals to understand the necessity of their own contributions to the economic commonwealth and to avoid an unrealistic sense of security in the labors of others.

The communism of Oneida was established while the nucleus of the group was still in Putney. The Oneida settlers showed excellent business sense in avoiding the usual communitarian error of overinvestment in land. Although they depended largely upon agriculture, particularly in their earlier period, they manufactured and marketed such diverse items as traveling bags, match boxes, and steel traps.

Oneida's economic activity was carefully planned. Forty-eight departments (e.g., hardware, publication, silk manufacturing, tin shop, clothing) administered the various segments of the economy. The heads of the departments constituted a "Business Board" which held regular open meetings on Sunday mornings. At these meetings the activities of the past week were discussed and plans for the future were drawn up. Formal approval of plans for the future came at a general meeting of the community on Sunday evening.[62]

Noyes thought of every phase of human experience as having a sacramental quality, and the economic arrangements of Oneida were designed to show the meaning of work in a redeemed society. Wrote Noyes, "In vital society, strength will be increased and the necessity of labor diminished, till work will become sport, as it would have been in the original Eden state." [63] Once the Perfectionists had become economically viable, the maximum workday for able-bodied men was seven hours, scarcely more than half the length of the normal workday of the period. Women worked fewer hours, as did

61. The most complete and authoritative account of Shaker economic life is Edward D. Andrews, *The Community Industries of the Shakers* (Albany, 1933).
62. Nordhoff, *op. cit.*, p. 279.
63. *History of American Socialisms*, p. 635.

men whose age or physical condition handicapped them. Men and women were mingled in their work assignments in a deliberate attempt to make their work more attractive. Frequent job rotation, supervised by a committee, guaranteed against drudgery. Futhermore, the Perfectionists hired outsiders—at excellent wages—to do the dullest and most difficult work.[64]

SEX RELATIONS. The Shakers and the Oneida Perfectionists agreed that monogamous marriage was incompatible with communal life, but they disagreed as to the best substitute for monogamy, with the Shakers adopting celibacy and the Perfectionists devising the institution of complex marriage.

As noted earlier, Shaker celibacy stems from Ann Lee's reported vision which revealed that sexual lust destroyed the divinely established order in Eden. Sexual lust disrupts the created order by perverting the sex act from its procreative function. Lust drives individuals to jealousy, envy, hatred, and murder. It drives nations to war and brings poverty and disgrace to families. In short, sexual lust is the root of all evils which afflict individuals and society.[65]

In an attempt to counter the argument that celibacy was a threat to the continuation of the human race and to the family's value as a cohesive force in society, the Shakers made it clear that celibacy is only for the regenerate minority. "We consider matrimony to be a civil institution, and as such, it is both useful and necessary for mankind in their natural state; but it does not belong to the true followers of Christ; and for that reason they have nothing to do with it." [66]

Nineteenth-century revivalism encouraged an activistic holiness, a state of embattled sanctification. The Shakers reflected this point of view by insisting upon celibacy under conditions which made sexual temptation inevitable. The Shaker celibates lived together in "families" of from thirty to ninety persons, both men and women, headed usually by four elders, two men and two women. A family—the basic unit in a Shaker com-

64. Nordhoff, *op. cit.*, pp. 279 ff.
65. For typical statements of this point of view, see Dunlavy, *op. cit.*, pp. 283 ff.
66. Green and Wells, *op. cit.*, p. 174.

munity—lived together in a big dormitory-like building. The rooms of the brothers and sisters were on the same hallways. They ate in the same dining hall, though at separate tables. They worshiped together, primarily through their sacred dances. They had an institution which might be called "communal dating." Four or five brothers would call on a similar number of sisters, usually in a sister's room. It must also be remembered that many of the brothers and sisters had lived in the world as husbands and wives. The Shakers, then, seemed to see more virtue in successfully resisting temptation than in insuring against any occasions of temptation.

This does not mean that the Shakers did not exercise caution in regulating the relationships between brothers and sisters. Indeed, the rules were numerous. There was, for example, what might be called the "five foot" rule, which decreed that a brother and a sister could approach one another no more closely than that distance. Nor might they exchange presents, nor meet on a stairway, nor shake hands, nor hold private conversation. A sister was not permitted to mend a brother's clothes while he had on the clothes, and she was required to be careful in keeping her own clothing strictly separated from men's clothing.[67]

In marked contrast with Shaker celibacy stood "pantagamous" or "complex" marriage, surely one of the most unusual attacks ever launched against monogamy. One of the key theological tenets of Noyes was the belief that the second coming of Christ occurred in A.D. 70, and, accordingly, that the kingdom of heaven was a present possibility for those who were aware of the spiritual presence of Christ. In the Kingdom of Heaven there is neither private property nor marriage. In a letter which he did not intend for publication, but which nevertheless appeared in the columns of a journal called the *Battle-Axe* in 1837, Noyes declared that in the Kingdom of Heaven it is as out of place for sexual relations to be regulated by the principle

67. For the official regulations of the Shakers, "The Millennial Laws," see Andrews, *The People Called Shakers*, pp. 243 ff. At first transmitted orally, these regulations were written down in 1821. New codifications were authorized in 1839, 1841, and 1845.

of exclusiveness as it is for persons at a meal to make exclusive claims upon particular items of food. "In a holy community, there is no more reason why sexual intercourse should be restrained by law, than eating and drinking should be—and there is as little occasion for shame in the one case as in the other." [68]

Among the evils which hold mankind in ruin, contended Noyes, the disruption of man's sex life is second in importance only to man's breach with God. The scheme of Christian redemption, Noyes insists, "begins with reconciliation with God, proceeds first to a restoration of true relations between the sexes, and then to a reform of the industrial system, and ends with victory over death." [69]

A redeemed sex life, then, is possible in a community in which men are at peace with God, and only a redeemed sex life conforms to man's natural capacity for "loving any number of times and any number of persons. . . ." [70] Complex marriage will work only in a redeemed community. Thus Noyes was extremely careful in screening applicants who sought membership in his society. "Holiness must go before free love." [71]

As practiced at Oneida, complex marriage did not give the license which at first glance it appears to allow. The system actually operated as a series of intermittent and temporary marriages. A particular man and woman would enjoy amorous relations for a few weeks or months before new partners would be chosen, or there would be a period of waiting for one or both parties. A woman who did not like a man was free to avoid him, and there is evidence that the women of Oneida were free to initiate amorous attachments. An important restraint on the relationship between the sexes was the fact that partners to an amorous relationship did not negotiate the attachment directly, but used the services of a third party, usually one of the older women of the community. These directors of the marital traffic undoubtedly served to reduce tensions and

68. Quoted by Parker, *op. cit.,* p. 44.
69. *History of American Socialisms,* p. 630.
70. *Ibid.,* p. 628.
71. *Ibid.,* p. 631.

complications, some of which were inevitable. A romantic attachment was expected to be temporary, and any undue prolongation was usually broken up through the system of mutual criticism.

The child population at Oneida was carefully controlled. Noyes emphasized the separation of the "amative" and procreative functions of sex, and he educated the men of the community to use *coitus interruptus* (which he called "male continence") as a method of birth control. Oneida was a ready-made eugenics laboratory, and Noyes personally decided upon the pairings for the procreation of children. In an ingenious move designed to placate those who, in his opinion, were risky genotypes, Noyes permitted each man who was not in the favored group of breeders, if he wished, to father one child —but no more.

Babies born at Oneida stayed with the mother only for the first eighteen months, after which they lived apart in the Children's House. Here they received expert care until they became full members of the community at fourteen. The child was regarded as belonging to the community rather than to its parents, although parents had the opportunity to show special affection to their own offspring.[72]

There is little evidence to support the suspicion that the Oneida Perfectionists were sexually promiscuous or that they were obsessively preoccupied with this feature of their experience. Rather there is indication that they were remarkably successful in keeping their sexual expression consistent with their religious and moral principles. A new member of the community sometimes had to wait for years before he was admitted to the complex marriage feature of community life, so that there was little chance that this institution should be abused by those with unworthy motives.

Both the Shakers and the Perfectionists thoroughly subscribed to the notion of equality of the sexes, a doctrine which was rooted theologically in the Shaker belief that Ann Lee was

72. Among the numerous descriptions of the sexual aspects of Oneida's history, one of the best is found in Parker, *op. cit.*, chap. iii.

the female incarnation of the Christ Spirit, and in the Perfectionist doctrine of the bisexuality of God. The sex ethic of Oneida is noteworthy in its respect for women, and especially in the protection which it afforded against unwanted and unwise pregnancies and against unwelcomed amatory advances. Whatever else may be said about the novel sexual innovations of Oneida, one can hardly escape the impression that there was indeed a quality of redemption in their sexual experience.

CONFESSION. The cohesiveness of a Shaker or Perfectionist community almost of necessity required that the individual member should have of himself the image which the community had. Confession met this need.

Among the Shakers confession was ordered somewhat along Roman Catholic lines, with each member making private confession to an elder. Admission to membership required a thorough confession, much in the fashion of the New England Puritans who required candidates for church membership to recount their moral failures and foibles to a "scanning committee." The Shaker system of confession required that one report not only his own sins but also such sins of his neighbors as he suspected were not being confessed. Confession came with great frequency, since the Shakers believed that unconfessed sins kept one from worshiping God.[73]

Certainly the most interesting and thorough confessional procedure employed by any communitarian group was that of "mutual criticism," a modification of a procedure used by the "Brethren," a secret society of theological students at Andover to which Noyes had belonged.

How did mutual criticism work? Usually an individual would request a criticism, or if it became obvious that he needed criticism, then he would be asked or even ordered to submit himself to it. Criticism might take place before the entire community, or the audience might consist only of a committee of six to twelve or more persons. The subject of the criticism had

73. See Green and Wells, *op. cit.*, for a statement of the Shaker arguments for confession, and Andrews, *The People Called Shakers*, pp. 261 f., for a description of the procedures used in Shaker confession.

an opportunity to speak for himself, but the emphasis was upon the testimony of others regarding his moral failures. There is nothing to indicate that spiteful or vindictive attitudes ever prevailed in the testimony presented at these criticism sessions. Criticism thus expressed undoubtedly kept backbiting at a minimum, and it undeniably helped to correct unlovely and irritating acts and attitudes which disturbed the harmony of Oneida. Along with the daily evening meetings (attended by all), mutual criticism was the chief instrument of government at Oneida. Noyes was interested in the connection between moral attitudes and health, and one of the most interesting uses of mutual criticism was in curing illnesses of psychosomatic nature.[74]

Conclusion

The very fact that the communitarian experiments were tolerated indicates the openness of American society in the nineteenth century, and a willingness to engage in social experimentation. Underlying this tolerance for radical social experimentation was a confidence in the special destiny and historic greatness of America, a destiny and greatness which were thought to be guaranteed against the threats of domestic heresy. To be sure, there were intense outbreaks of nativistic anti-Catholic feelings at various times and places from the 1830's onward, but even these ugly facts do not greatly mar the general picture of a society which was openly debating and experimenting with a great variety of conflicting social ideologies.

For all of their unorthodox beliefs and institutions, the religious communitarians shared the basic mood of America in the second third of the nineteenth century, the period of maximum influence of the communitarian movement. They were inspired by the general American confidence in progress and by the sanctificationist spirit of revivalistic Protestantism. They were fiercely democratic, and became radically unorthodox in their theology (i.e., the Shaker doctrine of the incarna-

74. Nordhoff, *op. cit.*, pp. 295 ff.

tion of Christ in Ann Lee, the Perfectionist doctrine of the bisexuality of God) in their attempts to justify the inclusion of women in all of the democratic privileges and processes of the group.

The communitarians sought the kind of purity which demanded isolation from the moral pressures and ambiguities inherent in the life of the world. Thus they contended that the community of earthly saints constituted a self-sufficient society in which, as Noyes said, "the church is the state, and the state is the church." [75] This emphasis overlooked, of course, the dependence of the communitarians on the social structures which formed the larger context of their experience. The very state from which they withdrew their allegiance continued to insure their existence, and they were dependent upon the economic order which they branded as selfish and worldly. They provide extreme examples of the continuing American Protestant proclivity for cloistered, apolitical morality.

The communitarians were fundamentally trying to restore the meaning of the church as fellowship or *koinonia*. They tried to maintain this fellowship of love and sanctification as a perpetual state by expanding their church life to include the world and by restricting their world to the church. Thus breaking down the barriers between church and world, the sacred and the secular, the Oneida group had no specifically religious services, and the main Shaker service was a dance which, it was hoped, would inspire one or more persons to bear messages to the community from the spirit world.

The communitarians, who sought escape from acculturation through the desperate resort of isolating themselves into self-sufficient communities, reveal nonetheless the depth of the acculturating power of America on her religious traditions. Looking back, as they thought, to the New Testament Church, the communitarians saw primitive Christianity refracted through glasses of faith in the essential goodness of man and the certainty of progressive realization of human brotherhood through the power of religious faith which perfects human character.

75. *The Berean,* p. 503.

Some Aspects of Religion on
the American Frontier

GORDON ESLEY FINNIE

Under normal circumstances the birth of George Brown on January 29, 1792, would have occurred in Brooke County, Virginia, on the bank of the Ohio River, "about opposite the middle of Brown's Island." [1] But he did not come into existence under "normal" circumstances, for his parents lived on the American frontier.

Like many other American families in 1789, the Brown family migrated from Maryland to western Virginia, seeking a new economic beginning. True to their expectation, they found an abundance of land and an opportunity to start anew.[2] They also discovered a strange new life. Immense uncleared tracts of timber awaited them and in part determined their daily routine, for until the land was prepared for cultivation there was no possibility of supporting a family of eleven.[3] The ever-recurrent fear of Indian attack, of severe winters, and of serious illness intensified the awareness of their isolation, which was occasionally relieved by the appearance of a Methodist circuit rider.[4] The exigencies of the moment and sparsely populated settlements made the education of their children almost an impossibility.[5] In that "half-civilized state," as

---

1. A sudden Indian uprising forced Hugh Brown to take his pregnant wife across the Ohio River to Washington County, Pennsylvania. There George Brown was born. Shortly thereafter the Brown family returned to their Virginia home. George Brown, *Recollections of Itinerant Life: Including Early Reminiscences* (3rd ed.; Cincinnati, 1866), pp. 26–27.

2. *Ibid.*, p. 30.

3. *Ibid.*, pp. 30, 32, 37, 39.

4. *Ibid.*, pp. 36–37.

5. *Ibid.*, pp. 30, 40.

Brown later referred to it, customary legal processes were often set aside, and disputes were decided in many instances "by a trial of manhood. He who could 'lick' his neighbor with whom he had a dispute, generally carried his cause." [6] In spite of these circumstances there were "thoughtful" men and women who attempted to carry on their traditional religious practices and "to bring up their children in the nurture and admonition of the Lord." [7]

Such were Brown's parents. Their ancestors had been supporters of the Anglican establishment in Virginia, but when the American Revolution occurred, "Church of England attachments gave way," and they—like many others in the colonies—transferred their allegiance to the Methodist Episcopal Church. Brown's parents were members of the first class of Methodists formed in Maryland. Consequently, when they migrated to the West in 1789, they sought out other Methodists with whom to worship.[8] Through their influence, through contact with itinerant Methodist ministers, through Bible reading, and through experience with denominational controversies, Brown early "deemed the Methodists to be right, and had . . . [his] controversial sword whetted up, and ready for a passage at arms with any boy of . . . [his] age in the neighborhood." [9]

With this conviction in his heart and with his "controversial sword whetted up," Brown began—as a lad of eight years—his spiritual pilgrimage and his relationship with the Methodist Episcopal Church. Nine years passed, however, before he experienced conversion and formally united with the Church he "deemed to be right." [10] Soon after these steps were taken, he entered the ministry and served the Methodist Episcopal Church as an itinerant and as a presiding elder during the years 1814–1829.[11] Toward the close of this period he increasingly came to believe that the episcopal form of ecclesiastical

6. *Ibid.,* pp. 30–31.
7. *Ibid.,* p. 31.
8. *Ibid.,* pp. 29–30.
9. *Ibid.,* pp. 36–37, 40–41.
10. *Ibid.,* pp. 60–63, 67, 74.
11. *Ibid.,* pp. 75–202.

polity, as it was then being administered in the Methodist
Episcopal Church, was inconsistent with "the rights of the
American freeman." When his efforts to correct the situation
failed and when he saw that there was no possible way for him
conscientiously to remain a part of such a "despotic" organization, he separated from the Methodist Episcopal Church in
June, 1829, and devoted the remainder of his life to furthering
the cause of "ecclesiastical liberty" through the medium of the
Methodist Protestant Church.[12]

When seen in retrospect, the events of George Brown's life
and ministry were in themselves of no particular significance.
Contrary to the belief of the editor of the *Western Methodist
Protestant* in 1866—that Brown would be remembered "as a
worthy representative of a noble class of men whose memories
will be ever green, and the recollection of whose Christian
virtues and faithful labors shall be imperishable in the
Church" [13]—he has not been remembered. Indeed, his endless
labors have slipped into an anonymity analogous to that which
the common name "George Brown" suggests.

But the details of his life and ministry are important, for he
is probably typical of a whole generation of itinerant ministers
in the Methodist Episcopal Church during the first half of the
nineteenth century in America.[14] As such, the details of his life
and ministry provide a basis for understanding some aspects of
the organization of the itinerant system in America and something of the men who were a part of it—their education, the
process through which they entered the itineracy, their roles as
itinerant ministers, the tools with which they worked, their
problems, and their theological and ethical emphases. The de-

12. *Ibid.*, pp. 130–456.
13. *Ibid.*, p. vi.
14. Cf. S. R. Beggs, *Pages from the Early History of the West and North-West:
Embracing Reminiscences and Incidents of Settlement and Growth, and Sketches
of the Material and Religious Progress of the States of Ohio, Indiana, Illinois,
and Missouri, with Especial Reference to the History of Methodism* (Cincinnati,
1868) ; John F. Wright, *Sketches of the Life and Labors of James Quinn Who
Was Nearly Half a Century a Minister of the Gospel in the Methodist Episcopal
Church* (Cincinnati, 1851) ; and Elnathan Corrington Gavitt, *Crumbs from My
Saddle Bags or, Reminiscences of Pioneer Life and Biographical Sketches* (To-
ledo, 1884) .

tails of his life and ministry also provide a basis for delineating some of the characteristics of religious life and practice on the American frontier during the first half of the nineteenth century. The purpose of this essay is therefore to characterize those aspects of the itinerant system and of religion on the American frontier which the life and ministry of George Brown reflect.

The itinerant system of which he became a part had a distinctive organization. Scattered settlements were organized into units or circuits. Each circuit ordinarily embraced an immense geographical area. The Stafford Circuit—to which Brown was appointed in 1818—included all of eastern Virginia between the Potomac and the Rappahannock rivers; [15] the Silver Creek Circuit in 1809 embraced all of the settlements in southern Indiana; [16] the Monroe Circuit in 1832 began four miles from Detroit with the Lacroix settlement, included an Indian mission on the Huron River, the town of Flat Rock, and the Bay settlement in Michigan, extended into Ohio—including all of the towns along the Maumee River—and ran along the Indiana state line within a few miles of Fort Wayne, thus requiring approximately four hundred miles of horseback travel every four weeks.[17] Included in each of these circuits were a number of places designated as preaching appointments. Farmhouses, barns, log schoolhouses, carpenter shops, courthouses, taverns, warehouses, and crude churches or meeting houses served as places of worship.[18] Each circuit was placed under the immediate supervision of a team of itinerant ministers, one of whom was in charge and was responsible for scheduling preaching engagements throughout the territory embracing the circuit.[19]

---

15. Brown, *op. cit.,* pp. 87–88.
16. Beggs, *op. cit.,* pp. 20–21.
17. Gavitt, *op. cit.,* pp. 175–176.
18. *Ibid.,* pp. 75, 80, 112, 129, 152, 172; Beggs, *op. cit.,* pp. 67, 76, 95, 113, 126, 133; Wright, *op. cit.,* pp. 57, 103, 202; Brown, *op. cit.,* pp. 31, 75, 80, 84; *Mutual Rights and Methodist Protestant,* I (June 24, 1831), 195; III (July 12, 1833), 217–218; William Warren Sweet, *Religion on the American Frontier, 1783–1840,* IV, *The Methodists* (Chicago, 1946), 406, 410, 418, 426, 442, 444.
19. In some instances one minister carried the entire responsibility for a circuit; however, one or two less experienced persons usually assisted the minister-in-charge.

Under this arrangement each minister made a preaching tour around the circuit once every four or six weeks, depending upon the number of appointments and the distance to be covered.[20] As a result the most isolated settlements were assured of some contact with the church, and Methodist circuit riders kept pace with the ever-expanding frontier.[21]

Brown was in one respect like most of the men who labored within the framework of this itinerant organization: he had little formal education.[22] From 1797 to 1800 he went to a school which he later characterized as "less than nothing and vanity." There he acquired the rudiments of reading and writing. Seven years later he went to school again. But the schoolhouse burned after he had been there for three days, and "there the matter ended . . . the neighbors divided about a site for a new one— each man wanting it near his habitation. So nothing was done. . . ." He then became a fuller's apprentice, but after nine months he decided to go back to his father's farm. These nine months of his life were as "good as thrown away, for . . . [he] had learned but little . . . save to make fuller's soap—a capital thing, by the by. . . ." In 1809 he went to Holliday's Cove, Brooke County, Virginia, where he attended school for two more years and received "what, in those days, was considered a good business education." This was his greatest educational opportunity, and he, like many other Methodist ministers in the nineteenth century, pursued the task of self-education in "Brush College." [23]

The process through which Brown entered the itinerant system was likewise similar to that which was followed by other Methodist ministers on the frontier.[24] In the summer of 1813 he experienced conversion in a camp meeting,[25] whereupon he became a "probationer" in the Methodist Episcopal Church.

20. Brown, *op. cit.*, pp. 75–94; Gavitt, *op. cit.*, pp. 175–176, 257, 264–265; Beggs, *op. cit.*, pp. 20–21, 50, 70, 75, 81, 83, 110; Wright, *op. cit.*, pp. 60, 92–93.
21. Brown, *op. cit.*, pp. 36–37.
22. Cf. Beggs, *op. cit.*, pp. 12–13; Wright, *op. cit.*, p. 16; Gavitt, *op. cit.*, pp. 54–55.
23. Brown, *op. cit.*, pp. 30, 40, 43–46.
24. Cf. Beggs, *op. cit.*, pp. 15–16; Gavitt, *op. cit.*, pp. 59–61, 66, 69; Wright, *op. cit.*, pp. 21–22.
25. Brown, *op. cit.*, pp. 60–63.

Under the leadership of older and more experienced Christians in the class to which he had been assigned, he was nurtured along in his Christian experience and soon began to assist "a very zealous class of pious men" who held prayer meetings periodically in various parts of the city.[26] Shortly thereafter he began to accompany local preachers to their appointments in the country. On such occasions he "was directed to give an exhortation after the sermon, and to close the meeting with singing and prayer, and it was not long before they laid on the cross more heavily, for they called upon . . . [him] to preach." During this period Brown carried on a course of reading which was designed to prepare him for the ministry. Upon the recommendation of his "elder brethren," he studied English grammar; and the Bible, John Wesley's *Sermons on Several Occasions,* Asa Shinn's *An Essay on the Plan of Salvation,* and Samuel Drew's *An Original Essay on the Immateriality and Immortality of the Soul* were his "constant companions." These "very profound works" made "advancement in theological and mental science . . . slow; still some progress was made, and . . . [his] mind became gradually inured to hard study." Early in 1814 he became a full member of the Methodist Episcopal Church and a local preacher. During the remainder of the year he labored with other local preachers and traveled throughout the Anne Arundel Circuit in Maryland as an assistant to the minister-in-charge. In March, 1815, the Baltimore Annual Conference appointed him to Prince George's Circuit in Virginia. With this appointment, Brown's life as an itinerant minister began.[27]

As an itinerant he had various responsibilities, the foremost of which were to proclaim the Gospel, to administer the rules and regulations of the Methodist Episcopal Church, and to defend Methodism and the Christian faith against all kinds of infidelity and attack.[28] Fortunately, he did not have to depend

26. At this time Brown was visiting his brother in Baltimore.
27. *Ibid.,* pp. 65–80.
28. See *The Doctrines and Discipline of the Methodist Episcopal Church* (New York, 1812) , pp. 37–49, for an example of the specific duties of a Methodist minister in 1812.

solely upon his native wit and ingenuity in order to carry out these responsibilities. John Claude's *An Essay on the Composition of a Sermon* and John Maury's *The Principles of Eloquence* were homiletical tools at his disposal; Hannah More's *An Essay on the Character and Practical Writings of Saint Paul* and John Fletcher's *The Portrait of St. Paul* were aids to a better understanding of his primary sourcebook—the Bible; Richard Baxter's *Gildas Salvianus: The Reformed Pastor* was his guide in matters pertaining to pastoral care; *The Doctrines and Discipline of the Methodist Episcopal Church* was his book of law in matters of polity and doctrine; and David Simpson's *A Plea for Religion and Sacred Writings* was his bulwark against the challenge of the Antichrist.[29]

As he labored to fulfill these responsibilities, he encountered problems which were inherent in the itinerant system itself. Upon entering the itineracy, he had to acquire enough money to pay for transportation to his appointment and for his sustentation along the way. If a man already owned a horse or was given one, as Brown was,[30] this was not too great a problem; however, it is possible that many itinerant ministers were not so fortunate as he. If such were the case, the problem of acquiring money for transportation to an appointment could become a great one. This would be especially true if the appointment were five hundred miles from the place where the Annual Conference convened, as it was in the case of S. R. Beggs in 1823. Indeed, an appointment in some instances could be as far as eight hundred miles from the seat of the Annual Conference.[31] The financial problem with respect to transportation did not end with the arrival of the itinerant to his charge, for a good horse was a perpetual necessity. Constant traveling in all kinds of weather and over every conceivable type of terrain shortened the life of an animal's usefulness. For example,

29. Brown, *op. cit.*, pp. 85–86; Wright, *op. cit.*, pp. 173, 261. *The Constitution and Discipline of the Methodist Protestant Church* became Brown's guide in matters of polity after his split with the Methodist Episcopal Church in 1829.
30. Brown, *op. cit.*, p. 78.
31. Beggs, *op. cit.*, pp. 56–57. On this particular occasion Beggs had to borrow money and a horse in order to get to his circuit, because he was "entirely out of money . . . ."

Brown wore out eight horses in the years 1831–1832. Since these were generally replaced at a "great sacrifice" and always at his own personal expense,[32] this was a continual drain on his meager salary, which was often not paid in full.[33] In addition to the expense of maintaining adequate transportation, he faced the more basic problem of providing shelter, fuel, food, and clothing for his family. The struggle continued throughout his active ministry and became more acute upon his superannuation, whereupon—at the close of a life's work and at a time when he was least able to earn a living —he found that he was without work and an income upon which to live.[34] His financial circumstances as an itinerant minister not only made it difficult to supply his family's physical necessities; but four- and six-week circuits, which necessitated almost constant absence from home, made normal relationships within the home almost impossible.[35] Thus, as he attempted to minister to the spiritual welfare of others, his own needs and the needs of his family were often disregarded.

In addition to these personal problems, Brown—like other itinerant ministers—constantly encountered practical problems directly related to his role as a preacher, as a disciplinarian, and as a defender of Methodism and the Christian faith. The nature of the itinerant system demanded that he preach almost every day; however, constant traveling and the nature of the rural homes he visited made sermon preparation and study extremely difficult.[36] His responsibility as a disciplinarian demanded that the "pruning-knife . . . be used in removing the improper and unfruitful branches." [37] But the line between

32. Brown, *op. cit.*, pp. 253–254.
33. *Ibid.*, pp. 110–111.
34. *Ibid.*, pp. 359, 361; cf. Wright, *op. cit.*, p. 212.
35. James Quinn considered himself fortunate in 1805 when he was able to spend two days out of every four weeks with his family. In order to do this, he had to travel an extra hundred miles and to preach twice a day for "nearly a week." Wright, *op. cit.*, p. 93.
36. Many of the frontier homes had only one room, which served as the parlor, the kitchen, and the bedroom. As a result, he was probably forced to do most of his studying upon horseback. Brown does not explicitly indicate this; however, see Beggs, *op. cit.*, p. 287; Gavitt, *op. cit.*, pp. 84, 87; and W. P. Strickland, *The Pioneers of the West; or Life in the Woods* (New York, 1856) , p. 140.
37. Wright, *op. cit.*, p. 145.

discipline and "tyranny" was a fine one, and he repeatedly faced the possibility of abusing his legal powers.[38] His responsibility as a defender of the faith demanded that he denounce Calvinism, Universalism, millenarianism, Unitarianism, Roman Catholicism, Judaism, deism, atheism, Anglicanism, Mormonism, and antinomianism;[39] however, in doing this, Brown always incurred the risk of producing what he called "sectarian bigots" rather than "thorough evangelical Christians."[40]

Brown's theology was anthropocentric in its emphases rather than theocentric or christocentric.[41] He apparently adhered to a Chalcedonian formulation of the Trinity;[42] however, this concept was probably a polemical weapon rather than an essential aspect of his theology, as his anthropology and his soteriology imply. Man, he believed, possessed the ability to discern right and wrong and the power to do the right.[43] Brown's own experience, however, convinced him that man— in his "fallen nature"—had such "a constant gravitation to the wrong" and such "a proneness to forget God" that he would, if left to take his own course, certainly find his way to "perdition."[44] But the "way of the cross" could save man from this fate. To Brown, the "way of the cross" was the life of self-denial,[45] the life of religious activity,[46] the life of making reparation for "injuries done to others."[47] He firmly believed that "it is impossible for the Lord Jesus Christ to save any of the depraved children of Adam, without, in a diversity of ways, laying the cross upon them."[48] Moreover, he believed that

---

38. Brown, *op. cit.*, pp. 103–104.
39. These were anathemas to the itinerant minister. *Ibid.*, pp. 80–81, 85, 88, 119–122, 137–139, 323–325; see also Beggs, *op. cit.*, pp. 96–97, 133; Wright, *op. cit.*, pp. 62–63, 85, 170; Gavitt, *op. cit.*, pp. 52–53, 62–65, 234; and Sweet, *op. cit.*, IV, 400, 433, 444, 447.
40. Brown, *op. cit.*, pp. 102–103.
41. Since none of his sermons are available, this discussion is based solely upon a few scattered remarks in his autobiography.
42. Brown, *op. cit.*, pp. 119–120.
43. *Ibid.*, pp. 40–41, 44, 57–59.
44. *Ibid.*, pp. 44, 65.
45. *Ibid.*, p. 65.
46. *Ibid.*, pp. 62–65.
47. *Ibid.*, pp. 68–69.
48. *Ibid.*, p. 65.

. . . God will forgive a penitent who promises reparation of in-juries done to others, so far as may be in his power; but if there is a willful failure to fulfill the promise, forgiveness will thereby be forfeited, happiness destroyed, and the soul be in danger of being lost. In all cases where reparation to another for injuries done is at all possible, it must be made; God requires it, and no man, with safety to his soul, can evade his requirements.[49]

Thus, Christ was the Saviour: but, to Brown, the efficacy of his salvation is dependent upon man's co-operation.

Brown's conceptions of life after death and of what is re-quired in order to produce a revival were also anthropocentric. He felt that *if* he were "faithful until death" he would see his parents again,[50] and he believed that a "working church" would inevitably produce a revival.[51] Indeed, the success or failure of God's kingdom in the church was dependent upon the character of the church's ministry. If the church employed "ministerial drones," the kingdom would surely fail.[52]

Brown's concept of the good life was likewise typical of that held by other Methodist itinerants. The good life was a nega-tive abstention from evil and a positive commitment to reli-gious duties. Even though he said that religion was an internal matter of "the head and heart and life," [53] he characterized the good life in terms of external activity. On the one hand, he condemned profanity, drinking, Sabbath-breaking, misbehavior in worship services, slaveholding.[54] On the other hand, he extolled public prayer, church and prayer meeting attendance, diligence in performing religious duties, the honor of being persecuted for religious belief, neighborly acts of hospitality, "soul-winning," family worship.[55] In so doing, he placed hardly any emphasis upon internal motivation or upon the more subtle sins of the spirit.[56] But he could hardly have been ex-

49. *Ibid.*, pp. 68–69.
50. *Ibid.*, p. 266.
51. *Ibid.*, p. 102. "Who ever saw a lazy, do-nothing church have a revival?" To Brown, there was only one possible answer.
52. *Ibid.*, pp. 242–243.
53. *Ibid.*, p. 453.
54. *Ibid.*, pp. 75–77, 88–89, 273, 288–289.
55. *Ibid.*, pp. 63–66, 77, 80–82, 84–85, 453–455.
56. Indeed, his own life on several occasions was ruled by what he called the "three-times rule": "When I have given an old friend three opportunities for Christian or even civil greetings, and he has treated me with rude contempt

pected to do so, for the religious life which he experienced on the American frontier made it imperative that he do otherwise.

As Brown discovered early in his childhood, religion on the American frontier was highly sectarian. Methodists, Baptists, Presbyterians, and other groups competed with each other as the frontier moved westward, and Brown later said of this: ". . . the struggle was long and arduous." [57] Baptists condemned Methodist ministers as "false prophets" because they taught that there were various modes of baptism, that the Lord's Supper was open to all who desired to partake of it, that redemption was for all who would accept it, that there was a possibility of "falling from grace," that good works were necessary for salvation, that infant baptism was Christian.[58] "Proud, High-Church Episcopalians, who rested in the outward form of godliness, and denied the power thereof, despised . . . [the Methodists] because in addition to form, they taught mankind a powerful spiritual religion, coming home to the heart and saving the soul." [59] Presbyterians, Roman Catholics, and Lutherans likewise condemned the Methodists, who "studied the questions at issue . . . well" and "deemed self-defense always in order." [60] Various factors led to these sectarian controversies: an uncritical and literal biblicism necessarily produced doctrinal disputes;[61] acts of destruction on the part of one group led to retaliation on the part of the other; [62] the lack

every time, then I shall take no further notice of him until he returns to his senses." He acknowledged in this "rule" that he could "not afford to cherish wrath or harbor ill-will against any man, especially an old friend." Yet, he had "a little too much spirit to admit . . . crawling in the dust to gain the friendship of any man who ignored the ecclesiastical liberties of a Christian people." *Ibid.*, pp. 225–227. Brown's unwillingness to "crawl in the dust" was not peculiar to himself; other Methodist ministers were also of a like temperament. Sweet, *op. cit.*, IV, 397–398.

57. Brown, *op. cit.*, pp. 36–37, 83–84, 88; Wright, *op. cit.*, pp. 213–218.
58. Brown, *op. cit.*, pp. 36–37, 88, 120–121; Wright, *op. cit.*, pp. 32, 50, 52–53.
59. Brown, *op. cit.*, p. 88.
60. *Ibid.*
61. *Ibid.*, pp. 36–37, 102–103.
62. Presbyterian opposition to Methodism was so violent in Granville, Ohio, in 1809 that a log schoolhouse which the Methodists had erected as a meeting house "was demolished and its contents scattered over the Public Square, and these opponents to Methodism were left to enjoy their honored rights; but not without Mr. Cloud's opinion of the Westminster Confession of faith." Gavitt, *op. cit.*, pp. 52–53.

of adequate facilities for worship necessitated that several denominations often share the same meeting house, thus providing a never-ending source of contention "as to the day and right
of occupancy"; [63] and the particular type of individualism
bred on the frontier produced a frame of mind that was basically competitive and self-assertive. Brown, like other itinerants, could not escape becoming involved in these sectarian
controversies. Indeed, he even viewed them as a positive good:
". . . after all, good was the result, for the whole community
went to searching the scriptures daily, to see who was right." [64]

The question of *"who* is right" was not always clear to
persons living on the frontier; the question of *"what* is right"
was even less clear. This was particularly true when frontiersmen attempted to regulate their religious practices according
to norms that had guided them in a more "civilized" environment. Many discovered, for example, that the frontier environment provided circumstances that made rigid observance of
the Sabbath almost impossible.[65] As a result of this difficulty,
many frontiersmen relaxed the rigidity of their norm concerning its observance.[66] The frontier environment also provided
circumstances whereby strict codes of personal behavior were
transformed into more relative ones. As the norms governing
religious practice and personal morality became more relative,
an abundance of "sins" were committed that could be "seen"
by itinerant ministers who, once having "seen" them, could not
conscientiously remain silent about them. Consequently, much
of the preaching on the American frontier—with its emphasis
upon the necessity of a positive commitment to religious duties
and upon the need for a negative morality—characterized religion in terms of something to do or not to do.[67]

63. *Ibid.*, pp. 112, 120–212; Brown, *op. cit.*, pp. 102, 207–211; Sweet, *op. cit.*,
IV, 400, 413; Beggs, *op. cit.*, p. 133. See Brown, *op. cit.*, pp. 207–211, for an example of a fight over the occupancy of a meeting house. This was carried on, not
on the basis of law, but upon the principle that he who got the key had the
right of occupancy. On this particular occasion a free-for-all was narrowly
avoided before the question was finally settled.

64. *Ibid.*, pp. 36–37.

65. Many were deprived of the opportunity to worship regularly; others were
forced to work even when given the opportunity of formal worship.

66. *Ibid.*, pp. 39, 334.

67. See notes 54–55.

The fruit of this preaching was not only a religion that was characterized by much "activity": it also produced a people who, having been made conscious of their sins of commission and omission, were especially vulnerable to the techniques of a frontier ministry who believed that preaching should be directed to the emotions rather than to the intellect.[68] This conviction, combined with the sectarian nature of religion on the frontier and with the nature of worship services and camp meetings, created a religion every aspect of which was highly emotional. Denominational controversies, which were often reduced to name-calling, engendered much heat and thereby inflamed the passions; worship services were often attended by boisterous singing,[69] by unreserved expressions of religious feeling,[70] by rude misbehavior,[71] and by sermons designed to send "a heavenly fire running through the assembly, melting all before it"; [72] and camp meetings were orgies of religious emotion.[73] Indeed, the religious life of the individual from birth to the grave was characterized by one intense emotional experience after another.

The frontiersman's religious life was not the only aspect of his existence that was attended by strong emotion. His political and economic life also provided occasion for the exercise of

68. The greatest homiletic mistake a frontier preacher could make was to preach a "metaphysical" sermon—that is, one "filled with literary quibbles and philosophical speculations." Brown, *op. cit.,* pp. 73, 127–128, 446; Wright, *op. cit.,* p. 136.

69. One of Brown's congregations sang with "a wild, rude grandeur . . . suited to the splendors of nature around them." Brown, *op. cit.,* p. 236.

70. Brown never allowed the "amens" and "hallelujahs" of the saints nor the "tears and sobs and cries of the penitents" to disturb him. *Ibid.,* pp. 73, 353.

71. *Ibid.,* pp. 75–77, 341; Wright, *op. cit.,* pp. 224–227.

72. Wright, *op. cit.,* p. 446.

73. H. Richard Niebuhr suggests, in *The Social Sources of Denominationalism* (Hamden, Conn., 1954), pp. 140–145, that the "isolation of frontier life fostered craving for companionship, suppressed the gregarious tendency and so subjected the lonely settler to the temptations of crowd suggestion to an unusual degree. In the camp meeting and in the political gathering formal, logical discourse was of no avail, while the 'language of excitement' called forth enthusiastic response. In addition to the isolation of the frontiersman other influences inclined him to make an uncritical emotional response to religious stimulation. The reduction of life on the border to the bare fundamentals of physical and social existence, the dearth of intellectual stimulation and the lack of these effective inhibitions of emotional expression which formal education cultivates, the awesome manifestations of nature, the effects of which were not checked by the sense of safety permanent dwellings and the nearness of other men convey—all these made the settler subject to the feverish phenomena of revivalism."

powerful feeling. Questions concerning political and economic freedom were of particular concern to him, and any attempt to deny him these privileges evoked his immediate protest. These were, to him, basic rights of an American freeman. To Brown, they were also among the basic rights of a Christian, as his break with the Methodist Episcopal Church in 1829 illustrates.

In the early days of his ministry Brown was convinced that everything in "Methodistical economy" was "exactly right." As he continued in the itineracy, however, he frequently saw Methodist ministers abuse their authority when dealing with their congregations.[74] A talk with David Stanton, the father of Edwin M. Stanton, Secretary of War under Abraham Lincoln, convinced him "that the Methodist Episcopal Church has as much right to a free representative government as the state; and that to be republican in the state and a monarchist in the Church involved a contradiction. . . ."[75] When his efforts to alleviate this situation failed, he separated from the Methodist Episcopal Church on the grounds that its ecclesiastical organization was "more arbitrary in its character than the civil government of King George III," that "it placed in the hands of the itinerant clergy alone all the legislative, the judicial, and the executive powers of the government, leaving the local preachers and lay members of the Church without due protection against this itinerant domination," that "the people . . . [bore] all the pecuniary burdens without the right of representation," and that the "foreign control" of church property exercised such "a power over a man's substance" that it actually amounted "to a power over his will." These, too him, were not only contrary to the basic rights of an American freeman; they were "anti-Christian" as well.[76] In asserting this, Brown made

74. Brown, *op. cit.*
75. *Ibid.,* pp. 104–106.
76. *Ibid.,* pp. 131–132, 193–198, 214–215, 416–417; see also Brown's famous "Timothy's Address to the Junior Bishop," written in November, 1826, *ibid.,* pp. 134–145, and "Reasons Why I Am Not an Episcopal Methodist," printed in *The Methodist Protestant Manual. A Concise Treatise upon the Principles of Government of the Methodist Protestant Church, in Contrast with the Polity of the Methodist Episcopal Church. With a Synopsis of Methodist Protestant Church History. By a Member of the Virginia Conference* (Baltimore, 1856), pp. 10–11.

his principle of political freedom and his economic bias against absentee control synonymous with Christian belief itself. Thus he identified his religious beliefs with his political and economic philosophy to such an extent that these aspects of the American "way of life" became a part of the Christian religion itself. The identification of religion with these aspects of the American "way of life" meant that religion was a vehicle for the propagation of the frontiersman's political and economic philosophy. Indeed, it meant in the minds of some Americans living on the frontier that the American "way of life" and Christianity were one and the same.

This, then, was the nature of religion on the American frontier, as reflected in the life and ministry of George Brown: religion was highly sectarian, religion was characterized in terms of something to do or not to do, religion was intensely emotional, and religion was synonymous in some respects with the political and economic idealism of the frontiersman.

To this religion George Brown devoted his life. In so doing, he helped Christianize America and Americanize Christianity.

A Centennial Appraisal of
James Henley Thornwell

A century ago, on August 1, 1862, in the midst of the Civil War and at his home in Columbia, South Carolina, death came to the Reverend James Henley Thornwell, D.D., LL.D., "probably the most influential southern minister of his day." [1] "The leading Old School Presbyterian minister in the South," is Clifton E. Olmstead's 1960 estimate published in *History of Religion in the United States,* where Thornwell is credited with having served the Southern cause by defining the relation of the church to slavery and by having incorporated in the Address of the Presbyterian Church in the Confederate States, 1861, a defense on Christian grounds of the Southern position.[2] William Warren Sweet wrote similarly of him as one of the most able Old School Presbyterian defenders of slavery on scriptural and moral grounds.[3] For these reasons Thornwell now is generally remembered.

One of the published articles of H. Shelton Smith was entitled, "The Church and the Social Order in the Old South as Interpreted by James H. Thornwell." [4] Here it was stated:

> The Church, like all bearers of culture (in the last generation of the *ante-bellum* South) had to reckon with the South's "peculiar institution." In this process of reckoning, Dr. James H. Thornwell played a master role. What Calhoun was to political theory in this period, Thornwell was to the social ethics of the church.

1. Margaret Burr Deschamps, "Union or Division? South Atlantic Presbyterians and Southern Nationalism 1820–1861," *The Journal of Southern History,* XX (1954) , 493.
2. (Englewood Cliffs, N. J., 1960) , pp. 375, 388.
3. *The Story of Religion in America* (2nd ed.; New York, 1950) , p. 308.
4. *Church History,* VII, No. 2 (1938) , 115–124.

During the time Dr. Smith was preparing that study, he introduced me as one of his graduate students to Thornwell. In the
effort of the intervening years to understand Thornwell in the
light of his environment and times, I have come to the conviction that any proper evaluation of Thornwell's place relative
to slavery and the Southern Presbyterian Church must take
into account the character of the whole of his thinking— philosophical, theological, social, political, ecclesiastical, and educational. The final estimate is not essentially changed for, as I
have stated elsewhere,[5] Thornwell, with his characteristic personal fondness for debate and professional polemical religious
thought and writing, can be considered a "Defender of the Old
South." What widening the perspective adds, however, is the
recognition that Thornwell's defense of the South's position
regarding slavery and the separation of the Southern church
were for him not isolated issues, but rather particular phases in
his defensive kind of thinking. His thought ranged widely, but
nearly always in exposition he viewed himself as having an
obligation, which to him seemed a moral duty, to defend traditional standards against dangerous attacks, especially those
which he considered ungodly and atheistic.

His Image

Any portrayal of Thornwell as protagonist of slavery and a
"fire-eating" South Carolina secessionist is inaccurate and unfair through lack of perspective. He was, however, ardently
fond of his state. There is a legend that returning from Europe
in 1841 (he was not yet thirty years old) , as the carriage which
took him to South Carolina crossed the state line, he sprang suddenly out, and reverently kissed the soil.[6] In 1852, addressing
the alumni of Yale College in New Haven, he confessed, "I
am a Carolinian by birth, by education and love my native

5. Paul L. Garber, "James Henley Thornwell: Defender of the Old South,"
Union Seminary Review, LIV (1943) , 92–116.
6. B. M. Palmer, *The Life and Letters of James Henley Thornwell* (Richmond, 1875) , 180.

State, and my own *Alma Mater,* with a love passing the love of woman." [7] Until the last eighteen months of his life, fondness for state was for him synonymous with fondness for nation. He wrote from Paris in 1841, "I candidly believe that America is the first nation on the globe; . . . I am proud of my nation, the prouder still, after having seen others." [8] In Europe again in 1860 he wrote to his wife, "There is no land like our own . . . and if we can have the grace to deal justly and honestly with one another, and to hold together as a people, the time is at hand when the distinction of being an American will be as proud and glorious as it ever was to be a citizen of Rome." [9]

A recent student of Presbyterians in the ante-bellum South Atlantic states has stated that until the winter of 1860–1861 these folk were generally "loyal toward both ecclesiastical and political organizations tying them to the North." [10] Some were disgruntled about Northern control of church and state, but spokesmen like editors of church papers advised against church division on the ground that ecclesiastical divisions would foster political divisions. In the Nullification crisis of the 1830's and in the 1850 Compromise controversy, Presbyterians championed the cause of Union.

Thornwell's influence was as spokesman rather than as maker of Southern Presbyterian conservatism. In 1832, just following his college graduation, he gave the aid of his pen to the "Union men" at Columbia who were opposing Nullification. In 1851, when support for secession was much stronger, Thornwell as editor of the *Southern Presbyterian Review,* sharply critical of five sermons published by Northern ministers, wrote glowingly of American destiny and urged the South seriously to consider national as well as sectional consequences of separation.

But [he concluded] for ourselves, we are linked to South Carolina, for weal or for woe. As long as our voice can be heard, we shall en-

7. Quoted, *ibid.,* p. 366.
8. Quoted, *ibid.,* p. 179.
9. Quoted, *ibid.,* p. 457.
10. Deschamps, *op. cit.,* p. 488.

deavour to avert calamity; but if what we regard as rash counsels finally prevail, we have made up our mind, as God shall give us to take what comes.[11]

In his Yale College address he had deplored "local jealousies" and "sectional distinctions." In 1855, involved, as president of South Carolina College, in state political affairs, Thornwell, in spite of opposition from friends, joined the Know Nothing party. He worked diligently to bring the whole South into that party, for he believed it was the only one which could save the country. Until the crisis of 1860, when Abraham Lincoln was elected to the presidency, Thornwell steadfastly maintained that withdrawal from the Union would bring "defeat and disaster, insecurity to slavery, oppression to ourselves, ruin to the State."

While in Europe during the summer of 1860, Thornwell determined that for the sake of peace, immediately upon his return, he would throw his influence on the side of gradual emancipation, but, he added, "When I got home, I found that it was too late; the die was cast." [12] It was in January, 1861, that his "State of the Country" article appeared in the *Review*.[13] It was a defense of secession which immediately attracted a great deal of favorable opinion.[14] In November, 1861, he wrote a lifelong friend, "I gave up the Union with great pain, but I saw no alternative. . . . We may have to suffer much, . . . but liberty is worth it all." [15]

A Mississippian had written to the Jackson paper in 1845, "The Presbyterian clergy . . . are whigs, not because they are aristocrats but because they are opposed to radicalism, and in favor of conservatism." [16] Thornwell, it would appear, reflected

11. *Southern Presbyterian Review*, III (1851); reprinted Appendix I, B. M. Palmer, *op. cit.*, pp. 482–483.

12. Quoted, B. M. Palmer, *op. cit.*, pp. 482–483.

13. *Southern Presbyterian Review*, XIII (1861), 860–889. It appeared in the *New York Observer* in February, 1861. Reprinted, Appendix III, B. M. Palmer, *op. cit.*, 591–610.

14. B. M. Palmer, *op. cit.*, pp. 487 f. Cf. Charles Hodge's remark, "never was a greater perversion of historical truth." A. A. Hodge, *Life of Charles Hodge* (New York, 1880), p. 446.

15. Quoted, B. M. Palmer, *op. cit.*, p. 498.

16. In the *Southron*, Jackson, Mississippi, Oct. 15, 1845. Quoted, Margaret Deschamps Moore, "Religion in Mississippi in 1860," *The Journal of Mississippi History*, XXII (1960), 235.

rather than invented the socio-political opinions of his denomination and region. In any case, he was not a "fire-eater." [17] On the contrary, his most characteristic thinking shows tendencies of moderation and restraint. Intrinsically and fundamentally the distinctive trend of his mind was toward preservation of inherited values. To the task of defending citadel walls, he gave himself not with heated emotion but with intellectual labor, on occasion in church and in public affairs, but more frequently in college and seminary chapel and classrooms.

His Shining Hour

When in 1855 Thornwell gave his inaugural as Professor of Theology at the Columbia Theological Seminary, he stated that on that particular occasion he could perceive how through his lifetime the Providence of God had been controlling, modifying, and shaping his training, studies, peculiar turn of mind, tastes, and "chosen speculations" "with reference to the solemnities of this hour." [18]

Another occasion in his life could be considered Thornwell's hour of destiny. On December 4, 1861, at Augusta, Georgia, there was convened a formal assembly of commissioners from forty-seven presbyteries making up ten southern synods of the Old School Presbyterian Church. Benjamin Morgan Palmer of New Orleans, a close friend of Thornwell and a pulpit orator widely known as a belligerent advocate of Southern independence, was elected Moderator.[19] On the motion made by Thorn-

17. The editor of the Philadelphia Old School weekly, *Presbyterian*, Aug. 23, 1862, commenting on Thornwell's death, stated that he "took great delight in propagating and defending the peculiar doctrines of that pompous and pragmatical people [Southerners?] upon all the great moral and political questions of the day" and added, "many were led into war . . . by his eloquent pleas."

18. John B. Adger, ed., *The Collected Writings of James Henley Thornwell* (4 vols.; Richmond, 1871), I, 574. Hereinafter cited as *Collected Writings*.

19. But for Thornwell's illness, he probably would have been elected Moderator. Palmer preached the stirring opening sermon of the Assembly and was elected unanimously. He was later to give Thornwell's funeral eulogy, and to write his biography. He was Thornwell's successor at the seminary. See Thomas Cary Johnson, *The Life and Letters of Benjamin Morgan Palmer* (Richmond, 1906), pp. 246, 262.

well the Assembly organized itself as an independent body and adopted the name of The Presbyterian Church in the Confederate States of America. During the morning of the fourth day of this Assembly Thornwell asked permission to read a paper he had prepared setting forth reasons for the separate organization. Palmer, who was presiding, stated that it was read "amid the solemn stillness of an audience whose emotions are hushed with awe." [20] On the tenth day the lengthy paper, "Address to All the Churches of Jesus Christ Throughout the Earth," once more was read in full and adopted. The manuscript was placed on the Moderator's table, and in silence each of the ninety-three commissioners came forward one by one to affix his signature to the document. Palmer recounted his feelings:

We were carried back to those stirring times in Scottish story, when the Solemn League and Covenant was spread upon the grave stone in the Grey Friar's churchyard, and Christian heroes pricked their veins, that with the red blood they might sign their allegiance to the kingdom and crown of Jesus Christ, their Lord and Head.[21]

The "Address" incorporates much of that which was "peculiar" and distinctive of Thornwell's deepest thought and conviction in ecclesiology and social thought as well as theology and ethics.

The Address

The Address, in "epistle" form, opens with "Dearly Beloved Brethren" and announces the formation of the new denomination as "taking its place among sister Churches of this and other Countries." [22] It asks that this new group not be considered guilty of schism, for "we are persuaded that the interests of true religion will be more effectually served by two independent Churches, under the circumstances in which the

20. Palmer, *op. cit.*, p. 504.
21. *Ibid*. The original manuscript with the signatures affixed is in the collection of the Historical Foundation, Montreat, North Carolina.
22. For the complete text, see *Collected Writings*, IV, 446–464; in abbreviated form, Maurice W. Armstrong *et al.*, *The Presbyterian Enterprise* (Philadelphia, 1956) , p. 211.

two countries (United and Confederate States) are placed, than by one united body." [23] The text follows in three numbered sections.

1. In a single Presbyterian Assembly, composed of commissioners drawn from two "enemy" nations, "political questions" "will be obtruded"; such an Assembly "would present a mournful spectacle of strife and debate" and "could have no security for peace."

"The only conceivable condition . . . upon which the Church of the North and the South could remain together . . . with any prospect of success, is the rigorous exclusion" of political considerations from Assembly debates. This observation provided opportunity for Thornwell to give classic expression to a Puritan interpretation of Church-State relations, a traditional Presbyterian theory known as that of the "spirituality of the Church." [24] This theory, though highly regarded today in some Southern Presbyterian circles, has recently come under attack by Ernest Trice Thompson, a former Moderator, as an "ultimate strangeness" to the Calvinistic heritage.[25] The key sentences are: "the provinces of Church and State are perfectly distinct, and the one has no right to usurp the jurisdiction of

23. Old School Presbyterians were fond of quoting a remark attributed to Cyrus McCormick that "the two great hoops holding the Union together were the Democratic party and the Old School Presbyterian Church." Lewis G. Vander Velde, *The Presbyterian Churches and the Federal Union 1861–1869* (Cambridge, Mass., 1932), p. 21.

24. The theory was not original with Thornwell. It was a part of his inheritance from Southern Presbyterian conservatism. For example, it had formed a basis for the separation of the Southern United Synod of the New School church in 1857. The theory was significant to conservatives outside of the South. One of the commissioners to the Philadelphia Assembly, May, 1861, Dr. A. G. Hall, protesting the Spring resolutions, stated it as the "duty of the Assembly . . . to confine itself exclusively to ecclesiastical action." *Minutes of the General Assembly,* XVI (1861), 338. Vander Velde (*op. cit.,* p. 65) found this to be "the only explicit objection of this kind," yet the judgment was assumed in Dr. Hodge's protest that the Spring resolution departed from Assembly precedent in such matters and, in deciding a political question, "violated the Constitution of the Church, and usurped the prerogative of its Divine Master." The Hodge protest had fifty-eight signatures, twenty-four from Northern commissioners. An editorial in the Philadelphia weekly, *Presbyterian,* April 27, 1861, anticipating the Assembly meeting, stated, "Our own settled conviction is that it would be prudent and wise in the Assembly to confine its attention to routine business . . . and to avoid all other questions which may engender difference of opinion and debate." Quoted, Vander Velde, *op. cit.,* p. 40.

25. *The Spirituality of the Church: A Distinctive Doctrine of the Presbyterian Church, U.S.* (Richmond, 1961).

the other." They are as planets moving in different orbits, and unless each is confined to its own track, the consequences may be as disastrous in the moral world as the collision of different spheres in the world of matter." To demonstrate the differentiation, Thornwell made detailed comparison at twelve points.

	State	*Church*
1. Institution of	Nature	Supernature
2. Founded on man as	Moral and social	Sinner, capable of Redemption
3. Designed to realize ideal of	Justice	Grace
4. Society of	Rights	Redemption
5. Aims at	Social order	Spiritual holiness
6. Concerned for	Visible and outward	Invisible and inward
7. Badge of authority	The sword	The keys of Heaven
8. Power of	Force	Exclusively spiritual
9. Constitution of	Determined by reason and circumstances	Given by divine revelation (the Bible)
10. Right excluded	To frame Church creed and polity	To construct or modify State government
11. Enjoins duty on man	As safeguard of social order	As obedience to God
12. Right of protest	When Church becomes seditious or disturber of peace	When State makes wicked laws, Church can make humble petition

The Address suggests that had this principle of polity prevailed in the May, 1861, Old School Assembly at Philadelphia, "the ecclesiastical separation of the North and South might have been deferred for years to come." (Note the word "deferred." Throughout the Address the permanency of the then still provisional Confederate States government is assumed; the culture of the North and the Federal government are already called "foreign.") Acknowledgment is given of the Old School Assembly's previously "conservative influence" as touching slavery and of the South's desire that this attitude would continue. "But, alas! . . . these golden visions were soon dispelled." In contrast to the results of current historical reviews of pre-1861 Presbytery and Synod minutes, the Address states, "The first thing which roused our Presbyteries to look the question of separation in the face" was the passage of the Gardiner Spring resolutions by the Philadelphia Assembly.[26] This action is declared to be a "political theory" "propounded" by the Assembly which made secession a crime and Southern citizens traitors. Herein the Church "transcended her sphere and usurped the duties of the State." The Philadelphia Assembly, "like Pilate . . . obeyed the clamour of the multitude, and, though acting in the name of Jesus . . . kissed the sceptre and bowed the knee to the mandates of Northern phrenzy." [27]

It is admitted that this one unconstitutional action by an Assembly would not "in itself [be] considered a sufficient ground of separation." However, the Address asserts that, since what has begun cannot soon be arrested, for the sake of peace, Christian charity, the honor of the Church and the glory of God, the Southern Presbyteries "have quietly separated, and we are grateful to God that . . . we ourselves have never given occasion to break the peace. We have never confounded Caesar and

26. Palmer repeated this claim in 1886 at the quarter-centennial Assembly. Prior to the Philadelphia Assembly, following as it did the secession of states, the fighting at Fort Sumter, and Lincoln's call for volunteers, sectional feelings ran high. Only about a third of the Southern Presbyteries sent commissioners. They must have been pro-Union men; no pro-secession utterances are reported in the Assembly debates. Unrepresented Presbyteries, such as those in South Carolina, had officially advised elected commissioners not to attend, withheld benevolent funds, and invoked God's blessing on the Confederacy. The Synod of South Carolina in principle approved these actions, November 29, 1860. See William S. Bean *et al., History of the Presbyterian Church in South Carolina since 1850* (Columbia, 1926) , pp. 74–102, and William C. Robinson, *Columbia Theological Seminary and the Southern Presbyterian Church* (Decatur, Ga.; 1931) , pp. 46–52. The Georgia Presbyteries reacted similarly; see Franklin C. Talmage, *The Story of the Synod of Georgia* (n.p., 1961) , p. 63. The Spring resolutions, after much publicity and debate, passed, 156 to 66. The strong conservative protest of Charles Hodge of Princeton was overruled. See Armstrong *et al.*, eds., *op. cit.*, p. 211, and Vander Velde, *op. cit.*, pp. 21–41.

27. Cf. Palmer referred to the Spring resolutions as an attempt "to place the crown of our Lord on the head of Caesar." Quoted, Johnson, *op. cit.*, p. 261. Note the 1951 formal exchange between the Northern and Southern Assemblies of statements of regret for past resolutions unworthy of Jesus Christ and His followers. *Minutes of the General Assembly, Presbyterian Church, U. S.*, 1961, pp. 64–66.

Christ, and we have never mixed the issues of this world with the weightier matters that properly belong to us as citizens of the kingdom of God."

2. As precedent for separation Thornwell observed that, historically, "in all Protestant countries, church-organizations have followed national lines." Division under such circumstance is no violation of the unity of the Church: "The Church catholic is one in Christ, but it is not necessarily one visible, all-absorbing organization on earth." This division of labor, like the division of the human race into countries and nations, is a benefit since "it stimulates holy rivalry and zeal" and "is a beautiful illustration of the great philosophical principle which pervades all nature—the co-existence of the one with the many."

Hence, Thornwell concluded, Southern Presbyteries "need no apology for bowing to the decree of Providence, which, in withdrawing their country from the Government of the United States, has, at the same time, determined that they should withdraw from the Church of their fathers." Rather, this separation gives opportunity for fuller development in the South of precisely those Presbyterian principles the Northern Church once stood for: "we have resolved . . . to realize its grand idea in the country, and under the Government, where God has cast our lot." The parallel is drawn with the American Presbyterian Church at the time of the Revolution separating itself from the church in Scotland. The difficulty in that case was not distance, "but the difference in the manners, habits, customs, and ways of thinking. . . . These same difficulties exist in relation to the Confederate and United States." Of these "there is one difference which so radically and fundamentally distinguishes the North and the South, that . . . the religious, as well as the secular interest of both will be more effectually promoted by a complete and lasting separation." "The North exercises a deep and settled antipathy to Slavery itself, while the South is equally zealous in its defence. Recent events can have no other effect than to confirm" the antagonism. By separation the Northern section of the Church will "get entirely quit of the subject" of slavery. The Southern section of the Church will have "unimpeded access to the slave population." "We cannot afford to give up these millions of souls [28] and consign them . . . to hopeless perdition for the sake of preserving an outward unity which, after all, is an empty shadow."

"And here we may venture to lay before the Christian world our views, as a Church, upon the subject of Slavery. We beg a candid hearing." The Address affirms that we are neither friends nor foes of slavery. Its existence or non-existence depends upon state action. Our business is with exclusively spiritual sanctions to proclaim and enforce the duties of masters and the duties of slaves. The church has no more right to preach the extirpation of slavery than she has to preach "republican equality" to the monarchies of Europe, unless, of course, slavery is a sin. Is it? The Church's only rule here is the Bible, her "positive Constitution," for she "has no right to utter a single syllable upon any subject, except as the Lord puts words in her mouth." The existence of slavery is found in both Old and New Testaments without any explicit word of condemnation. The Scripture's denunciations of oppression seem logically to involve condemnation of slavery, but, Thornwell insisted, since the Bible "expressly mentioned and treated [slavery] as a lawful relation," it follows that slavery as an institution is excepted. The Bible's law of love is to be regarded, not as against slavery, but simply as the "principle of universal equity," "that we should render unto [others] precisely the same measure which, if we were in their circumstances, it would be reasonable and just in us to demand at their hands." These conclusions, the Address declares, are nothing new; "we stand upon the foundation of the Prophets and Apostles, Jesus Christ Himself being the chief Corner-stone." "We may be denounced, despised, and cast out of the synagogues of our brethren. But . . . we shall

---

28. In 1860 there were nearly four million slaves in the South. Full recognition is often not given to the efforts of ante-bellum Presbyterian ministers like J. Leighton Wilson of South Carolina and Charles Colcock Jones of Georgia to evangelize the slaves, nor to support given official resolutions regarding this matter, as those of the Synod of South Carolina, 1831 and 1832. See an able discussion in Robinson, *op. cit.*, pp. 122–134; also Alex R. Batchelor, *Jacob's Ladder: Negro Work of the Presbyterian Church in the United States* (Atlanta, 1953). In 1961 there were 6,321 Negro members of the southern Presbyterian church in 75 congregations with 54 pastors.

go forward in our Divine work . . . ; It will be our aim to resist the real tyrants which oppress the soul—Sin and Satan." "We cannot but accept it as a gracious Providence that [our slaves] have been brought in such numbers to America, redeemed from barbarism and sin." Slavery to them "has been a link in the wondrous chain of Providence, through which many sons and daughters have been made heirs of the heavenly inheritance."

The system of slavery, the Address remarks in Thornwell's words, is kindly and benevolent in its general operation, an effective discipline without which the Negro can never be elevated. "As long as that race, in its comparative degradation, co-exists side by side with the white, bondage is its normal condition." True, the Negro does not have the rights which belong to other men, but human rights exist in "not a fixed, but a fluctuating quantity." "The truth is, the education of the human races for liberty and virtue is a vast providential scheme, and God assigns to every man, by a wise and holy decree, the precise place he is to occupy in the great moral school of humanity."

This section is concluded with a plea for approval: Are we not right in assigning slavery to the authority of the state? Are we not acting as Christ and His Apostles have acted before us? We have done our duty. We can do no more. We walk according to the light of the Written Word.

3. The Address declares the new denomination to have aims common to all Christian churches. However, "we are not ashamed to confess that we are intensely Presbyterian." "We embrace all other denominations in the arms of Christian fellowship and love, but our own scheme of government we humbly believe to be according to the pattern shown on the Mount [Sinai], and, by God's grace, we propose to put its efficiency to the test."

"And now we commend you to God and the Word of His grace." The Address concludes, "We devoutly pray that the whole catholic Church . . . may speedily be stirred up to give the Lord no rest until He establish and make Jerusalem a praise in the earth."

These pages were read in full in two sessions separated by six days before the Assembly adopted them in full ceremony. In them there is an evident plea for understanding and, in spite of high feelings, an effort at objectivity and fairness. Taking the position of a defense against novelty, the Address is a positive exposition of a Southern conservative attitude toward slavery and church-state relations. An underlying conviction of the Address is that God in Providence is responsible for the historical separation of states and churches, and that this separation is to be accepted with gratitude and with no regret.

As a considered expression of conservative Southern religious opinion, made while the states were still ratifying secession, the Address is a significant document. The adoption of the paper by the 1861 General Assembly of the Southern Presbyterian Church may well have been Thornwell's shining hour. In 1901 President William McPheeters of Columbia Theological Seminary, in reviewing the 1861 General Assembly, said of Thornwell, "Indeed, it is but history to add that to him, probably more than to any other single individual, our Church owes most of what is distinctive in her principles and her polity." [29]

A Hypothetical Student

A student who entered South Carolina College in 1851 would have been exposed through nearly the entire span of his collegiate career to the ideas of Thornwell as his college president. If, after graduating in 1855, he elected to continue his studies at the neighboring Columbia Theological Seminary, the student would have had three additional years in Thornwell's classroom. In the following pages we may discover the kind of thought influence Thornwell would have had on such a student. In imagination we can follow the student first through Thornwell's teaching of philosophy and ethics in college classroom

29. *Columbia Theological Seminary; A Retrospect* (n.p., 1901) , pp. 26, 27.

and chapel and then through the kind of theology Thornwell taught in the seminary.

Introduction to Philosophy and Ethics

From about 1800 to 1875 the prevailing American academic philosophy was Scottish Common Sense realism. Professors of philosophy at Harvard, Yale, Brown, Amherst, and Princeton "were all definitely in the tradition of British philosophy." They used as textbooks the work of such authors as Locke, Reid, Stewart, Brown, Paley, Butler, and Hamilton. Thereby Scottish realism seemed firmly established in American philosophy.[30] According to H. W. Schneider, the Common Sense school was an attempt to give grounds for moral and religious certainty in the face of what was regarded as the materialistic systems of Thomas Brown and Erasmus Darwin in their scientific works of physiological psychology and biology. "Idealism and agnosticism," Schnieder holds, "were both powerful forces in American thought, but neither had an academic foothold. The safe and sane system of Scottish realism, on the other hand, was an ideal pattern for preventing youth from indulging in speculative extremes." Within the framework of this philosophy it was possible to expound, as reasoned metaphysics, orthodox theology while at the same time demonstrating sympathy for science; here agnosticism and positivism could be met on their own ground. Scottish realism filled a desperate American academic need in the field of philosophy and ethics.[31]

Levi Hedge, a Scottish realist, was appointed by Harvard College in 1810 as America's first full-time professor of philosophy. Of the more usual sort was Francis Wayland, who, in addition to being Professor of Moral and Intellectual Philosophy at Brown from 1827 to 1855, was also President of the Uni-

30. Harvey Gates Townsend, *Philosophical Ideas in the United States* (New York, 1924), p. 102.
31. H. W. Schneider, *A History of American Philosophy* (New York, 1946), p. 249. See also S. A. Graves, *The Scottish Philosophy of Common Sense* (Oxford, 1960).

versity and a Baptist pastor. Wayland's *Elements of Moral Science* (1835) enjoyed numerous revisions and editions. Colleges in the South gave it an understandably warm reception. Princeton, its philosophical tradition of Scottish realism stemming from President John Witherspoon (who came from Scotland in 1768) and continued by his successor, Samuel Stanhope Smith, supplied four of the first five professors at the University of North Carolina. The first two or three presidents of the University of Georgia were Presbyterians and sometimes served as pastor of the local Presbyterian church. Princeton was so largely patronized by Presbyterian and other students from the South that until the war the college was thought by North and South alike as Southern in sympathy.

South Carolina College's first president was typical of both American philosophical and academic traditions. The Reverend Jonathan Maxcy, D.D., was a New England Baptist minister who had been trained at Brown. A kind of idealism and a sort of agnosticism soon came to be known in the college. The idealist was Robert Henry, a Charleston-born French Calvinist preacher, who in 1818 became Professor of Moral Philosophy and Logic, a position from which he was not to retire until 1854. Henry inclined toward Berkeleyan idealism, but his idealism was mild in comparison with contemporary New England transcendentalism. He regularly taught courses in the evidences of Christianity, and these, Thornwell wrote, effectively saved the faith of men at the college who were being tempted to agnosticism.

Agnosticism had academic representation in South Carolina College in the person of Maxcy's successor, the colorful Thomas Cooper, M.D. (hon.) . When he became the college's president, Cooper was more than sixty years old. Born in England, he was an intimate friend of the deist Joseph Priestly and had had personal associations with leaders of the French revolution. Jefferson thought highly of Cooper but failed to secure a chair for him at the University of Virginia because of Presbyterian opposition. Cooper was an Episcopal layman with liberal religious views; some thought him a Unitarian, others a Deist. Not a man to keep to himself his views on any subject, Cooper publicly pronounced the tariff act of 1828 adequate grounds for South Carolina's immediate withdrawal from the Union. He has been called "father of nullification in South Carolina." An Oxford-trained industrial chemist, he had no use for metaphysics and denied the existence of an immaterial soul. His rejection of the Mosaic authorship of the Pentateuch was ultimately responsible for his dismissal from the presidency in 1834. One of Thornwell's college mates wrote that Cooper was Thornwell's one-time "idol," but by his senior year Thornwell had become a student leader of the opposition to the college's president. It has been suggested that Thornwell's acceptance of a professorship in 1838 was part of an unofficial denominational effort to offset Cooper's influence on the institution.[32]

A survey of the footnote references in Thornwell's *Collected Writings* discloses that in the philosophical field he used mainly works of English and Scottish thought. After Thornwell's death his successor, John L. Giradeau, assigned his thought to the Scotch school. Thornwell had spoken his hearty approval of "the sturdy common sense of Englishmen." The training under Henry had given him this turn. In Scottish realism Thornwell found a philosophical tradition in which there was more than ample room for reasonable consideration of the theological beliefs he held as revealed truth. This too was in the tradition. Thornwell's memoir on Henry states he "never let slip an opportunity of vindicating religion, and the records of the Christian faith. We ourselves are particularly indebted to him for the able and satisfactory reply which he gave to us in private to Dr. Cooper's celebrated assault on the Pentateuch."[33] Here is a revealing picture of Thornwell, former student and now colleague, engaging privately with Henry, veteran professor, in critical analysis of their president's latest publication.

The task of apologetics suited Thornwell's mind. He was fond of debate and early stated that it was the Christian's duty

32. B. M. Palmer, *op. cit.*, pp. 145 ff., citing La Borde's history of the college.
33. "Memoir on Dr. Henry," *Southern Quarterly Review*, 3rd ser., I (1854) , 202.

to resist all efforts to corrupt the Church's pure doctrine and discipline.[34]

It becomes clear that in his philosophic utterances, Thornwell was an apologist as well as an expositor. As minister-professor he filled an accepted academic function in presenting within the curriculum and otherwise the evidences of Christianity. This he could do with enthusiasm for it was his habit of thought when considering a matter to evaluate it on the basis of its relation to the "authoritative standard of faith."

Instruction in Philosophy

Philosophy, Thornwell held, unfolds the mysteries of the universe—whence it came and how it has been produced. As such it deals with the deliverances of consciousness, regulating its conclusions according to these data. "The common sense of man is right, though language does not always adequately represent it." [35]

The pervading love of truth for its own sake, Thornwell held, is the standard of intellectual integrity. "He only deserves commendation . . . who begins with the predominating love of truth, and maintains it steadily and sincerely all the subsequent periods of his history." [36]

What disturbed Thornwell about philosophy as a discipline was its tendency, as he saw it, to accept unproved maxim-like hypotheses as absolute truths. He had in mind particularly Absolute Idealism, from the ascendency of which the world had been delivered by the work of Hume, who "prepared the way for a sounder metaphysics." [37] Philosophy, Thornwell was certain, is chiefly "defective from its ignorance of the fall, especially regarding the will." [38] Further, the self-knowledge of philosophy tends toward self-sufficiency and independence in contrast to Christian self-knowledge as entire helplessness in

34. See his commencement address, Oglethorpe University, Milledgeville, Georgia, October, 1861, in *Collected Writings*, III, 78.
35. *Ibid.*, II, 545.
36. *Ibid.*, II, 596.
37. *Ibid.*, II, 506.
38. *Ibid.*, I, 614.

ourselves and total dependence upon God. Fallen man errs in his philosophic thinking when he fails to take into account his fallen nature, but, conversely, even fallen man, if aware of himself as fallen, and, in light of the Gospel, has the powers with which to construct or to consider a sound philosophy, as Thornwell apparently considered Scottish realism to be.

Logic was a division of philosophy in which Thornwell had great interest. He once said in jocular understatement that he probably owned the largest collection of works on the subject in the whole country. He spoke in 1857 of his gratification over the increasing interest in this country in the study of logic, and he expressed the hope that he might some day write on the science of logic. He never wrote the book, but logic and its technical terminology came unbeckoned to his pen and tongue. Charles Hodge, who crossed points of view more than once with Thornwell, observed that one of Thornwell's books included a "profusion of the mere technicalities of logic." [39] B. M. Palmer, Thornwell's biographer and admirer, says that "his familiarity with [logic's formulae] tempted him, perhaps, too often to employ them, for the sake of precision, in his popular writings, and rendered them sometimes a trifle too technical for the ordinary reader." [40] Thornwell credited his initial interest in logic to Robert Henry, who, he held, established the tradition for logical thinking for which South Carolinians were nationally famed.

As to epistemology, Thornwell endorsed Sir William Hamilton's statement, "Philosophy proper is principally and primarily the *science of knowledge:* its first and most important problem being to determine, What can we know." [41] What we can know, said Thornwell, we know first by sense perception. There are no such things as innate ideas. Consciousness is dormant until experience awakens it by the presentation of an object. The mind, stimulated from the outside object, comes to know, "and whatever knowledge it obtains in obedience to

39. *The Princeton Review,* XVII (1845) , 269.
40. *Op. cit.,* p. 537.
41. *Collected Writings,* III, 79.

[the 'laws of thought'] is natural" and trustworthy.[42] Error comes through disobedience to the "laws of thought" and through man's depravity which renders it impossible for him to contemplate truth as he should. Error is a constant factor for which allowance must be made, but this, Thornwell insisted, is quite different from Kant's position that conceptions do not mirror the original objects of knowledge. "We can represent *all the essence* that we ever knew." [43]

The reliance on the ability of the mind to form exact ideas of reality leads readily to a defense of introspection as a dependable philosophic method. "Reflection is to psychology what observation and experiment are to physics." [44] Again, testimony is a real source of knowledge. All that is capable of being known through the experience of any one human individual is capable of being known to others through accredited testimony. This Thornwell supported by reference to God's revealing truth to the sons of men through testimony. Even so, for Thornwell all human knowledge is necessarily relative and limited. He wrote: ". . . all knowledge begins with the incomprehensible, and is bounded by the incomprehensible. . . . The longer I live, and the more I think, the more profound is my conviction of human ignorance." [45]

Thornwell's epistemology was directed against both absolute idealism and skepticism. For the epistemological conceptions of the idealists and those of the rationalists, Thornwell had no use. "Whoever," he said, "would seek to penetrate into properties of things to which our faculties are not adjusted, overlooks a fundamental condition of the possibilities of knowledge and his conclusions are entitled to no more respect than the speculations of a blind man upon colors or a deaf man upon sounds." [46] Knowledge is relative in its nature and sensual in its objects. The rationalist authoritatively pronounces that there can be no intelligible reality beyond the domain of hu-

42. *Ibid.,* I, 72.
43. *Ibid.,* III, 51.
44. *Ibid.,* III, 125.
45. B. M. Palmer, *op. cit.,* p. 344.
46. *Collected Writings,* II, 497.

man consciousness. According to the rationalist God cannot do with and in His world what He will and when He will; all that He can do must be known by man in advance. "Rationalism, in other words," Thornwell concluded, "if maintained as a logical necessity, subverts the first principles of Theism." [47]

On the basis of his epistemological principles Thornwell framed his apology for revelation and miracles. Some of his language suggests rigidly "fundamentalist" interpretation of the Bible. "The theory of 'verbal dictation' . . . is the only theory . . . which makes the Bible what it professes to be, the Word of God, and an adequate and perfect measure of faith." [48] Nevertheless, in response to the "Deist" and "infidel" attacks on Scripture, and in line with the early German critical studies of the Bible, Thornwell was prepared to admit that there might be errors in those parts of the Bible which pertain to geography, politics, customs, and manners. There is indication that he had read some of the early German Bible critics. He said of the essential significance of the Bible, "Christ crucified is its great subject; it is the knowledge of Him that saves the soul." [49] The central question regarding revelation, he held, is "Whether or not God *can* stand to man in the attitude of a *witness* to truth." [50] Since it is possible for all which can be known by any man to be received by other men by means of accredited testimony, then surely God can be a witness to truth, too. Revelation may be considered as God communicating truths to men or as God witnessing to man of the truth contained in some writings. The former way of revelation is illustrated by God's relation to writers of scripture; the latter by the way in which God in contemporary times, through the Holy Spirit, produces within the individual a faith that the Scriptures are true. How God inspired men, and how much human abilities were involved, Thornwell held, are simply curious questions to which the Bible gives no answers. The authority of the Scriptures rests in the fact that God moved the authors to write. Hence,

47. *Ibid.*, I, 46.
48. *Ibid.*, III, 51.
49. *Ibid.*, III, 197–198.
50. *Southern Presbyterian Review*, IV (1851), 503.

"the Word of God is truth, and . . . we are bound to receive all that it contains on the authority of its Author, independently of all other considerations. We are neither to question nor to doubt, but simply to interpret and believe. Philosophy and prejudice and everything else are to yield to the voice of God speaking in His Word." [51] Christianity, for Thornwell, has nothing to fear from true science: ". . . the real issue is between the Bible and a wild imagination." [52]

The credibility of miracles Thornwell supported through metaphysics. One's most immediate awareness in metaphysics is the self: that which is aware, conscious, and knowing. What is known of the material world may be regarded as objectively real; and this includes our own bodies. These bodies, however, are not of the same quality of existence, for our selves are immortal whereas our bodies "have not a single characteristic of personality." [53] The insistence on the body's relation to the self as solely instrumental was, clearly, a thrust at Cooper's denial of the soul.

In his analysis of the nature of the physical world, Thornwell relied upon the doctrines of Creation and Providence. The physical world manifests the principle of causality and so-called laws of nature; but these possess no efficiency in themselves. They are simply uniform effects of the agency of God as Creator and Providence. Providence, Thornwell was convinced, acts in such manner that many events seem to be fortuitous. This, however, has a divine intent to lift man's mind from the principles he can discover through observation and experience "to that sovereign Will which orders all things in heaven above and in earth beneath. Fortuitous [contingent] events are so many monuments of the Divine personality, so many memorials of God in the midst of a scene in which we are too prone to forget Him." [54]

Life in nature and man, Thornwell held, exists in a series of superimposed levels. Each possesses the characteristics of those

51. *Collected Writings,* II, 108.
52. *Ibid.,* III, 27.
53. *Ibid.,* I, 496; see also pp. 613–614.
54. *Ibid.,* II, 347; see also pp. 348, 351.

below it together with its own peculiar characteristics. These levels are in the main: vegetable, animal, rational, moral, and religious. The religious life is thus the perfection of earthly, spiritual nature. Thornwell, acknowledging his indebtedness, follows Aquinas in declaring the miracle is against the *order* of nature, but not against the *end* of nature. The enemy of the miracle is not the scientist who, like the geologist, begins and continues with miracles, but rather that pair of prejudiced systems to which science itself is opposed: Pantheism with its prejudicial outlook, and Naturalism, whose "blind devotion to the supremacy of laws" "is upheld against all extraordinary interventions of God." [55] A miracle, then, is to be regarded as "a direct interposition of an act of the will of some being whose will, having originally endowed all the causes with the powers by which they produce their effects, may well be supposed able to counteract them." [56] Thornwell concluded "Miracles," the third of his long articles on J. D. Morell's *The Philosophy of Religion,* in this oracular fashion:

Future generations will wonder that in the nineteenth century men gravely disputed whether God could interpose in the direct exercise of His power in the world He has made. The miracle a century hence will be made as credible as any common fact. Let the earth be explored, let its physical history be traced, and a mighty voice will come to us from the tombs of its perished races testifying in a thousand instances to the miraculous hand of God. Geology and the Bible must kiss and embrace each other, and this youngest daughter of Science will be found, like the Eastern Magi, bringing her votive offerings to the cradle of the Prince of peace. The earth can never turn traitor to its God, and its stones have already begun to cry out against those who attempted to extract from them a lesson of infidelity or Atheism.[57]

It is of interest to point out that in 1834 the state legislature of South Carolina, upon the resignation of Cooper as president of the college and professor of chemistry and geology, prohibited further teaching of these subjects at the college. Sixteen years later, 1849, Thornwell and others succeeded in reinstating geology to the curriculum. The following spring Louis

55. *Ibid.,* II, 275.
56. *Ibid.,* II, 258.
57. *Ibid.,* III, 275–276.

Agassiz, Harvard's scientist-apologete for Genesis, lectured at the college.[58] A faculty colleague of Thornwell's from 1856 was Joseph LeConte, the geologist who attained national reputation after his removal to the University of California in 1869. LeConte in his autobiography referred to Thornwell as one whose society at Columbia had stimulated his intellectual activity. In 1861 Thornwell heartily endorsed the addition of James Woodrow, Ph.D. in science from Heidelberg University, Germany, to the faculty of Columbia seminary. Woodrow was to hold the newly established Perkins Professorship of Natural Science in Connection with Revelation, the only chair of its kind in a Presbyterian seminary in the South; its incumbent became the center of a Presbyterian controversy over evolution in the late 1880's.[59] John Calvin McNair, who studied under both Woodrow and Thornwell, established a lectureship on the relation between science and theology which was inaugurated in 1909 and is still continued at the University of North Carolina.

Instruction in Ethics

When Thornwell became president of the college in January of 1852, he also became professor of moral philosophy. As a college teacher and administrator Thornwell stressed the significance of ethics. "Knowledge is not the principal end of College instruction, but habits. . . . the maturity of the habit is measured by the degree and accuracy of the knowledge; but still, the habits are the main thing." [60] The outstanding single publication of his career was his *Discourses on Truth* (New York: Robert Carter & Bros., 1855). It was widely circulated and had favorable reviews. R. S. Gladney in *The Southern Presbyterian Review* found it "especially valuable" in its insistence upon religion as a basis for true ethical judgment.[61] Sir

58. R. W. Gibbes, *The Present Earth the Remains of a Former World* (Columbia, S. C., 1849), p. 3.
59. Marion W. Woodrow, *Dr. James Woodrow* (Columbia, S.C., 1909), p. 13.
60. B. M. Palmer, *op. cit.*, p. 357.
61. IX (1855), 114.

William Hamilton acknowledged a copy Thornwell had sent him, stating, "I have read [the discourses] with great interest, and no less admiration." [62]

Every act of will, according to Thornwell, leaves permanent effect upon character. Ethical judgment of such acts springs from moral philosophy, in which the essential questions are: 1. How do we come to possess notions of right and wrong? 2. In what do the essential distinctions between right and wrong consist? 3. What, practically, are the actions that are right?

For Thornwell conscience was a simple element of our being, both natural and original. Decisions of conscience are not final considerations, but only preludes to God's higher pronouncements in the final judgment. Society must reinforce the consciences of its members with "punitive justice" as a part of moral order. "It is a fatal symptom that a nation is tending to anarchy when it becomes indifferent to ['punitive justice'], the first principle of prosperity." [63] Thornwell protested Bacon's assertion that all morality is supernatural, stating that morality as a subject falls within the province of natural reason. As such, systems of morality that do not accept the Scriptures as an authoritative rule of duty err in their omissions or in their additions or in their erroneous applications of right principles; "depravity of heart and the indulgence of corrupt and wicked passions . . . make out a false case, and hence a false judgment is necessarily rendered." [64]

The phase of practical ethics which Thornwell developed most fully was man's obligation in dealing with the truth. Ethical thinkers, he held, often overlook the fact that "there may be a virtuous or vicious exercise of the understanding;" "man is responsible for his opinions as . . . for the motives which impel him to intellectual effort, and for the diligence, caution and attention by which he avails himself of all the means of arriving at truth." [65] The moral character of a man is shown by his dealings with truth. "Why," Thornwell asked

62. Quoted, Palmer, *op. cit.*, p. 357.
63. *Collected Writings*, I, 411.
64. *Ibid.*, II, 508.
65. *Ibid.*, II, 492.

rhetorically in his discourse on sincerity, "am I bound to speak the truth? . . . Because it is the law of our nature; it is a fundamental datum of consciousness, a command of God impressed upon the moral structure of the soul." [66]

Much of Thornwell's writing was directed against utilitarianism. "We would utterly protest against the principle that expediency is any measure of duty or obligation. . . . The position . . . [is] much closer . . . to the atheistic philosophy of Epicurus . . . than to the Gospel of the Lord Jesus Christ." [67] As to theism and ethics Thornwell wrote, "Apart from the existence of a personal God, it is impossible to construct a consistent scheme of moral philosophy. . . . From God all moral distinctions proceed, and to God they naturally and necessarily lead." [68] The Bible, therefore, becomes necessary in ethics not as moral legislation, but as providing those principles of practical ethics against which the speculations of men can be tested. Redemption "opens a new chapter in the book of Ethics," and invites us to speculations as refreshing by their novelty as they are invigorating by their truth. In the same discourse Thornwell concludes: "There is a tenfold nearer approximation to the teachings of the Bible in Aristotle than there is in Paley; more affinity with the Gospel in Cicero than in the whole tribe of utilitarians." [69]

Instruction in Religion

It will be recalled that in his metaphysics Thornwell regarded the religious life as the highest form of earthly existence. He regarded man's whole being as involved in this and denied that there is a "religious sense" as conscience can be termed a moral sense. As such, religion is the true glory of man and its value a matter of universal human experience.

Nature and the supernatural are both parts of the same existence and cannot be separated.

66. *Ibid.*, II, 528.
67. *Ibid.*, IV, 167.
68. *Ibid.*, I, 505.
69. *Ibid.*, II, 462.

God has not left the world, as a watchmaker (Paley's) leaves his clock after he has wound it up, to pursue its course independently . . . ; He pervades the powers which He has imparted to created substances by His ceaseless energy. . . . He is the life of nature's life. In Him we live, and move, and have our being.[70]

The closeness of the Creator and Providence to creation was the ground upon which Thornwell viewed revelation as not only possible but probable. Thus, as noted, the Bible was for him authoritative revelation, though he considered present revelation as only mediate through the writings of the prophets and apostles by the Holy Spirit.

To deny the possibility of miracles, to Thornwell, was to make "matter more important than the life and health of the soul," and to degrade the Creator and ourselves.[71] Miracles were, he thought, "the criterion by which a real is distinguished from a pretended revelation, the mark by which we know that God has spoken." [72] "It is impossible to abandon the miracle, and cling to any other Christianity but that which is enkindled in our own souls from the sparks of our own reason." [73]

Thornwell's writings reveal that he shared Cooper's conviction that non-Christian religions were worth studying. His conclusion was that for Christians the authoritative Bible as miracle-attested revelation was the ultimate criterion: "the doctrine is the decisive test of spurious and true revelations," whether of Rome, Mohammed, or Joseph Smith. "Whatever is repugnant to a *known* truth, . . . cannot be Divine." [74]

In Thornwell's opinion the humanistic philosophy of religion, enamored of its portrait of man, accepts this as reality rather than partial representation of reality. The pantheist, too, is an artist, whose folly lies in his rebellion against the true position of man as a dependent being, and in his betrayal of the common-sense principles of human existence. Schleiermacher, Thornwell warned, had framed a type of "rationalism"

70. *Ibid.*, III, 230–231.
71. *Ibid.*, II, 273.
72. *Ibid.*, III, 249.
73. *Ibid.*, III, 227.
74. *Ibid.*, III, 193; also 191.

which would prove particularly insidious for Americans; "it invites by its warmth" and employs "the very language of piety." But, he continued, it repudiates all external standards of truth, reduces doctrine to feeling, strips sin of any moral import and is supported by a philosophy which is essentially pantheistic.[75] Appealing to college students in a sermon, Thornwell begged that they might never abandon the incarnation, the atonement, and the resurrection "while there is a sin to be pardoned, a grave to be feared, a hell to be dreaded, a God to be met—" [76]

Man, Thornwell said, is essentially a religious animal. He must have a God to pray to, as well as a God to swear by, and if he does not know the true God, then in His place man will have idols. Absolute dependence with the concomitant consciousness of his own mortality is the law of human nature. Thornwell labeled the interpretation of religion which denied the reality of evil and sin as "bastard liberality."

Man's historical life, which Thornwell often called "this sublunary state," is a school in which human beings are being trained for a higher and nobler state by being taught what is necessary to their happiness. Of the end of history we know little apart from revelation, but we do know by our mortality, by conscience, and by revelation that history is directed by God. And we know, too, that man's destiny at the end of history is in accord with the relations he has sustained to the moral government of God under which he has lived within temporal history.

The apologetic concerns of Thornwell in the philosophical and ethical instruction which he gave at South Carolina College, as professor and president, suggest similarity to the earlier efforts of Timothy Dwight at Yale. Thornwell sought by logic and learning in classroom and chapel to meet what he regarded as the current intellectual assaults on Christian doctrine and ethics. Apart from the revealed good news of God's scheme of reconciliation through Christ as mediator, he held, there is no means of attaining true integrity.

75. *Ibid.*, III, 250–251.
76. "Matt. XXII. 29," *Southern Presbyterian Review,* IV (1851), 524.

All your present excellencies are dead works, and when the influences which now embalm and preserve the corpse are gone, it will putrify [*sic*] and stink. The first step in real moral improvement is faith in the Son of God. When that step is taken, we begin to live; until then we are dead in trespasses and sin.[77]

The college's students and faculty who first heard the discourses were soon thrown into the vortex of the "irrepressible conflict." The fiber of their determination had been sensitized appreciably by such spirited certainty and conviction.

A good man struggling with the storms of fate, unshaken in his allegiance to God, and steady in his purpose never to be seduced into wrong, is the noblest spectacle which earth can present. There is something unutterably grand in the moral attitude of him who, with his eyes fixed upon the favour of God rises superior to earth and hell, and amid the wrecks of a thousand barks around him steers his course with steadiness and peace.[78]

Introduction to Theology

Thornwell's mother, a Calvinistic Baptist, was his earliest identifiable religious influence. During his college days he had prolonged periods of struggle with feelings of guilt and religious accountability; yet he had no formal church affiliation until he was twenty years old. In May, 1832, he united with the Presbyterian Church and within months had decided to prepare for the ministry. Later he recalled that as a college student he had purchased for 25 cents at a town bookstore a copy of the Westminster Confession of Faith to which he, being at the time unacquainted with the work, was attracted by its title alone. He was so fascinated with it that he read it through that same night. "For the first time," he commented, "I felt that I had met with a system which held together with the strictest logical connection; granting its premises, the conclusions were bound to follow." [79] Before entering college, Thornwell had studied some law in the office of a friend. At college he had continued

77. *Collected Writings,* II, 474–475.
78. *Ibid.,* II, 553.
79. Palmer, *op. cit.,* p. 80.

his study of classical languages and literature. The system of doctrine contained in the Confession of Faith, reflecting the thought of Calvin, who similarly was trained in the classics and law, became for Thornwell a coherent whole to be explored, to be explained, and to be defended, but one which he did not feel needed to be subject to further test or evaluation. As early as the first year of his theological studies, when he was for some months attending divinity lectures at Harvard, he showed in a personal letter the dual attitude of acceptance and defense:

I room in Divinity Hall, among the Unitarian students of theology; . . . I shall expect to meet and give blows in defence of my own peculiar doctrines; and God forbid that I should falter in maintaining the faith once delivered to the saints. I look upon the tenets of modern Unitarianism as little better than down-right infidelity.[80]

Palmer discovered more than a dozen points of parallel between the thought and career of Calvin and those of Thornwell and reported that Thornwell admired Calvin "above all, for his superior wisdom in founding his opinions upon the express declarations of Scripture, rather than upon the shifting speculations of human philosophy." Palmer also reports a student account of Thornwell's moving classroom description of his visit to Calvin's grave and of his concluding statement "that the emergencies of the conflict with Rationalistic infidelity were now forcing the whole Church more and more to occupy Calvin's ground." [81]

Thornwell's self-conscious role as expositor and defender of Calvinistic theology he held throughout his career. As a twenty-two-year-old theology student he confessed to a friend, "I have an eye on a Professorship in the Theological Seminary at Columbia." When he died, though not yet fifty years of age, he had held for six years in that institution the chair of Didactic and Polemic Theology. His thinking he did not regard as original, nor as grounded in any one historical church tradition,

80. Quoted, *ibid.,* p. 117.
81. *Ibid.,* p. 534.

much as he honored Calvin and repeatedly referred to the wording of the Church catechisms. Rather he thought of his theology as the necessary conclusions of biblical teachings. His students would recall his saying of a proposition that he could "see no flaw in my reasoning, but I am gravelled with one verse in the Bible," or again, "if there is but one passage against us, our speculation must go to the winds." Palmer explained, "Wherever he found a 'thus saith the Lord,' he ceased to reason, and began to worship." [82]

As a teacher Thornwell wrote out his lectures carefully. They comprise nearly 450 pages of the first volume of his *Collected Writings*. They were afterward used as basic text material in his own institution and also in the Presbyterian seminary at Richmond, Virginia, well into the twentieth century.

R. E. Thompson placed Thornwell among the three most influential systematic theologians of nineteenth-century American Presbyterianism.[83] Thornwell stood with Charles Hodge of Princeton and R. J. Breckinridge of Kentucky as champions of Old School Calvinism in distinction to the New School modifications which had been effected first by Jonathan Edwards and later by Nathaniel W. Taylor. The Old School claimed to represent the pristine Calvinistic system. It is clear, however, that in the case of Thornwell at least this representation was often colored by transmission through the English Presbyterian-Puritan thinkers like the Westminster divines as well as through continental Calvinistic scholastics like Cocceius, Turretin, and Van Mastricht. In discussing historical theology Thornwell repeatedly referred to the ancient catechisms, church council reports, and confessions of faith of which he possessed a fine collection. In his writings Thornwell practically ignored American religious writers while engaging in minute examination of writings by the Reformers, early church fathers, and Thomas Aquinas.[84]

82. *Ibid.*, p. 545.
83. *A History of the Presbyterian Churches in the United States* (New York, 1895) , p. 145.
84. For further analysis of Thornwell's sources in theological reading, see Paul L. Garber, "James Henley Thornwell: Presbyterian Defender of the Old South," *Union Seminary Review*, LIV, No. 2 (1943) , 14–17.

Instruction in Theology

Thornwell defined theology as "the science of religion; . . . the system of doctrine . . . which, when spiritually discerned, produces true piety." [85] Its truth is an objective and systematically organized body of knowledge resulting from the rational examination of God-given data in the external world of nature, in the internal realm of human nature, and in the unsystematized revealed truths of the inspired Holy Scriptures. As such, theology is "queen of sciences," which "must confessedly stand at the head of all human knowledge" [86] since it deals with all humanly available knowledge in the realms of nature and human nature as well as "the Gospel," "the facts of revelation."

Thornwell conceived the central consideration of theology to be justification, how man, a sinner, can be justified by the righteous God. This revealed message from God, Thornwell asserted, makes all earthly knowledge, possessions, and honors secondary, for upon man's attitude toward the Gospel depends "heaven or hell, life or death, eternal life or eternal death."

The elements of Thornwell's theology are the familiar ones of Calvinism: the unqualified sovereignty of God in Creation, Providence, and Decrees; unredeemed or "natural" man, as finite creature "who calls corruption his father, and the worm his mother," and as sinner, guilty by his own transgressions and also by "imputed" or "original sin" (the "thorniest problem in theology," as Thornwell admitted) ; sin as transgression and rebellion and the Devil as fallen being whose temptations the saints can repel only by an enduring "fear of God;" the covenant of works in Adam; the efficacious atonement through the covenant of grace in Christ; Christ as by His twofold nature God's effectual agent in atonement; adoption, regeneration, and holiness constituting individual, but not social, redemption; God's judgment sealing at death the eternal doom of immortal souls, either for good or for ill.[87]

85. *Collected Writings,* I, 36.
86. *Ibid.,* I, 25.
87. See the longer exposition in Paul L. Garber, "The Religious Thought of James Henley Thornwell," unpublished Ph.D. thesis, Duke University, 1939, chap. iv.

In Christology Thornwell left sketches of a book he proposed, but never wrote, on the Eternal Sonship of Christ.[88] His plan was an exposition based on the suggestions in Hebrews of Christ's atonement as an act of worship, an interpretation which he regarded as a helpful supplement to the more customary legal form of Calvinistic atonement imagery. A sermon, "The Priesthood of Christ," which Thornwell preached at the college in 1849, and later published, indicates the possibilities:

> . . . the whole work of Jesus was a solemn service of religion, . . . He was a priest in His death, a priest in His resurrection, a priest in His ascension. He worshipped God in laying His life upon the altar, He worshipped Him in taking it again, and it was an act of worship by which He entered with His blood into the very presence of the Highest to intercede for the saints.[89]

Vital for Thornwell in his systematic theology is his understanding of the relation of the Providence of God and the sense of duty. Thornwell's doctrine of Providence implies that nothing transpires within history which can ever take God by surprise. Yet God is not ethically responsible for all that happens. "God uses men without being a party to their crimes. The sun rouses the odour from the dung-hill, but is not itself defiled." "The design of the doctrine of Providence . . . is to prompt edification." [90] From these convictions, it followed, in Thornwell's thinking, that it was for the sovereign God in His good Providence and His good time to remove from the earth natural evils, the results of Adam's sin, such as disease and death; and it was equally for God, through the same offices, to remove from the earth social evils which were the results of Adam's sin, such as poverty and social classes. Meanwhile, it is possible by the Providence of God for these evils to be overruled for good to individuals. Death, for example, can be the means whereby a man, aware of the vanity of earthly things, gives his attention to his soul's eternal salvation.

There can be in God's world no "chance" occurrences; events

88. Palmer, *op. cit.*, p. 261.
89. *Collected Writings*, I, 280–284.
90. *Ibid.*, I, 616.

so designated actually constitute direct divine direction as to the believer's duty. Conscience is God's answer to prayer. So rigorously did Thornwell make practical application of this Puritanism that he confessed, "My friends sometimes charge me with a spice of fanaticism." [91]

In 1862 as he lay on what was to be his deathbed Thornwell was called upon by the South Carolina Tract Society to write something to strengthen public wartime morale. He entitled the pamphlet (#130) "Our Danger and Our Duty." In it Thornwell suggested that recent military reverses should be understood as "a call to break off our sins"—he mentions over-confidence, factionalism, public immorality, and all forms of materialism, and with an emphasis on the feelings of duty, concludes:

Do we feel the moral power of courage, of resolution, of heroic will, rising and swelling within us, until it towers above all the smoke and dust of the invasion? Then we are in a condition to do great deeds. . . . Let us seize the opportunity, and make to ourselves an immortal name, while we redeem a land from bondage and a continent from ruin.[92]

Three False Theologies

From Thornwell's theological writings it is possible to identify three types of thought which he regarded as challenges to orthodoxy.

1. ROMAN CATHOLICISM. Early in his journalistic writing Thornwell crossed swords in a series of articles with a Roman Catholic priest of Charleston, a Dr. (later Bishop) Lynch. The exchange began with an essay written by Thornwell at the request of R. J. Breckinridge on the "Claims of the Apocrypha to Divine Inspiration," which was published as an anonymous pamphlet. When a Columbia, South Carolina, newspaper editor published this material, he, knowingly but without permission, attached to it Thornwell's name. As Thornwell stated later, Dr. Lynch "naturally" regarded this as a challenge to

91. Palmer, *op. cit.*, p. 266.
92. *Ibid.*, pp. 589–590.

vindicate Rome "from the severe charges which were brought against her" [93] and made reply by long letters to the newspaper editor. The exchange was carried on over several years. Its scope ranged as widely as Protestant-Catholic differences. In his book *The Arguments of Romanists from the Infallibility of the Church, and the Testimony of the Fathers in behalf of the Apocrypha, Discussed and Refuted* [94] Thornwell published his parts of the exchange along with an appendix summarizing Lynch's replies. The acrimonious parts of the exchange, for which Thornwell later expressed private regret, were exscinded from the *Collected Writings*. Even so, the substance of the Apocrypha work makes up almost half of the eight hundred pages of Volume III. To these have been added another 129 pages of Thornwell's "Arguments against the Validity of Romish Baptism," published first in Richmond, 1846, and republished in 1851–1852 as a series in the *Southern Presbyterian Review* (Columbia, South Carolina) ; Thornwell was then its editor.

In ante-bellum South Carolina, as in the South generally except for certain urban areas, Protestants, who were busily engaged among themselves in controversies, did not regard the Roman Catholic Church as a threat to their domination of the region.[95] There were anti-Catholic actions in the United States from the 1830's through the 1850's, including movements, published vitriolic sermons, organizations, mob riots, and political parties, but these were in the North and West.[96] Thornwell, however, became involved as a religious journalist; in 1855 he wrote a close personal friend in Mississippi that he gave his most cordial approval to the anti-Catholic Know Nothing party, "if it fails, our last hope for the union is gone." [97]

Thornwell was not original in his attacks on Roman Catholic

93. *Collected Writings,* III, 280.
94. New York, 1845.
95. Margaret Deschamps Moore, "Religion in Mississippi in 1860," *The Journal of Mississippi History,* XXII (1960) , 226.
96. Olmstead, *History of Religion in the United States,* pp. 326–327. W. W. Sweet, *The Story of Religion in America* (2nd ed.; New York, 1950) , p. 273.
97. Palmer, *op. cit.,* pp. 478–479.

doctrine. He revived the customary Reformation and post-Reformation protests against Apocrypha as scripture, papal authority, transubstantiation, holiness as a supernatural grace, miracles as a present feature of Christian experience, and the doctrine of works of supererogation. Moral corruption, he warned his readers, is "the legitimate, natural, necessary" result of Romanism, "the bitter fruit of her graceless pretensions to infallibility." Thereby, he concluded, "the Church of Rome . . . declares herself to be a child of the devil and an enemy of all righteousness." [98]

2. PELAGIANISM AND ARMINIANISM. In view of the frequently bitter doctrinal disputes among Protestant champions in the South before the Civil War, particularly evident under the emotional strains of the widespread camp meetings or protracted revivals, Thornwell's handling of Pelagianism and Arminianism is strikingly moderate. He regarded both systems as being based on a misguided interpretation of the Bible in which human speculations had been made the determining principle; in this he compared them to the deists. Fortunately, Thornwell felt, in their Christian life, when loyalty to their systems of theology was laid aside, Pelagians and Arminians alike were found to be "sober and honest-hearted Calvinists, as their earnest prayers for grace and assistance unequivocally declare." [99] On the other hand, Socinians or Unitarians, he wrote, because of their denial of the Trinity, the depravity of man, the vicarious sacrifice of Christ, and eternal punishment, "are no more entitled to be considered as Christians than Mohammedans." [100]

3. RATIONALISM. The system of theology which Thornwell designated "rationalism" and which has come to be identified as Hegelian absolute idealism he regarded not as "the visions of crack-brained enthusiasts" but as the work of "men of the highest order of mind." He prophesied that it would have great

98. *Collected Writings,* III, 509.
99. *Ibid.,* II, 146.
100. *Ibid.,* I, 434.

vogue in this country and thus make the error of its theology more prevalent.[101] The German philosophers in the effort to discover the absolute, Thornwell held, "do not *rave,* but *reason.* They do not *dream,* but *think;* and that, too, with a rigour of abstraction, an intensity of attention, and a nicety of discrimination, which [we are] obliged to respect. . . . The difficulty with them is that they begin wrong." [102] The whole issue between Christianity and rationalism, as Thornwell saw it, "turns upon the question, Whether we have been left to ourselves, whether theology is in fact like all other sciences, the production of man, or whether God has framed it for us ready to our hands." [103] There is a subjective side to the religious experience, but, Thornwell insisted, it is never autonomous. The Bible as revelation was for Thornwell a God-given, objective, moral, and religious standard; he defended its authority with enthusiasm. "When men cry, Down with the Bible! the real meaning of their rage is, Away with Jesus and His Cross!" [104]

Thornwell regarded the appearance of the American edition of John Daniel Morell's *The Philosophy of Religion* [105] as a herald of rationalism's onslaught in this country. Morell had a scholarly reputation in America by reason of his widely used history of modern philosophy.[106] Thornwell's critical review of Morell's work on religion was long (occupying 171 printed pages in the *Collected Writings*) ; its three parts were published in 1849, 1850, and 1856. Here was occasion for Thornwell to express his own philosophy of religion: he did so in some of his closest reasoning. Reprints of the review were widely distributed, being regarded as including the best of Thornwell's critical thought. Thomas Smyth of Charleston, often a severe critic of Thornwell, sent copies with his com-

101. *Ibid.,* III, 27.
102. *Ibid.,* III, 99.
103. *Ibid.,* III, 29.
104. *Ibid.,* III, 155.
105. New York, 1849.
106. *An Historical and Critical View of the Speculative Philosophy of Europe in the Nineteenth Century* (2nd ed.; New York, 1847) .

mendation to friends in England.[107] The general evaluation is indicative of the spirit of the work:

> We do not hesitate . . . to rank Mr. Morell's book in the class of infidel publications. He has assailed the very foundations of the faith; and in resisting his philosophy we are defending the citadel of Christianity from the artful machinations of a traitor, who, with honeyed words of friendship and allegiance upon his tongue, is in actual treaty to deliver it into the hands of the enemy of God and man.[108]

Conclusion

If our hypothetical theological student who studied under Thornwell in college and seminary, 1851–1858, had, along with his studies, followed Thornwell's published sermons and editorial writings, he would have discovered basic materials for an identifiable philosophy of education and an interpretation of the nature of society and politics, as well as a full examination of the nature of the Christian church and its relation to society. He would have been exposed to Thornwell's treatment of the Negro as a human being of God's creation with a soul capable of Christ's redemption, and of slavery as an arrangement in Southern society which, though admittedly an exploitive form of labor economy, was nonetheless, as a gift of God's Providence, a benefit to the slave in cultural education, and a more humane system of employer-employee relations than that of industrial free labor.[109]

Through the full panorama of Thornwell's thinking, the dominant characteristic is that of "broad-minded conservatism." This paradoxical description is given by Vander Velde as the nation-wide reputation of Old School Presbyterians from the late 1830's to 1861.[110] These people were regarded as broad-minded because of their intellectual leadership and enthusiasm

107. B. M. Palmer to J. H. Thornwell, Sept. 10, 1850. Anderson-Thornwell letters, MSS Collection, University of North Carolina Library.
108. *Collected Writings*, III, 27.
109. For details on these topics, see Garber, *op. cit.*, chaps. v, vi, vii.
110. Vander Velde, *op. cit.*, p. 24.

for education. Moreover, they were less rigid in attitudes on communion than Baptists and Episcopalians, more flexible about centralized church authority and dancing than Methodists, and less bound regarding ordination rights and interchurch co-operation than Episcopalians. The Presbyterians seemed liberal-minded in their willingness to examine novelties. They were considered, however, conservative because of the high value which staunchly they placed on the thought-forms and behavior patterns of the past; from these they moved only when persuaded not by what was popular or logical, but by what they felt to be commanded by a "thus saith the Lord."

From the earliest period of his ministry to the end of his life Thornwell was in traditional spirit an Old School Presbyterian, committed to learning and conservatism by the temper of his mind and by his deepest feelings. The liberality gave room for his ambition to be a man of learning which, he confessed, "from the earliest knowledge of himself [worked] as a passion within him." [111] In this pursuit he achieved no little success. George Bancroft, the historian, presented Thornwell with a copy of Aristotle, inscribed in Latin, "A testimonial of regard to the Rev. Dr. J. H. Thornwell, the most learned of learned." [112] John C. Calhoun commented that in capacity of mind Thornwell was comparable to Timothy Dwight of Yale and added, "I was not prepared for the thorough acquaintance he exhibited with all the topics that are generally familiar only to statesmen." [113] Thornwell's urge to investigate by scholarship was not knowledge for the sake of knowledge. It was rather "love of truth," as he put it, which for a man of ethical integrity, he held, would be a predominating motivation sustained steadily and sincerely through life. For him this "love of truth" meant examination of the new in light of the old, always with the assumption that one would find it wise and possible to hold fast to the good which had stood the test of time and human experience. Therein lay his conservatism.

It is in this context that Thornwell's role as a defender of

111. Palmer, *op. cit.*, p. 20.
112. *Ibid.*, p. 537.
113. *Ibid.*, pp. 305–306.

the South is to be understood. Within his academic and theological "ivory tower," where he was more congenially at home than he was in public debate or social action, his first premise was that the Bible was God's revelation of what was true in theology and permissible in action. Although he was prepared to grant Christian fellowship, he was committed to Presbyterian theology and Presbyterian government, both being, as he saw it, in accord with the Scriptures and thus God's revealed truth. This disclosure he regarded as part of the redeeming work of the sovereign God Who, in Providence, continues to make evident through historical happenings the pattern of obedience for those who know and love Him.

Until late in 1860 Thornwell resisted proposals for secession, calling them "rash counsels;" and this was long after the abolition agitations of the 1850's had thrown many in his area into panic with fears of slave uprisings and social disorders.[114] The election of Lincoln Thornwell interpreted as signifying an extraconstitutional amending of the Federal Constitution. This event in history, an assault of novelty on the value of the past, was evidence for Thornwell of God through Providence giving direction in duty. Thereafter he gave himself, as faithful to God's mandate, to wholehearted support, even from his deathbed, to the Southern cause.

The case is similar with reference to the separation of the churches. Thornwell regarded the Spring resolutions less cause than occasion, for it was "the decree of Providence, which . . . determined that they [the Southern Presbyterians] should withdraw from the church of their fathers." God was responsible, by way of Providence in history, for the separation of the nations; it was the God-given duty of Presbyterians to heed and obey. Thornwell reveals his assumption that the separation of North and South was a *fait accompli,* as in other writings, in a letter which he sent to the Philadelphia Assembly in May, 1861, requesting his absence to be excused. He concluded this communication, which was read aloud to the Assembly:

114. Margaret B. Deschamps, "The Presbyterian Church in the South Atlantic States, 1801–1861," unpublished Ph.D. thesis, Emory University, 1952, pp. 147 ff.

Brethren, I invoke upon your deliberations the blessings of the Most High. I sincerely pray that . . . He may save the Church from every false way; that He may make her a messenger of peace in these troublous times, and that He may restore harmony and good will between your country and mine.

The reporter for the Philadelphia *Press* commented, "The last part of the letter created great laughter." And in Vander Velde's words, "thus in a burst of merriment perished the influence of one who in less troubled times had been respected as had few others in the Old School Church." [115]

It is likely that Thornwell never seriously considered that the life of the Old South would not continue without interruption; there is no evidence that he was ever aware of the breakdown which was to come. Although his father, a plantation manager, died when Thornwell was eight years old, his mother, with the aid of planter friends and relatives, was able to rear and educate the four children who survived infancy. Thornwell was testimony that a plantation-dominated society could find a place for a white man who with eager and alert mind was ready and able to give himself to learning and to the service of the church. Through his wife Thornwell acquired a small plantation in the upcountry which he romantically named Dryburgh Abbey for the Scottish burial place of Sir Walter Scott. Here he must have had a number of slaves; he speaks of "hosts of backs to cover." In his home there were several "servants" (in personal correspondence they are never called "slaves") ; one was a "body servant" named Charles, for whose welfare and religious experience Thornwell in his letters often expressed much concern.

The extent to which Southern Presbyterians were slaveholders is difficult to assess. A statement by the Reverend James Smylie of Mississippi, published in 1849,[116] is often cited, that three-fourths of all Presbyterian Church members in the South were slaveholders. This figure is probably excessive. Presbyterians in the South in 1860 numbered about 100,000. There

115. Vander Velde, *op. cit.*, pp. 43–45, citing the Philadelphia *Press*, May 21, 1861.
116. *Minority Report of a Committee of the General Association of Connecticut, on the Sin of Slavery* (Salisbury, Conn., 1849) , p. 4.

was an average of about ten slaves to each slaveholder. By Smylie's figures this would mean that Presbyterians held 750,-000 slaves out of a total of nearly four million.[117] Another index of uncertain value is the number of Negro members of the Presbyterian Church in the Old South; these have been estimated variously as seven thousand and twenty thousand, but, as Walter B. Posey comments, in either case "it is clearly evident that the Presbyterian Church held only a small percentage of the Negroes." [118]

Whatever their economic interests, Southern Presbyterian churches were generally self-consciously loyal to the "peculiar institution." By the time Thornwell entered the ministry, the Presbyterian critics of slavery in South Carolina as elsewhere had been silenced.[119] In 1818 the General Assembly had declared slavery to be "a gross violation of the most precious and sacred rights of human nature," "totally irreconcilable with the spirit and principles of the Gospel of Christ," and had encouraged Presbyterians to work earnestly for "a total abolition of slavery." [120] This position was protested to the Assembly of 1836 by twelve Southern presbyteries. One of these was Harmony Presbytery in South Carolina. Thornwell, more than a quarter of a century later, was to reflect that stand in the Address: "as the Kingdom of our Lord is not of this world, His church as such has no right to abolish, alter or affect any institution or ordinance of men, political or civil merely." [121] The request that the Assembly rescind its 1818 action failed to produce results at the 1836 Assembly. The 1837 General Assembly exscinded synods and presbyteries totaling five-ninths of its membership

117. For the number of Presbyterians, see Vander Velde, *op. cit.*, pp. 4–7; for the number of slaves and slaveholders, R. S. Cotterill, *The Old South* (2nd ed.; Glendale, Calif., 1939), pp. 274–275, and T. Harry Williams *et al.*, *A History of the United States to 1876* (New York, 1959), p. 476.

118. *The Presbyterian Church in the Old Southwest, 1778–1838* (Richmond, 1952), p. 92 with sources in notes 82 and 83.

119. Margaret B. Deschamps, "Antislavery Presbyterians in the Carolina Piedmont," *The Proceedings of the South Carolina Historical Association*, XXIV (Columbia, 1954), 6–13.

120. R. E. Thompson, *A History of the Presbyterian Churches in the United States* (New York, 1895), pp. 364–365.

121. MS Minutes, Harmony Presbytery, 1830–1848, Oct. 27, 1836, in the Montreat, North Carolina, collection; cited by Deschamps, *op. cit.*, p. 136.

in an action of doctrinal reform. This was Thornwell's first
Assembly. He seems to have taken little part in it save to give
support by his vote to Old School stalwarts like Robert J.
Breckinridge. In a letter to his wife from the Assembly, Thornwell makes no mention of slavery, but he does remark of the
New School group, "They never, constitutionally and regularly,
formed a part of the Church. . . . [The two parties] are wide
apart in spirit, principle, and doctrines; and nothing but confusion and disorder can result from their being united." [122]
There is a running historians' battle over whether this 1837
division was on doctrine, as appears on the face of the official
transactions, or, more covertly, on the basis of slavery-abolition
differences, as recent interpreters have held. [123] The fact is that,
from the year of the division until after 1861, the Old School
Assembly, following a markedly different policy from that of
the New School, declined to pronounce on methods of emancipation. Its stand throughout this period, the time of Thornwell's connections with it, was that stated by the Assembly of
1845, "that the existence of domestic slavery, under the circumstances in which it is found in the southern portion of the country, is no bar to Christian communion." [124] Thornwell was
consulted by the committee which framed this resolution and
at their request prepared a paper for their use; he told his wife
that by this Assembly action "abolitionism will be killed in the
Presbyterian Church, at least for the present." [125] The South had
a continuingly steady influence in the Assembly until 1861;
many Southern moderators were elected, among whom was
Thornwell, chosen in 1847 when he was thirty-four years old;
eight of the Assemblies between 1844 and 1861 were held south
of the Mason-Dixon line; and efforts were consistently made to
place Southern professors in seminaries under Assembly control. [126]

In the separation of the churches, therefore, as well as in the

122. Quoted, Palmer, *op. cit.*, p. 213.
123. For example, C. Bruce Staiger, "Abolitionism and the Presbyterian Schism
of 1837–38," *Mississippi Valley Historical Review*, XXXVI (1949), 391–414.
124. For the full text, see R. E. Thompson, *op. cit.*, pp. 269–272.
125. Quoted, Palmer, *op. cit.*, p. 286.
126. See Vander Velde, *op. cit.*, pp. 26–27.

separation of the nation, Thornwell saw himself morally bound to yield obediently to the lesson of Providence. The cause of church separation was not basically the passage of the Spring resolution, as he acknowledged, nor was it any slackening of the Old School Assembly's traditional conservatism regarding slavery. It was simply that God in His Providence had seen fit to divide the nation into two countries, and in light of this accomplished fact it was the duty of obedient Presbyterians quietly to separate.

Clement Eaton wrote in 1940, "The dynamics of Southern thought moved, after the death of Jefferson, in the direction of defense, a trend which explains much in the cultural history of the Old South." [127] This observation may be illustrated by an examination of the characteristic trends of Thornwell's thought in its broad aspects. However, in 1963, in view of more recent history, though some things are clear, it is difficult, even more difficult than in 1940, to be certain exactly what eternal verities Providence was teaching through the events of Southern cultural history a century ago.

127. *Freedom of Thought in the Old South* (Durham, N. C., 1940) , p. 332.

Puritan Character in the
Witchcraft Episode
of Salem

STUART C. HENRY

"It was in the latter end of February 1691,[1] when divers young Persons belonging to Mr. Parris's Family, and one or more of the Neighbourhood, began to Act, after a strange and unusual manner. . . ."[2] The consequence of the singular behavior of these Salem adolescents was dire and swift. On February 29[3] warrants were issued for the arrest of three persons[4] who the deluded children alleged "afflicted"[5] them by means of the black arts of witchcraft. Before the spring of the following year when Sir William Phips[6] "put an end to the Court and stopped the proceedings,"[7] and so "dissipated the blak cloud that threatened this Province with destruction"[8] an unknown number[9] had been apprehended on suspicion of witch-

1. 1692 of our calendar.

2. Robert Calef, *Wonders of the Invisible World or Salem Witchcraft* (Boston, 1828) , p. 196.

3. David Levin, *What Happened in Salem? Documents Pertaining to the 17th-Century Witchcraft Trials* ([Cambridge, Mass.], 1952) , p. 22.

4. Sarah Osburn, Sarah Good, and Tituba, the West-Indian servant in Mr. Parris' household. Calef, *op. cit.,* p. 197.

5. Calef, *op. cit.,* p. 204 and *passim.* This was the descriptive term generally used of the accusers.

6. Phips was the first governor under the new charter after the restoration. See Jedidiah Morse and Elijah Parish, *A Compendious History of New England, Designed for Schools and Private Families* (Amherst, 1809) , p. 288, hereinafter cited as *History.*

7. *Letters of Governor Phips to the Home Government, 1692–1693,* in George Lincoln Burr (ed.) , *Narratives of the Witchcraft Cases 1648–1706* (New York, 1914) , pp. 199–200.

8. *Ibid.,* p. 201.

9. Charles W. Upham, *Salem Witchcraft with an Account of Salem Village, and a History of Opinions of Witchcraft and Kindred Subjects* (2 vols.; Boston, 1867) , II, 351.

craft; two, at least, had died in jail; [10] twenty had been executed.[11] Phips's proclamation in May [12] which released those still imprisoned occasioned "such a jail-delivery as has never been known in New England." [13] Thus ended the frightful chapter of the "Devil in Massachusetts" [14] by which the "pillars of civil government were shaken to their foundation" [15] and a shadow cast on Puritan theocracy which has not yet been dispelled.

It is not the purpose of this essay to treat the philosophy or the theological implications of witchcraft (except as they impinge on our subject), nor to recount the distressing history of the trials before the courts which sat to hear the libelous charges that psychopathic witnesses (to describe them in the most charitable manner) made on the basis of "spectral evidence." [16] Rather the concern here is to show that there were certain admirable traits which the Puritans exhibited in the shocking episode at Salem, and that—examined as a whole and comparatively considered—the page of Massachusetts history usually regarded as the darkest in American annals is a story, in part, of a creditable light in which the Puritans walked earlier than their peers. There is no intention to deny the sinister mixture of sinful pride, aggressive ignorance, and shameful want of charity that was plainly manifested in Salem. It will be insisted, however, that one who examines the circumstances that gave rise to the delusion, evaluates the available evidence

10. *Ibid.*

11. *History,* p. 290, e.g.

12. John Hale, *A Modest Enquiry Into the Nature of Witchcraft, and How Persons Guilty of that Crime may be Convicted,* in George Lincoln Burr (ed.), *Narratives of the Witchcraft Cases 1648–1706* (New York, 1914), p. 422.

13. Thomas Hutchinson, *The History of the Colony and Province of Massachusetts-Bay,* ed. Lawrence Shaw Mayo (2 vols.; Cambridge, Mass., 1936), II, 46.

14. I am indebted to Marion L. Starkey, *The Devil in Massachusetts* (New York, 1949) for this phrase; her psychological study is based on careful study and use of original materials.

15. *History,* p. 288.

16. Deodat Lawson, *A Brief and True Narrative of some Remarkable Passages Relating to sundry Persons Afflicted by Witchcraft, at Salem Village Which happened from the Nineteenth of March, to the Fifth of April, 1692,* in George Lincoln Burr (ed.), *Narratives of the Witchcraft Cases 1648–1706* (New York, 1914), p. 154, e.g. Hereinafter cited as Lawson. Also see George Lyman Kittredge, *Witchcraft in Old and New England* (Cambridge, Mass., 1929), pp. 363–364, for discussion of the common admission of spectral evidence in the courts.

against the background of the times, and considers the outcome of the events will find it possible to see a commendable aspect of that little-understood and currently abused character: the Puritan.

The Puritans of New England were keenly aware of two worlds: the visible and the invisible. One had to reckon with more than cattle and crops. There was a world of invisible spirits, both good and bad, whose activities affected the visible world. Cotton Mather [17] knew of the good angels "who took Delight in helping" [18] man. Indeed, one had relieved him of a headache [19] once when other resources were powerless, nor was that the only occasion when the envoys of God had given him "singular Assistance of heaven." [20] Unfortunately, he knew, too, of the machinations of demons. Three sermons he had intended for publication "were *stolen . . .* with such Circumstances, that [he was] satisfied . . . Spectres, or Agents of the *invisible World,* were the *Robbers.*" [21] If he believed that his son Samuel was healed by a ministering angel,[22] he believed, no less, that the death of his daughter Mehetabel was accompanied by the work of demons.[23]

Mather, however, might have been regarded as something of a specialist in these matters. Clearer testimony of the popular connection between the circumstances of life and the power of the spirit world in the New England mind is seen in a quotation from Samuel Sewall's Diary, which is worth reproducing in its significant detail:

Generall Court on Adjournment Febr. 16. 1685. Publick Fast. This Court considering how apparent the threatening Hand of God is, by reason of the spreading of that infectious Disease of the

17. Mather, who was to play an influential role in the proceedings in Massachusetts, was at twenty-four years of age (1690) in full charge of one of the greatest churches in America, and, accordingly, a man whose word was important, for which see Worthington Chauncey Ford (ed.), *Diary of Cotton Mather* (Mass. Hist. Soc. Coll., seventh ser., Vols. VII and VIII [2 vols.; Boston, 1911]), I, 136 n. Hereinafter cited as *Diary.*
18. *Diary,* II, 140.
19. *Ibid.*
20. *Ibid.,* I, 249.
21. *Ibid.,* 171.
22. *Ibid.,* II, 8.
23. *Ibid.,* I, 185.

Small Pox in some Towns in the Countrey; (Portsmouth, Exeter.) ; together with other Evils impending our selves and the Churches of Christ abroad, as also the more than ordinary severity of the Winter, and the Loss of many of our Cattell occasioned thereby: Have appointed the 25th Day of March next to be kept as a day of Solemn Humiliation and Prayer throughout this Colony; That we may obtain Favour from God for the diverting these Tokens of his Anger, and his Smiles towards us in the Spring and Seed-Time approaching: And to this end do recommend it to the Elders and Ministers of the respective Churches, to promote this work on the said day; forbidding Servile Labour to all People within this Jurisdiction, thereon.[24]

The subsequent entry for March 25 represents the Reverend Samuel Willard as striving for the whole day to stay the hand of God's wrath against the colonists.[25]

With such sensitivity to the pervasive power of the invisible world on the part of the clergy and the courts, one can only imagine what phantoms peopled the minds of the less educated and duller inhabitants of Zion's state in the New World.[26] Indeed, if reality came to a choice between the two worlds, the Puritan knew that the weight of evidence lay with the invisible one; in the midst of the physical world he endeavored to follow the advice of Edward Reyner: "Get thy heart more and more weaned from the Creature, the Creature is empty. . . ." [27]

With such a conviction of the realm of the spirit and of the powers it comprised, belief in witches came natural to the Puritan. It must be specifically stated, however, that a belief in witchcraft was not an exclusive characteristic of the "pious," much less of the Puritans. The Salem episode was by no means

24. *Diary of Samuel Sewall* (Mass. Hist. Soc. Coll., fifth ser., Vols. V, VI, and VII [3 vols; Boston, 1878–1882]) , V, 127–128. Also see V, 402; VI, 404; VII, 215 for examples of Sewall's superstition. Sewall, along with Bartholomew Gedney, Wait Winthrop, Nathaniel Saltonstall, John Richards, William Sergant, and— after Saltonstall resigned—Jonathan Corwin were judges of the Special Court of Oyer and Terminer, of which Lieutenant-Governor William Stoughton was chief justice, appointed by Governor Phips to "hear and determine" the witchcraft cases, for which see Levin, *op. cit.*, pp. 12–13.

25. Sewall, *op. cit.*, V, 128.

26. Awareness of the invisible world was not restricted to the pious either, for which see *The Journal of Madam Knight* in Perry Miller and Thomas H. Johnson, *The Puritans* (New York, 1938) , pp. 432, 447. Hereinafter cited as *The Puritans*.

27. *Ibid.*, p. 289. The Puritan lived in the world, but he tried desperately not to be of it.

the first, nor the most horrible, nor the last occasion on which belief in witches manifested itself, either in the attempt to practice or the effort to suppress the black art. In answer to such easy, irresponsible generalities as that of Pennethorne Hughes to the effect that the "manifestations in New England, revealed with the sanctimonious piety by the various members of the Cotton family, themselves somewhat disreputable characters, were those of the last and worst phase of the English persecution" [28] we believe that there is specific evidence to substantiate the position indicated above.

The Massachusetts Puritans did not invent the idea of witchcraft. They brought it with them from England. In a letter written from Salem to Increase Mather on August 17, 1683, John Higginson related several cases of witches in England. One concerned a young man of London who was given a book by a stranger; when he "read in it, he was seized on by a strange kind [of] Horror, both of Body & minde, the hair of his head standing up, &c" [29] so that he concluded that the man who gave it to him "was the Devil." [30] Another tells of a man in Essex who sold his soul to the Devil in exchange for a reputation of "wisdome all the country over" but who "dyed miserably." [31] The third was of a man in Leicestershire. Though Higginson confessed himself "imperfect in the story" [32] in the latter case, he believed all that he wrote "to be certain." [33] These were instances of witchcraft, not in America, but in England, the memory of which might have been in the minds of American colonists, even of those who thought that "Satan took advantage" [34] of the unfortunate Mary Hacker, whose miserable circumstances are chronicled by John Hull.[35]

28. Pennethorne Hughes, *Witchcraft* (London, New York, Toronto, 1952), pp. 181–182.
29. *The Mather Papers.* (Mass. Hist. Soc. Coll., fourth ser., Vol. VIII [Boston, 1868]), 285.
30. *Ibid.,* p. 286.
31. *Ibid.*
32. *Ibid.,* p. 287.
33. *Ibid.,* p. 285.
34. *John Hull's Diary of Public Occurrences* (Vol. III in Transactions and Collections of the American Antiquarian Society), (Cambridge, Mass., 1857), p. 182.
35. *Ibid.,* pp. 181–182. This was in 1657.

And if the New England Puritans did not invent the idea of witchcraft after they came to America, neither was the English manifestation of the delusion an exclusively Puritan innovation. "The hanging of a great number of witches in Suffolk and Essex, by the discovery of one Hopkins [36] in 1645 and 1646," wrote Richard Baxter, "is famously known." [37] What, perhaps, is less famously known is that although Hopkins himself was, indeed, a Puritan,[38] he performed his services for Charles I,[39] who most certainly was not. Moreover, he did so under the provisions of the statute of 1604,[40] passed in the first year of the reign of James I (no Puritan himself) which provided the death sentence for various indulgences in witchcraft, including the second offense of even minor varieties of sorcery. More than that, it was James's *Demonology*,[41] with which Hopkins was familiar, that gave him sanction and authority for his outrageous procedure in its assertion that "by the Devils meanes, *can never the Devill be casten out* . . . it may wel serve for a shorte time, but at the last, it will doubtleslie tend to uter perdition. . . ." [42]

In both England and America Puritans were likely to remember that John Calvin, writing of the "unclean spirits," had pointed out that God

regulates this government in such a manner, that they exercise the faithful with fighting, attack them in ambuscades, harass them with incursions, push them in battles, and frequently fatigue them,

36. Upham, *op. cit.*, I, 351, notes that he was agreeable to his title, "Witch-Finder-General." Samuel Butler, *Hudibras* (London and New York, 1893), Part II, Canto III, pp. 215–217, satirizes him thus:

"And has not he, within a year
Hang'd three score of 'em in one shire?
Some only for not being drown'd. . . ."

37. Richard Baxter, *The Certainty of the World of the Spirits Fully Evinced* (London, 1834), p. 20.

38. Montague Summers, *The Discovery of Witches: A Study of Master Matthew Hopkins commonly call'd Witch Finder Generall together with a Reprint of The Discovery of Witches from the rare original of 1647* (London, 1828), p. 22: "It is obvious that he must have been an orthodox Puritan. . . ."

39. Charles I ruled 1625–1649.

40. Kittredge, pp. 282–283, and Wallace Notestein, *A History of Witchcraft in England from 1558 to 1718* (Washington, 1911), pp. 101–109, give illuminating discussions of this statute.

41. G. B. Harrison (ed.), *King James I Daemonologie (1597)* (London, 1924).

42. *Ibid.*, p. 49.

throw them into confusion, terrify them, and sometimes wound them, yet never conquer or overwhelm them; but subdue and lead captive the impious, tyrannize over their souls and bodies, and abuse them like slaves by employing them in the perpetration of every enormity.[43]

Here, indeed, was a voice of authority, speaking clearly on the subject of demonic powers, which described the agonies of the afflicted and ascribed them to their Satanic origin. The Puritans held this belief in common with others of their times, Puritans and non-Puritans, secular and ecclesiastical. Jeremy Taylor had written of how "devils, who are spirits . . . descend unto the daughters or sons of men . . ." [44] and took delight in "communicating with witches and impure persons in the corporal act. . . ." [45] Such "Witchcraft, or final impenitence and obstinacy in any sin, are," he wrote, "infallibly desperate." [46]

Sir Thomas Browne was one of the men of his day most prominently characterized by the "scientific" spirit. Vaguely agnostic about the possibility of miracles recorded in Scripture (which he accepted) being repeated in his own time,[47] he was definite in his position with regard to witchcraft and stated it plainly:

> For my part, I have ever believed, and do now know, that there are witches: they that doubt of these, do not onely deny *them*, but Spirits; and are obliquely and upon consequence a sort not of Infidels, but Atheists. Those that to confute their incredulity desire to see apparitions shall questionless never behold any, nor have the power to be so much as Witches; the Devil hath them already in a heresie as capital as Witchcraft. . . . I hold that the Devil doth really possess some men . . . that, as the Devil is concealed and denyed by some, so God and good Angels are pretended by others, whereof the late defection of the Maid of Germany hath left a pregnant example . . . I conceive there is a traditional Magick, not learned immediately from the Devil, but at second hand from his Scholars. . . .[48]

43. John Allen (trans. and ed.), *Institutes of the Christian Religion by John Calvin* (2 vols.; Philadelphia, 1844), I, 1, 165. Hereinafter cited as Institutes.
44. Reginal Heber (ed.), *The Whole Works of the Right Rev. Jeremy Taylor* (10 vols.; London, 1862), IV, Sermon vii, 412.
45. *Ibid.*, III, chap. ii, 57.
46. *Ibid.*, IV, Sermon xvii, 546.
47. Israel Gollancz (ed.), *Sir Thomas Browne's Religio Medici* (London, 1904), pp. 42–43.
48. *Ibid.*, pp. 44–45.

Browne wrote this in his youth. In 1664 he reasserted this belief when he was called into court as an expert in the infamous case of two old women who were fraudulently accused and executed for witchcraft. In Howell's *State Trials* [49] it is recorded that

Dr. Browne of Norwich, a person of great knowledge . . . was desired to give his opinion . . . and he was clearly of the opinion that the persons were bewitched; and said that in Denmark there had been lately a great discovery of witches. . . . And his opinion was, that the Devil in such cases did work upon the bodies of men and women . . . for he conceived that these swooning fits were natural, . . . but only heightened to a great excess by the subtility of the devil, cooperating with the malice of these which we term witches, at whose insistance he doth these villanies.[50]

It was at the same trial that Sir Matthew Hale, whose "motives were most laudable" but who "furnishes a memorable instance of the mischief originating from superstition," [51] charged the jury to determine only if the children in question were bewitched and if the accused were guilty. "That there were such creatures as witches he made no doubt at all," [52] citing Scripture and the law of the land in support of this conviction. In conclusion he reminded the jurors that "to condemn the innocent, and let the guilty go free, were both an abomination to the Lord." [53]

The sentiment implicit in the material considered thus far is, perhaps, given pointed summary by John Wesley *more than seventy-five years* after the Salem episode:

It is true . . . that the English in general, and indeed most of the men of learning in Europe, have given up all accounts of witches and apparitions, as mere old wives' fables. I am sorry for it; . . . the giving up of witchcraft is, in effect, giving up the Bible; and they [the enemies of Scripture] know, on the other hand, that if but one account of the intercourse of men with separate spirits be admitted, their whole castle in the air (Deism, Atheism, Materialism) falls to the ground. I know no reason, therefore, why we should suffer even this weapon to be wrested out of our hands.

49. T. B. Howell (ed.), *A Complete Collection of State Trials and Proceedings for High Treason and Other Crimes and Misdemeanors from the Earlier Period to the Year 1783* (20 vols.; London, 1816).

50. *Ibid.*, VI, col. 697.

51. John Lord Campbell, *Lives of the Chief Justices of England* (Philadelphia, 1851), p. 446.

52. Howell, *op. cit.*, VI, col. 700.

53. *Ibid.*, VI, col. 701.

Indeed there are numerous arguments besides, which abundantly confute their vain imaginations.[54]

It did seem to the Puritans that giving up belief in witches was a giving up belief in the Bible, from whose sacred pages witch-persecutors took a text which informed their actions and adorned the title pages of tracts: [55] "Thou shalt not suffer a witch to live." [56] Yet the cynical and the worldly men of latter eighteenth century were hardly less credulous of the spirit world.

While it is true that in his *Leviathan* (which was proscribed by churchmen and burned at Oxford),[57] Thomas Hobbes commented skeptically that "as for witches, I think not that their witchcraft is any real power," [58] he nevertheless added that he thought witches "justly punished, for the false belief they have that they can do mischief. . . ." [59] He confessed, moreover, "no doubt, but God can make unnatural apparitions. . . ." [60] The latter conception is somewhat naïve—to say the least—coming from a man who worked with Bacon and talked with Galileo.[61] Samuel Pepys, a worldly libertine if ever one was so described by his own admissions, was not a man to temper his judgments. However, after reading the extraordinary *Sadducismus Triumphatus*,[62] he wrote, rather mildly, that he read the "late printed discourse of witches by a member of Grescham College . . . the discourse being well writ, in good stile, but methinks not very convincing." [63] It is more interesting to note that Pepys received a long letter from Dr. George Hicks [64] which betrays

54. Nehemiah Curnock (ed.), *The Journal of John Wesley*, (9 vols.; London, n.d.), V, 265.
55. See Summers' reproduction of facsimile facing page 48.
56. Exodus 22: 18.
57. Homer A. Watt and William W. Watt, *A Dictionary of English Literature* (New York, 1946), p. 138. Hereinafter cited as *Dictionary*.
58. E. Hershey Sneath (ed.), *The Ethics of Hobbes* (Boston, 1898), p. 54.
59. *Ibid.*
60. *Ibid.*
61. *Dictionary*, p. 137.
62. Joseph Glanvil, *Sadducismus Triumphatus* (London, 1726). See Hale, *op. cit.*, p. 405: "Glanvil . . . hath strongly proved the being of witches."
63. Henry B. Wheatley (ed.), *The Diary of Samuel Pepys* (9 vols.; London, 1923), VI, 76–77.
64. J. R. Tanner (ed.), *Private Correspondence and Miscellaneous Papers of Samuel Pepys* (London, 1926), I, 367. Ed.'s note: "Hicks, the nonjuring Bishop of Thetford, Dean of Worcester, 1683–1690."

a definite belief in witchcraft and narrates the "well attested" story of "an elf-arrow that was shot at a venerable Irish bishop by an evil spirit" [65] and the case of Jannet Douglas, who was "famous for second sight and the discovery of witches. . . ." [66] And as for the *Sadducismus Triumphatus* which Pepys received, at least not hostilely, it was the work of Joseph Glanvil, Chaplain in Ordinary to Charles II and a Fellow of the Royal Society [67] and Henry More, "one of the leaders of the . . . Cambridge Platonists." [68] Yet this was the book which Kittredge says "was thought to have put the belief in witchcraft and apparitions on an unshakable basis of science and philosophy." [69]

In summary of the treatment thus far it seems possible to say on the basis of evidence submitted that a belief in witchcraft was not invented by the Puritans nor unique to them in their day. Rather the seventeenth-century belief in which both Puritans and non-Puritans shared was little altered from that of the Elizabethan age when Spenser wrote of witches who hid their "devilish deedes/ And hellish arts from people." [70] How much further back such beliefs go is not within the scope or purpose of this paper to examine, though surely it is well to notice here that Notestein says that it is "very old," [71] citing some examples as early as the ninth century.[72] In any case we believe that we can clear the Puritans of inventing a faith in witches, or of expressing novel views in the Salem trials. The views which they held were shared, or at least reflected, by men of scientific, legal, and philosophical interests and by others whose theological bent was by no means Puritan. Moreover, faith in witches outlived the men of Salem.

65. *Ibid.*
66. *Ibid.*, I, 370.
67. See Title Page of *Sadducismus Triumphatus,* n. 62.
68. *Dictionary,* p. 202.
69. Kittredge, *op. cit.,* p. 335.
70. J. C. Smith (ed.), *Spenser's Faerie Queene* (2 vols.; Oxford, 1909), I, Bk. III, Canto VII, p. 434.
71. Notestein, *op. cit.,* p. 2.
72. *Ibid.,* p. 3. Margaret Murray, *The God of the Witches* (London, 1933), p. v.: ". . . there is no doubt that the cult was spread in early times through Central Europe and [that it] survived, underlying . . . the official religion of the country."

It is hard to say with certainty what factors joined with this commonly held belief to produce the tragedy at Salem. Perhaps it is true that the "times were ripe for such an outbreak," [73] since the village was in a slough of unknown transition. A new generation had sprung up, a generation that was "wonted from youth to hardship and solitude, cruel from King Philip's War, less educated than their fathers, though of like faith, and actually falling backward into barbarism bred from the wilderness." [74]

The first vibration of the acute, high-strung Puritan mind to the demons of the spirit world was in Boston, 1688,[75] when the children of John Goodwin [76] were afflicted in the manner to become so familiar at Salem. Particularly was Martha "variously indisposed in her health, and visited with strange Fits, beyond those that attend an Epilepsy." [77] Sometimes the children would "be Deaf, sometimes Dumb, and sometimes Blind, and often, all this at once." [78] During attacks "they would make most pitteous out-cries, that they were cut with Knives, and struck with Blows that they could not bear." [79] The ignorant Irish laundress whom the children accused of bewitching them was executed.[80] But the effects of her supposed witchcraft were not dispelled finally until Cotton Mather had taken Martha—the greatest sufferer—into his own home,[81] prayed often and long with her,[82] after which, he writes, "we had no more such entertainments." [83]

Some four years later such entertainments as Mather had seen and written of in *Memorable Providences* occurred at Salem. The children referred to in the opening sentences of this essay were given to assuming "sundry odd postures and

73. N. H. Chamberlain, *Samuel Sewall and the World He Lived In* (Boston, 1898), p. 161.
74. *Ibid.*
75. Cotton Mather, *Memorable Provinces, Relating to Witchcrafts And Possessions* in George Lincoln Burr, *Narratives of the Witchcraft Cases 1648–1706* (New York, 1914), p. 100. Hereinafter cited as *Memorable Provinces.*
76. *Ibid.*, p. 99.
77. *Ibid.*, p. 101.
78. *Ibid.*
79. *Ibid.*, p. 102.
80. *Ibid.*, p. 105.
81. *Ibid.*, p. 110.
82. *Ibid.*, pp. 110–121.
83. *Ibid.*, p. 121.

antic gestures, uttering foolish speeches." [84] Physicians were
helpless; [85] prayer proved of no avail. [86] Eventually it was decided
that only witchcraft could explain the circumstances, and
Tituba, a West Indian servant in Mr. Parris' household, [87] was
"cried out" by the children and, accordingly, arrested. [88] Along
with her were imprisoned Sarah Good, "a *melancholy* or *distracted* woman," [89] and Goodwife Osborn, "an old bed-ridden
woman," [90] whom the children had also cried out and of whom
Calef says that they were "so ill thought of, that the accusation
was the more readily believed." [91] As the hysteria mounted
people of less questionable standing in the community were accused. [92] Also the charges became more frightening in detail.
Early indictments spoke of persons guilty of "Certain detestable
arts Called Witchcraft and Sorceries wickedly mallitiously and
ffeloneously . . . practiced and Exercised At and in the
Towne of Salem. . . ." [93] Soon many a prisoner was confronted
at the bar with the charge that she "a Covenant with the Devill
did make, and signed the Devills booke, and promised to serve
the Devill as long as shee Lived, and by the Devill was baptized; and renounced her former Baptisme, by which Diaboli-
call, And wicked Covenant with the Devill, Shee . . . [had]
become a detestable witch. . . ." [94] In order to show the darkest
side of the picture, the history of a single one of the victims is
presented. It is an illustration only, but not atypical.

Rebecca Nurse was the "venerable head of a large and prominent family, and a member of the mother-church of Salem." [95]

84. Calef, *op. cit.*, p. 196.
85. *Ibid.*
86. *Ibid.*, p. 197.
87. Hale, *op. cit.*, p. 413.
88. Calef, *op. cit.*, p. 197. "Cried out" was the term by which accusation was
described, p. 202: "Goodwife Proctor was brought thither, being accused or
cried out."
89. *Ibid.*, p. 197.
90. *Ibid.*
91. *Ibid.*, pp. 197–198.
92. As George Burroughs, graduate of Harvard, former minister of Salem
Church, for which see Cotton Mather, *Wonders of the Invisible World* in George
Lincoln Burr, *Narratives of the Witchcraft Cases 1648–1706* (New York, 1914),
pp. 215–217. Hereinafter cited as *Wonders*. Also Calef, *op. cit.*, pp. 222–223 for
the account of crying out the Reverend Samuel Willard.
93. Suffolk County Superior Court of Judicature Records.
94. *Ibid.*
95. Upham, *op. cit.*, II, 56.

Her character seems to have been matched by that of her husband, Francis Nurse, who in 1678 (when he was then fifty-eight years of age) contracted to buy the Bishop farm for four hundred pounds [96]—a move which marks him with a spirit equal to a bold undertaking. Upham says that he was "a very respectable person, of great stability and energy of character, whose judgment was much relied on by his neighbors." [97] Unthinkable as it was, the ugly accusation was made against such a household, and Rebecca Nurse was cried out. When it was known that the children had charged this woman of piety and simplicity of heart, certain of her neighbors went to see her.[98] At the time she was ill and had been confined to her home for some days. They naturally talked of the trouble abroad in Salem, not knowing, perhaps, how tactfully to tell the poor woman that she was the latest victim. From them we have a graphic description of what happened:

> But shee [i.e., Rebecca Nurse] said shee heard that there was persons spoke of that wear as Innocent as shee was shee belived and After much to this purpos: we told her we heard that shee was spoken of allsoe: well shee said if it be so ye will of the Lord be done: shee sate still awhille being as it wear Amazed: and then shee said well as to this thing I am Innocent as the child unborn but surely shee said what sine hath god found out in me unrepented of that he should Lay such an Affliction upon me In my old Age: and According to our best observation we could not decern that shee knewe what we came for before we tould her.[99]

On March 21 the girls afflicted by "Biting, Pinching, Strangling, etc." [100] testified before the court that they had seen Martha Corey's familiar, a "Yellow-Bird, that used to suck betwixt her Fingers," [101] and that they had seen Martha Corey and one whom they thought was Rebecca Nurse "Praying at the same time to the Devil." [102] On March 23 the Reverend Deodat Law-

---

96. *Ibid.,* I, 79. Starkey, *op. cit.,* p. vii, says Rebecca Nurse's house is still standing.
97. Upham, *op. cit.,* I, 79.
98. *Ibid.,* II, 58.
99. MS in the Essex Institute.
100. Lawson, *op. cit.,* p. 155.
101. *Ibid.*
102. *Ibid.,* p. 156.

son, former minister at Salem, went to call on the wife of Thomas Putnam, a woman who claimed that she was now afflicted by witches.[103] Hardly had he arrived when Mrs. Putnam began "to strive violently with her Arms and Legs" [104] and to cry out, " 'Goodw. N. Be gone! Be gone! Be gone! are you not ashamed, a Woman of your Profession, to afflict a poor Creature so? . . .' " [105] The next day Rebecca Nurse was "brought before the Magistrates," [106] and when she was asked about afflicting her accusers, "she pleaded her owne innocency with earnestness." [107] In the atmosphere of hysteria that pervaded the court, she quietly insisted, "I have got no body to look to but God." [108] The afflicted ones claimed that "the Black Man whispered to her in the Assembly, and therefore she could not hear what the Magistrates said unto her." [109] The first verdict of the jury before whom she was tried was that Rebecca Nurse was innocent.[110] Immediately "all the accusers in the court . . . made an hideous outcry"; [111] she was indicted anew and condemned. Before her execution, she was excommunicated. Says the church record:

1692, July 3.—After sacrament, the elders propounded to the church,—and it was, by unanimous vote, concented to,—that our sister Nurse, being a convicted witch by the Court, and condemned to die, should be excommunicated; which was accordingly done in the afternoon, she being present.[112]

Even then the "governor saw cause to grant a reprieve"; [113] but the "accusers renewed their dismal outcries . . . insomuch that the governor was . . . prevailed with to recal the reprieve," [114] and she was executed with the rest at the spot now called Gallows Hill. We have no record of how she died, but

103. *Ibid.,* p. 157.
104. *Ibid.*
105. *Ibid.*
106. *Ibid.,* p. 158.
107. *Ibid.*
108. MS of the cross-examination in the Essex Institute.
109. *Ibid.,* p. 159. Calef, *op. cit.,* pp. 220–221 offers evidence that Rebecca Nurse was deaf and could not hear all the questions put to her.
110. Calef, *op. cit.,* p. 219.
111. *Ibid.,* pp. 219 f.
112. Upham, *op. cit.,* II, 290.
113. Calef, *op. cit.,* p. 221.
114. *Ibid.,* p. 222.

the available evidence suggests that Arthur Miller has caught
the spirit of the woman when he pictures her in the last scene
of his moving play, *The Crucible,* still great of heart, and
strong of faith, encouraging those who go to meet their death:
"Rebecca: Let you fear nothing! Another judgment awaits us
all!" [115] It was on July 19 that she died.[116] There is no entry under this date in the diary of Cotton Mather, nor in that of
Sewall. When five more were executed at the same spot for the
same offense a month later,[117] Sewall records that

George Burrough, John Willard, Jno Procter, Martha Carrier and
George Jacobs were executed at Salem, a very great number of
Spectators being present. Mr. Cotton Mather was there, Mr. Sims,
Hale, Noyes, Chiever, &c. All of them said they were innocent,
Carrier and all. Mr. Mather says they all died by a Righteous
Sentence. Mr. Burrough by his Speech, Prayer, protestation of his
Innocence, did much move unthinking persons, which occasions
their speaking hardly concerning his being executed.[118]

In the margin by this report he has written "Dolefull Witchcraft!" [119] The latter description may well be taken as equally
true of the first execution. Rebecca Nurse remains the tragic
figure of a martyr, shamefully accused, cruelly treated, unjustly tried and sentenced, and horribly executed, but to the
end a great and good woman. How then can there be any case
at all for the Puritans who were guilty of this gross miscarriage
of justice and, as we believe, sin against heaven and before the
face of men?

To this point effort has been made to show only that the Puritans were neither unique nor original in their belief about
witches. The case of Rebecca Nurse is offered as that of an
unfortunate, innocent victim of the delusion at its worst. The
question now is not whether the Puritans were right or wrong
about witches. Rather it is whether there was not something
unique in the manner in which they conducted their trials, and
especially in the aftermath of the Salem madness.

115. Arthur Miller, *The Crucible, Theatre Arts,* XXXVII, (Oct., 1953) , 67.
116. Calef, *op. cit.,* p. 218.
117. *Ibid.,* p. 222.
118. Sewall, *op. cit.,* V, 363.
119. *Ibid.*

Let us consider this proposition from the standpoint of the part which two men, Cotton Mather and Samuel Sewall, played in this tragedy of errors. Mather, as will be shown directly, never changed his mind about witches. Sewall did. There were many others besides these two who played important roles in the proceedings at Salem, but the minister and the judge seem typical to us of the more unfortunate and the more enlightened attitudes ultimately maintained by those actively involved in the delusion.

"Mr. Cotton Mather was the most active and forward of any minister in the country in those matters" [120] wrote Calef, and indeed, witchcraft concerned and (be it remembered) distressed him. Baxter, in his preface to *The Certainty of the World of Spirits* to which he appended Mather's *The Wonders of the Invisible World* said that Mather's evidence was such as would "leave every Sadducee . . . either convinced, or utterly without excuse." [121] Mather shows a subtler concern in writing in his diary that he was obligated to do his "designed Service for His Glory," [122] and that his encounter with witchcraft had "enflamed [his] Endeavours this Winter to do yett more, in a direct *opposition* unto the Divel." [123] When the affairs at Salem began "to look formidable," Sir William Phips, the governor, "asked the advice of the ministers in and near Boston," [124] who in turn appointed Cotton Mather and his father, Increase,[125] to draw up a paper of advice.[126] They recommended to the Governor a "speedy and vigorous Prosecution of such as . . . rendered themselves obnoxious, according to the Direction given in the Laws of God . . . for the Detection of Witchcrafts." [127] This was not enough. The "loud cries and clamours of the

120. Calef, *op. cit.*, p. 316.
121. Baxter, *op. cit.*, p. xxvii.
122. *Diary*, I, 152.
123. *Ibid.*, I, 156.
124. Calef, *op. cit.*, p. 317.
125. Increase Mather was at that time president of Harvard, for which see Thomas Jefferson Wertenbaker, *The Puritan Oligarchy* (New York and London, 1947) p. 152: "Once more Harvard had one of the ablest men in the colony at its head. . . ."
126. Calef, *op. cit.*, pp. 317–319. Also see Wertenbaker, *op. cit.*, p. 272.
127. Increase Mather, *A Further Account of the Tryals of the New England Witches* (London, 1862), p. 291. Hereinafter cited as *Further Account*.

friends of the afflicted" [128] together with the persuasion of the Lieutenant Governor, William Stoughton, prevailed on Phips "to give a Commission of Oyer and Terminer for discovering what witchcraft might be at the bottome or whether it were not a possession." [129] Thereafter Mather had no further official connection with the business at Salem. Though he undoubtedly followed the trials carefully and reported them in detail,[130] he did so in no official capacity. In his writing about the subject and his comment on the cases one thing seems his paramount concern: to glorify God by fighting the devil vigorously. He wrote that George Burroughs "was Accused by Eight of the Confessing Witches, as being an head Actor at some of their Hellish Randezvouzes, and one who had the promise of being a King in Satan's Kingdom, now going to be Erected." [131] One can appreciate the gravity such charges would assume for Mather and others of his time if he reflects on the weight attached to accusations which self-confessed communists make against others in our own day. Seemingly, Cotton, scrupulously honest himself, did not consider the possibility that men might fabricate charges. Ignorant of the insights of modern psychology,[132] believing literally in the Bible and in a world of spirits, he had little choice but to regard the hysterical writhings of the afflicted as the work of Satan's imps and, indeed, after seeing one such exhibition was moved to write: "But all my Library never afforded me any Commentary on those Paragraphs of the Gospels, which speak of Demoniacs, equal to that which the passions of this Child has given me." [133] Through it all, Mather was insistent that such authorities as Keeble's *Common Law,* Sir Matthew Hale's *Trials of Witches,* and Bernard's *Guide to Jurymen* be followed.[134] It was not lightly that judges had been warned that

128. Phips, *op. cit.*, p. 196.
129. *Ibid.*
130. *Wonders*, pp. 215–222, e.g.
131. *Ibid.*, pp. 215–216.
132. See especially Starkey, *op. cit.*
133. *Memorable Provinces*, p. 123.
134. Hale, *op. cit.*, p. 416.

in the prosecution of these, and all such Witchcrafts, there is need of a very critical and exquisite Caution, lest by too much Credulity for things received only upon the Devil's Authority, there be a Door opened for a long Train of miserable Consequences, and Satan get an advantage over us, for we should not be ignorant of his Devices.[135]

Mather did not seek out witches. He simply spoke his mind when he was confronted with evidence. One cannot read his Diary and doubt his sincerity. Nor, for that matter, can one doubt the sincerity of the judges with whose judgment Cotton concurred. Thomas Brattle, who early saw the delusion for what it was, in the very letter he wrote questioning the whole procedure, referred to Nicholas Noyes as "certainly a learned, a charitable, and a good man, though all the devils in Hell, and all the possessed girls in Salem, would say to the contrary." [136] The same could have been said of Mather; indeed, it has, for Barrett Wendell says he was a "scholar unapproached by any one of his age [and] that his ecstatic prayers and fastings kept him in what he never doubted was direct communication with the angels of God." [137] Such a man took a dim view of the reproach of the world if he considered himself on the side of the angels. When the storm of abuse broke upon him with the publication of Calef's *More Wonders of the Invisible World* and the favorable reaction of the public to it, Mather "sett apart" a day "for the Duties of a secret fast" [138] by which he hoped to "obtain from [God] . . . Assistences to carry it patiently and cheerfully under . . . Trials, and bring forth such Fruits of greater Serviceableness" [139] as the Christian would be expected to do in such circumstances. It is difficult to free Mather from the charge of spiritual pride, but it is impossible to tax him with hypocrisy. His theme was ever: "There is ONE to whom all is due!" [140] The last pathetic entry in his

135. *Further Account,* p. 289.
136. *Letter of Thomas Brattle* in George Lincoln Burr, *Narratives of the Witchcraft Cases 1648–1706* (New York, 1914) , p. 172.
137. *Diary,* I, xiii; 136 n.
138. *Ibid.,* I, 383.
139. *Ibid.*
140. *The Puritans,* p. 179.

Diary that remains to us is a passionate petition for "an Healed Soul!" [141] He was not a man to take a position casually, or to relinquish it easily. He never lost faith in the invisible world or in witches, which the Bible so plainly taught; since he was committed to the service of God, he did not flinch when that obligation demanded that he take up arms against the powers of hell. Confronted by evidence that he could not deny, especially when he had seen it himself,[142] only one course was open to him. The sober, judicial conclusion must be, that one is allowed to pity, not to blame. We cannot agree with Mather, but we admire his consistency to an ideal whose obligations were often beyond his understanding.

By contrast to Mather, Matthew Hopkins, that "Witch-Finder General" for Charles I, showed a character of the "narrowest and most intolerant kind," [143] according to Montague Summers, who adds that Parliament would not have entrusted the business of witch finding "to a man of another sort." [144] He went about from place to place, searching for witches; his expenses were paid, and he required in addition regular fees for the discovery of a witch.[145]

Besides pricking the body to find the witch-mark, he compelled the wretched and decrepit victims of his cruel practices to sit in a painful posture, on an elevated stool, with their limbs crossed; and, if they persevered in refusing to confess, he would prolong their torture, in some cases, to more than twenty-four hours. He would prevent their going to sleep, and drag them over the rough ground . . . but his favorite method was to tie the thumb of the right hand close to the great toe of the left foot, and draw them through a river or a pond. . . . This monster . . . procured the death, in one year and in one county, of more than three times as many as suffered in Salem during the whole delusion.[146]

Yet this is the man who was sanctioned by Richard Baxter. His activity had been at its height during the summer of

141. *Diary*, II, 768. Many would have renounced faith in the face of circumstances which beset Mather in his last days; he contended with "restriction of his influence, the insanity of his third wife, the profligacy of his favourite son," for which see *The Puritans*, p. 163.
142. *Memorable Provinces*, pp. 110–121.
143. Summers, *op. cit.*, p. 22.
144. *Ibid.*
145. Upham, *op. cit.*, I, 351.
146. *Ibid.* See Summers, *op. cit.*, for Hopkins' justification of himself.

1645.[147] The number of witches executed during the rule of the Parliament which had commissioned Hopkins has been estimated as high as three thousand.[148] Notestein puts the figure, conservatively, at two hundred [149] at least and says that Hopkins was largely responsible for sending to the gallows "more witches than all the other witch-hunters of England can be proved . . . to have hung in the hundred and sixty years during which the persecution flourished in England." [150] And this was accomplished during fourteen months which were well within the memory of many of the principals in the Salem episode.

The cruel practices employed by Hopkins are duplicated in numerous instances in the records of witchcraft, occurring in greater and lesser degree: Witch-marks discovered on the body of Janet Paistoun [151] in Dalkeith, 1661, were pierced, although none "of the sd marks . . . did blood when they [the pins] wer takin out again." [152] In examining one of the nuns at Loudon "le Père lui prit la peau du bras & la perça d'outre en outre avec une épingle." [153] Too gruesome to recount here are the details of the examination of Dr. Fian [154] during the reign of James I. Yet we never find Mather or any of the others in New England who advocated the extermination of witches using torture or cruel physical abuse to extort confession. Prisoners were chained because common belief held that only so could the afflicted be relieved of their tortures.[155] Though the psychological suffering of the accused at Salem was unquestionably acute, at least the New England Puritans stand cleared of using the barbarous techniques which were known in their day. This, to their credit, is seen most clearly in the comparison of a man

---

147. C. L'Estrange Ewen, *Witch Hunting and Witch Trails* (London, 1929), p. 31.
148. Notestein, *op. cit.*, p. 194.
149. *Ibid.*, p. 195.
150. *Ibid.*
151. George F. Black (ed.), *Some Unpublished Scottish Witchcraft Trials* (New York, 1941), p. 45.
152. *Ibid.*
153. Aubin, *Histoire des Diables de Loudon* (Amsterdam, 1737), p. 231.
154. Notestein, *op. cit.*, pp. 94–96.
155. Burr, *op. cit.*, p. 349 n.

like Mather, generally regarded as the villain of the Massachusetts delusion, and Matthew Hopkins, a man of the same age. It was not a pleasant thing to be the instrument of God's justice, though it was sometimes necessary, and when it was, gravity—not sadism—became the office.

Moreover, the horror that overwhelms and sickens the imagination that considers the plight of Salem's pitiful victims has often obscured the fact that many of the accused were acquitted. The records speak, almost monotonously, of one after another who is apprehended, and then set free: "Elizabeth Johnson aforesaid to be discharged," "Abigaill Barker aforesaid, to be discharged," "Mary Tuler, aforesaid, to be discharged," "Marcy Wardwell, to be discharged," and so on and on in Suffolk County Superior Court of Judicature Records of case after case.[156]

On the other side of the picture there are certain individuals in the New England story who stand out as men advanced beyond their times. Thomas Brattle,[157] already referred to, comes in a class by himself. It must be remembered, however, that the letter which he wrote questioning witchcraft and condemning the procedure at Salem "did not see print in his own day." [158] Let us consider a man who was involved in the trials, a member of the court, who best demonstrates the Puritan character by what his contemporaries would doubtless have called his "carriage in the misery at Salem": Samuel Sewall.

Throughout March of 1692 the Salem storm gathered fury. On April 11 Samuel Sewall went to Salem

where in the meeting house the persons accused of witchcraft were examined; was a very great assembly; 'twas awful to see how the afflicted persons were agitated. Mr. Noyes prayed at the beginning and Mr. Higginson concluded. [In the margin] Voe, Voe, Voe, Witchcraft.[159]

Sewall was one of six associates of the special commission of Oyer and Terminer which Phips had appointed.[160] On Febru-

156. Suffolk County, Massachussetts, Superior Court of Judicature Records.
157. See above, p. 155.
158. Burr, *op. cit.*, p. 168.
159. Sewall, *op. cit.*, V, 358.
160. *Ibid.*, n.

ary 27 before his trip to Salem Sewall has been "startled by the roaring of a beast" [161] between four and five in the morning. It proved to be the bellowing of a cow bitten by a dog. The cow had to be killed, and as a commentary on the situation Sewall adds: "Happy are they who have God for their spring and breast of supplies." [162] A man who would interpret a barnyard crisis with reference to God would surely appeal to the divine in matters concerning the souls of men. Sewall's word would have carried weight, too. Graduated from Harvard in 1671 and made a fellow soon after,[163] he had married Hannah Hull,[164] daughter of John Hull, the wealthiest man in the colony. From that time on he was a man of substance. He was manager of the colony's printing presses between the years 1681 and 1684,[165] a deputy in the General Court in 1683,[166] a member of the Council from 1684 to 1725.[167] He had assisted Increase Mather in charter negotiations in 1688.[168] His career after the witchcraft trials was no less impressive, but suffice it to say here that Sewall at this time was well along the way to earning the right to an epitaph which was to read in part: "HE LEARNT THIS TRUTH, THAT ALL IS VANITY WHICH IS NOT HONEST, AND THAT THERE IS NO SOLID WISDOM BUT IN REAL PIETY." [169]

That Sewall did not take lightly his part in the witchcraft delusions is indicated by entries in his diary regarding it. On July 20, 1692, he was engaged in a "Fast At the house of Capt. Alden, upon his account." [170] At the time Alden was in jail for witchcraft.[171] Sewall, and a gathering of ministers including Cotton Mather,[172] were fasting and praying for Alden's salvation. Sewall was keen to catch news of other outcroppings of witchcraft. He took pains to note in his diary the escape from

161. *Ibid.*, p. 357.
162. *Ibid.*
163. *Ibid.*, p. 1.
164. *Ibid.*
165. *Ibid.*, p. 57.
166. *Ibid.*
167. Chamberlain, *op. cit.*, p. 319.
168. Sewall, *op. cit.*, V, 237–284.
169. Chamberlain, *op. cit.*, p. 308.
170. Sewall, *op. cit.*, V, 361–362.
171. *Ibid.*, V, 361 n.
172. *Ibid.*, V, 362.

Cambridge prison of a Mrs. Cary, "who was Committed for Witchcraft." [173] He has left a graphic account of the August 19 execution [174] which, beyond all question, moved him, as well as the "unthinking persons" who stood by. He records the tragic end of Giles Corey and comments that the efforts of his friends with him were "all in vain." [175] He reflects the Puritan conscience, always willing to submit itself to examination, in reporting a bill "sent in about calling a fast and convocation of ministers that may be led in the right way as to the witchcrafts." [176] It was done in such a manner that the Court of Oyer and Terminer counted "themselves thereby dismissed." [177] Entries in his diary represent Samuel Sewall as profoundly disturbed by the Salem episode. Believing in God quite as earnestly as did his contemporaries, this man (who had considered going into the ministry [178]) was, nevertheless, concerned to know if he had rightly understood the will of the Divine in the tragedy at Salem. He read "Mr. Willard's Epistle to Mr. Mather's book, as to Cases of Conscience touching Witchcraft," [179] and four days later went to Cambridge to see Mr. Danforth (one of the Salem judges) to "Discourse with Him about the Witchcraft." [180] In November he prayed that God "would chuse and assist our Judges, &c., and save New England as to Enemies and Witchcrafts, and vindicate the late Judges, consistent with his Justice and Holiness, &c., with Fasting." [181]

Yet when the gruesome ordeal had ended it was not finished. Sewall continued to speculate, and surely to pray, about the matters that had happened at Salem. By far the most poignant entry concerning the delusion is one that comes four years after the one just referred to, on December 24, 1696: "Sam recites to me in Latin Math. 12 from the 6th to the end

---

173. *Ibid.*
174. See n. 118.
175. Sewall, *op. cit.*, V, 364. Corey had the sad distinction of being the only one of the accused pressed to death for "standing mute," *ibid.*
176. *Ibid.*, V, 367.
177. *Ibid.*
178. *Ibid.*, V, 1.
179. *Ibid.*, V, 367.
180. *Ibid.*
181. *Ibid.*, V, 369–370.

of the 12th. The 7th verse did awfully bring to mind the Salem Tragedy." [182] That verse reads: "If ye had known what this meaneth, I will have mercy, and not sacrifice, ye would not have condemned the guiltless." [183] Never at ease about the matter or his part in it, Sewall now determined to do something about it. The Council had called a special day of fast for January 17, 1697,[184] at which time men should petition God's forgiveness and blessing,

> and especially that whatever mistakes on either hand have been fallen into, either by the body of this people, or any orders of men, referring to the late tragedy, raised among us by Satan and his instruments, thro the awful judgment of God, he would humble us therefore and pardon all the errors of his servants and people. . . .[185]

Sewall went to the fast, and like the brave, honest-hearted man that he was, took with him a document he had prepared to be read before the congregation, "giving it to Mr. Willard as he pass'd by, and standing up at the reading of it, and bowing when finished." [186] That document speaks for itself:

> Samuel Sewall, sensible of the reiterated strokes of God upon himself and family; and being sensible, that as to the Guilt contracted upon the opening of the late Comision of Oyer and Terminer at Salem (to which the order of this Day relates) he is, upon many accounts, more concerned than any that he know of, Desires to take the Blame and shame of it, Asking pardon of men, And especially desiring prayers that God, who has an Unlimited Authority, would pardon that sin and all other his sins; personal and Relative: And according to his infinite Benignity, and Sovereignty, Not Visit the sin of him, or of any other, upon himself or any of his, nor upon the Land: But that He would powerfully defend him against all Temptations to Sin, for the future; and vouchsafe him the efficacious, saving Conduct of his Word and Spirit.[187]

This is not only a testimony to the greatness of Sewall's character, but to that of the Puritans as well. For this confession was made by a Puritan, to Puritans, at a fast called by Puritans for

182. *Ibid.,* V, 443.
183. King James Version.
184. Calef, *op. cit.,* p. 299.
185. *Ibid.,* pp. 299–300.
186. Sewall, *op. cit.,* V, 445.
187. *Ibid.*

confession of sins of which Puritans believed themselves to be convicted by the judgment of God. Here is the Puritan conscience at its best—striving continually to conform to the will of the eternal, never willing to rest in self-complacency, but submitting itself ever anew to judgment by the inflexible norm. There is something awe-striking about the relentlessly deontological character which informs the Puritan ethic.

In one sense Sewall seems a greater man than Brattle. Brattle was given to see the truth about Salem from the start. Sewall erred, and erred badly; and just for that reason it required greatness of character to admit his error publicly. This was the greatness that, we believe, was radical to the New England Puritan character. Nor was Sewall the only one in whom it was expressed.

The members of the jury who had heard the evidence at Salem circulated a solemn declaration in which they confessed themselves to have brought "the guilt of innocent blood" [188] upon the community. The document reads in part:

We do heartily ask forgiveness of you all, whom we have justly offended; and do declare, according to our present minds, we would none of us do such things again, on such grounds, for the whole world,—praying you to accept of this in way of satisfaction for our offence, and that you would bless the inheritance of the Lord, that he may be entreated for the land.[189]

In 1697 John Hale, minister, published a study of the witchcraft persecutions in which he gave the reasons which led him to conclude that there was error in the proceedings at Salem.[190] On October 17, 1711, the General Court passed an act that "the several convictions Judgments and Attainders" [191] against victims (whose friends and families had petitioned the court) be "reversed, made and declared to be null and void to all Intents, Constructions and purposes whatsoever, as if no such convictions Judgments, or Attainders had ever been had or given." [192] On

188. Upham, *op. cit.*, II, 474.
189. *Ibid.*
190. See n. 12. Earlier Hale had persecuted witches vigorously, *ibid.*
191. Levin, *op. cit.*, p. 197.
192. *Ibid.*

December 17, 1711, Governor Dudley issued a warrant for "Damages sustained by Sundry persons prosecuted for witchcraft in the year 1692." [193] The sum amounted to £587 12s. [194] While it was neither adequate, nor fairly distributed, [195] it was remarkable that compensation of any kind should have been paid to "the said persons as are Living and to those that legally represent them that are dead." [196] Major Samuel Sewall, son of the Judge, made a zealous but unsuccessful attempt to rectify this matter. [197] Ann Putnam made public confession of her error and sin in "accusing several persons of a grievous crime [who were] innocent persons." [198] The Salem Village Church wrote a denunciation of the witchcraft delusion into the records in 1717. [199] The record of such a repudiation of error is without parallel in the annals of witchcraft.

After the storm in Salem there was never another trial for witchcraft, much less an execution for witchcraft in Massachusetts. This is considerably more than can be said for other regions. Several instances will suffice: Kingolfing, 1715, Walburga Pillering beheaded and burnt, her two sons, aged nine and twelve, made to see the execution and then soundly whipped; Freising, 1717, three men beheaded and burnt for commerce with incubi; Wasserburg, 1715, schoolmaster severely tortured, beheaded and burnt; Salzburg, 1717, five men condemned to galleys for lycanthropy; Freising, 1721–1722, twenty-two prosecuted for witchcraft, eleven of them executed; Eichstatt, 1723, Maria Rung, beheaded and burnt; Augsburg, 1728–1734, various executions for witchcraft; Landshut, 1754, Veronike Zerritschin, burnt; 1756, Maria Klossnerin, burnt. [200] These shocking instances (which can be duplicated again and again) [201] fall outside the wave of witchcraft hysteria in Eng-

193. *Ibid.*
194. *Ibid.*, p. 198.
195. Upham, *op. cit.*, II, 481.
196. Levin, *op. cit.*, p. 198.
197. Upham, *op. cit.*, II, 481.
198. *Ibid.*, II, 510.
199. *Ibid.*, II, 513.
200. Henry Charles Lea, *Materials Toward A History of Witchcraft*, ed. Arthur C. Howland (3 vols.; Philadelphia, 1939), III, 1134–1135.
201. *Ibid., passim.*

land of which the Massachusetts story was surely a part; they are offered in support of a generalization made earlier to the effect that the Salem prosecutions were by no means the last or the worst instances of the error. Yet for eighteenth-century England there are "cases in plenty," [202] as Kittredge points out. The last executions in England were in 1705 when Mary Phillips and Elinor Shaw were put to death.[203] In 1808 Ann Izzard, of Great Paxton in the county of Huntingdon, was attacked by a mob and cruelly treated because they believed her to be a witch.[204] Similar instances occur as late as 1880 in England.[205] In America Grace Sherwood was swum as a witch and committed to jail in Virginia in 1706.[206] As late as 1897 an old woman at Lyme, Connecticut, was ducked by a mob to drive the devil out of her.[207] But no such record darkens the pages of Massachusetts history after the delusion of 1692–1693.

There is one other aspect of the Salem witchcraft which must be mentioned as a credit to the Puritans of Massachusetts, and that is the behavior of the victims themselves under the trying circumstances of false accusation and in the face of death. By no means the least significant aspect of the ordeal, it is perhaps the most commonly conceded. The point here is that the heroic bearing which most of them maintained was itself a part of the Puritan character which gave the unique stamp to the Salem episode. The accused, like the accusers, were Puritans.

Joseph Putnam, little more than twenty-two years of age, in opposition to his brothers and both his uncles, denounced the proceedings and announced to a hostile community that if anyone attempted to arrest him it would be at peril of life (for the eventuality of arrest he kept a horse saddled, literally, for six months).[208] Martha Corey, accused and finally executed, expressed herself fearlessly and freely against the whole

202. Kittredge, *op. cit.*, p. 236.
203. George Lyman Kittredge, "Notes on Witchcraft," in *Proceedings of the American Antiquarian Society*, new series, XVIII (Worcester, 1907), 206.
204. Upham, *op. cit.*, II, 520.
205. Kittredge, *Witchcraft in Old and New England*, p. 237.
206. *The Virginia Case of Grace Sherwood* in George Lincoln Burr, *Narratives of the Witchcraft Cases 1648–1706* (New York, 1914), pp. 441–442.
207. Kittredge, *Witchcraft in Old and New England*, p. 237.
208. Upham, *op. cit.*, II, 457.

doctrine of witchcraft, which she utterly repudiated: she said the afflicted girls "were poor, distracted Children, and no heed [was] to be given to what they said." [209] She asked, but was denied, permission to pray at her examination.[210] Martha Corey, "protesting her Innocency, concluded her Life with an Eminent Prayer upon the Ladder." [211] John Proctor had said of the writhings of the earliest afflicted (one of whom was employed at his household) [212] that "if they were let alone so, we should all be devils and witches quickly; they should rather be had to the whipping-post." [213] The remark helped to hang him. The Reverend Francis Dane of Andover stood against witchcraft from the first.[214] Thomas Brattle has already been mentioned.[215] When the storm was at its worst there were those who were able to make actual in their lives a tenet of their faith regarding the misfortunes and trials of circumstance: "But whosoever has been taught from the mouth of Christ, that the hairs of his head are all numbered, . . . will seek further for a cause [i.e., of misfortune], and conclude that all events are governed by the secret counsel of God." [216]

It is not easy to write dispassionately of the Salem episode, especially in a world where again vitriolic prejudice and persecution threaten to engulf a society in a delusion of error. The Salem story is one of the few chapters of American history which seems to have a definite beginning, middle, and end. That is not to say that it is easy to evaluate what happened. Even a limited reflection on the rich bibliography available indicates that there is much still to be considered with reference to the origins of the delusion, the implications of the trials, and the connection between our own day and the tragic aspect of Massachusetts culture reflected in the delusion. The concern in this paper has been a rather special one: to examine

209. Lawson, *op. cit.*, 156.
210. Calef, *op. cit.*, p. 198.
211. *Ibid.*, p. 229.
212. Upham, *op. cit.*, II, 4.
213. *Ibid.*, II, 458.
214. Hale, *op. cit.*, p. 420 n.
215. See above.
216. *Institutes*, I, 184.

the behavior of the Puritan caught in the toils of the Salem misery as a situation which reveals the Puritan character. In the light of the evidence some conclusions are submitted.

The delusion which gripped the elders and the people in the Massachusetts village was by no means unique to them. They shared a common belief in witchcraft with the seventeenth century, with centuries that had gone before, and with those that were to come after.[217] When the madness overtook them, however, they displayed the vein of iron. With the exception of the "afflicted" themselves, for whom mental aberration is conceded, judges and accused alike met a difficult circumstance determined only to act in accordance with the inflexible norm which demanded unerring adherence to the truth. There is something relentlessly grand about this uncompromising meeting of the temporal in the power of the eternal. Faith for the Puritan was well thought out and carefully articulated, and—what is more impressive—faith was that vital power by which and in which the Puritan lived and had being. In the examination of the accused and the course of the trials there is evidence of injustice, but no such records of torture as blacken the chronicles of similar delusions. The hysteria in Massachusetts was less intense and sooner ended than such miseries in other places. Above all, the Puritan showed his character in Massachusetts by admitting his error publicly, and by trying—in a measure—to right the wrong he had done. Although this attitude toward Salem witchcraft is not unique,[218] it is not the only interpretation of evidence by any means.[219] And yet, the facts stand. The Puritans *did* renounce their error. Once having admitted their guilt, the people of Salem did not make the same mistake again, although instances of the delusion continued to occur elsewhere for almost two hundred years. The persecution of witches at Salem

217. For examples of belief in and practice of witchcraft in our own generation see William Seabrook, *Witchcraft, Its Power in the World Today* (London, 1941).

218. Kittredge, *Witchcraft in Old and New England, passim.*

219. For which see George H. Moore, "Notes on the Bibliography of Witchcraft in Massachusetts," in *Proceedings of the American Antiquarian Society,* new series, II (Worcester, 1883), 162–192, and George Lincoln Burr, "New England's Place in the History of Witchcraft," in *Proceedings of the American Antiquarian Society,* new series, XXI (Worcester, 1911), 185–217.

was not so much the torment of individuals as it was the expression of an Ideal, warped and distorted, but an Ideal nevertheless. The scope of this paper has allowed only inquiry regarding *what* the Puritans were, not *why* they were as they were. Seen against the background of their times and in comparison with other men, they appear possessed not of evil, but even admirable, character.

John Caldwell, Critic of the Great Awakening in New England

BARNEY L. JONES

In the historical treatment of the Great Awakening in New England, where he has been noticed at all, John Caldwell has been dismissed peremptorily as a minor irritant upon the revival movement and, ultimately, a forlorn and discredited figure. In 1748, Samuel Davies, at that time minister of the Presbyterian congregation in Hanover, Virginia, penned a resumé of Caldwell's abortive career in America and published it in the preface to his *The Impartial Trial, Impartially Tried and Convicted of Partiality*,[1] a sharp rebuttal to Caldwell's *Impartial Trial of the Spirits* (1742),[2] then being circulated as an antidote to the spread of the revival in Virginia.[3] On the basis of his information, Davies had this to say:

Mr. *Caldwell* was a Minister for some Time in *Ireland*; if I remember rightly, in *Dublin.*—Being reputed a Gentleman of tolerable

1. Samuel Davies, *The Impartial Trial, Impartially Tried, and Convicted of Partiality: in Remarks on Mr. Caldwell's, Alias Thornton's Sermon, Intituled, An Impartial Trial of the Spirit, &c, and the Preface of the Publisher in Virginia, to Which Is Added, a Short Appendix, Proving the Right of the Synod of New York to the Liberties Allowed to Protestant Dissenters, by the Act of Toleration* (Williamsburg, 1748). Hereinafter cited as *Impartial Trial, Impartially Tried.* The author is indebted to the Virginia State Library for the use of its photostatic copy of this pamphlet, the original of which is held by the Historical Society of Pennsylvania, Philadelphia.

2. John Caldwell, *An Impartial Trial of the Spirits Operating in This Part of the World: by Comparing the Nature, Effects and Evidences of the Present Supposed Conversion with the Word of God. A Sermon Preached at New Londonderry, October 14th, 1741. On 1 John 4:1 . . . Published at the Desire of the Old Congregation in the Said Town* (Boston, 1742). Hereinafter cited as *Impartial Trial.*

3. Wesley M. Gewehr, *The Great Awakening in Virginia, 1740–1790.* (Durham, N. C., 1930), pp. 81–83, and *Journal of the Presbyterian Society* (Philadelphia, 1941), XIX (1940–1941), 195 f. give the background for its employment in Virginia.

Sense and Learning, he flourish'd there for some Time; but went on a Course of *Pilfering* and *Stealing.*—His Theft being discover'd, he fled to New-England; and having *chang'd* his *Name,* impos'd upon some of the Ministers there, and was receiv'd by them for some Time as a *Presbyterian* Minister: During which Time he distinguish'd himself in virulent Opposition to the religious Concern which then prevail'd in the Land; and, among other Exploits, preach'd and printed this *Sermon,* and afterwards publish'd a *Pamphlet* in Defence of it, by way of Answer to Mr. McGregere's Confutation of it.—But his Triumph was but short.—For some Persons arriving there, who had known him before, gave an Account of his scandalous Conduct in *Ireland:* Whereupon he was judicially try'd in *Court,* and found guilty.—He then either declin'd the Exercise of the Ministry for Shame; or was authoritatively depos'd by the Ministers there.—Being sunk into just Contempt in *New-England,* he came to *Pennsylvania,* and remain'd a considerable Time near the Place of my former Residence, following the Practice of *Physic.*—He was obliged to renounce his New Name Cal'd-well, for really he was *Call'dill;* and to content himself with his *old* Name *Thornton* again.—In *Pennsylvania* in the Presence of the Rev. Mr. *McDowel* and his Congregation, he made open Acknowledgement of his bad Conduct; which he was oblig'd to do, in order to be admitted to Church-Privileges, from which he had been authoritatively suspended.—But after he had made this Acknowledgement, his Conduct was such, that I am *absolutely certain,* the *Ministers who* had excluded him, for whom he had been so *faithful* an *Advocate,* did not admit him to re-assume his ministerial Office.—Whereupon, as if he had thought the *Dreggs* of the *Presbyterians* pure enough for the *Church of England,* he went through *Maryland* seeking Recommendations to the Bishop of *London;* and then set out for *England.* But whether he has had a prosperous Voyage, or a safe Return, I know not.[4]

A personal attack of this nature, pressed so relentlessly by a man of Davies' stature, attested the vitality and effectiveness of Caldwell's opposition to the revival movement. Apparently, however, there was general public acquiescence to the veracity of Davies' narrative, and the settled estimate of Caldwell's character and reputation conformed to this portrayal.

Nonetheless, in his own right, Caldwell merits more consideration in a comprehensive study of the Great Awakening than he has received. Moreover, while biographical resources remain meagre and painfully fragmentary, sufficient data are

---

4. *Impartial Trial, Impartially Tried.*

presently available to require the qualification and correction of Davies' testimony against Caldwell in several important particulars.

Though for some months previous he had been pastor to the church at Blanford, Massachusetts,[5] Caldwell first achieved notoriety in New England when on October 14, 1741, before the "Old Congregation" in Londonderry, New Hampshire,[6] he attacked the Great Awakening in a notable sermon entitled *An Impartial Trial of the Spirits Operating in This Part of the World*. He prefaced his criticism of the revival by observing that God treats man as a rational creature [7] and thus expects him to employ his powers of reason to distinguish truth from error.[8] However, since man's reason has been darkened by original sin,[9] God has provided Scripture as the sure guide in matters of religion,[10] and upon an objective and impartial attendance to this rule, Caldwell purposed to try the spirit of "the present supposed Conversion in this Part of the World." [11] Accordingly, he observed:

To any Person, that with an unprejudiced Mind hath view'd the same [conversion experiences] for these six Months past, or more, I presume its Nature will appear to be this, or very near, (*viz*) A sudden and terrible Fear of Divine Wrath, or the Miseries of Hell, occasioning in some a Sensation of Cold, in most a very extraordinary Warmth all over the Body; causing People to cry as if distracted; to shed Tears in great Plenty; throwing many into Convulsions, and a few for some Time into Despair. This continues with the generality but for a very short Season (tho' some few feel it a little longer). In a few Days or less, the Terror is at an End, and a more than common Cheerfulness succeeds; all their Difficulties and Doubts are removed, and immediately a Certainty that all Sins are pardoned, and that they shall be saved, [takes] place; and that all their after

---

5. "In 1741 the town was incorporated by the name Blanford; previous to that it had borne the name of Glasgow." *Proceedings of the Massachusetts Historical Society*, LI (1917–1918) , 46 n.

6. John N. McClintock, *History of New Hampshire* (Boston, 1888) , pp. 138–143, gives the historical background on the Irish settlement at Londonderry.

7. Caldwell, *Impartial Trial*, pp. 5, 20.

8. *Ibid.*, p. 6.

9. *Ibid.*, p. 13.

10. *Ibid.*, p. 14.

11. *Ibid.*, pp. 16 f., 20.

Sins, how many or [what] soever they be, will be overlook'd, upon their confidently relying on the Merits of our Redeemer.[12]

Caldwell next described the result attendant upon such conversion experiences:

. . . a bold talking of Experiences, as soon as the Terror is over . . . a Contempt of all others, especially such as seem to question any Thing of what they say of their Experiences; boldly calling such carnal, and sentencing them to eternal Misery, who demand more Evidence than they think proper to give. . . . Its Effects upon many of their Teachers are very uncommon, divesting them of Charity to such as oppose, tho' ever so conscientiously, this present Scheme; moving them to shut the Gates of Heaven against the whole humane Race, but themselves and a few of their Friends, whose Sins God will not be offended at, as he will not approve the righteous and christian Behaviour of others. . . . Some of them it moves to leave their own particular Congregations destitute of the Ordinances of Christ, and travel to and fro upon the Earth, spiriting People against their Pastors, who are not of their Stamp, by representing them as carnal and dead Men, who have no more Right to preach than the Devil . . . to reproach People for not being affected with what they say, i.e. because they do not shed Tears, fall down into Convulsions, scream, prevent others from being benefited. . . . Its Effects upon People are Censoriousness and Uncharitableness . . . taking deluded Imaginations for Heavenly Visions . . . become Teachers of others, praying in Publick, and some laying aside all Labour for the Support of themselves and Dependants. . . . The Evidences upon which the Certainty of their Conversion is founded, are their being able to point out the Time of their first Convictions, or remember how some Expressions in a Sermon or Texts of Scripture, tho' not understood, filled them with Terror, caused them to weep, scream, or fall into Epileptick-like Fits; thus finding by some unknown Cause, or Text of Scripture, or humane Expressions, or Imaginations called Visions, and attributed to the Divine Spirit, this Uneasiness removed, and Chearfulness succeed: From these and such like Things, they judge that their own, and the Conversion of others, are undoubtedly certain.[13]

Thus contending that the preponderance of revival conversions were irrational and "more like a bodily Distemper, than a religious Conviction," [14] Caldwell proceeded to charge that the temper of the current revival was radically opposite to the

12. *Ibid.*, p. 20.
13. *Ibid.*, pp. 20–23.
14. *Ibid.*, p. 24.

spirit poured out upon the Apostles, evidenced by miracles and their willingness to reason with gainsayers, and was therefore unworthy to be denominated a work of God: [15]

That Spirit therefore that unqualifies Persons to receive Information, that begins with Imagination or Passions, that uses not the Way to promote Religion our Saviour and his Apostles did, that influences Men to take Imagination for Revelation, and Delusions of Fancy for heavenly Visions; that despises the Understanding, would make Religion and Reason opposite, makes Men rash Judgers, Confiners of Divine Operations to themselves and Friends, that leads them to endeavour Divisions among Christian People, between them and their Pastors, that despises what our Saviour has made necessary, (*viz.*) Morality; that lays a Stress upon Tears and bodily Gestures; that destroys Reason, and the *Candle of the Lord,* and excludes that from Conversion, without which there can be no Religion . . . that makes Men believe that they are converted, who are governed by Passion, or Appetite, or Ignorance; that despises Learning and Sense; that influences Men to assume more than our Saviour did, the judging such as believe them not . . . and ruin the Characters of such as are not of their Opinion (which 'tis self-evident is the Fruit of that Spirit now at work in this Part of the World) is not, nay, impossible it should be from God.[16]

Then declaring that a true work of God is invariably attested by the fruits of righteousness and love to all men,[17] Caldwell concluded his remarks by encouraging his listeners to try all things in matters of religion by their rationality [18] and to declare their minds with respect to the current revival, unintimidated by the charges of blasphemy, for as he observed, "this is no more than the common Cry of such as in all Ages have had more Impudence than Sense." [19]

Included in Caldwell's "auditory" on this occasion were "many" members of the Second Church in Londonderry over which the Irish Presbyterian David McGregore [20] presided as pastor. Since Caldwell had cast aspersions upon the "Work,"

15. *Ibid.,* pp. 23–26.
16. *Ibid.,* pp. 39 f.
17. *Ibid.,* pp. 41–43, 48.
18. *Ibid.,* pp. 46 f.
19. *Ibid.,* p. 47.
20. For biographical data, see William B. Sprague, *Annals of the American Pulpit; or Commemorative Notices of Distinguished American Clergymen of Various Denominations, from the Early Settlement of the Country to the Close of the Year Eighteen Hundred and Fifty-Five. With Historical Introductions* (New York, 1858) , III, 28 f. Hereinafter cited as *Annals.*

McGregore considered that it would be "a crimminal Silence and an inglorious Neutrality" [21] not to make answer. In a January 30, 1742, letter to his uncle David Cargill in New Castle, he recalled

one Caldwell who has been some time preaching at New Glasgow came here last 8 ben [*sic*] and being invited by Mr. Davids: to his Pulpit preach'd a Sermon from 1 Jo 4:1 the manifest Design was to rediccule & Burlesque the glor: work of God that is now carrying on in this Land and as the Sermon was preach'd at the Fair so that many of my Congreg: & Negh: in the Adjac: were pres: I tho't I could not be faithful to the cause if I was *intirely* Silent & therefore at Next Sabbath I gave Publick [Intin:] that the Friday following I designed to preach upon the Same Text and did accordingly at wch time appeared Mess. Caldwell & Davidson they used their pens during the Time of the Sermon & at the Close Davidson Introduced his Bro: who desired a Publick dispute I told him that if he desired such a dispute in order to vindicate his own Sermon it was needless for as I had not heard it so I had said nothing about it if he desired said dispute in order to Impeach mine that neither in that case did I judge it to Edificate: that he had the liberty of Scholars viz the Press and Pulpit &c. My people were some what disturbed to see the petulant *boldness* of the man being a meere Stranger so that in the end several of them spoke out with some [   ] wh: was said I know not however I commanded Silence and the affair ended—My Sermon upon the Sub: I preach'd some time after in Boston at the desire of some of the Min: & at their request and that of many other Gent: I gave a Copy of it to the press tho' with some reluctance I have sent you one bear:r as you desired Caldwells is not yet published.[22]

The appearance in print of McGregore's sermon, *The Spirits of the Present Day Tried,* with a preface by Thomas Prince, John Webb, and William Cooper, prompted Caldwell to publish his *Impartial Trial* and assured the continuation of the controversy between the two ministers. In the preface Caldwell noted that his sermon was published "under the Disadvantage of opposing fashionable Principles in Religion," and added:

'tis well known, that several Ministers and many People have lately fallen into the Extravagances about Conversions and the Divine

21. David McGregore, *The Spirits of the Present Day Tried. A Sermon at the Tuesday Evening Lecture in Brattle-Street, Boston, Nov, 3, 1741. With a Preface by Some Ministers of Boston* (2nd ed.; Boston, 1742), Appendix, ii. Hereinafter cited as *Spirits Tried.*

22. From the original copy in the *Lemuel Shaw Collection,* Massachusetts Historical Society.

Spirit mentioned in this Sermon, judging and condemning others as carnal, and resisters of the Spirit; to prevent the People where I have sometime preached from blindly running into such Things because fashionable, I first composed this Discourse, without any Design of appearing in this publick Manner before the World; the Occasion of which was a Sermon preached at Londonderry by Mr. McGregore upon the same Subject with this, and as was reported, intended as an Answer to it; Notes thereof being carried to him by a Preacher who heard me deliver the same.

When the second edition of McGregore's sermon appeared later in the year (1742), it contained an Appendix which gave in detail McGregore's version of the origin of the controversy, subjected Caldwell's sermon to a range of criticisms, and questioned darkly whether "Mr. Caldwell, in case he were indited before an *Ecclesiastical Court* for *Heterodoxy* in Principle, or before a *Civil Court* for *Stealing, Forgery,* or any other Crime" [23] would not insist upon adequate proof as a condition of his conviction. Caldwell's reply, which seems to have terminated this particular exchange, took the form of *An Answer to the Appendix of the Second Edition of Mr. McGregore's Sermon* [24] and was published in 1743. Beyond a review of the particular points at issue between the disputants, Caldwell observed that a "Mr. Abercrumbie" had taken notes during the delivery of his *Trial of the Spirits* sermon and had brought them forthwith to McGregore,[25] cited a recent public debate at Londonderry in which McGregore had been involved,[26] and identified Whitefield, Tennent, and Davenport as the intended recipients of his barbs against the principal "Instruments" of the revival.

Prior to this time, however, Caldwell had sent to the press two additional sermons which broadened and intensified his assault upon the revival—the first, entitled *The Scripture Character or Marks of False Prophets or Teachers,*[27] having been

23. McGregore, *Spirits Tried*, Appendix, ix.
24. John Caldwell, *An Answer to the Appendix of the Second Edition of Mr. McGregore's Sermon on the Trial of the Spirits, &c.* (Boston, 1743).
25. *Ibid.*, p. 3.
26. *Ibid.*, p. 5.
27. John Caldwell, *The Scripture Character or Marks of False Prophets or Teachers . . . Published at the Desire of Several Ministers and Other Gentleman Who Heard It* (Boston, 1742). Hereinafter cited as *False Prophets.*

delivered on May 26, 1742, before the "Presbytery of Boston" in the French Meeting-House. It was, for the most part, a transparent and scornful delineation of the worst attributes and most pernicious practices of the itinerant revivalist, as judged by the "Old Light" and the "Arminian" criteria. Illustrative of an extensive catalogue of vices was Caldwell's observation that such men (i.e., "false Prophets") were fond of popularity,[28] "lovers of themselves," [29]

Boasters; i.e. Persons who glory in their Performances, talk much of their superior Holiness and Endowments, to the Disparagement of others; who are perpetually telling us of their Success, of the Numbers that follow them, and the Satisfaction People have in their Performances, going away in general satisfied, and much melted whilst they stayed. . . .[30]

In the course of his remarks, Caldwell described the present season as a time in which "all Persons, even the most ignorant, are heard as Instruments: Men are believed more than ordinary Men, for no Reason, but their Ignorance and Impudence." [31] Among other concerns, he cautioned particularly against the schismatic, divisive spirit within and among the churches,[32] the general lowering of ministerial standards,[33] and the disparagement of morality and reason [34]—defects, he believed, characteristic of the revival movement.

Among the clergy in attendance upon the sermon was Ebenezer Parkman, who recorded in his "Journal" that the "drift was against false prophets, and not without bitterness, mixed with his wit and sense. I sat very uneasy and went out as soon as it was done." [35]

On July 11, again in the French Meeting-House, Caldwell resumed his caveat regarding the religion of the times with an address on *The Nature, Folly, and Evil of Rash and Uncharita-*

28. *Ibid.*, p. 7.
29. *Ibid.*, p. 14.
30. *Ibid.*
31. *Ibid.*, p. 31.
32. *Ibid.*, pp. 7, 9, 27.
33. *Ibid.*, p. 11.
34. *Ibid.*, pp. 10, 12.
35. For which see "Extracts from the Private Journal of the Rev. Mr. Ebenezer Parkman, of Westborough, Mass.," Joseph Tracy, *A History of the Revival of Religion in the Time of Edwards and Whitefield* (Boston, 1842), p. 208.

ble Judging.[36] In his analysis of the subject, he allowed that it was permissible to judge men who spoke nonsense,[37] who were "spiritually proud," who were "industrious in raising Divisions amongst Men, warming instead of cooling their Tempers," who took "Imaginations for Visions from Heaven, Fancy for Divine Impressions," and who damned "others for Difference of Opinion." [38] It was unwarranted and reprehensible, however, to

judge that a Man or Number of Men (who profess *to believe in GOD,* and in CHRIST as the Messias, SON of GOD and only Mediator between GOD and Man, the Brightness of Divine Glory, and the express Image of his Person, and all his Doctrines the very Truth) will be damned, or in a damned, or in a damnable State, by any other Way than the Wickedness and unrepented Immorality of their Lives. . . .[39]

Such judgment, Caldwell insisted, belonged to God's tribunal [40] and where it was exercised by men, it was based upon *"Pride, evil Affections* to Mankind, or a *blind, ignorant Zeal"* [41] and calculated to arouse resentment rather than repentance in the person against whom the judgment was directed.[42] It was the practice of those accustomed to judging all others in the lump as sinners [43] and to confining "God's Favour to themselves and Friends!" [44] Caldwell then appealed for a cautious, rational approach to the problem of judging [45] and urged that both sides of any controversy be carefully examined to insure a fair and objective decision.[46] To this end he staunchly defended the right of private judgment ("this is your unalienable Right as

36. John Caldwell, *The Nature, Folly, and Evil of Rash and Uncharitable Judging . . . Printed at the Desire of Several Gentlemen Who Heard It. With an Appendix, Containing an Answer to Some Observations in the Weekly Journal of June 8th 1742, on My Sermon upon the Trial of the Spirit, &c.* (Boston, 1742). Hereinafter cited as *Judging.*

37. *Ibid.,* p. 9.
38. *Ibid.,* p. 10.
39. *Ibid.,* p. 12.
40. *Ibid.,* p. 15.
41. *Ibid.,* p. 24.
42. *Ibid.,* p. 21.
43. *Ibid.,* p. 11.
44. *Ibid.,* p. 29.
45. *Ibid.,* p. 33.
46. *Ibid.,* p. 29.

Christians, and bounden Duty") [47] and advised his congregation to "be of the Temper of the *Bereans,* ready to receive GOD'S Word, but search the Scriptures, and be convinced therefrom that 'tis GOD'S Word before you believe it." [48]

The tenor of Caldwell's remarks on this occasion may very well have been prompted by the temporary success of a damage suit he had only days earlier initiated against John Moorhead,[49] Scotch-Irish minister to the Presbyterian congregation in Boston. As a friend of McGregore, an admirer of Whitefield, and a staunch supporter of the revival, Moorhead had ample cause for offense at Caldwell. When, on the basis of his own intelligence, he became convinced that Caldwell's ministerial credentials were fraudulent, he made this charge, and other damaging remarks of an unspecified nature, public in Boston and promised to substantiate his accusations should they be challenged in court. Caldwell obliged with a suit against Moorhead and the case was brought for settlement before the Inferiour Court of Common Pleas convened in Boston on July 6. After a full hearing, the jury returned a verdict favorable to Caldwell and awarded him "Two Hundred & Fifty Pounds Lawful Money of this Province & Costs of Suit." Thereupon, Moorhead appealed the verdict to the Superiour Court of Judicature.

Though the Boston press passed over the incident in silence, the record of the trials is preserved and is largely reproduced here not alone for its value in following in detail the progress of the suits but also for the supply of additional biographical data pertinent to a critical evaluation of Davies' Caldwell narrative. The transcript of the initial trial before the Court of Common Pleas reads in part as follows:

Alexander McCracken, Moderator of the Presbetery of Strabane within the County of Tyrene in the Kingdom of Ireland and Joseph Hemphill Clerk of the Presbetery on the 25th day of June AD 1740 by a writing they subscribed with their Names, in the

47. *Ibid.,* p. 32.
48. *Ibid.,* p. 37.
49. For a biographical sketch, see Sprague, *Annals,* III, 44–46.

Name of the Presbetery afores certified that the bearer of it afores John Caldwell after having passed his several courses at the University of Edinborough & studied some Years at home, was invited to enter tryals to the great Satisfaction of the Presbetery, that since the Presbetery had licensed him to preach the Gospel which they certified was on the eight of October AD 1736/ he had always behav'd virtuously, this public performance had given universal Satisfaction especially to the most judicious, that he being desirous to travel to New England to prosecute his Ministerial Office had obtained the s presbetery's Consent thereto & was by all Ministers and others to be encouraged in so good a design; and the afores John Caldwell bro't with him the afores Certificate into the Massachusetts Bay & made use of it as his Credentials for his Character & was thereupon well received in the Character of a preacher of the Gospell, & was invited by the Church & Inhabitants of the town of Blanford afores to settle with them as a Minister of the Gospel & received a Competent Maintenance from the s Church and Inhabitants & propty of s Town for preaching the Gospell there, and his Invitation was laid before the Presbetery of Boston afores & Consent to his Settlement as afores, & altho' the s John Caldwell was always of a blameless Character & Behavior & free from the Crime of making, forging or publishing false writings, and the s John Morehead well knew it, yet he the said John Morehead maliciously designing to destroy the Reputation and Character of the s John Caldwell and to bring him into Contempt, on or about the 28th day of February (then) last at Boston afores having spoken of the s John Caldwell Certificate before many of his Majesty's Subjects, falsely and maliciously say'd & publish'd of him in their presence & hearing the following false and opprobrious Word vizt he/ meaning the afores John Caldwell/ forged his Credentials (meaning the afores Certificate) and the s John Morehead of his own further Malice to the s John Caldwell & further to hurt and defame him as afores, on the 27th day of May last at Boston afores having had discourse with divers of his Majesties Subjects about the s John Caldwell & the afores Certificate falsely and maliciously say'd and publish'd of him in their presence & hearing the following false and opprobrious Word vizt if he (meaning the s John Caldwell) sues me, I am ready to prove it (meaning the afores Forgery) & by reason of these several false and Defamatory Words the s Caldwell has been greatly hurt in his Estate & Reputation & so much prejudiced in the Opinion of divers of his Majesty's Subjects that he is greviously injured in his afores Ministry and Maintenance. To the Damage of the said John Caldwell as he saith the Sum of Three Hundred Pounds; The Deft. came into Court Mr. Joseph St. Lawrence his Attorney & (Saving his pleas in Abatement which were Over ruled by the Court) for plea said that the Words by him Spoken & laid in the Writ are true & that he is ready to prove the same & of this he put himself on the Countrey. Upon which issue being joined the case after a full hearing was committed to the Jury who were sworn according to the Law to try the same and returned the Verdict therein upon Oath, that is to say, they find for the Plant. Two Hundred & Fifty Pounds Lawful Money of this Province & Costs of Suit. The Def. Appealed from this Judgment unto the next Superiour Court of Judicature to be holden for this County & Entered into Recognizance with Suretys as the Law directs for Prosecuting his Appeal to Effect.[50]

Moorhead's appeal was duly brought before the Superiour Court in Boston in August, 1742, and from thence continued from term to term until August 16 of the succeeding year; at which time, the record shows, "the Appellant [Moorhead] appeared and the Appelle [Caldwell] although solemnly called to come into Court did not appear but made Default." Whereupon, Chief Justice Benjamin Lynde ruled that "the former Judgmt be & hereby is reversed & that the s John Morehead recover against the said John Caldwell cost of Courts taxed at eighteen pounds twelve shillings."[51]

However tempting it is to conjecture, no sure explanation is available to account for Caldwell's failure to reappear in court. A strong presumption of guilt would reasonably attach to his default were it not for the existence of original affidavits, prepared for use against the appeal of the original verdict, which corroborate much of the testimony in Caldwell's behalf before the Court of Common Pleas.[52] The documents are herewith reproduced verbatim for the obvious bearing which they have upon the case.

Testimonials to the Character of Rev. John (Thornton, nov) Caldwell: from the minutes of Presbytery of Strabane. Attested Dec. 29, 1742.
 the
    Honourable ye Judges of ye
     Superior Court
      attn
      Boston New England
Andrew Welch of the parish of Ardstraw and County of Tyrone in the kingdom of Ireland testifieth that in June 1740 he gave Mr.

50. "Court Files Suffolk" (Boston) , CCCLV (July, 1742) , 63.
51. "Superior Court of Judicature, 1743–1747" (Boston) , pp. 17, 18.
52. From the original document, *Miscellaneous* XI (1738–1748) , Massachusetts Historical Society.

John Caldwell a letter of Commendation to the Rev. Willm Mc-Clenachan in New England in which he signified the change of his name and the reason of it, nor did he ever excommunicate said Mr. Caldwell or hear that any person ever did.

*   *   *

December 29th 1742

The Rev. Andrew Welch of ye Parish Ardstraw—appeared before me and swore to ye truth of ye above relating to Mr. Caldwell & yt he wrote ye same.

Willm Colhoun, Esq.

*   *   *

Newton Stewart Aprile the 5th 1739

Appeared before me Mr. James Caldwell of the Parish of Ardstraw and County of Tyrone, and Mr. John Thornton his Son in Law; when at the desire of Mr. James Caldwell, and according to agreement between them Mr. John Thornton consented to have his name changed to Mr. John Caldwell which according to common practice was then done before me.

Charles Crafart, Esq.

*   *   *

Dec. 29, 1742

Charles Crafart of Newton Stewart in ye Parish of Ardstraw Esq. appeared before me in Strabane and swore to ye truth of the above relating to Mr. James Caldwell & his son in law.

Willm Colhoun, Esq.

*   *   *

At the same time also appeared Mr. James Caldwell above mentioned and Mary Caldwell his wife who sware to ye above Mr. John Thornton had his name changed to Mr. John Caldwell at their earnest desire and yt his wife their daughter never had any child.

Willm Colhoun, Esq.

A Copy of the Minutes in the Presbytery of Strabane Relating to Mr. John Caldwell—

June 25, 1740 Ante Meridem, Mr. John Caldwell appeared before this Presbytery signifying his design to travel to New England and desiring a Certificate from us of his being Licentd by us to preach ye Gospel and Moral Character, this Presbetry having heard his reasons consented to his desire and ordered Mr. Joseph Hemphill to draw a Certificate for him against our next [illegible].

* * *

June 25, 1740 Post Meridem Mr. Joseph Hemphill produced the Certificate he had drawn for Mr. John Caldwell to ye Presbytery in which was signified the time we licentd him to Preach the gospel viz gber ye 8th 1736. Your Approbation of his learning and moral character &c. this Certificate being read and Approv'd this Presbetry order'd the same to be signed by the Moderator and Clerk in the name of ye Presbetry. Which was accordingly done by Messuirs Alexander McCracken Mod. and Joseph Hemphill Clerk.

Extracted December 28th 1742 by Joseph Hemphill We Alexander McCracken and Joseph Hemphill members of ye Presbetry of Strabane in the County of Tyrone and Kingdom of Ireland do testifie that the above is a true Copy of ye minutes in our Presbetry of June 25th 1740 relating to Mr. John Caldwell, and that the Certificate therein mentioned of the same date with the above was wrote by our Clerk, as this is, and signed by us thus.

Alexander McCracken. M.P:J
Joseph Hemphill. P.C.

* * *

December 29, 1742

The Revd Messuirs Alexander McCracken and Joseph Hemphill both members of the Presbetery of Strabane in ye County of Tyrone & Kingdom of Ireland appeared before me in Strabane, and swore to the truth of ye above particulars; and also that ye reason of their giving Mr. Caldwell a certificate in ye name of Caldwell was because his name was legally changed.

Willm Colhoun, Esq.

Although the cumulative evidence of the affidavits and the hearing before the Court of Common Pleas concerning the question of Caldwell's professional standing and deportment in Ireland, his change of name, his ministerial credentials and mission to New England, and his trial is impressive, it is insufficient to allow dismissal of Davies' allegations as devoid of substance. It does make it clear, however, that at least to the point of Caldwell's departure from New England, Davies' narrative is a seriously imprecise and defective document upon which to rest a final judgment of Caldwell's character and reputation.

From this point on to the termination of Caldwell's experience in America, this writer can add but little to the information provided by Davies. Of special importance, obviously, is the statement that "In *Pennsylvania* in the Presence of the Rev. Mr. *McDowell* and his Congregation, he [Caldwell] made an open Acknowledgement of his bad Conduct." In absence of a more precise citation, the McDowell to whom reference is made here is, presumably, Alexander McDowell who was "ordained sine titulo" by the Donegal Presbytery on October 28, 1741, "in order to Itinerate pro tempore in Virginia," and who was later transferred to the New Castle Presbytery.[53] It will be recalled that Davies himself was born in New Castle County, and that it was by the New Castle Presbytery that Davies was licensed to preach (July 30, 1746) and ordained evangelist to Hanover County, Virginia (February 19, 1747).[54] Caldwell is placed upon the scene by Davies' statement that "Being sunk into just Contempt in *New-England*, he [Caldwell] came to *Pennsylvania*, and remain'd a considerable Time near the Place of my former residence." Efforts to locate corroborating evidence for Caldwell's "open Acknowledgement" have proven fruitless, and the "Records of the New Castle Presbytery" for the years 1732–1758, where some reference might have been found, have been lost for some time.[55]

For the time being, the "Caldwell Case" must rest here and without elaboration upon the assertion that having failed in his efforts to be reinstated as a Presbyterian minister, "he [Caldwell] went through Maryland seeking Recommendations to the Bishop of *London;* and then set out for England." It seems unlikely, however, that persistent research will not yield the additional data required for a biographical summary and a confident appraisal of John Caldwell and his role in the Great Awakening.

53. "Records of the Donegal Presbytery," Ic (1741–1750), 337 f., 349, 351 f., 363, 365, 367, 370 f., 373, 375, and 391, and "Records of the Synod of Philadelphia (1717–1758)," pp. 73, 76 f. Both volumes are in the custody of the Presbyterian Historical Society, Philadelphia.

54. Sprague, *Annals*, III, 140.

55. The Presbyterian Historical Society possesses the complete records of the Presbytery of New Castle from the inception of the Presbytery in 1716 until the present day, with the exception of the second volume, which encompasses the years 1732–1758.

John Witherspoon: Academic Advocate for American Freedom

JAMES L. McALLISTER

When John Witherspoon rode into the town of Princeton in August, 1768, to become the sixth president of the twenty-three-year-old College of New Jersey, there was little expectation, either in the minds of those Presbyterian divines who had called him to that post or in his own mind, that within ten years he would become America's foremost academic propagandist for independence. He came because of his reputation and because the arguing Presbyterians could not agree on an American; he became, through his personal involvement as well as his academic leadership, a formidable force in the movement toward independence and representative democracy.

Significance of Witherspoon in America

The invitation to Witherspoon grew out of the financial difficulties of the College and some shrewd ecclesiastical maneuvering among the Presbyterian leaders in New Jersey and East Pennsylvania. The more conservative Old Side Presbyterians whose stronghold was in Philadelphia found that many of their ministerial candidates educated in the Old Country were being opposed in their Presbytery examinations by New Side ministers educated at the College of New Jersey.[1] Knowing that the College was in financial straits and hoping to gain some

[1]. Varnum Lansing Collins, *President Witherspoon: A Biography* (Princeton, 1925), I, 75.

control over it, a group of Old Side laymen from Philadelphia proposed to send their sons to be educated in Princeton, thus making it possible for the College to hire three additional professors and secure a president, provided that the president and one of the professors be chosen from the Old Side group.[2] However, the New Side trustees of the College were unwilling to share control of their College and chose as president one whose presence in Scotland removed him from the squabbles of American Presbyterianism but whose reputation as a scholar and conservative theologian was sufficient to attract the sympathies of the affluent Old Side supporters.[3]

Coming to America at the age of forty-six, Witherspoon was well prepared to assume his ecclesiastically delicate and academically penurious position. At the age of thirteen in 1736, he began college studies at the University of Edinburgh, received his A.M. degree three years later, and completed his theological studies in 1743.[4] In Edinburgh young Witherspoon studied natural philosophy under the aging Robert Stewart and logic under young John Stevenson,[5] a man who, "possessed of the modern spirit," introduced the philosophy of Locke into Edinburgh and substituted Heineccius and Locke for Aristotle and Ramus.[6]

Ordained in April, 1745, at the age of twenty-two, Witherspoon soon aligned himself with the more conservative Popular party, which was opposed in the Scottish Church by the Moderates. The latter party was more liberal in its interests, more complacent toward traditional Presbyterian doctrines, and supported the law of patronage, which placed the disposition of church livings in the hands of patrons who installed in the churches whomever they willed without regard for the wishes of the particular congregations. The Popular party was

2. *Ibid.*, I, 76. Cf. Charles Hodge, *The Constitutional History of the Presbyterian Church* (Philadelphia, 1851), II, 302; John MacLean, *History of the College of New Jersey* (Philadelphia, 1877), I, 291–292.
3. Collins, *op. cit.*, I, 78.
4. *Ibid.*, I, 12, 18, 20.
5. *Ibid.*, I, 2.
6. Sir Alexander Grant, *The Story of the University of Edinburgh During Its First Three Hundred Years* (London, 1844), II, 328–329.

more conservative in theology, more pietistically evangelical, and supported the demands of local church people that they have the liberty of choosing their own pastors.[7] It would appear that Witherspoon's evangelical interests, together with his reputation for being a sound scholar and an opponent of centralized ecclesiastical control, were the chief characteristics which commended him to the New Side American Presbyterians; and it is certain that his theology was sound enough to satisfy the Old Side, for he repeatedly reaffirmed the Federal theology which was so dear to most eighteenth-century American Presbyterians, particularly those of the Old Side party.

In his sermons and doctrinal lectures Witherspoon followed the main principles of the Federal covenant theology: The idea was that God had made a Covenant of Works with the first man, Adam, by which he was constituted the "federal head and representative of the human race, as he was then the natural head." The consequences of his action, either obedient or disobedient, would be shared by all of his descendants.[8] Because Adam sinned the result was, and is, that "man now comes into the world in a state of impurity or moral defilement;"[9] and the history of the world is a history of unhappiness arising from "the envy, malice, covetousness, and other lusts of men."[10] The guilt and general corruption which came upon Adam is communicated from him to his descendants down through the ages by the body, because there is "so close a union between the soul and body, that the impressions conveyed to us through the bodily organs, do tend to attach the affections of the soul to things earthly and sensual."[11] Witherspoon affirmed the typically Federal doctrines; but the Augustinian influence is quite readily seen in the fact that whereas he said the history of the

7. Collins, *op. cit.,* I, 28–29.
8. John Witherspoon, "Lectures on Divinity," *The Works of John Witherspoon* (Edinburgh, 1804), VIII, 120–121. Unless otherwise noted all references to Witherspoon's writings are to be found in this nine-volume edition, hereinafter cited as *Works.*
9. *Ibid.,* VIII, 125.
10. John Witherspoon, "The Dominion of Providence Over the Passions of Men," *Works,* V, 181.
11. "Lectures on Divinity," p. 127.

world is the history of human guilt, his major emphasis was on the corruption of the human race.

In saying that man is so depraved that "every action of an unregenerate man is essentially defective as a moral duty," however, Witherspoon was very clear that he did not mean man can do no good and is incompetent of moral judgment. "The human race in general, with all its defects, is certainly the most valuable in this lower world, and therefore the most worthy of cultivation." [12] In spite of the fact that in depraved man "the supreme desire of the mind, and leading principle" [13] is wrongly directed so that man loves the creature more than the creator, yet there still remains the "power of natural conscience." [14] The net result of original sin, therefore, is to corrupt the reasoning powers of man but to leave intact the capacity of his conscience to pass judgment immediately upon truth and error "with little danger of mistake" and to "reject what is evil, and yield its approbation to what is good." [15]

In spite of this apparent optimism about the power of conscience in men, Witherspoon repeatedly affirmed that all mankind is by nature under sin, and by sin he meant want of conformity unto or transgression of the law of God, even as the Westminster Confession said.[16] Although depraved man retains in the moral sense a power to discern the ultimate nature of right and wrong, he does not have the power to reason out rightly the consequences of this natural light. Sin, therefore, is rebellion against the law of God, failure to be in total conformity with his will. Even though the divine image is not obliterated in man but remains in the power of the conscience or the moral sense, man is too self-directed to make right use of the light which he has. He lacks the power to reason the first principles of truth and morality, or to follow the promptings of his conscience. Were it not for the grace of God, there could be no ultimate hope for man.

12. John Witherspoon, "The Druid," *Works,* IX, 227.
13. "Lectures on Divinity," p. 126.
14. John Witherspoon, "Lectures on Moral Philosophy," *Works,* VII, 13.
15. John Witherspoon, "The Trial of Religious Truth by its Moral Influence," *Works,* IV, 306.
16. John Witherspoon, "All Mankind by Nature Under Sin," *Works,* II, 26.

Witherspoon understood salvation in the characteristically eighteenth-century Calvinist manner of the Covenant of Grace. This Covenant is

a compact or agreement between God and elect sinners to give freely and of mere mercy Christ to die for them, and with him a pardon of sin and a right to everlasting life, together with the Spirit of sanctification to make them meet for it; all which the believer received and accepts in the manner in which it is offered and rests his eternal state upon it.[17]

By means of the death of Christ as a substitutionary sacrifice, God's justice is satisfied and men can be saved. The only condition is faith, which renounces "all self-dependence, accepts and closes with the promise of recovery and salvation just in the manner in which it is offered freely, without money, and without price." But, receiving this gift does not relieve the believer of responsibility for good works, which serve as "the proper evidence of our relation to God." [18]

Obviously Witherspoon reflected that union of Federal covenant theology and Scotch Common Sense philosophy which was to become the foundation of the "Princeton Theology" of the nineteenth century. His understanding of Adam as both federal and natural head of the race; his definition of sin as want of conformity to God's Law; his explanation of redemption by means of the substitutionary sacrifice of Christ, the second Adam, through whom is granted pardon and "the Spirit of sanctification"—all of these affirmations made this Scottish pastor fully acceptable to both Old Side and New Side Presbyterians. His Common Sense insistence upon the dependability of the moral sense or conscience provided both a theological understanding of man's responsibility for sin and a philosophical framework within which he urged his students to effective political action based not on naïve optimistic rationalism but on a realistic appraisal of the potentialities of human nature.

When John Witherspoon landed on the shores of the Ameri-

17. John Witherspoon, *The Miscellaneous Works of the Rev. John Witherspoon* (Philadelphia, 1803), p. 111. Hereinafter cited as *Miscellaneous Works*.
18. *Ibid.,* p. 115.

can continent, August 7, 1768, the struggle for American independence had barely begun—indeed had not begun except in the minds of such radicals as Samuel Adams and Patrick Henry. The incidents which had occurred centered primarily upon the right of the British government to impose revenue taxes upon the American colonies without colonial representation in Parliament. The Revenue Act of 1764, the Stamp Act of 1765, and the Townshend Acts of 1766 had brought widespread American protest but no general sentiment toward independence. The Boston Massacre and the rousing Tea Party lay in the future, and the American pot was only beginning to simmer.[19] The stocky forty-six-year-old Scotsman, who, followed by his forty-eight-year-old wife and five children, walked onto a Philadelphia wharf and peered with keen blue eyes through his thick eyebrows at the party sent to greet him, could never have anticipated the coming struggle for American independence in which he would be engulfed within half a decade. He was soon to find that at some crucial times there is little interval between the simmering and the boiling over of the historical pot.

During his first few years as president of the College of New Jersey, Witherspoon was too busily involved in administration, teaching, and preaching to aid those of his new countrymen who were adding more wood to the fires of independence. As early as 1773, however, his personal sympathies with the American cause were known to some friends, but "since the church under whose jurisdiction he had placed himself had not yet raised the ban of silence, as a clergyman he felt bound to respect the tacit convention that was keeping politics out of the pulpit." [20] Indeed, not until May, 1776, did he promote or even mention the independence movement from his Princeton pulpit; [21] but long before his students must have known his sympathies. In the summer of 1770 they had seized a letter sent by

19. Samuel Eliot Morison and Henry Steele Commager, *The Growth of the American Republic* (New York, 1950), I, 147–159.
20. Collins, *op. cit.*, I, 156.
21. "Dominion of Providence," pp. 176–236.

some New York merchants who were breaking the colonial non-importation agreement and inviting their Philadelphia colleagues to do the same. The students burned the letter with ceremony in front of the College's lone building, Nassau Hall. The president remained conveniently in his house next door. At the following September graduation one of the senior Latin theses argued that subjects were bound to resist their king and defend their liberties if the laws of the state were ignored and the subjects cruelly treated; and no thesis was publicly propounded at the College until the president had privately read and approved it.[22] Less than a month after the Boston Tea Party of December, 1773, the entire student body burned Governor Hutchinson of Massachusetts in effigy, "having a tea cannister about his Neck";[23] but the president's well-known disciplinary wrath was not heard.

Indeed, by this time Witherspoon's sympathy with the colonials was known to more people than his students and close friends. In July, 1774, he was a leading member of the Somerset County Committee of Correspondence, which sent him and William Livingstone to "a representative body of 72 men from eleven of the thirteen counties of the province" which met for the purpose of electing New Jersey delegates to the first Continental Congress. At that meeting the Somerset representatives urged a more radical opposition to the British than the other Jerseymen were willing to make.[24] At the same time this lately come American was making friends of those who were soon to be the most prominent leaders of the independence movement. At the first Commencement over which Witherspoon presided in 1769 an honorary master's degree was awarded to John Hancock and an honorary doctorate of laws to John Dickinson.[25] Witherspoon's best known pupil of these early Princeton years was James Madison. Another, Henry Lee, was, like Madison, from Virginia. John Adams visited Witherspoon's home en

22. Collins, *op cit.*, I, 133–134.
23. *Ibid.*, I, 158.
24. *Ibid.*, I, 161.
25. *Ibid.*, I, 125.

route to the Continental Congress, drank wine with him, and later wrote that he was "as high a son of liberty as any man in America." [26] That Witherspoon continued to give the colonial independence leaders cause to respect him is evident. In June, 1776, he was leading the New Jersey movement to depose its royal governor, Benjamin Franklin's unfortunate son, William; when the New Jersey provincial congress reported to the Continental Congress its intention to arrest and try the governor, John Hancock transmitted the Congress' approval via the president of the College of New Jersey.[27]

Witherspoon's best known political action was in connection with the Declaration of Independence, although he was a member of the Continental Congress for nearly five years. In June, 1776, he and four other New Jersey men were appointed as representatives to the second Continental Congress. They arrived on either the first or the second of July and immediately joined in the last rounds of discussion about the Declaration being prepared. Although Witherspoon was the only clergyman to sign the Declaration, he contributed nothing significant to its writing.[28] Until 1782 he continued to serve in this Congress most of the time,[29] during which period he frequently acted on committees dealing with financial affairs and the care of prisoners; advocated a sound fiscal policy of paying interest on the mounting public debt in order to assure the Congress' credit,[30] and of giving Congress more effective central control over commerce and trade; [31] opposed a New England recommendation to regulate prices; [32] argued against Ben Franklin's proposal that the number of votes allotted to each state should be in proportion to population by maintaining that the proposal would serve

26. Charles Francis Adams (ed.), *The Works of John Adams* (Boston, 1850–1856), II, 356.
27. Collins, *op. cit.*, I, 207–210.
28. *Ibid.*, I, 213–219.
29. *Ibid.*, II, 3.
30. John Witherspoon, "Part of a Speech in Congress on Finances," *Works*, IX, 125 ff.
31. Oscar Theodore Barck, Jr., and Hugh Talmage Lefler, *Colonial America* (New York, 1958), pp. 699–700.
32. "Diary of Dr. Benjamin Rush," quoted in Henry Steele Commager and Richard B. Morris (eds.), *The Spirit of Seventy-Six* (New York, 1948), II, 784.

only to divide the Congress and thus cause the people to lose confidence in it; [33] and otherwise promoted the aims of the smaller and landless states, urging that Congress dispose of western lands.[34] In 1776 he was a member of the Committee on Foreign Affairs with chief responsibility for securing French financial aid, and in this capacity he frequently defended the activities of Franklin and argued for giving him a freer hand.[35] All of these activities demonstrate that John Witherspoon's lectures dealing with political philosophy were based on an intimate acquaintance with the practical aspects of his subject, and that his direct influence was rather more widespread than is commonly realized.

However, Witherspoon's most lasting influence on the American scene is not to be found in his political activities but in the power that he mediated through the lives of his students. As one would expect, Witherspoon's College made a decided imprint on the American churches, Anglican and Congregational as well as Presbyterian.

Of the four hundred and sixty-nine graduates of the College during Dr. Witherspoon's presidency, one hundred and fourteen became ministers of the Gospel; and of these ministers nineteen became Presidents or Professors in different institutions in the States of New York, New Jersey, Pennsylvania, Virginia, North Carolina, South Carolina, Georgia, and Tennessee.[36]

Some indication of Witherspoon's influence on late eighteenth-century American Presbyterianism is reflected in the General Assembly's *Minutes* for 1789 which report that of the 188 ministers then included on the Presbyterian roster, 52, or 28 per cent, had been trained under Witherspoon. Moreover, in excess of 11 per cent of Witherspoon's clerical graduates became college presidents in eight different states.[37] The first two presidents of Hampden-Sydney College in Virginia, the first two teachers in what is now Washington and Lee Univer-

33. Thomas Jefferson, *The Writings of Thomas Jefferson* (Washington, D. C., 1905), I, 47–48.
34. Collins, *op. cit.*, II, 73. Cf. Barck and Lefler, *op. cit.*, p. 683.
35. Collins, *op. cit.*, II, 15.
36. MacLean, *op. cit.*, I, 402.
37. Collins, *op. cit.*, II, 223.

sity, President Robert Finley of the University of Georgia in the early nineteenth century, five of the trustees at the University of North Carolina when it was chartered and its first two presidents [38]—this is a random sampling of Witherspoon's students and an indication of his extensive influence on American higher education.

One would expect that the former Scottish Presbyterian would be concerned about clerical education and training teachers; but the surprising thing is that, in spite of the impressive statistics given above, the primary emphasis at the College of New Jersey seems to have shifted during Witherspoon's presidency from training ministers to educating men for public affairs.

Witherspoon found the college, if not a theological seminary, at least a place where religion struck the dominant note and where a very large percentage of the graduates went into the ministry; he left it a place devoted to training men for public life. . . . Under Witherspoon the number of ecclesiastical students gradually became less, while those destined to become governors of states, congressmen, senators, judges, lawyers, and doctors steadily increased.[39]

To be sure, one factor in the transformation was the widespread disinterest in religion during the years following the Revolutionary War; but more than that seems to have been involved at the College in Princeton. A tabulation by President Witherspoon's biographer suggests the extent of his influence on politics in the new American nation.

One of his layman graduates, James Madison, became President of the United States, and Aaron Burr, a Vice-president; and ten became cabinet officers. Young though they were at the time, six were elected members of the Continental Congress. Thirty-nine became United States Representatives and twenty-one were United States Senators; twelve were Governors of States and fifty-six were chosen to State Legislatures. Thirty became judges, three others being appointed Justices of the United States Supreme Court. Of the

38. *Ibid.*, II, 225–229.
39. Thomas Jefferson Wertenbaker, *Princeton: 1746–1896* (Princeton, 1946), p. 76.

twenty-five college graduates in the Federal Convention, nine were Princetonians and six of these had President Witherspoon's signature on their diplomas.[40]

Even a brief examination of that part of the College curriculum for which Witherspoon was personally responsible will show why he must have considerably influenced the thinking of his students. Among the President's courses required of every graduate were: first principles of philosophy, chronology and history, moral philosophy, and composition and criticism in the English language. In all four years of their studies the students had regularly to make speeches and publicly to defend theses of their own composition,[41] all of which activities were under Witherspoon's sovereign direction. These exercises, and particularly the required and wide-ranging course in moral philosophy, must have made a lasting impact on most of the young men who studied under Witherspoon.

There can be little doubt that this Scottish preacher, called to American shores partly because of the ecclesiastical struggle in American Presbyterianism, contributed significantly to a much larger contest than those who invited him had intended. Although his theological, moral, and political views were not always consistent, nonetheless, he established the theological thought which dominated American Presbyterianism for a century and a half and greatly influenced the thinking of other denominations of American Christians as well. Philosophically, he established Princeton as the bastion of the Scottish Common Sense philosophy in America.[42] Politically, he presided over a foremost school for statesmen in the new American republic.

John Witherspoon did not publish any finished treatises in political philosophy. The nearest approach to such is his "Lec-

40. Collins, *op. cit.*, II, 229. Cf. MacLean, *op. cit.*, I, 359–362, for the names of these and other prominent graduates of the College of New Jersey in the Witherspoon era.
41. John Witherspoon, "Address to the Inhabitants of Jamaica, and other West-India Islands, in behalf of the College of New Jersey," *Works*, VIII, 318–319.
42. I. Woodbridge Riley, *American Philosophy: The Early Schools* (New York, n.d.), pp. 485–486.

tures in Moral Philosophy," of which subject political philosophy was a part; however, even these are barely adequate because,
not being intended for publication, they consist of summary
paragraphs and statements which Witherspoon quite apparently elaborated and illustrated extemporaneously. Nonetheless,
these lectures, supplemented by sermons, articles, speeches, and
other lectures, are the main source of the political philosophy
to which Princeton graduates were introduced for a quarter of
a century.

The Moral Basis of Politics

Witherspoon's political philosophy was part of his "moral
philosophy" and must be understood within that context. Politics was the second division of moral philosophy; the first was
ethics, dealing with the nature of man, the principles of
moral action, and moral law in relation to man's duty to God,
to his fellow man, and to himself; the third was jurisprudence, treating the right enactment and administration of civil
laws in conformity to the moral law. Obviously, Witherspoon's
understanding of the nature and purpose of political philosophy was rooted fundamentally in his analysis of man's nature,
as a morally responsible being, a being with inherent rights,
and a social being.

Witherspoon defined the nature of man's sin in such way
as to leave ample room for moral responsibility in terms of conscience and moral sense.

It pleased God to write his law upon the heart of man at first. And
the great lines of duty, however obscured by our original apostasy,
are still so visible, as to afford an opportunity for judging, what
conduct is, or is not agreeable to its dictates. It will be found from
experience, that men are able to determine on this point, with far
greater certainty, than on any other subject of religion: that is to
say, they can perceive the excellency of the end, when they are in
much doubt about the means, in themselves or separately considered. Such authority hath natural conscience still in man, that it
renders those who, in their conduct, despise its reproofs, inexcuse-
able in the sight of God.[43]

43. "Trial of Religious Truth," p. 310.

Clearly, the insights of the moral sense are dependable in spite of man's sin. Although Witherspoon objected to Francis Hutcheson's vigorous opposition to reason as a principle of virtuous conduct, the Princetonian recognized that he shared Hutcheson's view that a sense of moral good and evil is really a principle of human nature; it is the law of God written indelibly "upon our hearts, and both intimates and enforces duty, previous to all reasoning." [44] Thus, the moral sense is the foundation of all virtue, the springboard of all moral decision. To say this does not mean that man intuitively knows what is right and wrong in all cases. Witherspoon recognized that the conscience cannot judge right from wrong unless it has correct information.[45] His point was that moral accountability presupposes that man, whose reason is incapable of arriving at the first principles of truth and morals, possesses a sense of what is his duty, i.e., of moral right and wrong, simply because he is man.

This moral sense is more than knowledgeable insight—it involves obligation:

The moral sense implies also a sense of obligation, that such and such things are right and others wrong; that we are bound in duty to do the one, and that our conduct is hateful, blameable, and deserving punishment, if we do the contrary; and there is also in the moral sense or conscience, an apprehension or belief that reward and punishment will follow, according as we shall act in one way, or in the other.[46]

Thus, the moral sense of man involves three things: an insight into the fundamental difference between right and wrong; a sense of our obligation to do what is right; and an expectation that right acts will bring their rewards and wrong acts their punishments. It follows that the moral sense is the foundation of virtue. Witherspoon rejected that theological position which would say that an act is virtuous merely because God commanded it.

This would be taking away the moral character even of God himself.
. . . to say, that God, by his will, might have made the same temper

44. "Moral Philosophy," p. 25.
45. *Ibid.*, p. 73.
46. *Ibid.*, p. 29.

and conduct virtuous and excellent, which we now call vicious, seems to unhinge all our notions of the supreme excellence even of God himself.[47]

Since the moral sense is the law of God written on man's heart, a "transcript of his moral excellence," and since—as Witherspoon implied—God's will is not free to act in discord with his very nature, therefore even God is bound by the moral sense in man. Witherspoon presupposed that there is a fundamental morality governing the creation; the moral sense gives man infallible insight into its basic principles and places on him a sensible obligation to do right and avoid wrong; even God acts according to this moral law, but he cannot be said to be limited by it because the moral law is the law of his own nature. Although John Witherspoon did not carefully spell out the connection between the moral sense, the moral law, and the will of God, this formulation certainly appears to be consistent with what he did write.

Witherspoon's own summary of the nature of virtue in relation to the moral sense is careless and over-inclusive. After summarizing in lecture four of the various "schemes" by which others such as "Hutchinson," [48] Samuel Clarke, William Wollaston, Adam Smith, David Hume, and Jonathan Edwards had analyzed virtue, the Princeton professor laid down four propositions essential to any formulation of the nature of virtue with reference to the moral sense: what God is and what he commands; the "general good"; a difference in the nature of things "between virtue and vice; and private and public interest." Making no real attempt to combine these into a coherent whole, he concluded:

The result of the whole is, that we ought to take the rule of duty from conscience, enlightened by reason, experience, and every way by which we can be supposed to learn the will of our Maker, and his intention in creating us such as we are. And we ought to believe, that it is as deeply founded as the nature of God himself, being a transcript of his moral excellence, and that it is productive of the greatest good.[49]

47. *Ibid.,* pp. 35–36.
48. Witherspoon consistently referred to Francis Hutcheson as "Hutchinson."
49. "Moral Philosophy," p. 38.

Witherspoon preached about reason being unfit to pass judgment upon truth and error and about the leading principle of the mind being depraved because it is wrongly directed; but his references to "conscience, enlightened by reason" make clear that he did not mean that man can make no correct rational judgments. Indeed, he repeatedly expressed or implied his considerable confidence in the rational judgments of men. Lecturing on the uniqueness of man, he reviewed inconclusively the variety of ways that this subject had been treated and observed:

A general distinction, which deserves particularly to be taken notice of in moral disquisitions, is, that man is evidently made to be guided and protected from dangers and supplied with what is useful more by reason, and brutes more by instinct.[50]

When he was arguing against those who claimed that fallen men had no justification for revolting against their rulers and trying to set up a new basis for civil society, he waxed eloquent:

Shall we establish nothing good, because we know it cannot be eternal? . . . it only requires the more watchful attention, to settle government upon the best principles, and in the wisest manner, that it may last as long as the nature of things will admit.[51]

Far from arguing that sinful man can make no right rational judgments, Witherspoon was simply taking the realistic position that a recognition of the limits and perverse character of man's reasoning abilities only "requires the more watchful attention" to see that government be according to the best possible principles. The position is very similar to that of Witherspoon's famous pupil, Madison, in the *Federalist* papers, Number 10. Indeed, as a Continental Congressman, Witherspoon's confidence in the accomplishments and possibilities of reasoning men reached great heights.

. . . I do expect, Mr. President, a progress, as in every other human art, so in the order and perfection of human society, greater than we have yet seen; and why should we be wanting to ourselves in urging it forward? . . . There have been great improvements, not

50. *Ibid.*, p. 15.
51. *Miscellaneous Works*, p. 256.

only in human knowledge but in human nature; the progress of which can easily be traced in history.[52]

One may dismiss the difference between Witherspoon's preaching and his philosophical lectures and political exhortation as another sign of a careless mind's inconsistency. A more charitable and perhaps a more accurate judgment is that in speaking of man's rational incapacity, Witherspoon meant merely that reason alone cannot be man's principal guide in moral actions, because its scope is more limited than many rationalists of the Enlightenment believed. Reason, for Witherspoon, is always directed by man's self-centered will, and it is supplemented by another more dependable human faculty, the moral sense. Both the existence of the moral sense and the subordinate role of reason must be regarded as essential to Witherspoon's understanding of man as a morally responsible being.

Two other aspects of Witherspoon's view of human nature must be mentioned as part of the purpose of his political philosophy, although they can best be developed more fully in connection with his social contract theory of society and government: his stress on man as an individual, with certain rights that are fundamental to his nature; and his insistence that, nonetheless, man's nature demands and is enhanced by society. Both of these affirmations, together with the claim that man is a morally responsible being, must be kept in mind as necessary background for understanding Witherspoon's analysis of political philosophy.

Therefore, the purpose of political philosophy as part of moral philosophy in general is to explain "the principles of social union, and the rules of duty in a state of society." More broadly considered, since "political law is the authority of any society stamped on moral duty," [53] and since the moral sense of duty is fundamental to human nature, the purpose of political philosophy is to describe the norms of human society conformable to the moral law known by the conscience or moral sense,

52. "Speech in Congress Upon the Confederation," *Works,* IX, 140.
53. "Moral Philosophy," p. 75.

which is enlightened by reason and made manifest in the accumulated social experience of man.

The Social Contract: Consent and Human Rights

Two political ideas of fundamental importance to John Witherspoon's political philosophy are: that government should be by consent of the governed, and that all government in its formation and administration must protect certain essential human rights and provide others which man needs for his greater well-being. Both of these ideas lie at the heart of his reformulation of the social contract theory of society and government.

The historical fact of human society, i.e., man understood as Witherspoon understood him, presupposes certain covenants or contracts by which individuals agree to live together in harmony.[54] But this contractual aspect of society implies the prior existence of a state of nature.

The existence of a society founded upon clear established laws obliges us to form an idea of a state previous to the formation of society, or before such, or any laws, were made and acknowledged to be in force. This is called a state of nature.[55]

What Witherspoon had to say about this state of nature was not very precise, as it usually was not among seventeenth- and eighteenth-century contract philosophers, but he does make clear that he was not sympathetic to any radically individualistic type of contract. He was sensitive to the historical criticism of the social contract which had already begun in such men as Montesquieu, "the oft-proclaimed herald of the historical school," [56] and also he retained much of the scholastic and Aristotelian concept that man is by nature a social being.

Actually, Witherspoon's understanding of the state of nature appears to be much like that of Pufendorf, who with Montes-

54. "Lectures on History by the Rev. John Witherspoon, President of New Jersey College, Abel Johnson, scripsit" (manuscript notes on lectures given in 1784, Princeton University Manuscript Collection) , p. 21.
55. "The Druid," p. 234. Cf. "Moral Philosophy," p. 76.
56. John Wiedhofft Gough, *The Social Contract: A Critical Study of its Development* (2nd ed.; Oxford, 1957) , p. 157.

quieu, was on the recommended reading list for the course on moral philosophy.[57] He even says that "the principles of our nature lead to society." [58] Accordingly, he appears to have had in mind Pufendorf's concept of the "sociability" of man, the idea that although men do join together in society for their convenience, nonetheless, men are naturally sociable, i.e., have a natural inclination to join societies.[59] Man cannot be man except in some societal relationship. Moreover, Witherspoon acknowledged the historical and natural argument that family society precedes any state of human individuality. Nevertheless, he maintained that there is a point in man's development when he is thrown on his own and becomes individually responsible for his own being and welfare.

The truth is, though man, for wise reasons, afterwards to be noticed, continues longer in family-dependence than any other animals, yet in time he becomes *sui juris;* and when their numbers are increased, when they either continue together, or remove and form distinct societies, it is plain that there must be supposed an expressed or implied contract. Some say there is no trace or record of any such contract in the beginning of any society. But this is no argument at all; for things inseparable from, and essential to any state, commonly take place so insensibly, that their beginning is not observed.[60]

After this fashion Witherspoon tried to understand the state of nature in such way as to include both individual responsibility and societal relations as essential to it.

Witherspoon preferred to avoid controversy about the historical existence of the state of nature. The so-called "state of nature" was largely his device for explaining and defending the thesis that there are some rights which are fundamental to man as an individual and which, therefore, ought never to be curtailed by his society. To be sure, there are certain rights which man cannot have except in society, and it is the purpose of government to provide and insure them; but logically prior to these rights of society or civil rights are certain rights which belong essentially to individual man. Hence, Witherspoon was interested less in the historical reality of the state of nature than in what was commonly called the natural and inalienable rights of man.

There are many references to natural rights in Witherspoon's writings, and all of them are more reflective of an abiding conviction that there *are* natural rights than of any clearly conceived idea of *what* they are. In his lectures he began with the claim that the source of all human rights is "the supreme law of moral duty; for whatever men are obliged to do, that they have a claim to, and other men are considered as under an obligation to permit them." Since the lectures dealing with ethics explained man's moral duty in a threefold sense—to God, to man, and to oneself—human rights and human obligations are seen to be different aspects of man's relation to his Creator. Moreover, human rights are directed to the end of human happiness, but, Witherspoon cautioned, an individual has the right "to promote his own happiness only by those means which are not in themselves injurious to others." [61]

One discussion of human rights distinguished between (1) *natural* and *acquired* rights, the former being essential to human nature, e.g., self-preservation, and the latter being either "the fruit of industry or the effects of accident or conquest"; (2) *perfect* and *imperfect* rights, the perfect being "clearly ascertained in their circumstances," defensible by force and protected by human laws, e.g., self-preservation and justice, and the imperfect being "such as we may demand, and others ought to give to us," although we have no title to compel them, e.g., a grateful return for a favor; (3) *alienable* and *"unalienable"* rights, the first being those which man may "according to justice and prudence" give up, e.g., goods, lands, or money, and the second not being dispensable, e.g., the right to judge for one's self in religious matters, self-preservation, and self-provision. The distinction between alienable and unalienable rights differs from that between natural and acquired rights in the sense that some universal and natural rights, e.g., self-

61. *Ibid.*, p. 62.

defense and doing justice to ourselves in property matters, may be given up in the state of society for "the good of the whole"; whereas unalienable rights may never be given up.[62]

The above listing is in the context of Witherspoon's ethical discussion of "our duties to man." [63] When he discussed "politics" proper, he had another listing of "the perfect rights in a state of natural liberty": life; employment of a man's faculties for his own use; things that are "common and necessary, as air, water, earth"; "personal liberty"; power over one's own life, "not to throw it away unnecessarily, but for a good reason"; private judgment in matters of opinion, e.g., religion; association with those to whom one inclines and can so persuade but not force, e.g., marriage; and "character." [64]

Toward the very end of his course, in the part entitled "Jurisprudence," the Princeton professor distinguished between rights of necessity and common rights. The discussion is in the context of civil rights, but it is mentioned here because rights of necessity would seem to have some connection with natural rights.

Were a man perishing with hunger, and denied food by a person who could easily afford it him, here the rights of necessity would justify him in taking it by violence. . . . Much more would men, in cases of urgent necessity, make free with the property of others, without asking their consent, but presuming upon it.[65]

In answer to those who rejected such a distinction on the grounds that it reasserted the utilitarian doctrine that usefulness has priority over justice, Witherspoon replied:

. . . those rights of necessity have in general property as their object, or at most the life of particular persons—and it seems to be inseparable from the establishment of property in the social state, that our property is to be held only in such manner, and to such degree, as to be both consistent with, and subservient to the good of others. And therefore these extraordinary cases are agreeable to the tacit or implied conditions of the social contract.[66]

62. *Ibid.*, pp. 62–65.
63. *Ibid.*, Lecture VIII.
64. *Ibid.*, p. 77.
65. *Ibid.*, p. 145.
66. *Ibid.*, p. 146.

Rights of necessity cannot be prescribed by law because any right which the law prescribes is then "no longer a right of necessity but a legal right." Rights of necessity are by definition illegal in the sense that the law does not cover them, "and if necessity does not excuse, the person who pretends them may be punished." Over against rights of necessity are common rights.

> There are certain things called common rights, which the public is supposed to have over every member: the chief of them are (1.) Diligence. As a man must eat, the community have a right to compel him to be useful—and have a right to make laws against suicide. (2.) They have a right to the discovery of useful inventions, provided an adequate price be paid to the discoverer. (3.) They have a right to insist upon such things as belong to the dignity of human nature. Thus all nations pay respect to dead bodies. . . .[67]

The relationship is not clear between these rights of necessity and common rights, on the one hand, and the prior listings of rights on the other. Rights of necessity are contrasted with civil or legal rights, and the rights of necessity that are mentioned have to do with such earlier designated natural rights as self-preservation of the individual or of the community. The common rights appear to be of the type which Witherspoon had called imperfect rights.

Although these listings of different types of human rights do not fit readily into a coherent scheme, they do make clear two circumstances. (1) Although Witherspoon's listings of basic human rights overlap and are not precisely conceived, they do exhibit his conviction about the existence of some inviolable human rights, which he attempted to understand in relation to man's duty to God, his fellow man, and himself. Witherspoon thus sought to establish a connection between rights and obligations. (2) During the time Witherspoon was president at Princeton the students there were acquainted with the idea of fundamental human rights, which played a significant role among the leaders of the early American republic. In fact, the

67. *Ibid.*, pp. 147–148.

idea of a state of nature only served Witherspoon as an effective myth for expounding his belief in these rights of man.

Like most social contractarians, Witherspoon moved from discussion of the state of nature into a consideration of the state of society. He was clear in affirming that all society implies a compact or contract between the individuals, as his definition of society makes clear:

Society I would define to be an association or compact of any number of persons, to deliver up or abridge some part of their natural rights, in order to have the strength of the united body, to protect the remaining, and to bestow others.[68]

He was equally clear about why individuals in the state of nature formed society.

That the principles of our nature lead to society, that our happiness and the improvement of our powers are only to be had in society, is of the most undoubted certainty; and that in our nature, as it is the work of God, there is a real good-will and benevolence to others; but, on the other hand, that our nature as it is now, when free and independent, is prone to injury, and consequently to war, is equally manifest; and that in a state of natural liberty, there is no other way but force, for preserving security and repelling injury. . . .

One class of the above-mentioned writers say, that nature prompts to society; and the other, that necessity and interest obliges it; both are equally true.[69]

One can hardly deny that there was some considerable confusion in Witherspoon's discussion of the state of society. He was trying to include in his theory of society conflicting elements that can hardly be reconciled. The root of the confusion lay in his discussion of the state of nature, i.e., in his failure to identify the individual or the societal aspect of man's nature as more fundamental. Witherspoon was not clear about the aim of men in forming society: in one place he said that "the single purpose of society, indeed, is to protect the individual, and to give him the strength of the public arm, in defense of his just

68. *Ibid.*, p. 78.
69. *Ibid.*, pp. 76–77. The writers referred to are Hobbes, "Hutchinson," and Shaftesbury.

and natural right"; [70] in another he maintained that "the public good has always been the real aim of the people in general,
in forming and entering into any society." [71] He maintained
both that society is natural to man and that it is an artificial
creation for utilitarian reasons. He seemed unable to make up
his mind whether man is by nature benevolent or warlike; perhaps he meant that man as created by God is benevolent, while
man as sinner is warlike, but he did not clarify this difference.
Witherspoon wanted to hold to the social contract idea with its
emphasis on the priority of the individual in relation to society,
but he was sensitive to criticism from history and nature that
family society is prior to any self-contained individual status.
He did not make clear precisely what rights, except the self-
defense and self-execution of justice, man sacrificed upon entering society.[72] Plainly, just as the state of nature seems to
have been Witherspoon's device for explaining the existence of
inviolable human rights growing out of man's moral duty, so
the idea of a state of society served chiefly as a vehicle for his
conviction that the principles on which a society is founded
must be based on the consent of the individuals involved. Indeed, one can hardly escape concluding that Witherspoon was
interested not so much in the state of nature or society as such,
but rather in using these myths to explain his concept of civil
government in such way as to insure that the rights of human
beings were not trespassed. His real interest was made clear
when he lectured:

From this view of society as a voluntary compact, results this principle, that men are originally and by nature equal and consequently
free. . . . Liberty either cannot or ought not to be given up in the
social state. The end of the union should be the protection of
liberty, as far as it is a blessing.[73]

The conflicting elements in Witherspoon's political philosophy
and the passion of his real interests make it possible to conclude that in his classroom as in his political activities this re-

70. "The Druid," p. 235.
71. "Moral Philosophy," p. 80.
72. *Ibid.*, p. 64.
73. *Ibid.*, pp. 79–80.

cently arrived American was less interested in careful and consistent political philosophizing than in justifying and spurring on the cause of American independence.

Civil Society

Witherspoon's views about the contractual nature of civil society suggest that he thought in terms of two contracts: a social contract proper and a civil contract. He did not make this distinction explicitly, but the arrangement of materials in his "Lectures on Moral Philosophy" together with the content of Lectures XI and XII suggests that such distinction was implicit in his thinking. In the "Lectures" he discussed first his theory of society, including the state of nature and the state of society; then, after considering slavery and property as belonging to the social state, he turned to civil society in its two aspects: domestic life (including the relations of marriage, parents and children, and masters and servants) and civil life.

Again and again he reaffirmed the importance of recognizing that consent is the foundation of all society, in both social and civil state.

(1) The consent of every individual to live in, and be a member of that society. (2) A consent to some particular plan of government. (3) A mutual agreement between the subjects and rulers; of subjection on the one hand, of protection on the other. These are all implied in the union of every society, and they complete the whole.[74]

His belief in the right of unjustly treated citizens to resist their government was founded on this doctrine of consent. Although some rulers have historically gained dominion over their subjects by inheritance or conquest, the only just basis for dominion is consent.[75]

Two features are apparent in Witherspoon's idea regarding the way in which civil society is formed: First, he did not hold any radically atomistic views about the formation of civil society. Rather, following again the lead of Pufendorf, he

74. *Ibid.*, p. 94.
75. *Ibid.*, pp. 103–104.

thought of men living in the social state of the family, which is contractual by nature, and joining to form the civil state for their mutual benefit.[76] Once again one sees Witherspoon's individualism modified by the idea of sociality. Second, characteristically, Witherspoon did not spell out how the civil society was formed, although his lists of the three necessary implications of every civil society seem to be in line with the theory of Pufendorf's disciple, Christian Thomasius, who held that civil society involves two contracts and a "decretum": the first contract was between individuals living in natural freedom and agreeing to form a perpetual union as fellow citizens; there followed the "decretum" by which a mutual decision was made about the form of government to be adopted by the rulers and the ruled according to which the former promised protection and the latter promised obedience so long as the purposes of this civil contract were promoted.[77] These three aspects are all involved in Witherspoon's understanding of the nature and formation of government. Thus he, like Pufendorf and his disciples, was trying to account for civil government in contractual terms without placing the ruler's sovereignty above the reach of the governed, after the manner of Hobbes.[78]

This understanding of civil government always raised a question about the consent and obligation of children and others who had not given their actual consent at the time the contract was made. Generally, Witherspoon detoured this obstacle in the commonly accepted way of Locke's implied consent: "Though every individual has not given an actual consent, yet his determination to live with every society implies it." As for the children: they receive the benefits and partake of the rights of the society during the whole time of their education, and as they come to the use of reason, they "both claim the privilege and acquiesce in the duties of citizens." Moreover, persons may remove themselves from any society which they do not like, so long as it be in time of peace; although during war

76. *Ibid.*, p. 94. Cf. Gough, *op. cit.*, p. 120.
77. Gough, *op. cit.*, pp. 150–152.
78. *Leviathan*, chap. xviii. See Gough, *op. cit.*, p. 122.

"they may be hindered from emigrating at that time and compelled to contribute their share in what is necessary to the common defence." [79]

Once the civil society is formed, the individuals or individual families involved must be treated as a body, but only so long as the purpose of the formation guides the course of the civil society. Of innocent subjects who frequently suffer for rulers' folly, Witherspoon wrote:

> The whole individuals that compose a state are considered but as one body. It would be impossible for an enemy to distinguish the guilty from the innocent. When men submit to a government, they risk their own persons and possessions in the same bottom with the whole, in return for the benefits of society. [80]

Any valid contract is by definition "a stipulation between two parties, before at liberty, to make some alteration of property or to bind one or both parties to the performance of some service." [81] In the civil contract, regardless of the form of government, the mutual services of the two parties involved were explained in terms of the rights of the rulers and the ruled, the magistrates and the subjects:

> The rights of rulers may be divided into essential and accidental: the essential, such as in general must be vested in rulers of every society; the accidental, such as may be given to the rulers in some societies, but not in others.
>
> The essential rights of rulers . . . are divided into greater and lesser essentials.
>
> Of the first kind are, (1) Legislation. (2) Taxation for the public expense. (3) Jurisdiction, or the administration of justice. (4) Representation. . . .
>
> The less essential rights of rulers are many, and they are called less essential, because they may be more varied than the others; such as, coining of money, possessing or managing public edifices, conferring honors on officers.
>
> The rights of the subjects in a social state cannot be enumerated, but they may be all summed up in protection; that is to say, those

---

79. "Moral Philosophy," p. 95. Cf. John Locke, *An Essay Concerning the True Original, Extent and End of Civil Government,* chap. viii, par. 118–120.
80. "The Druid," pp. 236–237.
81. "Moral Philosophy," p. 129.

who have surrendered part of their natural rights, expect the strength of the public arm to defend and improve what remains.[82]

As Witherspoon acknowledged, this listing of the rights of the ruled is incomplete, and as it stands it would be in agreement with Hobbes' theory. However, it is apparent throughout all his writings that Witherspoon had no intention of following Hobbes' line, as, for example, his claims (1) that subjects give up only "part of their natural rights," (2) that "it is but a bad maxim, that we may force people for their good"; [83] and (3) that the right of resistance and rebellion is a natural right which the subject always retains.

The emphasis given to the citizen's right and obligation to resist an unjust government makes clear how central the correlated ideas of consent and personal liberty were in Witherspoon's political philosophy.

When persons believe themselves, upon the whole, rather oppressed than protected in any society, they think they are at liberty, either to rebel against it, or to fly from it; which plainly implies that their being subject to it arose from tacit consent.[84]

Though people have actually consented to any form of government, if they have been essentially deceived in the nature and operation of the laws, if they are found to be pernicious and destructive of the ends of the union, they may certainly break up the society, recall their obligation, and resettle the whole upon a better footing.[85]

However, Witherspoon was aware of the dangers which this resistance doctrine opened up. He looked for ways to guard against its being misused, but he was too practical of mind and too Pauline in orientation to countenance political insurrection. He distinguished between civil war and "solemn war between nations," the former being "an unreasonable or unprovoked insurrection of disorderly citizens"; but he acknowledged that "there are many cases in which the pretences on both sides are so plausible that the war should be in all respects considered as solemn." [86] Of course, he thought the American

82. *Ibid.*, pp. 95–96.
83. *Ibid.*, p. 97.
84. *Ibid.*, p. 79.
85. *Ibid.*, p. 97.
86. *Ibid.*, p. 114.

struggle for independence was not such an "unprovoked and unreasonable insurrection of disorderly citizens," because the decision to overthrow the tyrannical British government was made by "the subjects in general, every one for himself." He argued that he was not advocating a doctrine which would make the rebel the judge, which doctrine "is subversive of all order." Recognizing this danger, he consoled himself and his students by saying that "it is not until the whole people arise, that resistance has any effect, and it is not easy to suppose that a whole people would rise against their governors, unless they had really received great provocation," and that whereas experience shows "there are many instances of rulers becoming tyrants," there are "comparatively few of causeless and premature rebellions." [87] Clearly, Witherspoon knew that the right of rebellion must be kept by the contracted subjects in order to avoid a Hobbesian tyranny, but he could not find any adequate and self-consistent criteria within the framework of his dual taproots in Pauline theology and contractarian political philosophy for keeping this highly explosive right of rebellion within limits. His argument boiled down to saying (1) that the right of resistance, so necessary for individual liberty, is a lesser risk than the possibility of tyranny, and (2) that since men essentially possess a benevolent and reasonable spirit, they will not rebel without due provocation.

Regarding the forms of government, Witherspoon generally accepted and slightly modified the types listed by Aristotle: [88] there are three "general and simple kinds" of government— monarchy, aristocracy, and democracy. The distinctive principle of democracy is that "the supreme power is left in the multitude" which may exercise it either directly or representatively, although Witherspoon did not think pure democracy could last long or be very extensive because "it is very subject to caprice and the madness of popular rage." Whatever the form of government, four things are required of any effective

87. *Ibid.*, pp. 103–104.
88. *Politics*, Bk. III, chap. vii.

type: (1) wisdom to plan proper measures for the public good; (2) fidelity to the public interest instead of private wishes; (3) secrecy, expedition, and dispatch in executing measures; and (4) unity and concord among the different departments or branches of government. Of the different types, monarchy has an advantage in the third requirement, aristocracy in the first, and democracy in the second. Following the lead of Montesquieu, he insisted that monarchy tended to politeness, elegance of manners, and usually luxury; aristocracy "narrows the mind exceedingly, and indeed cannot long subsist in a large state"; and democracy "tends to plainness and freedom of speech, and sometimes to a savage and indecent ferocity." Furthermore, "democracy is the nurse of eloquence, because, when the multitude have the power, persuasion is the only way to govern them." Therefore, in summary, to Witherspoon it appeared "that every good form of government must be complex, so that the one principle may check the other." Although there should be as much "virtue among the particular members of a community as possible, . . . it is folly to expect that a state should be upheld by integrity in all who have a share in managing it. They must be so balanced, that when every one draws to his own interest or inclination, there may be an over-poise upon the whole." [89]

What Witherspoon had to say about the forms of government and the most effective type is interesting to the extent that it reflects the main sources of his thinking and reveals a similarity between the Princeton professor and some of his graduates. The influence of Montesquieu has already been noted, and is further seen in Witherspoon's observation that "in a well-formed state, the subjects should not be too numerous or too few"; too many are difficult to govern, and too few cannot successfully suppress internal insurrection or repel external attacks. [90] Even more interesting is the similarity between Madison's discussion of fac-

89. "Moral Philosophy," pp. 91–104. Cf. *Spirit of the Laws*, Bk. IV, chap. ii.
90. "Moral Philosophy," p. 102. Cf. Montesquieu, *Spirit of the Laws*, Bk. VIII, chap. xiv, and Bk. IX, chap. i.

tions in *Federalist* No. 10 and John Witherspoon's view that it is foolish to found government on universal human integrity instead of on a harmony of the conflicting interests.

However, to suggest that Witherspoon's political views might have been one, perhaps the earliest, source of some of Madison's political theories is not to suggest for a moment that the former was as foresighted as the latter. Indeed, Witherspoon did not have much ability intellectually to anticipate the future political course which many of his students were to chart. For example, although he insisted that "the great essential rights of rulers must be divided, and distributed among the different branches of the legislature," [91] he did not anticipate the highly developed separation of powers which was written into the American Constitution under Madison's leadership; indeed, Montesquieu, whose *Spirit of the Laws* was used as a text in the moral philosophy course, developed this principle far more fully than John Witherspoon.[92] The professor had in mind the developing British system of separation of power between Parliament and King, not the threefold separation of legislative, executive, and judicial powers, such as the student helped to constitute. Actually, Witherspoon did not have much to say about the judiciary at all: he noted the need for judges of equity and thought this could best be insured if judges were chosen from the district in which they were to act. Further, he developed the idea that a multiplicity of laws tends to cause endless litigation but thought that the difficulty of electing impartial judges made a detailed constitution with a multiplicity of written laws more likely to be workable.[93] How much wiser the student than the professor in this regard. Nonetheless, it does not require much imagination to see Witherspoon as one who stimulated the thinking of Madison and some of his constitutional colleagues.

Witherspoon made no attempt to detail the structure of a good constitution, but he did sketch some of his ideas on the

91. "Moral Philosophy," pp. 101–102.
92. Bk. XI, chap. v.
93. "Moral Philosophy," pp. 123–124.

nature of civil law and civil liberty, which ideas strongly reflect the influence of Montesquieu.

The meaning of the term "law" to Witherspoon must be inferred because he never stated it explicitly. He thought in terms of a universe ruled by natural moral law which is grounded in the very nature of God the Creator and is known in the moral sense or conscience of man. He spoke of this law of nature having a sanction in man's "sense of duty and accountableness to a supreme Judge; to which may be added, such a sense of utility, as makes men fear" to go conversely lest they incur "reproach and infamy among all nations . . . and probably resentment and indignation by common consent." [94] Therefore, Witherspoon's conception of "law" seems to have involved two elements: a command with a sanction, and a fundamental principle in created reality. As we shall see, one of the objects of civil laws was said to be that of transcribing the natural moral law into positive or political laws for a particular society. "Political law is the authority of any society stamped upon moral duty." [95] The sense of moral duty is the law of God written on the heart of man.[96]

The general purpose of civil laws in relation to the society of men is "to prevent offenses, and make men good, as much as to punish them when they do evil." [97] At first this sounds like a blend of the Pauline and the Scholastic-Aristotelian concept of law, but when Witherspoon explains, it becomes apparent that laws make men good not by training them in virtue so much as by providing for the magistrates to promote true religion.

If, as we have seen above, virtue and piety are inseparably connected, then to promote true religion is the best and most effectual way of making a virtuous and regular people. Love to God, and love to man, is the substance of religion; when these prevail, civil laws will have little to do.[98]

94. "The Druid," p. 236.
95. "Moral Philosophy," p. 76.
96. "Trial of Religious Truth," p. 310.
97. "Moral Philosophy," p. 118.
98. *Ibid.*, pp. 118–119.

This insistence on the role of religion in relation to the civil laws suggests some kind of state support of religion, and such is more directly implied by all that Witherspoon said about the relation of religion and the civil officials. The magistrate ought to encourage piety by defending the "rights of conscience" and tolerating all in their religious sentiments, "if such are not injurious to their neighbors," by guarding against religious persecution ("because such as hold absurd tenets are seldom dangerous") and by enacting laws to punish profanity and impiety. Witherspoon added that there was "a good deal of reason" for the view of many persons that "the magistrate ought to make provision for the worship of God, in such manner as is agreeable to the great body of the society; though at the same time all who dissent from it are fully tolerated." Clearly, this idea that the laws must be designed to make good men put Witherspoon in the camp with those who favored state-supported religion, but with full toleration being provided for dissenters. Although the state needs to support true religion that the general purpose of its laws may be realized, the state has no right to interfere with the religious views of any individual because one of the perfect rights of man is "that every one should judge for himself in matters of religion." [99]

Witherspoon made two other general remarks about civil laws before detailing the three ways in which civil laws operate in a society. Reflecting the influence of Montesquieu, he remarked that "laws should be so framed as to promote such principles in general as are favorable to good government, and particularly that principle, if there be one, that gave rise to the constitution, and is congenial to it." [100] He did not specify that "principle," although he mentioned "sobriety, industry, and public spirit" as among the most important principles of any good constitution. In addition, he noted that every "constitution of note" includes two kinds of laws, those that are written and those that are "in the hearts of the magistrates." His own preference was for writing down the laws as fully and clearly as possible so as to leave no more room than necessary for de-

99. *Ibid.,* pp. 119–121.
100. *Ibid.,* p. 121. Cf. *Spirit of the Laws,* Bk. III, chaps. i–iii.

pendence upon the other type.[101] This preference for a multiplicity of laws seems to reflect a realistic view about the way in which man's selfish interests may interfere with justice, and at the same time it assumes a highly optimistic estimate of man's ability to form a constitution that is comprehensively effective.

Civil laws were described as having three particular objects:

1. To ratify the moral laws by the sanction of the society. The transgressions of such laws are called *crimes*. . . .

2. To lay down a plan for all contracts in commerce or intercourse between man and man. . . . The transgressions of such laws are called *frauds*. They chiefly regard the acquisition, transmission, or alienation of property.

3. To limit and direct persons in the exercise of their own rights, and oblige them to show respect to the interfering rights of others. . . . And the transgressions of such laws are called *trespasses*. A number of things in this view may become illegal, which before were not moral.[102]

The first of these objects makes apparent Witherspoon's understanding of civil law in the context of moral law. He believed that the universe is governed according to moral law, which man knows by means of the moral sense; therefore, the responsibility of the legislator is to formulate civil laws based on the moral law. Since rightly constituted civil laws are concrete forms of the moral law, the committing of crime is, in its ultimate context, a violation of the natural moral law.

The second object of civil law is concerned with property, more especially private property, which Witherspoon defined as the exclusive right of every person "to a portion of the goods which serve for the support and conveniency of life." Private property is acquired by "(1) Prior occupation, (2) Our own industry." The terms meant about the same thing since the former was analyzed as follows:

Of the things that lay in common for the use of man, I have a right to take what is convenient for me; and after I have taken it, no body can have a better right, nor consequently any title, to take it away from me.[103]

101. "Moral Philosophy," pp. 122–124.
102. *Ibid.*, p. 124.
103. *Ibid.*, p. 85.

Hence, "prior occupation" is the effect of someone's industry. Private property is limited by use, in that a man has no right to more than he can use,[104] and by the public good, in that one has no right to whatever is harmful to his fellow men.[105] Therefore, the second object of civil laws is to see that transactions involving property specifically and commerce in general are regulated for the good of all individuals within the society.

Witherspoon's statement of the third object of civil law is open to an easy misinterpretation unless one remembers that limiting and directing persons in the exercise of their own rights and requiring them to respect the rights of others extends only to what he has distinguished as "perfect rights."

Human laws reach only, in ordinary cases, to perfect rights. Sometimes imperfect rights, by being carried far, become perfect, as humanity and gentleness in a parent to a child may be so grossly violated as to warrant the interposition of human authority.[106]

Therefore, the scope of civil law does not extend to imperfect rights or to "unalienable" rights. There can be no question here of the civil laws regulating the whole life of man in the manner of a totalitarian state.

Witherspoon's discussion of civil law is elaborated and more fully developed in his views on civil liberty. "By liberty I mean . . . a completely ordered and well balanced plan of civil government, where justice and equal laws take place, and are well supported." [107] A person being in a state of nature is not truly free, because he who lives unencumbered among other men who have the same degree of license is always threatened in property and person. Therefore, civil liberty is absolutely necessary if men are to be truly free.

Liberty has been sometimes very justly called the dominion of laws and not of men; it is in its most perfect state when no man, how great soever, can or dare hinder another from doing that which he ought to do, and when every man is most effectually hindered from doing that which he ought not.[108]

104. *Ibid.*, p. 86. Cf. Locke, *op. cit.*, chap. v, par. 31.
105. See the distinction between rights of necessity and common rights, "Moral Philosophy," pp. 145–148.
106. "Moral Philosophy," p. 64.
107. "Dialogue on Civil Liberty," *Pennsylvania Magazine,* II (April, 1776), 163.
108. *Ibid.*, p. 164.

Witherspoon did not mean that a person cannot be virtuous or privately happy in the absence of civil liberty; men who are both are found under every form of government. What he did mean is that civil liberty is possible only in a government which keeps within its proper limits and seeks to direct its members in their political, commercial, and communal relations according to the moral law written in the heart of man; and he seldom missed an opportunity to wax eloquent on the advantages of civil liberty.

Upon the whole, I take the essential benefit of civil liberty, . . . to be, its tendency to put in motion and encourage the exertion of all the human powers. It must therefore evidently improve the human mind, and bring with it, in highest perfection, all the advantages of the social state. It is the parent or nurse of industry, opulence, knowledge, virtue, and heroism.[109]

Moreover, civil liberty promotes "the knowledge of God and his truths," [110] lessens the impact of war, famine, and pestilence,[111] and furthers the national prosperity of a people. One can readily imagine the impact which such an advocate of civil liberty must have made on his young American students during the 1770's and 1780's. Indeed, it is possible that the convictions which his political philosophy rationalized helped to cover up some of its inconsistencies.

One final question needs to be asked in this discussion of Witherspoon's concept of law, and civil law particularly. Since Witherspoon was of a rather conservative theological bent and argued that "the wisest way for us, with regard to all revealed truth, is to receive it as revealed," [112] how large a role did the biblical revelation play in his theory of civil law? His "Lectures on Divinity" repeatedly illustrates his literalistic method of interpreting Scripture; but when he raised the question about whether the laws of Moses are of "perpetual obligation," he argued that they are not because of their being particularly suited to conditions of the Jews in Canaan. Nonetheless, he

109. *Ibid.*, p. 167. Cf. "Moral Philosophy," p. 106, and Montesquieu, *Spirit of the Laws,* Bk. XIX, chap. xxiii.
110. "Dominion of Providence," p. 203.
111. "Reflections on the Present State of Public Affairs and on the Duty and Interest of America in this Important Crisis," *Works,* IX, 68.
112. "Lectures on Divinity," p. 83.

believed that criminal laws based on the principle of *lex talionis* were "founded upon so much wisdom, that it is a question whether the departure from them in punishing of crime has ever been attended with advantage." [113] Therefore, the answer to the question regarding the biblical contribution to Witherspoon's teaching about civil law and liberty is: almost nothing. We claimed that his theory of society and civil law was based not on revelation but on the moral sense enlightened by reason and common experience. Although his theological method was based on a literalistic view of the Scripture, he somewhat inconsistently explained away a large part of the scriptural revelation which he had said must be merely accepted without the believer's "presuming to be wise above what is written."

The Law of Nature and Nations

Witherspoon recognized that any adequate political philosophy must have application to the relations between nations, and these, he said, are to be conducted according to the "law of nature and nations."

. . . the law of nature and nations is nothing else but the law of general reason, or those obligations of duty from reason and conscience, on one individual to another, antecedent to any particular law derived from the social compact, or even actual consent. On this account it is called the law of nature; and because there are very rarely to be found any parties in such a free state with regard to each other, except independent nations, therefore it is also called the law of nations.[114]

Since there is no contract to which the nations have initially consented, their relations with each other must be governed by the prompting of natural conscience enlightened by reason. Without any contract there can be no positive law, and "when they disagree, they have no common umpire or judge to resort to, but must decide their quarrels by the sword." [115] Therefore, there is no sanction of the law of nature and nations "other

113. *Ibid.*, pp. 156–157. Cf. "Moral Philosophy," p. 128.
114. "Speech in Congress on the Convention with General Burgoyne," *Works,* IX, 112–113.
115. "The Druid," pp. 234–235.

than a general sense of duty, and such a sense of common utility," as makes men fear that if any nation notoriously breaks these laws, it will bring down upon itself the reproach, resentment, and indignation of other nations.[116]

That some such law exists was evident to Witherspoon from "the universal acknowledgement of men, and the practice of nations from the earliest ages," as well as from "the nature of the thing." The duties which are binding on nations are those which are binding on men in the state of natural liberty prior to any contract.[117] The "chief or only object" of this law is to deal with "the manner of making war and peace," and Witherspoon's discussion of this subject involved such characteristics of just war as its causes, the time for its beginning, its duration, and the means of conducting it, as well as some characteristics of just peace.[118]

There is little new material in this discussion of the law of nature and nations; nothing more needs to be noted here. The discussion merely approves the way men fought war and made peace in the days when men of "right reason" agreed that certain customs, such as wholesale destruction of those who do not directly participate, were despicable even in war. The real significance of the law of nature and nations in Witherspoon's thought is threefold: it makes clear how little concerned he was about the historical existence of a state of nature among men prior to any societal relations; once again, it emphasizes the doctrine of consent of the governed; and it further illustrates his conviction that the light of nature or moral sense is the fundamental impulse guiding the thought and actions of men.

Schoolman of Statesmen

Anyone who studies the writings of John Witherspoon, both before his arrival at Princeton and after, is impressed by the wide range of subjects to which he addressed himself—every-

116. "Moral Philosophy," p. 108.
117. "The Druid," p. 235.
118. "Moral Philosophy," pp. 108–117.

thing from training infants to be submissive under parental rule [119] to the law of nature and nations. No philosophical view was too abstract and no issue too minute for his extensive interests. In such diversity there were eclectic and sometimes inconsistent views.

Above all else Witherspoon was a teacher, as his lectures, his sermons, and even his speeches in Congress illustrate; and very often the most effective teachers make lasting impact not so much by originality and consistency of argument as by opening intellectual doors for their students. The role of such professorial doormen is frequently forgotten as more prominent students proceed along the paths of celebrity. Perhaps something of this sort happened to Witherspoon. Although he did not lack recognition from his contemporaries, any effort to trace Witherspoon's contribution to the thinking of his prominent students is frustrated because so few of them acknowledged the ways in which their Scottish teacher had contributed to their intellectual development. His most prominent student, James Madison, a prolific political pamphleteer and correspondent as well as the "father of the Constitution," never gave any written acknowledgement of Witherspoon's influence upon his own thinking. One reason may be the apparent inconsistencies in many of the professor's views; another may be that intellectual consistency in the teacher was, and frequently is, less important for the students than intellectual stimulus.

There is little if any originality to be found in Witherspoon's thought. He was no explorer of new realms. Indeed, he was not even a good absorber of the intellectual insights uncovered by greater minds than his own.[120] In any case, the unresisted pressure of his duties, as pastor and college president, left him little time for constructing a theoretically consistent approach in his philosophizing, even had he possessed the ability and desire to do so. He was more interested in action than in reflection, and action was what his situation most demanded. Called to the College of New Jersey because of its need for

119. See "Letters on the Education of Children," *Works*, VIII, 165 ff.
120. Cf. Riley, *op. cit.*, p. 491.

uniting and increasing the support of rival factions in American Presbyterianism, Witherspoon immediately faced enormous problems in raising its academic standing and finding money at a time when the supporters of the College were increasingly involved in the struggle against England. In this contest also he soon was actively involved.

With his manifold duties in the New Jersey College, the Provincial Convention and the Continental Congress, he had little time for meditation and less for the production of philosophic works.[121]

But more than the pressures of responsibilities must be noted in any accounting of Witherspoon's role as a teacher: there is a strongly practical and even utilitarian tendency running through much of his writing. When his son, David, was an instructor at what is now Hampden Sydney College, the father wrote:

Next to the one thing needful [apparently, salvation] you know that I am chiefly concerned for your improvement in useful knowledge, and fitness for the duties of active life.[122]

When he lectured to his students on the general principles of taste and beauty and spoke specifically about the beauties of the natural world, his utilitarian tendency became apparent.

The beauties of nature, we are sensible, are greatly heightened by adding to their delightful appearance, a reflection on their utility, and the benevolent intention of their author.[123]

The same he thought to be true of the "fine arts": their beauty is largely to be found in their contribution to the improvement of mankind.

An admirable poem, or an eloquent discourse, or a fine picture, would be still more excellent, if the subject of them were interesting and valuable; and when any one of them are perverted to impious or wicked purposes, they are just objects of detestation.[124]

Not being content with the arguments which reason can muster to defend natural liberty, Witherspoon felt the necessity of

121. *Ibid.*, p. 484.
122. Collins, *op. cit.*, II, 204.
123. "Lectures on Eloquence," *Works,* VII, 315.
124. *Ibid.*, p. 316.

adding that "common utility commends it." [125] Again, in his Congressional speeches urging the delegates to pay the interest on loans made for the conduct of war, he appealed not to any abstract moral principle but to common utility: if such payment were not made, the states united could not expect to maintain good credit and thus be able to borrow needed money in the future.[126] How effectively Witherspoon communicated his practical emphasis to his students seems to be reflected in James Madison's repeated insistence in the *Federalist* and his other writings that republican government generally, and the newly formed Constitutional version of it specifically, was not perfect government but the "least imperfect" and therefore deserved ratification and an opportunity to be tested in experience.[127]

When one probes yet deeper into the prevailing character of Witherspoon's views he discovers a background conflict between conservative theology and Enlightenment philosophy which the Princeton professor never synthesized. He had not the time and probably not the ability to live, as Paul Tillich has tried to do, "on the boundary" between conflicting schools of thought. From the very beginning he attempted to live in two different, but not unrelated camps: Federal theology and Enlightenment philosophy. Among the circumstances which account for the situation are his youth in a pious Scottish home; his education at Edinburgh (where professors were beginning to introduce the study of Locke, Montesquieu, and other philosophers of the Enlightenment); his alignment in the Scottish Church with the conservative Popular party in opposition to the more enlightened and liberal Moderates; the necessity in America of maintaining good theological relations with conservative Old Side Presbyterians while grounding students in the "Enlightened" political philosophy which undergirded the founding of the American republic. It is a rare teacher who can

125. "Moral Philosophy," p. 80.
126. "Speech in Congress on a Motion for Paying the Interest of Loan-Office Certificates" and "Part of a Speech in Congress on Finances," *Works,* IX, 117–134.
127. See *Federalist,* Nos. 14 and 37; and James Madison, *Letters and Other Writings* (New York, 1884), IV, 328–329, 334.

avoid intellectual inconsistencies which are more apparent to others than himself, especially when his background and present situation are as varied and demanding as John Witherspoon's.

Without seeking to absolve Witherspoon of responsibility for his shortcomings, one can admit that a major problem with his political philosophy reflects not only his own inabilities but also the inadequacy of the contractarian political philosophy which he adopted and which was widely accepted in his generation. As the critics of the Social Contract have made clear, the elements that make up an historically effective society cannot all be logically included within the idea of a contract. Witherspoon had some inkling of the limits of contractarian thought. He defined a contract as a lawful and free covenant between two responsible parties according to which they agree about their future relations with each other. He also acknowledged that, as matter of historical and natural fact, in all human relations some societal aspect had preceded the aspect of individual consent. The truth of the matter is that in some respects man's political obligations and privileges are best analyzed by means of the contract analogy; in other respects other analogies, such as the organism, are more appropriate.[128] In his use of the contract analogy Witherspoon was doing as he very commonly did: adopting rather uncritically a scheme of thought that proved a useful vehicle for his cherished convictions about civil liberty and human rights.

Regardless of the fact that Witherspoon did not synthesize adequately some views of others which he adopted, to one conviction he held consistently: the moral freedom and responsibility of man as a child of God. Philosophically, this conviction was developed within the structure of the Scottish Common Sense philosophy with special emphasis on the moral sense in man. Politically, it was manifest in his steadfastly expounding the correlated doctrines that all just government must be by the consent of the governed and that every government ought

128. Gough, *op. cit.,* pp. 247-249.

to be so constituted as to protect and enhance the rights and duties of man. His total impact on his students may be measured more in terms of the depth of this underlying conviction than with regard to the inconsistency of which he was sometimes guilty. When these abiding convictions are understood within the context of Witherspoon's role as one who taught such a large number of prominent American political leaders, perhaps the best way in which to characterize his contribution to the young republic is to call him an academic advocate for the civil liberty of man.

Under Witherspoon's direction the College of New Jersey during the crucial years from 1770 to 1790 became less a theological seminary, more a school for statesmen. At its sesquicentenial celebration in 1896 the College officially became Princeton University. The development from college to university, which received its major impetus under another Scotsman, James McCosh, had been initiated by the first Scottish president, John Witherspoon.

Bronson Alcott: Emerson's "Tedious Archangel"

H. BURNELL PANNILL

Professor Smith, in his study of the religious context out of which New England transcendentalism arose, has pointed out that "one clear-cut mark of a transcendentalist was that he believed in intuitive knowledge and rejected the Lockean claim that all knowledge is limited to that of external sensory perception."[1] A study of the *Journals* and *Orphic Sayings* of Bronson Alcott reveals that, by this test, Alcott was the arch-transcendentalist of them all. This enigmatic figure, so often praised and equally as often ridiculed, dreamer of great dreams and colossal failure, filled his literary efforts with one central theme: an unbounded confidence in the "divine ray in his own breast; . . . the light drawn from within."[2] This central theme of an intuitive epistemology is the fulcrum upon which the life and thought of Alcott lay balanced. Out of it he erected, albeit in tedious, disjointed fashion, an idealistic theory of metaphysical creativity; for its sake and out of its promptings he modeled his utopian Fruitlands, endeavoring to incarnate the vision which the oracle of his heart had given.

The decade between 1835 and 1845 may be taken as the climactic period in the development of Alcott's transcendentalism. During these years his friendship with Emerson and Thoreau ripened; his years of reading in the accumulated wisdom of mankind were bearing their fruit as the thoughts of

---

1. H. Shelton Smith, "Was Theodore Parker a Transcendentalist?" *The New England Quarterly*, XXIII (1950), 355.
2. A. Bronson Alcott, "Days from a Diary: V. Inspiration. An Epistle," *The Dial: A Magazine for Literature, Philosophy, and Religion,* II (1841–1842), 417.

Plato and Plotinus, of the German idealists and romanticists, of Wordsworth, Coleridge, and Carlyle, began to merge into his own distinctive eclecticism. These years were to mark his "triumph" at Alcott House in England and his "failure" at Fruitlands. They were to close a period in which he almost attained the "genius" of which he prophesied, and they began a lengthy twilight period of accomplishments which mark his place in the history of American idealism. These ten years were his "years of trial," when the realization of his vision always seemed just over the horizon, when his reforming zeal was at its strongest and his failures the most bitter. They were also the years in which he was unafraid to trust his own advice, "Believe, youth, that your heart is an oracle; trust her instinctive auguries, obey her divine leadings; nor listen too fondly to the uncertain echoes of your head." [3]

In October, 1841, Alcott spoke to a Bible Convention meeting in Boston. His topic was "Transcendentalism." A reporter for the Boston *Daily Advertiser* summarized his reaction to Alcott's speech with these words:

We have never heard any exposition of the Transcendental doctrines so intelligently made or placed in so favorable an aspect,— though the speaker implicitly contended that this knowledge, or attainment, or divine *afflatus* (whatever it is) could not be known or understood from others, but must be acquired, learned, and felt only by the soul itself, by means of its own efforts,—by purity, obedience, meditation, freedom (as far as possible) from actual sin, and by progress in goodness and piety.[4]

This report emphasizes the individualism with which any discussion of Alcott's epistemology must begin. In February, 1836, he had written, ". . . I believe no revelation can be made to the consciousness of an individual through that of another. The intuition must come from the direct vision of the subject, without other intervention." [5] The ideas which made up the sum of any individual's true knowledge were considered by Alcott to be revelations of the infinite and spiritual Reality

---

3. Alcott, "Orphic Sayings: II. Enthusiasm," *The Dial*, I (1840–1841), 85.
4. Quoted by F. B. Sanborn and W. T. Harris, *A. Bronson Alcott. His Life and Philosophy* (2 vols.; Boston, 1893), I, 328–329.
5. *The Journals of Bronson Alcott*, ed. Odell Shepard (Boston, 1938), p. 75.

within the universe. The reality and the truth of the ideas depended upon the extent to which the transmission of these revelations could be kept pure and unaffected by external interference. In its pure state, the human consciousness transcended space and time; the intuitions available to man in this state, therefore, stood beyond history, historical institutions, written "scriptures," and the other usually accepted sources of perceptual and conceptual knowledge. The soul had had a "primordial experience in the infinite Spirit," and out of this experience it drew both its inherent dignity and its commission to bring the light of Truth into history. The historical empirical and rational epistemologies, as Alcott interpreted them, had ignored this assumption of the primacy of innate, intuitive ideas, and had consequently failed to provide an adequate basis for knowledge of reality.

The human faculty operative in intuitive knowledge was, for Alcott, the "conscience." This faculty was the human pole of a relationship of knowledge to which he referred variously as "revelation" and "inspiration." At times he was willing to interpret the former term broadly enough to include that information received through "sense" and "reason," and to let the distinctiveness of the intuitions rest upon a qualitative emphasis. "Revelation is mediate or immediate, speculative or intuitive. It is addressed to conscience or reason,—to sight or sense. Reason receives the light through mediums and mediators; conscience direct from its source. The light of one is opake [*sic*]; of the other, clear." [6] As a faculty of knowledge, however, the conscience had for Alcott two significant attributes. These attributes were distinctive enough to warrant a radical separation of its "truths" from those of reason and sense. First, the conscience was considered to be free from the bondage into which man's other cognitive faculties had fallen and, being innocent, was "quick with instincts of unerring aim."

. . . she knows by intuition what lapsed reason defines by laborious inference; her appetites and affections are direct and trustworthy. Reason is the left hand of instinct; it is tardy, awkward, but the

6. "Orphic Sayings: LXXVIII. Revelation," *The Dial,* I (1840–1841), 357.

right is ready and dextrous. By reasoning the soul strives to recover her lost intuitions; groping amidst the obscure darkness of sense, by means of the fingers of logic, for treasures present alway and available to the eye of conscience. Sinners must needs reason; saints behold.[7]

This "impeccable, immaculate, immutable" conscience stands aloof in an isolated purity from man's corrupted faculties. Since it had never been a party to man's guilt, its judgments of right and wrong, of true and false, were infallible; it alone could lay valid claim to being "the oracle and interpreter, the judge and executor of the divine law." [8] The conscience is seen, therefore, as the supremely transcendental fact. It is of God, not of this temporal world; suprahistorical, it is above all pretended authority except that which it recognizes as its own source. In his less transcendentalist moments, however, Alcott knew that some limitation upon the scope of universal conscience was indicated. He preferred to make that limitation by restricting it to the "saints" or "prophets." These, the "innocent ones," were the partakers of the divine omniscience; they were the "Incarnate Words, . . . silent or vocal, as the divine influx retreats to its source, or flows over their cloven tongues, bringing glad tidings to all who have access to the urns of being." [9] The prophet, his eye "purified of the motes of tradition," could pierce the veil of sense that surrounded him, bridge the gap between faith and sight, and commune, face to face, with God. But the logic of the saint and the prophet is too subtle, too occult, for ordinary men. For them there is only "reason," only the dreams of that which the innocent soul already knows as a present fact, only the plodding way of analysis that reveals but the shadows of truth.[10]

This occult logic of the saint gives to his conscience a second characteristic. Through it the soul is enabled to grasp the unity of all things.

7. "Orphic Sayings: XIV. Instinct and Reason," *The Dial*, I (1840–1841) , 88.
8. "Orphic Sayings: XVI. Conscience," *The Dial*, I (1840–1841) , 89.
9. "Days from a Diary: V. Inspiration. An Epistle," *The Dial*, II (1841–1842) , 416.
10. "Orphic Sayings: XXV. Prophet," *The Dial*, I (1840–1841) , 91.

It is the perpetual effort of conscience to divorce the soul from the dominion of sense; to nullify the dualities of the apparent, and restore the intuition of the real. The soul makes a double statement of all her facts; to conscience and sense; . . . Yet though double to sense, she remains single and one in herself; one in conscience, many in understanding; one in life, diverse in function and number. Sense, in its infirmity, breaks this unity to apprehend in part what it cannot grasp at once. Understanding denotes diversity; conscience alone divines unity, and integrates all experience in identity of spirit.[11]

This intuition of the conscience gives true metaphysical knowledge. Only through it can a man come at last to grasp that Being which is the living, creative Fact of the universe. The true Life of the universe eludes scientific analysis. "God, man, nature, are a divine synthesis, whose parts it is impiety to sunder. Genius must preside devoutly over all investigations, or analysis, with her murderous knife, will seek impiously to probe the vitals of being." [12] Back of this emphasis on unity is Alcott's belief that difference is not as metaphysically significant as sameness, not as real and not as permanent. Identity becomes a necessary category in the mind's true apprehension of reality. Thus we must come to look upon nature, not as something remote and detached, but as that which is one with us. "In moments of true life," he wrote, "I feel my identity with her; I breathe, pulsate, feel, think, will through her members, and know of no duality of being. It is in such moods of soul that prophetic visions are beheld, and evangeles published for the joy and hope of mankind." [13] This sense of identity, with the source of creative activity on the one side, and with nature on the other, was to provide Alcott with a basis for his theory of metaphysical creativity. As far as theory of knowledge is concerned, the emphasis on identity means that man does not stand over against nature in a subject-object duality which must somehow be reconciled in order for knowledge to take place. All facts, material and spiritual, are but the emerging realizations of something greater than either manifestation. It

11. "Orphic Sayings: XV. Identity and Diversity," *The Dial,* I (1840–1841) , 88.
12. "Orphic Sayings: XXXIII. Each and All," *The Dial,* I (1840–1841) , 93.
13. "Orphic Sayings: XXXV. Nature," *The Dial,* I (1840–1841) , 94.

is this something greater which is grasped by the prophet's intuition, and this grasping is the first step in man's participation in God's continual creativity.

This same emphasis on unity and identity appears in Alcott's treatment of memory and history. History, he wrote, was of use in the enlightenment of man only as man was conscious of the facts of history in his own experience.

All history is contemporaneous with my present life. It is a commentary on my experience. My light illuminates the darkness that antiquity may cast over it. I pierce this darkness and see the same old eternal verities that once charmed the ancient world. I become a contemporary of truth, not of men. I am beyond the range of history. I antedate its records, which can only testify to the facts of which my own soul bore prior testimony.[14]

The soul is eternal, "coeval with God," and memory is but the account of her eternal history, just as hope is the prophecy of this eternity. The "facts" written upon the memory are, therefore, not an adequate basis for knowledge. Self-intuition alone makes us wise, both as to that which we call "past" and that which we call "future." Only the present "is," but it is eternally. The biography of the saint or the prophet thus becomes the only truly accurate history, and this only when it is a biography of "spiritual causes" rather than of physical changes and the "vicissitudes of external life." In the spiritual biographies of such men we see humanity," not in the soiled glory of its original prerogatives but in its native dignity." [15] Even these spiritual biographies eventually fail to capture the truth of the union of reality and the spirit of genius that makes intuition possible. Biography, once written, ceases to be true biography and becomes "scripture," subject to codification and loss of vitality. Life that is reduced to "letters" ceases to retain its spirit and becomes an object to be thought about rather than lived. In the final analysis, virtue and genius cannot be written. The attempt to do so results in the reclothing of the living spirit in the superstitions and tradition-determined attitudes of the

14. *Journals* (Oct., 1838) , p. 106.
15. *Journals* (Jan. 2, 1835) , pp. 50–51.

scribe.[16] The true meaning of life is to be found only in action; virtue is not a system, but a life; truth is not "discovered," but grasped intuitively and made explicit only in facts that are creative rather than static. Once a fact is reported and recorded, said Alcott, it becomes false. Thus the scriptures of the men of genius are really no more authentic than those of other men. Intuition alone is the legitimate carrier of truth, and intuition is a living fact, not an object which can be subjected to perceptual or conceptual analysis and systematization. "Not only all scripture, but all thought is fabulous. Life is the only pure fact, and this cannot be written to sense; it must be lived, and thus expurgate all scriptures." [17]

This emphasis upon the significance of the "living intuition" was to have its effect in determining Alcott's attitude toward any organization that attempted to codify its precepts and prescribe action. Out of this emphasis was also to come his evaluation of the role he was to play, as prophet to his age. He was being quite consistent with the premises expressed above when he questioned Emerson's judgment that "my medium of success to the public must be made through the pen rather than by practical action." [18] Alcott did make several attempts at the literary presentation of his thoughts, and Emerson was to criticize these rather severely, largely from the standpoint of style.[19] Alcott's own judgment upon his work can be found, however, in a statement from his Journal for May 13, 1839.

. . . I am not a scholar. My might is not in my pen. This is feeble. I do no justice to myself in literary composition. My organ is action and voice, rather. I am an actor and a sayer, rather than a writer. I do not detach my thoughts from my life. I am concrete. Thought manifests itself in deed and spoken words.

I act rather than observe. . . . I am of the race of prophets; and I should put out my eyes and damp my enthusiasm by seeking to

16. "Orphic Sayings: LXXI. Life," *The Dial,* I (1840–1841) , 355.
17. "Orphic Sayings: LXXVII. Fact and Fable," *The Dial,* I (1840–1841) , 357.
18. *Journals* (April, 1837) , p. 89.
19. *Journals* (March 5, 1836) , p. 75. Here the reference is to Alcott's manuscript copy of "Breath of Childhood." Emerson's most critical comments were reserved for the later revisions of this work, now entitled "Psyche." The criticisms were so adverse that Alcott decided to take Emerson's advice that he "withhold it from publication." *Journals* (June, 1838) , p. 102.

play the philosopher or the critic. I analyze life and nature not by speculation but action. . . . I must think, and set my thoughts in the drapery of action and living speech. . . . My genius is epic.[20]

Alcott came increasingly to look upon himself as the creator of a "new era in the history of man" as well as the founder of a "new school of theology." His work here, however, as he saw it, was not to be that of a system builder. His life itself was to be his contribution. Others might derive new forms of expression and new spiritual laws from the intuitions imprisoned in his words, in the record of the life he lived. Here philosophers might find new facts upon which they could base broader generalizations than had hitherto been possible. But such tasks were not fit for men of genius, being suitable only for those to whom the creative insight had not been given. So convinced was Alcott of the "prophetic" character of the role he was to play that he could make a virtue out of his lack of preparation in the schools and institutions which, through their dependence upon traditions and scriptures, would have violated the integrity of his intuitions. "Character," he wrote, "is the only legitimate institution." Before it all pretensions of power, all authorities save its own, and all states, social, religious, and political, would eventually capitulate. Until that day came, however, the prophet must expect antagonism and condemnation from those whose vested interests, order, and perpetuity his revolution threatened. His lot would be a lonely one and he would have little to sustain him except his faith in the validity of his intuitions. In the strength of that faith he would have to work, confident that character-in-action would finally destroy the old and build the new. The prophets are men "attempered in the fires of heaven; they are mailed in the might of principles, and God backs their purpose. They uproot institutions, erase traditions, revise usages, and renovate all things." [21] The destructive work of the prophet—that for which he is in his own age condemned—is, therefore, but the reverse side of true

20. *Journals,* p. 128.
21. "Orphic Sayings: LII. Reformers," *The Dial,* I (1840–1841) , 351.

creation. Out of his work shall emerge, as existent fact, that which is now in the prophet's vision.

Knowledge of Reality, intuitively given, thus gives rise, through action, to creation. Metaphysics is secondary to theory of knowledge, and the nature of knowledge itself specifies the essential nature of what is to be. Intuitions are more than the bearers of truth; conscience is more than a faculty of knowledge. Both are creative rather than imitative, and within the individual they well up with a compelling urgency, reminding man of his divine origin and his divine commission. True to his basic individualism, Alcott saw the creative process as beginning within the prophet himself.

> . . . change must originate within and work outwards. The inner being must first be reorganized. And the method of regeneration must be learned, not by prescription, but from Experience—from self-conquest—self-insight: its law revealed by fidelity to the spiritual constitution. Renovation of being must precede all outward reformation of organs and functions, and the whole man be first sanctified by the wholesome discipline of a true life.[22]

Reform will begin with the individual; his labors will initiate in the precincts of his private life and will be limited to "the simplest ministeries of families, neighborhoods, fraternities, quite wide of associations and institutions." The fruits of these labors will appear not as sets of rules, not as descriptions of what has been done nor as pledges of what is to be done, but simply as a life, a creative impulse commensurate with human existence, a tendency toward "perfection of being." [23]

The distinction which Alcott made between the saints or prophets and other men required a parallel distinction between the "reality" which each group knows and with which it works. The understanding (man's rational powers) is fit to receive only the appearance which analysis can present as the facts of nature and history. Seen with the eye of prophetic vision, however, "natural facts are symbols of spiritual laws." To the

---

22. "Days from a Diary: XV. Reform. An Epistle," *The Dial,* II (1841–1842), 434–435.
23. *Ibid.*

"worldling" the saint appears as a mystic; to the saint the worldling is seen as one "living to sense, . . . identified with the flesh," who dwells amidst the dust and vapors of his own lusts. His vision thus obscured, he cannot attain to the heights of that reality which is the object of the prophet's vision.[24] The dualism implied here, both of knowledge and being, is historically severe, and although Alcott was to attempt to resolve the dualism, he was aware that such resolution would not be easy. In April, 1834, he wrote:

I have so long lived an inward, reflective life that the relations of external things to my temporal prosperity have been almost lost sight of. I am not perhaps sufficiently inclined to yield to the dictates of earthly prudence. I cling too closely to the ideal to take necessary advantage of the practical, and my wife and children suffer from this neglect.[25]

Apart from this very practical consideration, there was the additional difficulty which the prophet faced in making his visions intelligible to the ordinary man and effective in concrete changes. Alcott observed that his thoughts were often so general, so composed of maxims and ideal principles, that he could not illustrate these ideals through common imagery. The result was that he found it difficult to "let these principles down to the details of fact, circumstance, common relations, in which they are intended to work and to which they are practically adapted." [26]

These difficulties did not, however, cause Alcott to waver in his basic conviction that a proper understanding of the role of the prophet would reveal that this dualism was apparent only and could be resolved. Fruitlands was his own attempt to give substance to this conviction, but back of that attempt was a reasoned defense of the truth which Fruitlands was supposed to verify. He once said that the whole purpose of life was to incarnate the abstract, the universal and infinite truth, to bring this truth within the scope of the senses, to give to it flesh and blood, and to make its "shadow in the finite and the particular"

24. "Orphic Sayings: VII. Spiritualism," *The Dial*, I (1840–1841), 86.
25. *Journals* (April 27, 1834), p. 41.
26. *Ibid.* (Aug. 4, 1835), p. 60.

obvious to all men.[27] This abstract, ideal truth, which was both the object of the prophet's vision and the ultimate metaphysical reality, was referred to as "Spirit" and as "God." Alcott used the latter term to designate Reality as it is in itself; the former was used specifically to refer to the creativity of God at work in the world. Through the work of the Spirit all material things could eventually become, to the creatures of sense and reason, revelations of the "invisible, spiritual Creator." A significant aspect of this revelation, however, was creativity itself; being was not to be seen as static, else the living Spirit would disappear from view and in its place there would remain only the dead husks of the outer, sensate covering. Growth, production, and progress were to be seen as indications of a living reality, as stages in the revelation of the spiritual Being. Thus interpreted, the creative facts could be taken as denoting "the Spirit struggling to represent, reveal, shadow forth itself to the sense and reason of man." [28]

This emphasis on the progressive, creative aspect of God's nature kept Alcott's metaphysical idealism from becoming pantheism. God was present in all his created works, but never wholly extant in any of them. His attributes were never fully or completely organized in any single structure. Thus Nature can never "contain" God, and the universe, at any given time, cannot be said to reveal the mysteries of his being. "He subjects his noblest works to minute and constant revision; his idea ever transcends its form; he moulds anew his own idols; both nature and man are ever making, never made." [29] Spirit is the efficient cause of this creativity. In the historical world the work of Spirit is to be seen in the dead and decaying forms of once-living things that have now been left behind in the process of creative revelation. New forms are constantly being created to contain the ever-flowing Spirit. The work of Spirit in these new forms of visible nature proceeds from the center to the circumference; thus the activity remains hidden from the senses

27. *Ibid.* (Sept. 26, 1835) , p. 66.
28. *Ibid.* (Sept. 21, 1835) , p. 65.
29. "Orphic Sayings: XXXIV. God," *The Dial,* I (1840–1841) , 93–94.

until the creativity has organized itself into concrete forms. The nature of sensory experience requires that the senses must begin their attempt to understand reality with the "appearances" of natural objects. But these appearances are dead: the "bodies" of Spirit are fleeting, historical phenomena, concretized and solidified for a moment of time, while they obscure the true working of the Spirit within. The "apparent," wrote Alcott, "is the corpse of the real; and undergoes successive sepultures and resurrections." [30] Solidity is but an illusion of the senses; beneath the apparent stability of things is a constant creativity which is the only true reality, and it is this truth that the prophetic vision grasps.

Sense looking at the historic surface beholds what it deems matter, yet is but spirit in fusion, fluent, pervaded by her own immanent vitality and trembling to organize itself. Neither matter nor death are possible: what seem matter and death are sensuous impressions, which, in our sanest moments, the authentic instincts contradict. The sensible world is spirit in magnitude, outspread before the senses for their analysis, but whose synthesis is the soul herself, whose prothesis is God. Matter is but the confine of spirit limning her to sense.[31]

Only as individual men can rise above their attention to the historical and grasp this constant creative flow can they truly know the Spirit's real work and the Reality which is made known through it. Their apprehension of this is, at one and the same time, the emerging of Spirit within themselves; it marks the dawning of their own creativity. They become new men, "reformed" beings who are now the true "reformers" of that which their lives touch. To this end, said Alcott, we need to develop "a spiritual calculus, a novum organon, whereby nature shall be divined in the soul, the soul in God, matter in spirit, polarity resolved into unity." [32] This calculus will teach the men of vision how that "power which pulsates in all life, animates and builds all organizations" can be channeled effectively through their own lives into the new forms yet to be.

30. "Orphic Sayings: XXXVI. Flux; XXXVII. Sepulture and Resurrection," *The Dial,* I (1840–1841) , 94.
31. "Orphic Sayings: XLI. Spirit and Matter," *The Dial,* I (1840–1841) , 95.
32. "Orphic Sayings: XXXI. Calculus," *The Dial,* I (1840–1841) , 93.

The application of this idea to the natural world was to provide a part of the rationale behind the Fruitlands experiment. It was not limited to the reformation or rejuvenation of natural objects, however. Alcott believed that this description of reality was true for all institutions and organizations, whether they are what we call "natural," "human," or "social." All such organizations, in their outward form, are mortal. Indeed, the "seal of death" is upon them from the moment of their birth, and they appear historically as "corpses of the real." Within them, however, to a greater or lesser extent, is Spirit with its creative, life-giving impulse. Here again, as in the natural world, the key is to be found in the men of genius. It is in the human organism, with its kinship to the material world on the one hand and its participation in a social order on the other, that Spirit has found its most acceptable and most effective residence. Through the human organism it will be enabled to carry on its work, transform all things, until its realization is complete.

This central importance of man marks him as God's noblest creation. Man is Spirit's most glorious achievement, and as such comes closest of all creatures to the achievement of that state toward which Spirit ultimately tends. This fact gives hope for man's immortality; it also gives to the man of genius a confidence in his ability to build a new and eternal Eden. Man has an "inborn immortality," the intuition of which was lost in the descent of man into the "worship of the idols of flesh and sense." [33] Since that fall from his pure Promethean state, man has been subjected to the same generation and decay which characterize all physical objects and organizations. Into this mortal matter Spirit has entered, and it emerges as the soul of man on its journey through time to immortality. But the archway which this mortal material thus forms over the bridge of time is not enduring and must continually be renewed by the creative Spirit lest the journey of the soul be interrupted. [34] Alcott did not believe, however, that this process was neces-

33. "Orphic Sayings: XI. Discontent," *The Dial,* I (1840–1841) , 87.
34. *Journals* (March 12, 1836) , p. 77.

sarily eternal. The continual refinement of the human soul by the Spirit's inhabitation might eventually lead to the freedom of the soul from its mortal dwelling place.

Possibly organization is no necessary function or mode of spiritual being. The time may come, in the endless career of the soul, when the facts of incarnation, birth, death, descent into matter and ascension from it, shall comprise no part of her history; when she herself shall survey this human life with emotions akin to those of the naturalist, on examining the relics of extinct races or beings; when mounds, sepulchres, monuments, epitaphs, shall serve but as memoirs of a past state of existence; a reminiscence of one metempsychosis of her life in time.[35]

The soul's present aspirations furnish us with intimations of this immortality. In every attempt which the soul makes to realize her potentialities, she finds herself frustrated and disappointed. And yet she never gives up the "perpetual effort to actualize her divinity in time." There is within man an instinctive tendency to fulfil his destiny, and this tendency can be seen as an "authentic augury" of the soul's original divinity and its ultimate possibilities.[36]

In the man of prophetic vision this recovery of inborn immortality is now almost complete. The Spirit within him is already strong enough to be causally effective in his creative efforts to build the true society.

Most men are on the ebb; but now and then a man comes riding down sublimely in high hope from God on the flood tide of the soul, as she sets into the coasts of time, submerging old landscapes, and laying waste the labors of centuries. A new man wears channels broad and deep into the banks of the ages; he washes away ancient boundaries, and sets afloat institutions, creeds, usages, which clog the ever-flowing Present, stranding them on the shores of the Past. Such deluge is the harbinger of a new world, a renovated age.[37]

It is important to keep in mind, in any evaluation of Alcott's actions, his conviction that the creative capacities of the "new man," the man of genius, were not limited to simple reorganization of existing social institutions. The "reform" of which he

---

35. "Orphic Sayings: XL. Organization," *The Dial,* I (1840–1841) , 95.
36. "Orphic Sayings: IX. Aspiration; X. Apotheosis," *The Dial,* I (1840–1841) , 87.
37. "Orphic Sayings: XXI. Originality," *The Dial,* I (1840–1841) , 90.

spoke was to be metaphysically significant. It would draw its effective essence from the Source of all Being as that Being found residence in the ideas of the men of genius. These ideas would "exalt and deify the thinker" and stimulate him to action. His labor would transmit this essence to the things with which he worked, reforming and renovating them and shaping a new era. Action would translate death into life as it became the means by which the Spirit, encrusted in material forms, would be freed to continue its aspiring climb to the Reality from whence it came.

This theory of creative idealism was to come to full flower in Alcott's thought in the decade preceding the Fruitlands experiment. In 1834 he had asked the crucial question:

> May we not believe that thought gives life and meaning to external nature, that what we see, hear, feel, taste, and experience around us acquire these properties by the self-investing power of our spirits, and do they not, through the vivid action, the picturing, life-starting agency of this same Spirit, rise up, tinted and shaped before us. . . ? [38]

Five years later he was beginning to give his answer to this question. He referred to the "solidarity of nature" as an illusion; to matter as "a mote floating in the beams of Spirit" and casting its "shadow on the screen of time." [39] He spoke of his bestowing "a benison on Nature whenever I walk forth in hope and joy and breathe forth my Soul into her atmosphere. I give more than I take." Man breathed, he wrote, not just to sustain life in his own body, but to renovate the "common body of Nature," the extent of the healing, salutary influence one would have upon Nature depending upon one's own virtue—his "spiritual health." [40] Theodore Parker, upon hearing Alcott voice the opinion on a particularly beautiful day that, "men must have behaved well in order to have such fine sunshine," had asked Alcott what he would do with the Mosaic account of creation that gave priority in creation to the elements rather than to man. Alcott's reply was given in terms of his theory of

38. *Journals* (June 18, 1834) , p. 44.
39. *Ibid.* (April 17, 1839) , p. 124.
40. *Ibid.* (April 27, 1839) , p. 125.

"historical account" being the reverse of "true genetic account." The Mosaic story was given "in the order of the senses"; in the "order of generation" the Soul was prior to all elements and was both the "base of matter" and that from which light was generated.[41] Alcott was to become so obsessed with this idea of the creative power of Spirit that he was even willing to stake the well-being of his family on his acceptance of it as a workable plan of action. On one occasion his wife had questioned a proposed move to the country, observing that she did not see "whence shall come bread for herself and little ones." Alcott's reply reveals how deeply rooted his idealism had become. "Neither do I see with the eyes of sense; but I know that a purpose like mine must yield bread for the hungry and clothe the naked, and I wait not for the arithmetic of this matter." [42] From that day in June, 1838, when Emerson returned Alcott's manuscript of "Psyche" with his criticisms and his suggestion that it ought not to be published, Alcott had come increasingly to the decision that he must "act." The disappointment he felt in the realization that he could not put down in words the vision he held became the catalyst that led him eventually to set these thoughts in "living speech."

His educational activities in Boston during the years immediately preceding 1838 provided him with one outlet for testing his theory. His work in this area resulted in the publication of the very controversial *Conversations with Children on the Gospels* (2 vols.; Boston, 1836, 1837). About the same time (1836), he wrote the pamphlet entitled *The Doctrine and Discipline of Human Culture,* which was later used as an introduction to the *Conversations.* Here he defined "Human Culture" as the "art of revealing to a man the true Idea of his Being—his endowments—his possessions—and of fitting him to use these for the growth, renewal, and perfection of his Spirit. It is the art of completing a man." [43] The method to be

41. *Ibid.* (April 22, 1839), pp. 124–125.
42. *Ibid.* (April 23, 1839), p. 125.
43. Alcott, *The Doctrine and Discipline of Human Culture* (Boston, 1836), in *Essays on Education (1830–1862)* by Amos Bronson Alcott, Facsimile reproductions with an Introduction by Walter Harding (Gainesville, Florida, 1960), pp. 31–32.

used in this process of human culture Alcott found exemplified in the practice of Jesus, Socrates, and Plato: the dialectic method which Alcott was to label "conversation." Through this method the latent Spirit within man was to be stimulated and brought to fruition.

In this all the instincts and faculties of our being are touched. They find full and fair scope. It tempts forth all powers. Man faces his fellow man. He holds a living intercourse. He feels the quickening life and light. The social affections are addressed; and these bring all the faculties in train. Speech comes unbidden. Nature lends her images. Imagination sends abroad her winged words. We see thought as it springs from the soul, and in the very process of growth and utterance.[44]

In order for such education to proceed the teacher must be a man already in possession of the Spirit—a man of genius, a "human nature rising superior to things and events, and transfiguring these into the image of its own Spiritual Ideal." [45] Instruction is really inspiration, and only Genius can inspire. The true teacher must remember that "instruction is something more than mere impression on the understanding." He must feel it to be a kindling influence; he must know that, in himself alone, is "the quickening, informing energy; that the life and growth of his charge preexist in him." [46]

Although Alcott's attempts to implement this theory in Boston won approval from Elizabeth Peabody and some defense from Emerson, the people of Boston reflected their general preference for more traditional methods by withdrawing their children from his school, and soon after the publication of the *Conversations* Alcott's last formal experience as a teacher came to an end. For a time thereafter he was content with his more informal "Conversations," hoping thereby to find a means of "quickening the mind of the people" and "of publishing myself." [47] But the "Conversations," while variously received, did nothing to achieve that release of Spirit which Alcott knew was necessary if the new Eden was to be realized.

44. *Ibid.*, p. 38.
45. *Ibid.*, p. 41.
46. *Ibid.*, p. 46.
47. *Journals* (Sept., 1838) , p. 103.

It is easy to caricature Alcott as a dreamer whose actions were limited to the mouthing of idealistic theories. Emerson, who knew him best perhaps, sensed the truth which such a caricature would contain. In 1842, seven years after their first meeting, Emerson wrote of him: "It must be conceded that it is speculation which he loves, not action. . . . When the conversation is ended, all is over. He lives to-morrow as he lived today, for further discourse, not to begin, as he seemed pledged to do, a new celestial life." [48] Later, after the collapse of Fruitlands, Emerson spoke of it as an illustration of those "projects that so often seem without feet and hands." Alcott, he wrote, "is an intellectual Torso,—he has vision without any talent,— a colossal head and trunk without hands or feet." [49] But Emerson was too astute an observer not to realize that this picture of his "tedious archangel" was not the complete truth. Alcott was a poet, with a poet's temperament, but unlike other poets whom Emerson knew, he believed in his images. Sanborn and Harris quote Emerson as once remarking that Alcott "exists to see and multiply" his poetic images, "to translate by them evermore history, natural and civil, and all men and events into laws." [50] Thoreau, who knew him too, spoke of him as "almost the only friend of human progress," as one in whose presence "the heavens and the earth had met together, since he enhanced the beauty of the landscape." Thoreau called him "one of the last of the philosophers," and prophesied that "though comparatively disregarded now, when his day comes, laws unsuspected by most will take effect, and masters of families and rulers will come to him for advice." [51] In later years William T. Harris was to observe this same characteristic and give to it a more precise statement. He gave to Alcott the credit for his own conviction that the soul contained certain "higher native powers, . . . by which the limits of man's sensuous experience

---

48. (March 23, 1842), *The Heart of Emerson's Journals,* ed. Bliss Perry (Boston, 1926), p. 176.
49. Quoted by Sanborn and Harris, *op. cit.,* II, 347.
50. *Ibid.,* I, 345–346.
51. *Walden,* ed. Sherman Paul (Riverside Editions; Boston, 1957), XIV, "Winter Visitors," 183–184.

could be passed over or transcended." [52] More than this single idea, however, was the influence of the person of Alcott himself: ". . . here was a living and commanding personality who held a doctrine of the supremacy of the soul and the ideality of the material world. Idealism was not a mere fanciful theory to him, but the sober truth." [53] To the task of making this truth a reality Alcott was committed, and the fact of his commitment was as real as the ideals themselves. That the vision could be made real he did not question, and he knew that the way of achievement led from the individual outward. The reformer, armed with his intuitions, his ideals, and valor, could wage successfully the war against the encrusted institutions, traditions, and customs which the centuries had built up to obscure and confuse the truth. Already the axe lay at the roots, and the man of genius needed only to give the final stroke and the wilderness of human affairs would be cleared for progressive husbandry.

These convictions were all firmly fixed in Alcott's mind before he made his trip to England and Alcott House in 1842. While there, in the company of Charles Lane and Henry Gardiner Wright, he gave to his convictions their most systematic statement. In a meeting held at Alcott House on July 6, 1842, following discussions by Wright and Lane on the need for reforms in many existing institutions, Alcott proposed the method by which such reforms were to be achieved. "In order to attain the highest excellence of which man is capable, not only is a searching Reform necessary in the existing order of men and things, but the Generation of a new race of persons is demanded." [54] This was but a restatement and extension of the earlier assertions about the significance of the man of prophetic genius. But now Alcott was ready to spell out the next step.

52. Sanborn and Harris, *op. cit.,* II, 549.
53. *Ibid.,* II, 550. Emerson, in reflecting upon those men whom he had known who "gave flesh to what were, else, mere thoughts," wrote the following: "It were too much to say that the Platonic world I might have learned to treat as a cloudland, had I not known Alcott, who is a native of that country, yet I will say that he makes it as solid as Massachusetts to me." Emerson's *Journals* (July, 1852) , p. 260.
54. Odell Shepard, *Pedlar's Progress; The Life of Bronson Alcott* (Boston, 1939) , p. 325.

. . . the elements for a superior generation consist in an innocent fertile mind and a chaste healthful body, built up from the purest and most volatile productions of the uncontaminated earth, thus removing all hindrances to the immediate influx of Deity into the spiritual faculties and the corporeal organs.[55]

By late summer of 1842, Lane and Wright had decided to return to America with Alcott and establish the "New Eden" in which to plant the "divine seed" that would restore man to this superior status. The influence which Lane and others had upon Alcott during this period cannot be ignored; yet it is true that for Alcott the opportunity seemed to open up the possibility for the "action" needed to give substance to dreams he had held for years. His enthusiasm over the prospects was so genuine that it began to infect Mrs. Alcott, although she had reservations about certain details of the plan from the beginning. Alcott had written to her of the plans, and while she could agree with Emerson that "Mr. A. lives in such a region of high hope that he does not feel the atmosphere of less elevated humanity, who are perishing in the chills of a cold and selfish world," the closing entry in her Journal for August 22, 1842, reveals a sympathy for his hopes: "With what trust has my husband felt that this great ideal, which has filled his mind and at times occupied his whole being, would be actualized! Is it not about to be realized?"[56]

In June, 1843, the great experiment began at Fruitlands, near the village of Harvard, Massachusetts. Alcott had written his rationale for the experiment in May, 1841, and published it in *The Dial* one year later. There he had spoken of the destructive tendencies of "present modes of agriculture" and of the adverse effects these tendencies had upon men. Then he described the cure and the glories of the Eden thus to be wrought:

55. *Ibid.*
56. Quoted in *Journals*, p. 146. Emerson had financed Alcott's trip to England, but he was not happy with the proposed result of his visit. While Alcott was abroad he had written to Emerson that he was bringing Lane and Wright home with him to establish a community. Emerson tells us that "I wrote him a letter, which I required him to show them, saying, that they might safely trust his theories, but that they should put no trust whatever in his statement of facts." Emerson's *Journals* (May, 1846), p. 218.

This Beast, named Man, . . . must first be transformed into very man, regenerate in appetite and desire, before the earth shall be restored to fruitfulness, and redeemed from the curse of his cupidity. Then shall the toils of the farm become elegant and invigorating leisures; man shall grow his orchards and plant his gardens,—an husbandman truly. . . . Labor will be attractive. Life will not be worn in anxious and indurating toils; it will be at once a scene of mixed leisure, recreation, labor, culture. The soil, grateful then for man's generous usage, debauched no more by foul odoures, nor worn by cupidities, shall recover its primeval virginity, bearing on its bosom the standing bounties which a sober and liberal Providence ministers to his need,—sweet and invigorating growths, for the health and comfort of the grower.[57]

The story of the failure of Fruitlands has been told too often to need repeating here. By mid-January, 1844, after seven months of hardship and increasing dissension among the members of the "household," it became obvious even to Alcott that the dream was ended. Emerson remarked that the "fault of Alcott's community is that it has only room for one."[58] He had once suggested to Alcott, as they were discussing the latter's plans for the utopian community, that Alcott's concern for his family was evidence that he was not the man who should undertake the experiment.[59] The advice went unheeded, but it placed a finger upon the fatal flaw in Alcott's dream. He was not an insensitive man, and however great his dreams, he was not unaware of what his failure meant to his family. And yet, his theory made no place for such an awareness. He was an individualist, extremely so, from first to last. While he looked upon the family as the most sacred of all institutions, he always held that the "voice of the private heart" was alone authentic.[60] He did what he could to make his family's life a pleasant one at Fruitlands, from helping with the preparation of meals to encouraging the children in their enjoyment of the pastoral setting, but his eyes were fixed on scenes too ideal to include the hardships which Mrs. Alcott and the four daughters found quite real. The clearest recognition of this comes from Mrs.

57. "Days from a Diary: VIII. Husbandry," *The Dial*, II (1841–1842), 426.
58. Emerson's *Journals* (March 24, 1846), p. 216.
59. *Ibid.* (Nov. 19, 1842), p. 191.
60. "Orphic Sayings: XVII. Theocracy," *The Dial*, I, (1840–1841), 89; "Days from a Diary: I. The Family," *The Dial*, II, (1841–1842), 410.

Alcott herself. Several weeks after the end of Fruitlands, when she had sold nearly all of her negotiable possessions in order to feed her brood and was reduced to begging from friends, she wrote, with a tinge of understandable bitterness,

> Should like to see my husband a little more interested in this matter of support. I love his faith and quiet reliance on Divine Providence, but a little more activity and industry would place us beyond most of these disagreeable dependencies upon friends. . . . Mr. Alcott is right in not working for hire, if thereby he violates his conscience; but working for bread does not necessarily imply unworthy gain.[61]

We have already noticed, however, that what Mrs. Alcott intended by "activity" and "work" was not what her husband meant. He once spoke of the prophet as having "bread in his exile which mammon knows not of," and for this bread he was willing to work—as he had worked in spading the ground at Fruitlands. But he firmly believed that the efficient cause of the bread to be produced was the spiritual power that would flow from the universal Spirit through the pure conscience of the individual. To corrupt this conscience by descending to the world of mammon would be to deny the last bridge to Eden. He could more easily accept the thought of his wife's begging for his food than he could accept the suggestion that he was wrong in his belief that "organic changes are wrought by spiritual powers." When the cold and hunger of the Massachusetts winter and the demands of his family and friends made him finally realize the futility of his dream, he fell ill, physically and mentally, and almost died of disillusionment. Two years later he expressed his hope again, but now it was the hope of a true idealist whose days of "reform" were ended.

> I fancied that of this earth a heaven could be fashioned, and set in good earnest to mould it to my ideal. My youth and early manhood was given to a strenuous and ardent toil for this end, and not till later manhood did I acquire the fruits of this endeavour—a serene and hopeful resignation to build my heaven in the mind. And lo! as this thought was born was my heaven itself born also.[62]

61. Quoted in *Journals* (Jan. 28, 1844), p. 157.
62. *Journals* (March, 1846), p. 174.

Fruitlands was a failure, but in the history of American transcendentalism it must be counted as a glorious failure. Its failure was the proof of the subjective, intuitive character of the transcendentalist ideal. Alcott tried to incarnate the ideal in a world in which it would not fit; in so doing he forgot that the "archangel" belongs not to this world, and in that forgetting he became less the transcendentalist. But his failure brought him around again to see that "One cannot people a world of ideas with clowns and brutes, nor create an apartment in the ideal mansion of road-dust and locust thorns." [63]

63. *Journals* (April 25, 1846) , p. 177.

Ontology and Christology: The Apologetic Theology of Paul Tillich

JOHN PEMBERTON

Ever since the famous debate between Karl Barth and Emil Brunner in 1934 regarding the Christian conception of general revelation and special revelation Protestant theologians have again had to come to grips with the question of whether apologetics is a legitimate activity of Christian theology.[1] In that debate, as well as later, Barth, armed with deep insight into the biblical revelation concerning man and the gospel and with theological virtuosity, called into question and denied a legitimate place to apologetics in Christian theology. In the "introduction" to the first volume of his *Church Dogmatics* Barth declared:

Really responsible, up-to-date theological thought, in genuine rapprochement with its contemporaries, will reveal itself to be such even today (if by God's grace it is all this!) by refusing to discuss the basis of its ground, questions such as whether God is, whether there is such a thing as revelation, etc., but also . . . by actually achieving its own consummation as thought on this ground and by being thereby actually on the spot, as the witness of faith against unbelief. There is no dispute about the fact that dogmatics too, together with the Christian Church generally, has to speak all along the line as faith opposing unbelief, and that to that extent all along the line her language must be apologetic, polemical. But there has never been any other effective apologetic and polemic of faith against unbelief than the unintended one (impossible to

1. For the controversy between Barth and Brunner, see Emil Brunner, *Natural Theology*. Comprising "Nature and Grace" by Emil Brunner and the reply "No!" by Karl Barth, trans. Peter Fraenkel (London, 1946).

intend! purely experiential!) which took place when God Himself sided with the witness of faith.[2]

Impressed by Barth's insight and fidelity to the biblical and Reformation doctrine of *gratia sola,* but undaunted by his charge of "natural theology," many Protestant theologians have sought in the last two and a half decades to understand anew the place and function of the apologetic task of Christian theology. H. H. Farmer's *The World and God* (1935) and *Towards Belief In God* (1943), Karl Heim's *God Transcendent* (English translation, 1936) and *Christian Faith and Natural Science* (English translation, 1953), Edgar P. Dickie's *Revelation and Response* (1938), John Baillie's *Our Knowledge of God* (1939), Emil Brunner's *Revelation and Reason* (English translation, 1941), H. Richard Niebuhr's *The Meaning of Revelation* (1941), and Alan Richardson's *Christian Apologetics* (1947) are familiar to American students of the problem. As important as their individual contributions have been, however, no one of these theologians has defended the apologetic task more vigorously or with greater perception than Paul Tillich. It is Tillich who has emerged as a theological colossus in the American scene and who has responded to Barth's challenge in the name of apologetic theology with an artistically ingenious system, a rigid discipline, and a high intellectual quality.

Tillich's Concern

In contrast to the majority of the apologists who have preceded him, Tillich's approach to the apologetic task is not based upon a concern to delineate a region within human experience which can be called "religious" and which can be considered safe from the threats posed by the rest of man's cognitive activities. He rejects both the Thomistic concern to provide for an emancipated reason by which man can reach through his own

2. Karl Barth, *The Doctrine of the Word of God* (*Prolegomena to Church Dogmatics,* being Vol. I, Pt. 1), trans. G. T. Thomson (Edinburgh, 1936), p. 31.

efforts a body of theological truth and the liberal Protestant concern to demonstrate how the Christian faith can be derived from man's natural state—a creation of man's religious self-realization.[3] Tillich is not interested in making the Christian faith acceptable to its cultured despisers, or concerned to be "modern" in the sense in which Schleiermacher in his addresses *On Religion* sought to participate in the deepening cultural awareness of the Enlightenment and to speak in good conscience of the human spirit and its religious potentialities.[4] Rather, Tillich is concerned to witness to the redeeming truth of the Christian faith in a chaotic world. His fundamental desire is to speak the healing word of Christ to the man of today: "the autonomous man who has become insecure in his autonomy" and "who no longer possesses a world view in the sense of a body of assured convictions about God, the world, and himself." [5] This is the task of theology: to mediate "between the eternal criterion of truth as manifest in the picture of Jesus as the Christ" and the cultural situation of the man of today.[6]

There are, I believe, two principle sources for Tillich's understanding of the apologetic task in Christian theology. The first is the insight provided by his revered teacher, Martin Kahler, into "the all-controlling character of the Pauline-Lutheran idea of justification." [7] This central "material" principle of Protestantism Tillich discovered was not only relevant to the religious-ethical situation as defined and emphasized by the Reformation, but also to the religious-intellectual life of man:

Not only he who is in sin but also he who is in doubt is justified through faith. The situation of doubt, even of doubt about God, need not separate us from God. There is faith in every serious doubt, namely, the faith in the truth as such, even if the truth we can express is our lack of truth. But if this is experienced in its depth and as an ultimate concern, the divine is present; and he who doubts in such an attitude is "justified" in his thinking. . . . It is

3. Paul Tillich, *Systematic Theology* (Chicago, 1951) , I, 65.
4. Note especially the second and third speeches. Friedrich Schleiermacher, *On Religion: Speeches to its Cultured Despisers,* trans. John Oman (New York, 1958) , pp. 26–145.
5. Tillich, *The Protestant Era,* trans. James L. Adams (Chicago, 1948) , p. 192.
6. *Ibid.,* p. xiii.
7. Tillich, *The Interpretation of History,* trans. N. A. Rasetzki and E. L. Talmey (New York, 1936) , p. 32; also *The Protestant Era,* pp. xiii-xiv.

this radical and universal interpretation of the doctrine of justification through faith which has made me a conscious Protestant.[8]

Tillich's broad understanding and use of the Pauline-Lutheran
insight will be discussed later in this essay. It is sufficient now
to note that the discovery of "the Protestant principle" of justification through faith and above all its relevance to the whole
of man's life, cognitive as well as ethical, was a determinative
factor in directing Tillich to the apologetic task.

A second principle source of Tillich's apologetic concern is
his experience of the church's failure in the revolutionary twenties and thirties in Europe.[9] The horror and tragedy of World
War I ended much of the power and relevance of liberal theology; the shallowness of its optimistic estimate of man was revealed to all. The postwar period saw social and economic
revolution spread throughout Europe, bringing collapse of imperial Germany and threatening the church with a similar
fate because of its identification with the ruling groups. Protesting groups emerging from industrialized masses—speaking
with social conscience through the arts, Marxist philosophy,
and labor institutions—increasingly divorced the proletariat
from the socially and politically conservative Lutheran churches.
The ensuing political struggle, centered upon the problem of
authority and the nature and destiny of political community,
betrayed the inability of the church to speak the redeeming
Word to the situation, and produced the demonic institutions
of National Socialism. What did such upheavals mean? Why
had the Christian churches been unable to speak? Whence
came the few words of prophetic insight and protest spoken
outside the church? Had the church any power to speak effectively to the present age?

Searching for answers to these questions, Tillich examined
the religious and cultural situation of his day in terms of the
Protestant principle, seeking a new interpretation of history

8. *The Protestant Era,* pp. xiv, xv.
9. Tillich, "Autobiographical Reflections," C. W. Kegley and R. W. Bretall
(eds.) , *The Library of Living Theology; The Theology of Paul Tillich* (New
York, 1952) , I, 12–16; "Author's Introduction," *The Protestant Era,* ix–xxix, and
"Storms of Our Times" in the same volume, pp. 237–252; *The Religious Situation,* trans. H. R. Niebuhr (New York, 1956) , pp. 103–219.

and culture to provide a theological basis for Christian social ethics. For Tillich the apologetic task of theology is concerned with the redemption of, not an accommodation to, culture. Apologetic theology must be ethically and sotereologically concerned to be Christian.

Religion and Culture

In 1926 Tillich published *Die Religiöse Lage der Gegenwart*,[10] in which he sought to assess various developments in Western culture that had taken place during the twentieth century. By "religious situation" Tillich refers to more than churches and creeds.

Human religion from this point of view is only a part of the total phenomenon; it is that part which testifies to the ultimate meaning and which has been especially called to do so since by nature it seeks to be in relation to the eternal. But it is not the only phenomenon which bears witness to the ultimate and in some periods it is not even the most important of the witnesses or the most effective in expression and symbolism.[11]

"Religious situation" refers to "the unconscious faith which is . . . the presupposition of life and is lived rather than thought of." [12] Thus, to seek to discover the religious situation of an age is to analyze the "ultimate concern" expressed in the productions of its science and art, in the political and economic structures, and in the philosophical and ethical principles that it adopts. It is as much from "secular culture" that one discovers the religious situation of an age as from ecclesiastic institutions and theological pronouncements. Every form of cultural expression contains both immediate concern (for example, the ordering of social relations) and reflection of ultimate concern. It contains a judgment about "the whole of human reality, the structure, the meaning, and the aim of existence." [13] Such judgment is religious, essentially decisional, not

10. Tillich, *Die Religiöse Lage der Gegenwart* (Berlin, 1926). Subsequent references are to H. R. Niebuhr's translation, *The Religious Situation* (New York, 1956).
11. *Ibid.*, p. 37.
12. *Ibid.*, p. 40.
13. *Systematic Theology*, I, 14.

open to experimental verification. Religion, therefore, is not a special function of the human spirit, having to do with cultic as over against moral, cognitive, and aesthetic functions. Religion is the ultimate concern manifest in *all* these functions. The unconditional seriousness of the moral demand, the passionate longing for ultimate reality, the infinite desire to express ultimate meaning—all of these concerns are states of "being grasped by something unconditional, holy, absolute." [14] Hence, Tillich took as the central proposition of his philosophy of religion: "Religion is the substance of culture, culture is the expression of religion." [15]

As Tillich noted, his definition of religious faith as ultimate concern is "rather near" Schleiermacher's "feeling of absolute dependence." [16] So important is the similarity that it is worth quoting Tillich at length:

No present-day theology should avoid a discussion of Schleiermacher's experiential method, whether in agreement or disagreement. One of the causes for the disquieting effect of neo-orthodox theology was that it detached itself completely from Schleiermacher's method, consequently denying the theological development of the last two hundred years. . . . The crucial question of theology today is whether or not, or to what degree, this denial is justified. Certainly it would not be justified if it were based only on a mistaken interpretation of Schleiermacher. But more than this is involved in the neo-orthodox judgment. A psychological interpretation of Schleiermacher's famous definition of religion is mistaken and even unfair, inasmuch as it can easily be avoided. When he defined religion as the "feeling of absolute dependence," "feeling" meant the immediate awareness of something unconditional in the sense of the Augustinian-Franciscan tradition. "Feeling," in this tradition, referred not to a psychological function but to the awareness of that which transcends intellect and will, subject and object. "Dependence," in Schleiermacher's definition, was, on the Christian level, "teleological" dependence—a dependence which has moral character. . . . Schleiermacher's "feeling of absolute dependence" was rather near to what is called in the present system "ultimate concern about the ground and meaning of our being."

14. *The Protestant Era*, p. 59. See also "Religion," *Perspectives U. S. A.*, No. 15 (Spring, 1956), pp. 43–48; *Dynamics of Faith* (New York, 1958), pp. 1–29; *Systematic Theology*, I, 11–15.

15. *The Protestant Era*, p. xviii.

16. *Systematic Theology*, I, 42.

Understood in this way, it lies beyond much of the usual criticism directed against it.[17]

This acknowledged appreciation of, if not return to, Schleiermacher's theological method is of the first importance for understanding Tillich's reaffirmation of the apologetic task in Christian theology.

The common soil of German idealism in which the thought of both roots in part effects Tillich's deep respect for Schleiermacher. In Tillich's estimation German idealism was in some measure a recovery of the Augustinian-Franciscan tradition in the philosophy of religion. In its "re-establishing the *prius* of subject and object," [18] the Absolute which precedes everything that has being and in virtue of which knowing and acting can take place, idealism recovered the Augustinian-Franciscan principle of the immediate awareness of being itself *(esse ipsum)*, which is, at the same time, truth itself *(verum ipsum)*, or God.[19]

While Schleiermacher acknowledged with idealism a prior reality, an epistemological and moral prius transcending the observable world and immediately known, he rejected the turn that realism took in the metaphysical and speculative orientation of Hegel and Schelling. For him the speculative turn was incompatible with the theological enterprise. He wrote to Lücke, "I shall never be able to accept the idea that my belief in Christ stems from knowledge or philosophy, which ever philosophy it might be." [20] But Schleiermacher's fundamental reliance upon "the Augustinian" dimension of idealism is evidenced throughout his theological system.

In the fourth proposition in the "Introduction" to *The Christian Faith* Schleiermacher wrote:

The common element in all howsoever diverse expressions of piety, by which these are conjointly distinguished from all other feelings, or, in other words, the self-identical essence of piety, is this: the

17. *Ibid.,* I, 43.
18. Tillich, "Two Types of Philosophy of Religion," *Theology of Culture,* ed. R. C. Kimball (New York, 1959), p. 21.
19. Tillich quotes Augustine: "When I have found the truth, there I have found my God, the truth itself." *Theology of Culture,* p. 12.
20. Quoted in Karl Barth, *Protestant Thought: from Rousseau to Ritschl,* trans. J. Pelikan (New York, 1959), p. 329. Hereinafter cited as *Protestant Thought.*

consciousness of being absolutely dependent, or, which is the same thing, of being in relation with God.[21]

Schleiermacher sought to establish, if not a point of identity, at least a basis for an awareness of something unconditional, a *prius,* which overcomes the separation of being and knowing, and which would provide an intelligible basis for commending the Christian faith to the non-Christian thinker. This he claimed to have discovered in the "highest" knowledge of human self-awareness.

Schleiermacher identified three grades of self-consciousness: "the confused animal grade," in which the antithesis between self and other cannot arise, as the lowest; "the sensible self-consciousness," which rests entirely upon the antithesis, as the middle; and "the feeling of absolute dependence," in which the antithesis again disappears and the subject unites and identifies itself with everything which, in the middle grade, was set over against it, as the highest.[22] In his experience of the world man always stands over against an "other," an object with respect to which he knows or acts. Furthermore, man is relatively free, relatively dependent: dependent upon the object for knowing, he may respond to the object with some freedom, i.e., self-determination. Man's situation, however, precludes the possibility of the experience of absolute freedom, not the experience of absolute dependence. There is the experience of that which is not the world upon which we are dependent, "the consciousness that the whole of our spontaneous activity comes from a source outside us." [23] It is that moment in which the self is aware of "the consummating point of the self-consciousness," [24] the *"whence* of our receptive and active existence which," according to Schleiermacher, "is to be designated by the word 'God.' " [25] Our experience of the whence of our being cannot be referred to in terms of an objective reference point, for to deal with God as an object is not to deal with God, but

21. Schleiermacher, *The Christian Faith,* trans. H. R. Mackintosh and J. B. Stewart (Edinburgh, 1928) , p. 12.
22. *Ibid.,* pp. 19–20.
23. *Ibid.,* p. 16.
24. *Ibid.,* p. 21.
25. *Ibid.,* p. 16.

with some aspect of the world. "God" signifies the co-determinant of man's feeling of absolute dependence, not an object of human knowledge.[26]

As Barth has observed, Schleiermacher, having rejected speculative theology by setting knowledge and being in opposition, sought to establish "a bracket beyond the antithesis," namely, the feeling of absolute dependence or an immediate self-awareness in its correlation to God.[27]

Tillich, like Schleiermacher, begins with the general religious premise discoverable in the experience of ultimate concern. But unlike Schleiermacher, Tillich does not proceed with the same ease from reflection upon sensible self-consciousness to a pious self-consciousness, the correlate of which is God. It is important that the similarity and the difference be made clear.

Like Schleiermacher, Tillich maintains that one cannot speak literally of an object of religion, for that which is ultimate, unconditional (hence holy and sacred) "gives itself only to the attitude of ultimate concern. It is the correlate of an unconditional concern but not a 'highest thing' called 'the absolute' or 'the unconditional,' about which we could argue in detached objectivity." [28] Tillich agrees with Schleiermacher's conviction regarding the necessity of the religious premise in human experience, but he does not treat it with the ease or good conscience of Schleiermacher.

Behind Tillich's use of the term *Das Unbedingte* ("the unconditional") is Schelling's *Das Unvordenkliche* ("that which is prior to thought"). Schelling had held that the subject-object dualism of empirical knowledge presupposed a prior unity in virtue of which the distinction was possible. This prior identity of opposites can never itself be an object. It is rather the "absolute Prius" and "absolute Productivity" which makes possible thinking and creative activity.

"The ultimate question is ever, Why is there something, why is there not nothing?" This cannot be shown through thinking, but the Idealist's doubt as to whether there is a something truly existing

26. *Ibid.,* pp. 16–17.
27. Barth, *Protestant Thought,* pp. 328–330.
28. Tillich, *Systematic Theology,* I, 12.

presupposes a truly existing (Ib. 242), something that precedes everything that goes forth out of potency. . . . It may be designated "pure actuality itself" (W. II, 1, 391) or "The self-Existing, auto to on (Ib. 314)." [29]

Schelling was primarily concerned to establish the first principle of all philosophy in terms of which to understand both empirical knowledge and artistic creation. It would appear that Tillich's use of "the unconditional" refers not only to the idealistic, self-developing principle of Schelling, but also involves something of Rudolf Otto's idea of the "holy," the *mysterium tremendum,* and something of the biblical prophetic protest against idolatry. In its positive function "the unconditional" is the "power of being . . . of everything that has being." [30] It also performs the negative function of protesting against the spirit of self-sufficient finitude and destroys every attempt to render the *prius* an object. [31]

Tillich expresses man's experience, individual and social, of the unconditional with two New Testament terms: "Kairos" and "the demonic." In the New Testament Kairos means "the fulness of time" and "describes the moment in which the eternal breaks into the temporal, and the temporal is prepared to receive it." [32] Kairos is not perfection or completion in time, as in the idea of the Golden Age: it is experienced in tangible and, thus, manageable form. It is rather a quality of experience which invades the temporal order at some particular moment, transforming chronology into history, bestowing upon time direction, purpose, and meaning. To experience Kairos is to be turned toward, and to know, the eternal either as judgment upon the self-sufficient attitude of one's own life or culture or as salvation in the disclosure of "depth" and "power" to one's

29. Rowland Gray-Smith, *God in the Philosophy of Schelling* (Philadelphia, 1933), p. 81.
30. Tillich, "The Two Types of Philosophy of Religion," *Theology of Culture,* p. 25. See *The Religious Situation,* pp. 58, 63; *The Protestant Era,* p. 32, n. 1.
31. James Luther Adams writes: "As Tillich uses it, the German term *Das Unbedingte* connotes . . . the sovereign, the commanding, that which cannot be tampered with, that which makes demands that cannot be ignored with impunity" ("Tillich's Concept of the Protestant Era," *The Protestant Era,* p. 300). See Tillich, *The Religious Situation,* pp. 73, 191 ff.
32. *The Protestant Era,* p. xix; See Tillich's essay "Kairos," *The Protestant Era,* pp. 32–54; *The Religious Situation,* pp. 18 f.

individual or social situation. Every individual and every period stands in relation to the eternal, but this relation is not always acknowledged and known.

To account for man's ignorance of the eternal and his failure to receive Kairos as salvation Tillich employs the New Testament concept of "the demonic." Biblically the demonic refers to man's possession by that which is destructive of personality: the experience of the power of evil.[33] The demonic is not mere negation. It is the perversion of the creative into the self-destructive. Like "the carpenter" of Isaiah who chooses a tree and takes part of it and warms himself, kindles a fire and bakes bread, and makes a god of the residue, praying, "Deliver me, for thou art my god!" the propensity of man in every age to make unqualified claims for that which is finite stands under the prophetic judgment: "He feeds on ashes; a deluded mind has led him astray, and he cannot deliver himself or say, "Is there not a lie in my right hand?" [34] Like Augustine, Tillich transforms the biblical notion into a concept applicable to social movements. Every period has its cultural forms in terms of which it seeks to realize and express itself. But accompanying the element of creative responsibility is the possibility of the creation of destructive forms: political, economic, social, and religious. In our age, according to Tillich, these are the forms of self-sufficient finitude expressed in the spirit of capitalist society, of religious-political nationalism, or of ecclesiastical institutionalism. And these structures produce individual and social tragedy as they overwhelm the freedom and destroy the meaningful creations of men.[35] It is not historical conditioning or finitude which corrupt the creative possibilities of the forms and structures of a culture and an age. Rather, it is the consequent of the universal character of man's existential situation:

33. *The Protestant Era*, p. xx.
34. Isaiah 44:18–20. Although Tillich always refers to the New Testament notion of the demonic, the Isaiah passage presents, I believe, the real clue to the New Testament use of the demonic. In the New Testament the terms "Satan," "Be-elzebul," and "demon" give figural realism to man's experience of the demonic, and the exorcism scenes portray the structure of evil that haunts human existence. See *Romans*, especially chaps. 7 and 8.
35. See *The Religious Situation*, pp. 105–154.

"his estrangement from his essential being." [36] The demonic is thus the profaning of the holy, the disavowal of that which is truly unconditional, the attempt by individuals or an age to say, "Come, let us build ourselves a city, and a tower with its top in the heavens. . . ." [37]

With the concepts of "the unconditional," "Kairos," and "the demonic" Tillich develops a new interpretation of history and culture. In terms of the "material" principle of Protestantism, and the concepts just discussed, one can discern three types of periodization in history: the autonomous, the heteronomous, and the theonomous.

By *autonomy* Tillich means "obedience to reason," [38] man's rational response to the rational structure of reality; the response of the logos of the human mind to the Logos immanent in reality. Autonomy is "the dynamic principle of history," [39] creating cultural forms and structures as men respond to demands of their existence. However, when autonomy becomes not only "the dynamic principle" but also "the substance and meaning" of history, it becomes destructive. For in its valid concern to order, control, relate, and express through forms and structures, there is the temptation to claim for reason a self-sufficiency, rendering the means of form-creating an end in itself. The inevitable result is the substitution of some aspect of the finite world for the infinite, the conditioned for the unconditional. It is, as Tillich observes, to confuse *sapientia* with *scientia*, the level of being and truth as such with the level of the antithesis of subject and object, thereby reducing the realm of truth to the realm of observable and calculable relations. Man's rational capacity for the creation of forms and structures becomes identified with a technical employment of reason, producing an attitude of self-sufficiency and therewith "the loss of control by human reason over man's historical existence." [40]

In contrast to autonomy the periods of history characterized

36. *Systematic Theology*, II, 74.
37. Genesis 11:4.
38. *The Protestant Era*, p. 44.
39. *Ibid.*, p. 45.
40. Tillich, "The World Situation," ed. H. P. VanDusen, *The Christian Answer* (New York, 1945), p. 4.

by *heteronomy* have been those in which "an alien law, religious or secular," has been imposed on man's mind. Heteronomy, according to Tillich,

disregards the logos structure of mind and world. It destroys the honesty of truth and the dignity of the moral personality. It undermines creative freedom and the humanity of man. Its symbol is the "terror" exercised by absolute churches or absolute states. Religion, if it acts heteronomously, has ceased to be the substance and life blood of a culture and has become a section of it, which . . . betrays a mixture of arrogance and defeatism.[41]

The late medieval doctrine of papal infallibility, post-Edwardean New England Puritanism and the doctrine of predestination, and the American South and the doctrine of racial segregation all illustrate Tillich's thesis.

Over against both autonomy and heteronomy and their cultural expressions Tillich poses *theonomy,* the law of God, and the theonomous culture, in which all cultural forms appear in their relation to the unconditional. "The divine, for such a state of mind, is not a problem but a presupposition." [42] Theonomy is the recognition of the structure of grace that underlies and provides the substance for the structure of reason. And that culture which in its autonomy transcends itself, saying "no" to every attempt to absolutize the finite, and affirms the structure of grace is a culture open to and directed toward the divine.

Tillich's analysis of culture proceeds from a concern to provide a new basis for social ethics: And before the church can speak the redeeming Word to the present situation, it must recognize the true nature of the religious situation. The sense of responsibility for the cultural world was a part of Tillich's heritage from his German intellectual forebears. Schelling maintained that behind the plurality of cultural forms was a fundamental unity, the "divine essence," "informing" every cultural production.[43] And Schleiermacher, as Barth has observed,

41. *The Protestant Era,* p. 46.
42. *Ibid.,* p. 43.
43. Commenting on the relation of religion and art, Schelling wrote: "The inner bond that unites Art and Religion . . . raises to a necessity the scientific

. . . also felt responsible . . . for the intellectual and moral foundations of the cultural world into which a man was born at the end of the eighteenth century. He wanted in all circumstances to be a modern man as well as a Christian theologian. . . . He took part in the philosophy, science, politics, social life and art of his time as if they were his own concern, as the man who was responsible in all these fields, the man who was called to achieve and to lead in the general achievement.[44]

But it is also important to realize that Schleiermacher was not concerned to share in the cultural developments just to show that Christianity and Enlightenment culture were compatible. As Barth notes, Schleiermacher was concerned to show the continuity between cultural achievement and the Christian faith by establishing the continuity between sensible self-consciousness and pious self-consciousness, and to establish "religion as a necessary manifestation of human intellectual life." [45] Barth continues:

Without that highest unity of intuition and feeling, as Schleiermacher said in his *Addresses,* or without the feeling of utter dependence, as he puts it in the *Doctrine of Faith,* cultural awareness would be incomplete, a headless torso.[46]

Tillich is concerned to restore to twentieth-century theology Schleiermacher's notion of religion as the all-embracing function of man's spiritual (i.e., dynamic-creative) life.[47] Furthermore, Tillich shares Schleiermacher's "ethical" concern to establish the continuity or necessary relationship of not only religion and culture, but Christianity and culture. In an early essay entitled "The Interpretation of History and the Idea of Christ," Tillich wrote: " 'Christ and history' is the combination of two concepts, neither of which can be treated completely without reference to their connection. At some point Christology meets the concept of history, and at some point the analysis of the nature of history inevitably leads to the question of Chris-

---

knowledge of Art on the part of the genuinely pious man" (quoted in Gray-Smith, *op. cit.,* p. 44) . Cf. Tillich's discussion of religion and art in *The Religious Situation,* pp. 85–102; "Existentialist Aspects of Modern Art," ed. C. Michalson, *Christianity and the Existentialists* (New York, 1956) , pp. 128–147.

44. Barth, *Protestant Thought,* p. 314.
45. *Ibid.,* p. 330.
46. *Ibid.*
47. Tillich, *Systematic Theology,* I, 15.

tology." [48] Some years later Tillich wrote: "Apologetic Theology must show that trends which are immanent in all religions and cultures move toward the Christian answer." [49]

But there is, I believe, a significant difference between the religiously informed cultural awareness of Schleiermacher and that of Tillich. Tillich has a far greater sense of the tension between the forms of cultural expression and "the unconditional" disclosed in and through the forms. Tillich is never unaware of the prophetic and Protestant principle of grace. Furthermore, Tillich's experience of the political and social tragedy of the twentieth century leads him to place greater emphasis upon the reality of destructive structures in man's cultural experience. There is for Tillich a far greater discontinuity between man's essential nature and his existential situation than for Schleiermacher, under the influence of the Enlightenment, could be aware of: a discontinuity that did not permit the easy conscience of liberal Protestantism in explicating the fundamental relationship of religion and culture.

It is now necessary to ask the question about the relation of Tillich's analysis of religion and culture to his conception of the apologetic task of Christian theology.

Philosophy of Religion and Apologetic Theology

Tillich in the first volume of his *Systematic Theology* writes thus of theology:

A theological system is supposed to satisfy two basic needs: the statement of the Christian message and the interpretation of this truth for every new generation. Theology moves back and forth between two poles, the eternal truth of its foundation and the temporal situation in which the eternal truth must be received. [50]

Too often Tillich's critics, and his followers, have placed their emphasis upon "the interpretation" and upon "the temporal situation." In so doing they have failed to see Tillich's appreciation of the kerygmatic basis of all theological state-

48. *The Interpretation of History*, p. 242.
49. *Systematic Theology*, I, 15.
50. *Ibid.*, I, 3.

ments and have failed to heed Tillich's warning against trying to derive the contents of the Christian message from man's "religious situation." [51]

As Tillich recognizes, it is the kerygma, the gospel of God's action in Jesus Christ, that is the distinctively Christian dimension of Christian theology. This and this alone is the unchangeable truth standing over against the changing demands of every age and situation. In large measure the history of Christian thought is the record of those voices calling the church back to her center. This according to Tillich was the mission of Martin Luther in the sixteenth century and of Karl Barth in our own day.

> Luther's criticism of the Roman system of mediations and degrees in the name of the decisive biblical categories of judgment and grace, his rediscovery of the Pauline message, and, at the same time, his courageous evaluation of the spiritual value of the biblical books were a genuine kerygmatic theology. Barth's criticism of the neo-Protestant-bourgeois synthesis achieved by liberal theology, his rediscovery of the Christian paradox, and, at the same time, the freedom of his spiritual exegesis of the Epistle to the Romans and his acceptance of radical historical criticism were a genuine kerygmatic theology. In both cases there was an emphasis on the eternal truth over against the human situation and its demands. Without such kerygmatic reactions theology would lose itself in the relativi- t..s of the "situation." [52]

But kerygmatic theology alone is not enough. It must be related to and received by men in their situation, and in terms of the peculiar questions raised by their generation. Thus, for Tillich, "the task of theology is mediation, mediation between the eternal criterion of truth as it is manifest in the picture of Jesus as the Christ and the changing experiences of individuals and groups, their varying questions and their categories of perceiving reality." [53] The greatness of Barth, according to Tillich, is not only his recovery of the gospel for twentieth-century theology, but his capacity to correct himself again and again in the light of the situation. Yet Barth, insofar as Tillich can see, does not realize that in doing so he ceases to be a merely keryg-

51. See *ibid.*, I, 42.
52. *Ibid.*, I, 5.
53. Tillich, *The Protestant Era*, p. xiii.

matic theologian.[54] Barth is so concerned to preserve the freedom of God and so acutely aware of man's propensity to transform the gospel through culture that he denies the mediating task of theology and professes, as a Christian theologian, to be unconcerned with man's cultural expressions. But for Tillich theology without concern for the situation becomes either idolatrous by baptizing the language and world view of a particular period or irrelevant by trying to speak an esoteric language divorced from every day and age. Kerygmatic theology, according to Tillich, has traditionally fallen prey to both of these dangers. And in the process it has become irresponsible in its failure to answer the question of how the message can be received, let alone expressed.[55]

If the task of theology is to mediate between the eternal truth manifest in Jesus as the Christ and the cultural situation of a particular period, then theology is "apologetic," i.e., "an answering theology." [56] To proclaim Christ is to answer the questions raised by men about the meaning of their existence. The task of theology is "to correlate the questions implied in the situation with the answers implied in the message." [57] The theologian attempts to bring together Christ and culture in such a way that Christ transforms culture by saying "no" to every attempt at the exaltation of the finite, and by speaking the redemptive word of reconciliation to the man made insecure by the world of judgment, and thereby providing a new basis for cultural development.

As Barth and Tillich are both aware, apologetic theology exists on the assumption that there is a common ground, however vague it may be, between the eternal message and the human situation. The question of the validity of this assumption separates Barth and Tillich drastically in their understanding of the task of theology. In his essay on Schleiermacher Barth defined apologetics as "an attempt to show . . . that the de-

54. *Systematic Theology*, I, 5.
55. See Tillich, "The Present Theological Situation in the Light of the Continental European Development," *Theology Today*, VI (Oct., 1949) , 305.
56. *Systematic Theology*, I, 7.
57. *Ibid.*, I, 8.

termining principles of philosophy and of historical and natural research at some given point in time certainly do not preclude, even if they do not directly require, the tenets of theology, which are founded upon revelation and upon faith respectively." But Barth adds: "as long as he is an apologist the theologian must renounce his theological function. In so far as the apologist approaches the educated among the despisers of religion . . . *He must present himself to them in a part which is provided for in their categories,* which really occurs or can occur there." [58] Tillich agrees with Barth that the first task of "theology is the methodical interpretation of the contents of the Christian faith," but adds, in sharp contrast: "It is the task of apologetic theology to prove that the Christian claim also has validity from the point of view of those outside the theological circle." [59]

Although fully aware that a theology which acknowledges a common ground with those outside the "theological circle" can destroy the uniqueness of its message through accommodation, Tillich insists that theology by its very nature must take this risk, and that this risk continually reminds the theologian that his task, while the consequence of a divine action, is nonetheless a human enterprise.[60] What is the common ground upon which the theologian ventures with risk, but also with the hope of mediating between the eternal message and the situation of the unbeliever? Already in Tillich's analysis of religion and culture the common ground appears as the universal experience of "ultimate concern."

Tillich defines revelation in *Systematic Theology* as "the manifestation of what concerns us ultimately." [61] But now the question must be asked: What is the cognitive status of revelation which permits it to become the common ground of the apologetic task?

In *Systematic Theology* in the study of religious knowledge, Tillich makes a basic distinction "between an ontological and

58. *Protestant Thought*, pp. 320–321, 323–324. (Italics mine.)
59. *Systematic Theology*, I, 15.
60. *Ibid.*, I, 6–11.
61. *Ibid.*, I, 110.

a technical concept of reason."[62] This distinction is not new with Tillich. The distinction he feels pervades all philosophical reflection; although most philosophers fall into traditions emphasizing one understanding of the function of reason or the other. The technical concept of reason is reason reduced to the capacity for "reasoning," concerned with and competent for knowledge and management of the world which lies to hand— the "I-it" world of Martin Buber or Karl Heim. Ontological reason, on the other hand, is the structure of the mind (or logos) by which human reason is primordially conformed to the structure of Being (Logos), and it is the transparency of this reason to its "depth," to the "abyss" of Being, which is revelation of Being.[63]

This distinction of ontological and technical reason serves Tillich in two ways. In the first place, it enables him to point to the limits of controlling reason and to technical reason's dependence upon ontological reason. The special function of technical reason is to enable man to establish a consistent, logical, and correctly derived organism of thought, but it cannot grasp structures, Gestalt processes, values, or meanings without ontological reason. Technical reason unaided dehumanizes man. In the second place, the distinction provides for scientific knowledge without jeopardizing distinctive religious truth. The world of technical reason is the world of subject-object polarity and the means-end relation. Neither are its findings relevant nor do they pose a threat to religious truth. Thus "theology cannot accept the support of technical reason in 'reasoning' the existence of God. Such a god would belong to the means-end relationship. He would be less than God."[64]

But reason is not merely finite. It constantly reaches beyond its technical employment in quest of an ultimate destiny by which to guide the activity of technical reason, or in its rejection of limited, finite ends that destroy reason's freedom and deny the depth of rational experience. This depth of reason, or on-

62. *Ibid.,* I, 72.
63. *Ibid.,* I, 75, 79.
64. *Ibid.,* I, 74.

tological reason, is the acknowledgement not only of the rational structure of reality in terms of which the mind can grasp reality. It is also the acknowledgement of the prius or as Tillich describes it, the " 'substance,' which appears in the rational structure, of 'being-itself' which is manifest in the *logos* of being, or the 'ground' which is creative in every rational creation, . . . or the 'infinite potentiality of being and meaning' which pours into the rational structures of mind and reality, actualizing and transforming them." [65] The overcoming of the cleavage between subject and object, therefore, is in virtue of their prior (ontological and hence logically understood) participation in being-itself.

To speak of reason in terms of its ground, or being-itself, is to speak of the divine. It is to raise the question of pure actuality, and hence the question of freedom and destiny. It is to raise the question of the Unchangeable, and hence the question of truth and goodness.[66] To speak thus is to speak of revelation: "the manifestation of the ground of being for human knowledge." [67] And for Tillich "the religious word for what is called the ground of being is God." [68] What is the meaning of such an identification and how is it possible?

There is a story that once at Harvard a brave, if not brazen, sophomore asked Tillich "Does God exist?" Immediately Tillich replied: "Of course not! God is the ground of being which makes existence possible." Tillich dismisses all arguments for the existence of God as of no consequence, except as their very existence reflects man's concern for ultimate meaning. Existence cannot be a predicate of God, for God does not exist in the way things or persons exist. God is not part of the world. God is "being-itself beyond essence and existence." [69]

The term "being-itself" is the one nonsymbolic, completely

65. *Ibid.*, I, 79.
66. "The Two Types of Philosophy of Religion," *loc. cit.*, p. 14.
67. *Systematic Theology*, I, 94. The question, "What precedes the duality of self and world, of subject and object?" is one in which reason looks into its own abyss—an abyss in which distinction and derivation disappear. Only revelation can answer this question (*ibid.*, I, 174) .
68. *Ibid.*, I, 156.
69. *Ibid.*, I, 205.

literal way of denoting God.[70] It does not designate a highest being, but is an essentially negative way of expressing that which is not subject to polarities and finitude. When one speaks positively of that which is designated by the term being-itself, he must speak metaphorically; for being-itself or God transcends everything, including human language, which is bound to the polarities of the subject and object world. But to speak nonsymbolically and negatively is to speak in a manner which falsifies man's experience of ultimate reality. Man's experience of being is of the "power of being." It is an acknowledgement of "the self-affirmation of being-itself, . . . the power of being which prevails against non-being." [71]

Can a doctrine of God be derived from an ontological system? Tillich's answer is that it cannot. For philosophical speculation God remains the ultimate mystery. Moreover, man cannot be concerned about being-itself. His concern always involves his finite situation, through which the experience of ultimate concern is mediated. But our existence participates in the ground of being and thus being-itself may be disclosed under the conditions of existence. Such disclosure is always partial and always symbolic: partial because being-itself can never be exhaustively identified with a segment or the whole of existence, and symbolic because the disclosure is partial—revealing, yet pointing beyond itself.[72]

In summary, the common ground upon which apologetic theology depends for commending the Christian message to the non-believer is, subjectively expressed, the universal religious experience of ultimate concern, objectively stated, the power of being-itself embracing finitude, that which is the prius of all thought and action. It is the task of apologetic theology to correlate the questions raised in man's experience of ultimate concern, questions having to do with the meaning of being and hence existence, with the answers implied in the Christian message.[73] As a theology of culture systematic theology formu-

70. *Ibid.,* I, 156; II, 10.
71. *The Courage to Be* (New Haven, 1952), pp. 180–181.
72. *Systematic Theology,* I, 241.
73. *Ibid.,* I, 9, 59–66; II, 13–16.

lates the questions implied in human existence, and as a Christology formulates the answers implied in the divine self-manifestation. The "theological circle" therefore includes both Christian message and the situation of the unbeliever. As a circle with two foci, it is actually an elipse. Yet Tillich insists on referring to the "theological circle"; for as theology moves between the foci of the eternal message and the human situation, "it drives man to a point where question and answer are not separated. This point . . . belongs to man's essential being, to the unity of his finitude with the infinity in which he was created and from which he is separated." [74]

As apologist, Tillich must concentrate first upon establishing the common ground shared by believer and unbeliever. He must make the general religious premise the initial concern of his theology, and present it in such a manner that the unbeliever will at least be persuaded of its intelligibility. Thus Tillich, like Schleiermacher, introduces his theological system by presenting revelation as a distinct mode of human cognition. Tillich's point of departure appears to be "above" Christianity.[75] Tillich begins with the experience of ultimate concern, and then attempts to establish the fact of the divine correlate: the personal, redemptive reality which, however, remains unknown apart from the knowledge of God in Jesus as the Christ. Apologetic theology is therefore a practical science, an inductive process, beginning with the universal religious experience of faith (ultimate concern) and proceeding to a position at which the unbeliever is confronted by the Word of God.

For Tillich apologetics is not a substitute for "natural theology" which acts as philosophical prolegomena to dogmatics. Apologetics is "an omni-present element and not a special section of systematic theology." [76] Its concern with intelligibility is not for the sake of "proving" the faith, but with "commending" the faith. Theology must enable men to perceive the fundamentally religious nature of their situation and constrain

74. *Ibid.*, I, 61.
75. Barth, *Protestant Thought*, p. 325.
76. Tillich, *Systematic Theology*, I, 31.

them to acknowledge the correlation between their situation and the eternal message. In Tillich's judgment it was precisely this that Calvin intended in the opening sentences of the *Institutes*.

He [Calvin] speaks of man's misery, which gives the existential basis for his understanding of God's glory, and of God's glory, which gives the essential basis for man's understanding of his misery. Man as existing, representing existence generally and asking the question implied in his existence, is one side of the cognitive correlation to which Calvin points, the other side being the divine majesty. In the initial sentence of his theological system Calvin expresses the essence of the method of correlation.[77]

However, in spite of his clear disavowal of natural theology and his appeal to Calvin, it must be asked whether Tillich has left himself open to the charge of "Cartesianism" in his theology.

In the first volume of *Church Dogmatics* Barth, discussing Kantian influence upon theology,[78] used "Cartesianism" to refer to that procedure in theology which seeks to derive the knowledge of God and of the world from the prior knowledge of the self. For Barth such a move denies the knowledge of the Word of God:

The fact of the Word of God in no respect nor yet in the very slightest degree receives its worth and validity from a presupposition which we apply to it; its truth for us, like its truth in itself, is based purely upon itself. The procedure in theology therefore is to

77. *Ibid.*, I, 63. Among the sentences to which Tillich refers are the following: "I. *Without knowledge of self there is no knowledge of God.*

"In the first place, no one can look upon himself without immediately turning his thoughts to the contemplation of God, in whom he 'lives and moves' [Acts 17:38]. . . . Thus, from the feeling of our own ignorance, vanity, poverty, infirmity, and—what is more—depravity and corruption, we recognize that the true light of wisdom, sound virtue, full abundance of every good, and purity of righteousness rest in the Lord alone. To this extent we are prompted by our own ills to contemplate the good things of God; and we cannot seriously aspire to him before we begin to become displeased with ourselves. . . . Accordingly, the knowledge of ourselves not only arouses us to seek God, but also, as it were, leads us by the hand to find him" (*Calvin: Institutes of the Christian Religion*, ed., John T. McNeill, trans. F. L. Battles, *The Library of Christian Classics* [Philadelphia, 1960], XX, 35–37.) See also Karl Barth's reservations regarding these opening sentences, *The Doctrine of the Word of God*, p. 191.

78. Barth, *The Doctrine of the Word of God*, p. 223. For a full discussion of this problem for Barth and for theology in the days to come, see Robert E. Cushman, "Barth's Attack upon Cartesianism and the Future in Theology," *The Journal of Religion*, XXXVI, (Oct., 1956), 207–223.

base self-certainty upon God-certainty without waiting for this beginning to be legitimised by self-certainty. . . . Men can know the Word of God because and so far as God wills that they should know it. . . . The question cannot be how man in general and as such can know the Word of God. . . . The question is how these men to whom it is spoken concretely can actually know it.[79]

Robert Cushman has called attention to the "realism" in Barth's epistemology, and to the fact that for Barth "knowledge . . . obtains when, as distinguished from ontic, there is nonetheless noetic identity or conformity between the known and the knower. . . . In knowledge there is a necessary and inward determination of the subject's existence by the object. . . . Speaking of knowing subjects, he [Barth] says: 'As knowers they are got at by the known object.' " [80] This epistemological position is the only possible one consistent with Barth's constant affirmation of the sovereign freedom (i.e., the ontological priority) of God. Barth's vivid sense of antecedent reality in the order of being demands that in the order of knowing he must regard the object as determining the subject.[81]

Measured by Barth's statement Tillich's theological system is vulnerable to the charge of Cartesianism, for his theological circle includes philosophy of religion and the theological analysis of man's situation, as well as Christology. Tillich's theology is apologetic, and does move from questions implied in man's existence to answers implied in God's manifestation in the Christ. But it must not be hastily dismissed as Cartesianism. Granting Tillich's dependence upon Schleiermacher, it would be most unfair to place his *Systematic Theology* in the tradition of Kantian phenomenalism which so strongly influenced an uncritical Protestant theology after Schleiermacher, and which is the real object of Barth's attack. Two observations are in order.

In the first place, if there is any point at which Tillich's theology is vulnerable to the charge of Cartesianism, it is the ontological analysis of anxiety and courage from which he derives

79. Barth, *The Doctrine of the Word of God*, pp. 223–224.
80. Cushman, *op. cit.*, p. 214. Quotation is from Barth, *The Doctrine of the Word of God*, p. 214.
81. *Ibid.*, p. 211.

what he calls "the God above God." [82] In this analysis Tillich takes seriously the experience of radical doubt, describes the courage of such doubt and self-affirmation in the midst of apparent meaninglessness, and designates the source of such courage as the power of being or "the God above God." This is "to transcend the God of theological theism," who is spoken of in terms of the conditions of existence.[83] But even here Tillich provides neither speculative theology and argument for God's existence (Aristotelianism in theology) nor uncritical movement in thought from self-consciousness to God-consciousness (Cartesianism in theology). On the contrary, his concern here as elsewhere is to reaffirm the logos doctrine in and for Protestant theology: "the doctrine of the identity of the absolutely concrete with the absolutely universal." [84] By identity Tillich refers to God's freedom, symbolized in the theological doctrine of creation, and expressed philosophically by "the power of being." Tillich's concern is to account for the depth of man's religious experience manifest in the forms of cultural expression as well as for the possibility of man's knowledge of God in Christ. Tillich *also* has a vivid sense of the antecedent reality in the order of being, and in this is motivated not by an apologetics of accommodation, but by an apologetics of transformation.

Accompanying Tillich's restoration of the logos doctrine is a reaffirmation of the Protestant principle. It is this juxtaposition that bewilders those who would dismiss Tillich as "liberal" because of his appreciation of Schleiermacher, and those who desire to dismiss him as "neo-orthodox" because of his affirmation of the principle of justification through grace. Tillich sees these affirmations as fundamentally related. Philosophically this relation rests on Tillich's indebtedness to Schelling's rejection of the philosophy of identity. With Schelling Tillich acknowledges that being as such and finite existence are integrally related, yet radically distinct. Finite existence is "being limited

---

82. *The Courage to Be, passim.*
83. *Ibid.*, pp. 182 ff.
84. *Systematic Theology*, I, 17.

by non-being. . . . It is being in process of coming from and going toward non-being." [85] This dialectical relationship Tillich finds expressed in the logos and justification doctrines. The logos doctrine expresses the participation of finitude in being, and the antecedent reality of being. The doctrine of justification gives expression to the distance and estrangement of being itself and finite existence which is overcome in God's self-manifestation. Cartesianism in Tillich's theology is essentially insistence on taking seriously the grace of God in creation, which alone is the adequate basis for raising the question of God, to say nothing of receiving the answer.

In the second place, Tillich nowhere claims that the Christian answer to man's situation can be derived from the human situation. Fully aware of the illusion of Schleiermacher's followers (that Christian faith could be derived from religious consciousness) which legitimately raised the cry of Cartesianism,[86] Tillich observes that the attempt fails to take seriously the estrangement of finite existence from its ground and the priority of God in knowing as well as being:

The existential question, namely, man himself in the conflicts of his existential situation, is not the source for the revelatory answer formulated by theology. . . . Man is the question, not the answer. . . . Man as man knows the question of God. He is estranged, but not cut off from God.[87]

Even in the most "Cartesian" of all Tillich's writings, *The Courage to Be,* he states in the concluding paragraphs:

And one can become aware of the God above the God of theism in the anxiety of guilt and condemnation when the traditional symbols that enable men to withstand the anxiety of guilt and condemnation have lost their power. When "divine judgment" is interpreted as a psychological complex and forgiveness as a remnant of the "father-image," what once was the power in those symbols can still be present and create the courage to be in spite of the experience of an infinite gap between what we are and what we ought to be. The Lutheran courage returns *but not supported by the faith in a judging and forgiving God.*[88]

85. *Ibid.,* I, 189.
86. *Ibid.,* I, 42.
87. *Ibid.,* II, 13–14; see also *Systematic Theology,* I, 42, 46–47, 64. In this Tillich is not as far from Barth as some writers have suggested.
88. *The Courage to Be,* pp. 189–190. (Italics mine.)

Tillich is as acutely aware as Barth that "Christian theology is based on the unique event Jesus the Christ" and that it remains "the criterion of every religious experience. This event is given to, not derived from it." [89] Tillich may begin his system with an attempt to establish the cognitive status of revelation, but this beginning is nonetheless informed and guided by the Christology and the doctrine of the church that come later. [90]

Here again is Barth's question: "Why later?" Why all the preparation for the proclamation of God's Word, unless one cannot rely upon the action of God? And if we cannot wait upon the Lord, are we not turning *pistis* into *gnosis?* Is not the theologian guilty of turning Christology into an "art"? We must now address ourselves to these questions.

Ontology and Christology

Commenting on nineteenth-century Protestant theology, Barth wrote:

> There was in fact no need for the Copernican conception of the universe to acquire the significance of a command that theology should in the future be anthropocentric theology. It might have perhaps been both more spirited and wiser to take up and carry through the Reformed theology . . . in instructive opposition to the trend of the age . . . as a pure theology of the Word, it offered opportunity enough to do justice to the tendency of the age by an honest doctrine of the Holy Spirit and of faith. [91]

Barth contended that Schleiermacher and other nineteenth-century theologians had reversed the order of Reformation thought and were more interested in man's action in regard to God than in God's action in regard to man. Two consequences followed for trinitarian theology.

The first had to do with the doctrine of the Holy Spirit. According to Barth, Reformation theology was a theology of the Word and, as such, at once a theology of the Holy Spirit and a theology of faith. That is, Reformation theology had to take

89. *Systematic Theology,* I, 46.

90. *Ibid.,* I, 11. It is the great weakness of many of Tillich's followers that they have failed to see his whole theological system as christologically founded and informed.

91. Barth, *Protestant Thought,* p. 340.

account of the Holy Spirit as the divine reality in which the Word is heard.[92] It is by and through the Spirit that man receives the Word; not by or through any natural capacity of man. It does not depend on the subject. And since the receiving of the Word, "the objective moment," as Barth refers to the experience of faith, is objectively assured, it is kept from dissolution into the subjective.[93]

In contrast to Reformation theology Schleiermacher made the Holy Spirit, not the Word, the center of his theology. The reason, according to Barth, lay in Schleiermacher's emphasis upon pious (human) self-awareness and concern as an apologist to construe revelation in such a way as to make it comprehensible as a mode of human cognition.[94] Schleiermacher could not use a doctrine of the Holy Spirit which preserved the radical objectivity of the Spirit, and guarded the Divine freedom and sovereignty, as in Reformation thought. Schleiermacher had to construe the doctrine so that man's role was preserved in the process of religious knowledge. Schleiermacher's solution was to speak of the Holy Spirit as the objective guarantee of the validity of pious self-awareness. It was the principle of mediation between the Word of God in Jesus Christ and man's highest self-consciousness. As such it remains a question, in Barth's estimation, "whether . . . the divinity of the Spirit which seemingly formed the centre of his [Schleiermacher's] theology was really the divinity of the Holy Spirit." [95]

The second consequence of the Copernican revolution in nineteenth-century theology concerned Christology. If the primary interest of a theology is man's religious consciousness, then the historical element in religion, the objective motif, becomes an embarrassment. And the consequence is, according to Barth, that theology must "rework the biblical presentation in order to produce the particular Christ who might be considered adequate from this point of view." [96] The concern of theology

92. *Ibid.,* p. 340.
93. *Ibid.,* p. 354.
94. *Ibid.,* pp. 339, 343–344.
95. *Ibid.,* p. 343.
96. *Ibid.,* p. 342.

is now to show the relation of the objective historical moment and the timeless original revelation in pious self-awareness. The positive quality of the Christian revelation is identified in Jesus as the *Urbild,* the "original image." As the Christ, Jesus effects the transition to pious self-awareness as awareness of redemption.[97] But Schleiermacher, primarily concerned with man's relation to God, rather than God's relation to man, cannot speak of the eternal significance of Christ. He must always acknowledge the eternality of other religions.[98]

Extended reference has been made to Barth's criticism of Schleiermacher, for it provides the basis for raising similar questions about Tillich's Christology.[99] Although numerous articles treat Tillich's concept of being, his understanding of revelation, and his theology of culture, few have discussed Tillich's Christology. Yet this, in Tillich's estimate, is as crucial as any part of his system, and, in fact, is "presupposed" in his discussions of being and existence, revelation and history.[100]

Tillich defines the task of theology as mediation between the Christian message and the situation of man. Christian theology is "answering theology," offering the healing Word to the questions raised by man's existential situation: "The early church was well aware that Christology is an existentially necessary . . . work of the church. . . . It is 'soteriological,' i.e. determined by the question of salvation." [101]

The question of salvation is the question of God implied in man's awareness of estrangement.[102] The word *estrangement* is central in Tillich's analysis of the human situation. It describes the human dilemma of the distance between man's existential situation and essential nature.

Like recent existentialist thinkers, Tillich rejects the Hegelian essentialist view of man and history. Existence "is the

97. *Ibid.,* p. 351.
98. *Ibid.,* p. 352.
99. See R. E. Cushman, "Barth's Attack upon Cartesianism and the Future in Theology," *loc. cit.;* E. A. Dowey, Jr., "Tillich, Barth, and the Criteria of Theology," *Theology Today,* XV (April, 1958) , 43–58.
100. Tillich, *Systematic Theology,* I, 11.
101. *Ibid.,* II, 146.
102. *Ibid.,* II, 78 ff.

process in which man becomes a thing and ceases to be a person. History is not the divine self-manifestation but a series of un-reconciled conflicts, threatening man with self-destruction. The existence of the individual is filled with anxiety and threatened by meaninglessness." [103] But in contrast to most existentialist thinkers Tillich draws heavily upon the biblical description of the human predicament, especially the symbol of "the Fall" which "is a decisive part of the Christian Tradition" and "has universal anthropological significance." [104]

For Tillich "the Fall" symbolizes the transition from essence to existence. The possibility of such a transition is in man's freedom, manifest in man's creative activity and in his capacity to contradict his powers of creative activity. Man is also finite. This is the other condition making possible the transition from essence to existence. As "finite freedom" man's situation is therefore one of constant transition from essence to existence —a universal quality of finite being.[105] The transition involves a distortion of man's essential nature.

Finite freedom produces anxiety, an awareness of finitude, and the threat of non-being. Under the conditions of existence this "ontological anxiety" is known in the confrontation of death, meaninglessness, and guilt. Ontological anxiety, the basis of human despair, also arouses man's freedom, and in "aroused freedom" [106] man seeks to provide his own answers. In this actualization of freedom the transition from essence to existence becomes a Fall, which though inevitable, is experienced as a personal responsibility by man.[107]

The consequences of the Fall—the experiences of man under the conditions of existence—are summed up in the word "estrangement." One form is sin, "the personal act of turning away from that to which one belongs. . . ." [108] Sin is thus the disobedience of man in his refusal to conform his will to the divine will. A second form of the experience of estrangement is the

103. *Ibid.,* II, 25.
104. *Ibid.,* II, 29.
105. *Ibid.,* II, 32, 36, 39.
106. *Systematic Theology,* II, 35.
107. *Ibid.,* II, 40 ff.
108. *Ibid.,* II, 46.

discovery of the inadequacy of the self as a determining center and the inability to discover any other object worthy of trust as a center for himself and his world. Nothing finite can give freedom and meaning. Estranged from his essential being, man is left in his finitude with death as the adequate symbol for his existence, for it is the conqueror of his existence.

The acute realization of the finitude of existence is expressed by the words despair, fate, and bondage of the will. Such words express man's inability to save himself, but they also provide the condition for man's realization that salvation must come from outside the human situation. Before man can *act* in freedom, he must *be* free and participate in a destiny. Being precedes acting, and "only a New Being can produce a new action." [109]

Religion is man's attempt to discover a New Being. It suffers under the ambiguity of existence, but "it is also the place where life receives the conqueror of the ambiguities of life, the divine Spirit." [110] Thus, for Tillich, religion is the indication that man is not without hope. "The quest for the New Being presupposes the presence of the New Being. . . ." [111] Again: "The universal quest for the New Being is a consequence of universal revelation." [112]

Has Tillich like Schleiermacher defined the work of the divine Spirit in order to guarantee the reality of man's universal religious experience and thus revealed more concern with man's relation to God than with God's relation to man?

Tillich, I believe, would consider the question inappropriate. His understanding of ultimate concern, coupled with his continuous affirmation of the Protestant principle, and his analysis of man's predicament place him at considerable distance from nineteenth-century theology. With Barth and Heim, Tillich seriously maintains the "infinite qualitative distinction" between the Creator and the creature. But he does not assert the

109. *Ibid.*, II, 80.
110. *Ibid.*
111. *Ibid.*
112. *Ibid.*, II, 89.

transcendence of God in such a manner as to isolate, abstract, and absolutize the "wholly other," a position to which earlier Barth came perilously close and one which, as Barth acknowledged, "showed greater similarity to the deity of the God of the philosophers than to the deity of the God of Abraham, Isaac, and Jacob." [113] The biblical notion of the transcendence of God involves, as Karl Heim points out, not only the acknowledgment that "God dwelleth in the light which no man can approach unto" (1 Timothy 6:16), but the awareness that the transcendent God is he who "compassest my path and my lying down, and understandest my thought afar off" (Psalm 139:3). "God is," Heim writes, "the omnipresent Thou of every I, the Being who is immediately close to us, before whom we stand always, before whom we do all our deeds, and before whom we think even our most secret thoughts." [114] It is this same insight that Tillich has glimpsed. Man may be estranged, but he is not cut off from God.

Finally, Tillich like Schleiermacher is aware of man's experience of the divine Spirit apart from the revelation of God in Christ. But he is also aware with Barth that trinitarian theology demands not only the distinction of the persons but also the fundamental unity of the Godhead. This Reformation thought affirms in asserting the integral relation of the work of the Spirit with the Word—hence the centrality of the Word rather than the Spirit in Reformation theology. For Tillich the distinction is too sharp, though the point is a valid one. The Word is central; but this need not mean that the doctrine of the Holy Spirit be understood solely with reference to the doctrine of the Word. Does not this threaten the sovereignty of God and fail to consider "the cosmic and un-incarnate functions of the Word of God?" [115] Tillich employs precisely this idea: "The question

---

113. Barth, *The Humanity of God,* trans. J. N. Thomas (Richmond, 1960), p. 45.
114. Karl Heim, *Christian Faith and Natural Science,* trans. N. H. Smith (New York, 1953), pp. 212–213.
115. The phrase is Albert C. Outler's used *re* Augustine's early Christology. See "The Person and Work of Christ," *A Companion to the Study of St. Augustine,* ed. Roy W. Battenhouse (New York, 1955), p. 349.

of salvation can be asked only if salvation is already at work, no matter how fragmentarily. . . ." [116] In other words, one can neither dissociate the Spirit from the Word nor restrict the Holy Spirit to the advent of the Redeemer. Thus, to speak of man's experience of ultimate concern is not to speak of revelation apart from the Word, but of the activity of the un-incarnate Word through the divine Spirit. And to speak of the knowledge of God in Christ is to speak of the manifestation of the divine Spirit, appearing under the conditions of existence.

Tillich early defined the Christological problem thus: "To develop Christology means to describe the concrete point at which something absolute appears in history and provides it with meaning and purpose. . . ." [117] Three questions must be asked of this statement: Why does Christology involve the historical category? What does it mean to "describe" the concrete point? What is the nature of the absolute that provides meaning and purpose?

As Tillich notes, the history of the expectation of the New Being can be divided between non-historical and historical types of expectations. Of the two, the latter is the more profound. The non-historical type of expectation seeks to escape history and finitude by "the negation of all beings and the affirmation of the Ground of Being alone." [118] In contrast the historical expectation recognizes that history is the bearer of true human nature, that the whole of reality, finite as well as infinite freedom, is essentially good, and that redemption must occur for man under the conditions of existence. Man's predicament is that the structures of existence, space and time, have become meaningless. The essential nature of man is restored only through the gift of the New Being.

Tillich begins discussion of Christology in his *Systematic Theology* with the following observation:

Christianity is what it is through the affirmation that Jesus of Nazareth, who has been called "the Christ," is actually the Christ, namely, he who brings the new state of things, the New Being. . . .

116. *Systematic Theology*, II, 80.
117. *Interpretation of History*, p. 242.
118. *Systematic Theology*, II, 82.

Christianity was born, not with the birth of the man who is called "Jesus," but in the moment in which one of his followers was driven to say to him, "Thou art the Christ." And Christianity will live as long as there are people who repeat this assertion. For the event on which Christianity is based has two sides: the fact which is called "Jesus of Nazareth" and the reception of this fact by those who received him as the Christ.[119]

Obviously the christological task is not the work of the historian. Schweitzer's critique of the search for the empirical truth about Jesus remains valid. And the extension of this critique in Bultmann's program of "demythologization" demonstrates "that there is no picture behind the biblical one which could be made scientifically probable." [120] The docetic problem will ever haunt the church's confession.

Tillich, however, is fully aware of the necessity of the historical category for the church's faith. "Only if existence is conquered concretely and in its manifold aspects, is it actually conquered." [121] What, then, is the concreteness of the biblical witness? Tillich answers: "the power which has created and preserved the community of the New Being." [122]

According to Tillich there is an *analogia imaginis,* that is, "an analogy between the picture and the actual personal life from which it has arisen. It was this reality, when encountered by the disciples, which created the picture. And it was, and still is, this picture which mediates the transforming power of the New Being." [123]

The historical concreteness of the biblical witness is not guaranteed by empirical factuality, but in terms of transforming power. The biblical witness is dependent upon the historical event, and both depend upon participation in the transforming power of the Christ for historical reality. To know Jesus as the Christ is to know the power of the New Being through personal participation with others in his being. The distinctive witness of biblical literature is primarily concerned with words,

119. *Ibid.,* II, 97.
120. *Ibid.,* II, 102.
121. *Ibid.,* II, 114.
122. *Ibid.*
123. *Ibid.,* II, 115.

deeds, and suffering of Jesus as the Christ as they bear witness to his being which "has the quality of the New Being beyond the split of essential and existential being." [124] And for Tillich this reference to the power of Jesus' being manifest in his personal life forms the basis of the biblical doctrine of grace.[125]

The biblical doctrine of grace is at the heart of Tillich's Christology. Jesus represents to man his essential nature.[126] But the work of Christ extends beyond representation and its effect upon man's God-consciousness. Christ must be understood as the Mediator, bestowing the reconciling will of God.[127] He is the power of God to man, participating in the historic and tragic situation of man and at the same time overcoming the estranged condition by the power of being, by his unity with God.

Tillich's doctrine of atonement clearly indicates intention to preserve the "objective" side of redemption: "The doctrine of the atonement is the description of the effect of the New Being in Jesus as the Christ on those who are grasped by it in their state of estrangement." [128] He acknowledges the divine act and the human reaction, but designates as of primary importance the principle "that the atoning processes are created by God and God alone." [129] God's act precedes man's ability to respond.

124. *Ibid.*, II, 121, 166. Tillich's position is strongly reminiscent of the thought of Wilhelm Hermann. In *The Communion of the Christian with God* Hermann wrote: "In the Christian fellowship we are made acquainted, not merely with the external course of Jesus' lot in life and of His work in history, but we are also led into His presence . . . of His inner life. For this we are certainly dependent . . . upon other men. . . . We need communion with Christians in order that, from the picture of Jesus which His church has preserved, there may shine forth that inner life which is the heart of it" (trans. J. Sandys Stanyon [New York, 1909], pp. 72–73). Tillich recognizes that Hermann's attempt to penetrate into the "inner life of Jesus" was not free from psychological concerns. "Significantly, the biblical reports about Jesus do not psychologize. More correctly," Tillich writes, "one could say that they ontologize. . . . Our records do not give a psychological description of his development. . . . They show only the presence of the New Being in him under the conditions of existence. . . . By recording his anxiety about having to die, the New Testament writers show his total participation in human finitude. . . . They also show his conquest of anxiety. . . . In all cases it is an occasion of the encounter of the New Being with the forces of estrangement, not some specific psychological behavior involved" (*Systematic Theology*, II, 124–125).

125. *Ibid.*, II, 125; I, 285–286.
126. *Ibid.*, II, 93.
127. *Ibid.*, II, 169–170.
128. *Ibid.*, II, 170.
129. *Ibid.*, II, 173.

In this is expressed the idea of predestination as the "religious correlate" to justification by faith alone.[130]

The atonement centers attention upon the situation of man with respect to his experience of guilt. The Fall is inevitable, but man nonetheless stands responsible; and he knows it. Furthermore, man cannot forgive himself. Alienated from his "original" destiny and in bondage to that which is less than human, he must be forgiven. The doctrine of atonement refers to both the wretchedness of man's situation and the act of the Cross of Christ in redeeming man.

The Cross is the center of the biblical witness. In the Cross "the divine participation in existential estrangement becomes manifest."[131] By "manifest" Tillich means effectively expressed, *known* in the Platonic-Johannine-Augustinian sense of transforming the knower. To *know* the Cross of Christ one must perceive in the being of the crucified the participation of one's own being, and also perceive the New Being which is not conquered and which is now a possibility for him. Atonement refers, therefore, both to God's act in His participation in the human situation and to man's response in his "participation in the divine participation, accepting it and being transformed by it."[132]

Karl Barth accused Schleiermacher of turning Christology into "a product of art," of developing a Christology compatible with his anthropology.[133] Can this same charge be appropriately lodged against Tillich as well? Three observations are in order.

In the first place, it is important to remember that the church has always asserted dogmatically the divinity of Christ's "person," but never declared any particular doctrine of the "work" of Christ. This has permitted discussion of the reality of the Christ's person as if it were independent of knowing God's action in Christ. Arianism is the inevitable result. In its wisdom the church has usually acknowledged that one must speak of the work of Christ before one can speak of Christ's person. To

130. *Ibid.*, I, 286.
131. *Ibid.*, II, 175.
132. *Ibid.*, II, 176.
133. Barth, *Protestant Thought*, p. 342.

know Christ as God-for-us is to know the Christ. The church has also recognized that only God in Christ can redeem and it is this that the orthodox doctrine of the person seeks to preserve. But "how" the redemption takes place cannot be formulated once and for all in dogma, but is variously expressed, depending upon man's situation:

> If theology gives the answer, "The Christ," to the question implied in human estrangement, it does so differently, depending on whether the reference is to existential conflicts of Jewish legalism, to the existential despair of Greek skepticism, or to the threat of nihilism as expressed in twentieth century literature, art, and psychology.[134]

In this sense, every christological statement is "a product of art." It is the church's attempt to express the central, determinative, saving event of its life. Each age in the life of the church must take counsel with every other age, but it must also affirm and express anew the power of God as it has known that power, and witness to its own day of the new life that it has received.

Barth has at times needed to be reminded of the above, yet essentially his problem with Schleiermacher is that Schleiermacher moved from anthropology to Christology, reversed the order of revelation.[135] That Tillich is not open to this charge is clearly indicated in a paragraph in which Tillich compares his own christological position with that of Schleiermacher.

> Some traits of the christological position taken here are similar to Schleiermacher's Christology. . . . The similarity is obvious; but it is not identity. Essential God-Manhood points to both sides of the relation and this in terms of eternity. It is an objective structure and not a state of man. The phrase "essential unity between God and man" has an ontological character; Schleiermacher's God-consciousness has an anthropological character. . . . In *Urbild* the idealistic transcendence of true humanity over human existence is clearly expressed, while in "New Being," the participation of him who is *also* the *Urbild* ("essential man") is decisive. The New Being is new not only over against existence but also over against essence, in so far as essence remains mere potentiality. The *Urbild* remains unmoved above existence; the New Being participates in

---

134. *Systematic Theology*, II, 15–16.
135. Barth, *Protestant Thought*, p. 313. See *The Doctrine of the Word of God*, p. 148.

existence and conquers it. Here again an ontological element makes the difference.[136]

Important is the reference to the "essential unity between God and man" in the New Being. Here is the difference in the formal and material principles of theology as stated by Tillich and Schleiermacher. Barth and Tillich both recognize that Schleiermacher's formal and material principles are identical— Christian pious self-awareness contemplates and describes itself.[137] The material principle, Jesus as the *Urbild,* is dependent upon the formal principle, the feeling of utter dependence. Christ effects man's higher self-consciousness, provides the Whence of our being, and is therefore identical with what has already been given to man as man: God's "original revelation." In contrast, Tillich clearly distinguishes: The formal principle of his theology is the experience of ultimate concern.[138] But the experience of ultimate concern is not synonymous with Schleiermacher's highest self-consciousness or God-consciousness. Ultimate concern is essentially the experience of estrangement and despair. The only positive significance of man's experience of ultimate concern is that he is constantly driven to reject objects unworthy of ultimate trust and thus is brought to an awareness of the courage to be in the midst of his despair. The material principle or norm in Tillich's theology is the New Being in Jesus as the Christ. Christ is the fulfilment of man's need for an ultimate concern, not as completion, but as restoration. This clear distinction lacking in Schleiermacher's thought permits Tillich to refer to the "ontological character" of his own thought and the "anthropological character" of Schleiermacher's theology. By ontological character Tillich means the power of being that precedes knowing and acting; the philosophical expression most adequate to the biblical notion of the sovereignty and grace of God.

This distinction leads to one other important point of contrast between Tillich and Schleiermacher. Schleiermacher can

---

136. *Systematic Theology,* II, 150.
137. Barth, *Protestant Thought,* p. 338; Tillich, *Systematic Theology,* I, 42.
138. *Systematic Theology,* I, 12.

never affirm the absoluteness of Christianity. Lacking an adequate distinction between the formal and material principles, he had always to acknowledge the eternality of other religions. Tillich, however, because of his distinction between formal and material principles and because of his analysis of man's predicament, can and must assert that Jesus as the Christ has universal significance for every human being and, indirectly, for the universe as well.[139] In his Cross and Resurrection there is final subjection to and conquest of existence through one "who is united with the ground of his being and meaning without separation and disruption." [140] Only such a one can be called the medium of "final revelation." [141]

From this discussion it should now be clear that Barth's attack upon Cartesianism in nineteenth-century theology cannot be brought against Tillich's theological system with the same devastating results. Apologetic theology is not incompatible with or corrupting of Christology. On the contrary, Tillich has to a remarkable degree brought ontology and Christology together in the service of an apologetic theology that is confessional and not accommodating. Observations must now be made about the present debate between Barth and Tillich and apologetic theology in the days to come.

The Foundation of Christian Apologetics

Barth recently wrote: "Certainly existentialism may have reminded us once again of the elements of truth in the old school by introducing once more the thought that one cannot speak of God without speaking of man. It is to be hoped that it will not lead us back into the old error that one can speak of man without first, and very concretely, having spoken of the living God." [142] Barth here repeats what has always been his central

139. *Ibid.*, II, 151–165.
140. *Ibid.*, I, 133.
141. *Ibid.*
142. Barth, *The Humanity of God*, pp. 56–57. This volume, heralded as a new direction in Barth's thought, I find not substantially different from the second and fourth volumes of the *Church Dogmatics*. It is, however, more readable.

concern: that the knowledge of God is the knowledge of faith and that the knowledge of faith "both with regard to the perception of its goal and the human effort to reach it" is a matter of grace.[143]

Apparently, the question for theology in the days to come is whether a distinction can be made between the christocentric and theocentric poles of theology without transforming the latter into an anthropocentric pole. For Barth the distinction between christocentric and theocentric is virtually impossible.

In an early (1930) and very important study of Anselm's *Proslogion* Barth found an answer to the problem of how theology could be understood as a rational task, safeguarded from the intrusion of non-rational elements, and distinguishable from the speculation of a faithless human reason. The answer was in Anselm's conception of a *ratio* peculiar to the object of faith.

Anselm, according to Barth, distinguished between the knowing *ratio* and an ontic *ratio* or the *ratio fidei,* which is reason summoned by faith to describe and declare the object of faith. The claim of truth by the noetic *ratio* is essentially a matter of decision based upon empirical evidence. But in the case of the *ratio fidei* "truth," Barth claims, "is conferred upon it with the creation of the object of which it is the *ratio.*"[144] The point that Anselm and Barth are concerned to make is that the truth of the *ratio fidei* is not dependent upon the activity of the knowing *ratio* but upon the participation of the *ratio fidei* in a third and ultimate ratio, a *ratio veritatis,* or "the *ratio* of God."[145] Thus, Barth writes: "It is not because it is *ratio* that it [the *ratio fidei*] has truth but because God, Truth, has it."[146]

From this it is clear that there is no self-redemption and no movement of human reason to the knowledge of God apart from the grace of God. God is remote from man, experienced

---

143. Barth, *Anselm: Fides Quaerens Intellectum,* trans. I. W. Robertson (Richmond, 1960) , p. 40.
144. *Ibid.,* p. 47.
145. *Ibid.,* p. 45.
146. *Ibid.,* pp. 45–46. See also pp. 52–53.

by sinful man as "an objective remoteness of God himself." [147]
Thus, if God is to be known, it will be because and only because God " 'shows' himself to the thinker and in so doing modi-
fies 'correct' thinking to an *intelligerse esse in re*." [148] "Anyone," Barth writes, "who wants to ask more questions at this
limit can only be a fool who, though he hears the revealed Word
and has it *in intellectu*, yet because the *res,* the fact of revelation, escapes him, still asks for an external necessity, a *quo-
modo,* which he can find only in the inner necessity, in the *esse,*
of the truth itself which is being proclaimed and which he is
calling in question." [149]

Barth's development of this thesis involves positive doctrines
of analogy and ontology, "profoundly, indeed exclusively,
Christological and Christocentric." [150] All of man's expressions
about God are false, since they have necessarily to do with objects that are not identical with God. God in his grace therefore provides a knowledge of himself. Such knowledge is
analogical, for human knowing is bound to the world of subject-
object relations. But the validity of the analogical expressions
is guaranteed by the ontological basis established in the determination of the knower by the known, the creature by the
Creator. In the Incarnation God "establishes the one truth, His
own, as the truth of our views, concepts and words." [151]

With a positive doctrine of analogy and ontology Barth provides a new basis for the apologetic task. The theologian does
not and cannot seek a truce with the unbeliever, attempting to
meet the unbeliever on some lofty place "above" Christianity.
And yet, as Anselm reminds Barth, the theologian must meet

147. *Ibid.,* p. 38. Barth observes that the continuity between man and the
world makes possible human apprehension of the world. "But between God and
man there is no such unity." *Church Dogmatics,* (New York, 1957) , II, 1, 189.
148. *Ibid.,* p. 39. Barth later wrote: "God is known only by God. . . . The
veracity of our human knowledge of God, consists in the fact that our viewing
and conceiving is adopted and determined to participation in the truth of God
by God Himself in grace" (*Church Dogmatics,* II, 1, 179) .
149. *Ibid.,* p. 28.
150. Hans Frei, "Niebuhr's Theological Background," *Faith and Ethics: The
Theology of H. Richard Niebuhr,* ed. Paul Ramsey (New York, 1957) , p. 51.
151. Barth, *Church Dogmatics,* II, 1, 229.

"the worldling" on the assumption that there is "a solidarity" between them.[152] For Anselm this assumption is based upon

the power of the objective *ratio* of the object of faith that enlightens and is enlightened from above by the *summa veritas* and which . . . was able to teach and all along did teach truths that are beyond the power of one human being to teach another. . . . Perhaps [Anselm] . . . did not really remain standing on this side of the gulf between the believer and non-believer but crossed it, . . . as conqueror whose weapon was the fact that he met the unbelievers as one of them and accepted them as his equal.[153]

Tillich's theology is also christologically centered. The central thesis is justification by grace alone, derived from his understanding of the Cross of Christ. Tillich does not feel constrained to center theological discourse in as restrictive a fashion as Barth upon the second person of the Trinity. Let us be careful to understand precisely what Tillich intends.

Recall that for Tillich Christian theology understood as apologetic theology includes not only Christology but philosophy of religion. As an "answering theology" Christian theology must take seriously the questions implied in human finitude; the questions of freedom, meaning, and the nature of ultimate reality. These questions raise the question of God. The ontology which forms the prolegomenon to Tillich's theology is derived from an analysis of the human situation as finite freedom and not, as with Barth's ontology, derived from Christology.

Tillich denies that a doctrine of God can be derived from an ontological analysis. But out of such an analysis emerges the idea of God, or as Tillich prefers to say, the question of God. This question arises not only in the notion of the power of being, but primarily in man's awareness of and quest for the Unconditional which is implied in his experience of freedom and destiny, form and dynamics, individualization and participation, as these elements of the structure of finite being remain unresolved in his existential situation. To what extent

---

152. Barth, *Anselm: Fides Quaerens Intellectum*, p. 68.
153. *Ibid.*, p. 71.

is man's awareness of the Unconditional, or confrontation with the question of God, knowledge of the living God? Tillich's answer might be twofold.

In the first place, the phrases "awareness of the Unconditional," "the question of God," or "ultimate concern" are all negative. It is not a personal, living God to whom reference is made, but rather it is an acknowledgement on the one hand of man's existential situation, of his finitude and his inability. On the other hand, these phrases refer to man's awareness of an "original relationship" (*Urbeziehung*) as Heim refers to it,[154] the experience of being known by a divine reality which remains mysterious and remote. Subjectively, that is, from man's side, it provides no redemption. Objectively, that is, from the divine side, it is the necessary condition for man's knowing God through his Word. Obviously, one cannot speak of the objective side apart from a prior knowledge of God in his self-manifestation in Jesus Christ. Ontological analysis cannot speak of this awareness as the divine presence except as that analysis is christologically informed. Without the Word of God, the divine self-manifestation under the conditions of existence, ontology must inevitably proceed either to metaphysical monism or metaphysical dualism.[155]

This leads to the second observation. I believe that Tillich would agree with Barth that it is impossible to speak of the work of the Holy Spirit *prior to* knowing the work of Christ, or of the knowledge of God as Holy Spirit prior to the knowledge of God in Christ. But Tillich would disagree with Barth's apparent contention that one cannot speak of the work of the Holy Spirit *apart from* Christ. For Tillich the Holy Spirit is the Christian symbol for the actualization of the power of the Godhead, of the divine depth which makes God God, and which provides for the divine *logos*.[156] It is thus the presence of the living God who is known by man in his experience of the

154. "Zur Frage der philosophischen Grundlegung der Theologie," *Zeitschrift für Theologie und Kirche*, XL, No. 13, 188.
155. See Tillich, *Biblical Religion and the Search for Ultimate Reality* (Chicago, 1955), pp. 36–37.
156. Tillich, *Systematic Theology*, I, 250–251.

searching mind, the restless heart, and the guilty conscience.

Tillich has sought to restore the notion of the immanence of the divine presence to theological reflection upon divine causality. For Tillich the theologian is not faced with the question of whether he will understand divine causality as immanent, or reserved and adventitious.[157] Divine immanence need not be identified with human self-understanding. The safeguard against Cartesianism in theology is not a rejection of the notion of divine immanence but a restoration of the doctrine of the Holy Spirit. It is with this that Tillich responds to Barth's radical christocentrism. The God who is transcendent, whose Being is incomprehensible, is also present to man as Spirit providing for man's being and his knowing.

There is, then, for Tillich, a theocentric and a christocentric pole about which theology circles; the un-incarnate presence of the transcendent God and the incarnate presence of the transcendent God. The human cannot be substituted for the divine at either of these points as the subject of theological reflection, although the presence of the living God as Spirit or as Word always involves man. It is this understanding of the basis or context of theological discourse that enables Tillich to define the theological task as apologetic. For Tillich carries not only the power of the Word of God in Christ to the nonbeliever. He also is aware of the power of the presence of God, a Gestalt of grace, in which the nonbeliever already exists and in terms of which the Christian apologist is enabled to meet the nonbeliever and be heard by him. It is as true for Tillich as for Barth that by God alone is God known.

157. Cushman, *op. cit.,* p. 222.

Jonathan Mayhew: American Christian Rationalist

McMURRY S. RICHEY

In Jonathan Mayhew of pre-Revolutionary Boston we see an early and vivid illustration of the impact of moderate English rationalism upon American colonial religious thought. The rationalism of John Locke and Samuel Clarke, to take two of the leading thinkers whose works Mayhew knew, may be described as "moderate," "evangelical," or "Christian" rationalism, in contrast to the more radical deistic rationalism of Tindal, Toland, and Voltaire. It is not here suggested that Mayhew was a disciple of Locke and Clarke alone, or that he followed them slavishly, or that they did not have other followers in this country. Mayhew read widely, thought independently, and expressed with uncommon zeal and courage the spirit of the coming Age of Reason in America. Something of the character and invigorating force of that spirit may be seen through a study of his views of reason and revelation, and of natural and revealed religion, against the background of that "Christian" rationalism. For this purpose we shall be concerned mainly with Mayhew's first book of *Seven Sermons,* his first "Thursday lectures" in which he carefully worked out his views and laid them down for Boston and the world to see.

Mayhew and His Times

Jonathan Mayhew was born in October, 1720, on Martha's Vineyard, one of the Massachusetts islands. His father, Experience Mayhew, was for some years missionary to the Indians there, as Mayhews had been for three generations since Thomas

Mayhew had become the island's first English settler and pro-
prietor.[1] Jonathan followed a brother to Harvard, which had
awarded his father an honorary A.M. in 1720. Studious, literary, moral, and pious, he was graduated in 1744, and seems to
have spent the next three years in teaching and further study.[2]
He was ordained to the pastorate of West Church and Society,
Boston, in June, 1747. Too unorthodox for the Boston Association of Congregational Ministers, he instituted his own series
of weekly lectures, the publication of which in 1749 won him
acclaim even in the mother country, led to a D.D. from Aber-
deen University in 1751, and launched him on a career of liberal pulpit and literary leadership in theological and ecclesiastical controversy and public affairs.[3] He was married in 1756,
at the age of thirty-five, to Miss Elizabeth Clark of Boston.[4]
They had two children.[5] Mayhew died in 1766, not yet forty-
six years old, after illness resulting from exposure on a home-
ward trip from a church council. He had been pastor only nineteen years.[6]

   To list and characterize Mayhew's more important publications is virtually to tell the story of his public career and main
interests during those nineteen years. His first book of "Thursday lectures" was entitled *Seven Sermons upon the Following
Subjects; viz. The Difference betwixt Truth and Falshood*
[sic], *Right and Wrong . . . The Right and Duty of Private
Judgment.*[7] Preached only a year after his ordination, these
sermons were a ringing declaration of theological independ-

   1. Alden Bradford, *Memoir of the Life and Writings of Rev. Jonathan Mayhew, D.D., Pastor of the West Church and Society in Boston, from June, 1747, to
July, 1766* (Boston, 1838) , pp. 12 f.
   2. *Ibid.*, pp. 15, 21.
   3. *Ibid.*, pp. 25, 28, 32.
   4. *Ibid.*, p. 169.
   5. *Ibid.*, p. 440 n.
   6. *Ibid.*, pp. 430 f.
   7. *Seven Sermons upon the Following Subjects; viz. The Difference betwixt
Truth and Falshood, Right and Wrong, The Natural Abilities of Men for Discerning These Differences. The Right and Duty of Private Judgment. Objections
Considered. The Love of God. The Love of Our Neighbour. The First and Great
Commandment, &c. Preached at a Lecture in the West Meeting-House in Boston
Begun the First Thursday in June, and Ended the Last Thursday in August,
1748* (Boston, 1749) . (Capitalization in Mayhew's titles has been regularized in
these footnotes.)

ence, if any further declaration was needed where he was already taken for an Arminian. That his rejection of theological authority was related to a like rejection of ecclesiastical and political authoritarianism was forcefully illustrated in his next publication, a January 30, 1750, sermon called *A Discourse concerning Unlimited Submission and Non-resistance to the Higher Powers*,[8] in which Mayhew turned the centenary anniversary observance of the "martyrdom" of Charles I into an occasion for opposing all for which the unhappy authoritarian "saint" had stood. His more positive views on civil government were expressed in his 1754 General Election sermon, in which he acknowledged his intellectual debt to Plato, Demosthenes, Cicero, Sidney, Milton, Locke, and Hoadly.[9] In 1755 Mayhew published a long book of *Sermons upon the Following Subjects; viz. On Hearing the Word*[10] and added greatly to the earlier expression of his rational and scriptural religion. In these sermons he outlined his views of "evangelical obedience," freedom of the will, and moral power, and specifically attacked as un-Christian and unscriptural the orthodox and Edwardean doctrines of imputation, justification by faith, total depravity, and the need of irresistible grace.[11] An earthquake that same year called forth his *Two Sermons . . . Earthquakes . . . The Expected Dissolution of All Things, a Motive to Universal Holiness*,[12] an example of his facility in making homiletical and

8. *A Discourse Concerning Unlimited Submission and Non-resistance to the Higher Powers: with Some Reflections on the Resistance Made to King Charles I. and on the Anniversary of His Death: in Which the Mysterious Doctrine of That Prince's Saintship and Martyrdom Is Unriddled* (Boston, 1750).

9. *A Sermon Preach'd in the Audience of His Excellency William Shirley, Esq.: Captain General, Governour and Commander in Chief, the Honourable His Majesty's Council, and the Honourable House of Representatives, of the Province of the Massachusetts-Bay, in New England, May 29th, 1754. Being the Anniversary for the Election of His Majesty's Council for the Province* (Boston, 1754).

10. *Sermons upon the Following Subjects: viz. On Hearing the Word: On Receiving It with Meekness: On Renouncing Gross Immoralities: On the Necessity of Obeying the Gospel: On Being Found in Christ* (Boston, 1755).

11. *Ibid., passim.* See also Bradford, *op. cit.*, pp. 136–166.

12. *The Expected Dissolution of All Things, a Motive to Universal Holiness. Two Sermons Preached in Boston, N. E. on the Lord's Day, Nov. 23, 1755; Occasioned by the Earthquakes Which Happened on the Tuesday Morning and Saturday Evening Preceeding* [sic] ([Boston], 1755). According to Bradford, a great fire in Boston was another such sermon occasion; and other Boston ministers preached on these same subjects (*op. cit.*, pp. 167 ff.).

doctrinal capital even out of natural catastrophe. Of less importance for our present purpose were his *Two Discourses Delivered November 23d. 1758, being the Day Appointed by Authority to be Observed as a Day of Public Thanksgiving*,[13] and his 1761 *A Discourse Occasioned by the Death of King George II. and the Happy Accession of His Majesty King George III*,[14] both of which showed Mayhew's political loyalty to able and constitutionally bound political sovereignty, as well as his expectation that such authority carry out its obligations to its constituency. His *Discourse Occasioned by the Death of the Honourable Stephen Sewall*[15] was a 1760 funeral sermon for one of the numerous outstanding public figures attending his church and sharing his liberal theological and political views.

In 1763 Mayhew published another book of sermons, the full title of which shows another side of his appeal: *Christian Sobriety: Being Eight Sermons on Titus II.6. Preached with a Special View to the Benefit of the Young Men Usually Attending the Public Worship at the West Church in Boston*, published, as his preface shows, in response to the petition of some fifty of these young men who doubtless found in Mayhew a fresh and vigorous intellectual and spiritual leader.[16] Two other sermons were published the same year or before on *Striving to Enter in at the Strait Gate*, in which Mayhew considered the question of the connection between the sinner's striving and his salvation, and in which he again asserted his anti-Calvinistic views of man's nature and moral ability.[17] Another book about

13. *Two Discourses Delivered November 23d. 1758, Being the Day Appointed by Authority to be Observed as a Day of Public Thanksgiving: Relating, More Especially, to the Success of His Majesty's Arms, and Those of the King of Prussia, the Last Year* (Boston, n.d. [probably 1758]).
14. *A Discourse Occasioned by the Death of King George II. and the Happy Accession of His Majesty King George III. to the Imperial Throne of Great-Britain; Delivered Jan. 4th 1761* (Boston, 1761).
15. *Discourse Occasioned by the Death of the Honourable Stephen Sewall, Esq; Who Departed This Life on Wednesday Night, September 10, 1760* (Boston, 1760). Sewall was provincial Chief Justice and close friend of Mayhew, according to Bradford (*op. cit.*, p. 175), and as the sermon itself shows.
16. Boston, 1763. In one of these sermons Mayhew counseled the young men not to argue with the orthodox until they had successfully argued with the whirlwind and Niagara—apparently a precipitate from his personal experience.
17. Cited in Bradford, *op. cit.*, pp. 203 ff.

the same time consisted of two Thanksgiving Day sermons *On the Nature, Extent, and Perfection of the Divine Goodness.* A published attack on these by a Mr. Cleaveland elicited from Mayhew a very severe and sarcastic rebuttal which not only showed his rejection of the Trinity and the Athanasian and Nicene Creeds in favor of a somewhat Arian view of Christ and a Grotian view of the Atonement, but also exhibited Mayhew at his controversial worst in personal attack entirely out of keeping with the Divine Goodness.[18]

At this same time Mayhew was involved in a more significant controversy over the efforts of the Episcopalians to secure a bishop for New England. He first published a tract of *Observations on the Charter and Conduct of the Society for the Propagation of the Gospel in Foreign Parts,* followed an answering pamphlet with *A Defence of the Observations . . . against an Anonymous Pamphlet Falsly Intitled, A Candid Examination of Dr. Mayhew's Observations &c.,* and later added his further *Remarks on an Anonymous Tract.*[19] For Mayhew, as for his friend James Otis and the Congregational clergy in general, this effort to secure an Episcopal establishment in New England was a threat to both political and religious liberties.[20] The political significance of Mayhew's vigorous polemic earned also John Adams' later approving comment.[21] Two further published addresses may be mentioned: Mayhew's Dudleian Lec-

18. *Ibid.,* pp. 237, 383 ff. Bradford dates these sermons in 1762; Frank Hugh Foster, in *A Genetic History of the New England Theology* (Chicago, 1907), p. 133 n., has 1763. Foster discusses Samuel Hopkins' answer to Mayhew.

19. *A Defence of the Observations on the Charter and Conduct of the Society for the Propagation of the Gospel in Foreign Parts, against an Anonymous Pamphlet Falsly Intitled, A Candid Examination of Dr. Mayhew's Observations &c* (Boston, 1763); and *Remarks on an Anonymous Tract, Entitled, An Answer to Dr. Mayhew's Observations on the Charter and Conduct of the Society for the Propagation of the Gospel in Foreign Parts. Being a Second Defence of the Said Observations* (Boston, 1764). With the original *Observations* (not seen in preparation of this paper), these afford material worth further study in connection with the problems of religious liberty and Church and State.

20. William Tudor, in *The Life of James Otis, of Massachusetts: Containing Also, Notices of Some Contemporary Characters and Events from the Year 1760 to 1775* (Boston, 1823), pp. 140–147, discusses Mayhew's opposition to the episcopate, his Charles the Martyr sermon, and (with quotations) his last sermon on repeal of the Stamp Act. Tudor draws an interesting comparison between Otis and Mayhew (p. 142).

21. Bradford, *op. cit.,* p. 276.

ture on *Popish Idolatry;* and his sermon on the repeal of the
Stamp Act, which was preached shortly before his death in
1766, and in which he again expressed his views on natural
rights and liberty.[22]

This review of most of his publications yields a portrait of
Mayhew as an outspoken and courageous religious and political
liberal, a preacher to young men, a friend of prominent men
in public life and of future revolutionary leaders, an ardent
patriot, a vigorous controversialist. It is apparent that his interest was predominantly ethical, as his theological concern was
primarily anthropological. His earlier controversial preaching
was largely theological, but he was increasingly interested in
and involved with public affairs.[23] This represented not so
much a change in views as their application to the problems of
the day. Mayhew's forthright liberalism in pulpit and press
not only allied him with like-minded New Englanders such as
Sewall, Otis, Samuel Adams, Winthrop the scientist, and
Charles Chauncy, but also made him friends across the ocean
among English liberals who responded to his books by initiat-
ing correspondence.[24] Notable among these was Thomas Hollis,
an English Dissenter, Baptist, advocate of religious and civil
liberty, founder of the Hollis chair of divinity at Harvard in
1723,[25] who for years maintained cordial correspondence with
Mayhew, sent him books—including editions of Sidney and
Locke, symbols of their mutual interest—and sent books
through him for Harvard College.[26]

New England in Mayhew's time was slowly but surely coming
of the Age of Reason. Mayhew was not so much the intellectual innovator as the pulpit herald of the changing political

22. *Ibid.,* pp. 414 ff. Bradford also relates that one of Mayhew's last acts was to
write to Otis suggesting an effort to cement the colonies against oppression. See
ibid., p. 428, for Mayhew's letter.
23. Joseph Henry Allen, "Historical Sketch of the Unitarian Movement Since
the Reformation," in Allen and Richard Eddy, *A History of the Unitarians and
the Universalists in the United States* ("American Church History Series," Vol. X
[New York, 1894]) , p. 179.
24. Bradford, *op. cit.,* pp. 472 ff., 179 ff.
25. Allen, *op. cit.,* p. 188.
26. Bradford, *op. cit.,* pp. 185, 202. Hollis even sent a generous gift of money
to Mrs. Mayhew after Mayhew's death *(ibid.,* p. 440) .

and theological views. For decades the New England clergy and laity had discussed problems of church government which prepared their minds for the new winds of political doctrine from England and the Continent. John Wise had published in 1716 his *Vindication* of local church autonomy and democracy, and rested his defense partly on the natural rights evident from the Light of Nature, "emphasizing the natural equality and liberty of all men and their right to judge for themselves what was most for their happiness and well-being." [27] In 1744, not long before Mayhew's lectures on private judgment and his 1750 sermon against "unlimited submission," a pseudonymous pamphlet by "Philalethes" proclaimed *The Essential Rights and Liberties of Protestants, a Seasonable Plea for Liberty of Conscience and the Right of Private Judgment in matters of Religion, without any control from Human Authority.*[28] The author drew heavily on Locke in explaining the natural right to property and the natural and unalienable right of men to religious freedom.[29] The annual Election Sermons offered many prominent New England ministers the opportunity of declaring their views on political rights and duties. These views increasingly reflected not only biblical grounding but also the influence of Locke and the natural-rights, social-compact theorists in general.[30] If Mayhew went on to advocate political revolution, he was but bringing out more radically the logic of their premises.

It might have been expected that the changing New England culture and the influx of English rationalism would foster theological changes as well. The early settlers had been almost uniformly Covenant Calvinists in theology. Homogeneity was so assumed that many of the early church covenants were nondogmatic in form, a fact which left the way open to a gradual doctrinal modification less perceptible than its ecclesiological correlates in the Half-way Covenant and the use of the Lord's

---

27. Alice M. Baldwin, *The New England Clergy and the American Revolution* (Durham, N. C., 1928) , p. 53.
28. Attributed to Elisha Williams, a follower of Whitefield (*ibid.,* p. 65) .
29. *Ibid.,* pp. 66 f.
30. *Ibid., passim,* especially chap. i.

Supper as a "converting ordinance." [31] To be sure, efforts were made to secure doctrinal conformity, but against them were ranged sociological changes and the aforementioned political restiveness, which together made the older Calvinism incongruent with the social and economic order. The "Arminian" and rationalist estimates of human nature were more congenial to a people of growing independence, developing middle class, and prosperous commerce.[32] Well might a Jonathan Edwards, in his Thursday lecture in Boston in 1731, recall a "God Glorified in the Work of Redemption," and warn against the growing Arminianism.[33] Mayhew's biographer lists thirty-three New England preachers of Mayhew's day who openly opposed or quietly refrained from teaching and advocating such Calvinistic doctrines as total depravity, election and reprobation, and the Trinitarian theology.[34] But few were outspoken in their Arminianism. The Awakening had come to Boston and gone, and left its legacy of theological disputation, recrimination, and criticism of liberal tendencies. Harvard in particular, where Mayhew had read Locke and Samuel Clarke and other rationalists, was condemned for its rationalism. So cautious had some become that the Boston clergy, even liberals like Charles Chauncy, were conspicuously absent at Mayhew's ordination, for he was "the first openly-avowed Arminian to ascend a New England pulpit." [35] The older orthodoxy and its New Light renewal of Calvinism were still too strong for a frontal attack by the liberals—at least until the "new gospel of reason" found utterance through Mayhew, the "boldest preacher of his day." [36]

31. Allen, *op. cit.*, pp. 171 ff.
32. Perry Miller, *Jonathan Edwards* (New York, 1949) , pp. 112 f.
33. *Ibid.*, pp. 15 ff.
34. Bradford, *op. cit.*, pp. 24 ff. (source also of lines to follow) .
35. Miller, *op. cit.*, p. 322. "When the economic and social order evolve of themselves into a system that contradicts the ideology, it takes courage to repudiate venerable formulae. This courage Jonathan Mayhew showed in the 1740's when he openly defied Calvinism and preached a theology compatible with rational and commercial Boston, although Boston was aghast when he did it" (*ibid.*, p. 113) . Miller mentions also "the writhings of the free and catholic sect as Mayhew embarrassed them by blurting out what was in their own minds" (*ibid.*, p. 323) .
36. Allen, *op. cit.*, p. 177.

The Background of Mayhew's Thought

Formative influences on Mayhew's thought may be sought both at home and abroad. His father, Experience Mayhew, engaged in theological controversy with the Awakening leaders Whitefield and Jonathan Dickinson, and wrote *Grace Defended* to show that man has moral power and must be active to receive grace.[37] That young Jonathan early shared his father's antipathy to the extravagances of the revival and of Whitefield in particular is apparent from letters written during his student days.[38] To probable paternal influence against orthodoxy and the Awakening may be added the Harvard of Mayhew's time with its covert "Arminianism" and its rationalist books.[39] Dr. Ebenezer Gay of Hingham, with whom Mayhew spent some time during his later student days, and who had the courage to preach the young radical's ordination sermon, seems to have been a further liberalizing influence.[40] But the larger intellectual environment of this forthright herald of the new truth was the Age of Reason in its English expressions, through Locke, Clarke, and others whom Mayhew read at Harvard, in the interim before his pastorate, and in the years which followed.[41] A brief notice of the Christian rationalism of Locke and Clarke, both quoted in Mayhew's first book, will provide background for a consideration of Mayhew's own ideas of reason and revelation.

For the rationalists in general, from the Socinians to the deists, the central point of departure from traditional Christianity was anthropological, the chief interest ethical. Man could no longer be thought of, as classical Christianity and Calvinism in particular pictured him, as too depraved morally and intellectually to work out his own salvation. Rather, natural human reason was the adequate guide to the good life; the

---

37. Bradford, *op. cit.*, p. 14.
38. *Ibid.*, pp. 18, 102.
39. *Ibid.*, p. 16.
40. *Ibid.*, pp. 21, 25 ff., 436.
41. *Ibid.*, pp. 18 ff. (especially n.) , and p. 21. Mayhew copied extracts from Locke and Clarke during this interim.

good life was the essential element in religion; and man was morally able to live it, with religious beliefs providing motives and sanctions of morality.[42] The essentials of religious belief must be those discernible by reason, for religion, like all else, must now justify itself at the bar of this new omnicompetent judge. As Leslie Stephen suggests, the old Vincentian formula for the essentials of the faith, *"quod semper, quod ubique, quod ab omnibus,"* received a radically new twist: If *omnibus, ubique,* and *semper* are extended to take in not only Christians but all men everywhere in all ages, as seemed required by reason, "then the true faith must be identified with that universal religion of nature, implanted in all men's hearts by their Creator," the fundamentals of which could be rationally ascertained.[43] Lord Herbert of Cherbury had given an early (1624) deist formulation of these fundamentals as "the existence of God, the duty of worshipping him, the importance of piety and virtue as the chief parts of this duty, the propriety of repentance, and the existence of a future state of rewards and punishments." [44]

For Christian rationalists like Locke and Clarke, as for Tillotson, who set their pattern, the crucial problem was to maintain both the adequacy of reason and natural religion on the one hand, and the necessity of revelation and of the Christian revelation on the other. The first they assumed; the second they must now establish. This meant that they must not only show revelation to be rational in itself and consistent with natural religion; they must also show incontrovertible evidence for the divine authorship of the Christian revelation in particular.[45] John Locke undertook this dual validation in *The Reasonableness of Christianity, as Delivered in the Scriptures* (1695). He readily discovered New Testament Christianity to be pri-

---

42. Arthur Cushman M'Giffert, *Protestant Thought before Kant* (New York, 1936) , pp. 186, 252; and John Herman Randall, Jr., *The Making of the Modern Mind: A Survey of the Intellectual Background of the Present Age* (rev. ed.; Cambridge, Mass., 1940) , pp. 284 ff.

43. *History of English Thought in the Eighteenth Century* (London, 1876) , I, 83 f.

44. *Loc. cit.*

45. Randall, *op. cit.,* p. 289.

marily moral in character and therefore in accord with reason. But why was a Saviour needed, and what were his credentials? Miracle was the proof: "The evidence of our Saviour's mission from heaven is so great, in the multitude of miracles he did before all sorts of people; that what he delivered cannot but be received as the oracles of God and as unquestionable truth. . . ." Though the Deity has sufficiently manifested himself in nature to reason, men have made little use of their reason, blinded by sense, lust, fear, and priests who have divorced reason and religion. The thinking few who found "the one, supreme, invisible God" lacked authority to persuade the multitude. The revelation by Moses "was shut up in a little corner of the world," and afforded the Gentiles none of the "attestation of the miracles, on which the Hebrews built their faith." But Christ dissipated the darkness with his clear revelation, and he and then his apostles after his resurrection brought the world a miraculously attested message restoring the knowledge of God.[46]

Besides the knowledge of God, men needed "a clear knowledge of their duty," which, though ascertainable by philosophers, was corrupted by priests, and in general was too piecemeal and lacking in force to secure morality. The people needed principles enforced by divine commands, and received them: "It is all pure, all sincere; nothing too much, nothing wanting: but such a complete rule of life, as (the wisest men must acknowledge) tends entirely to the good of mankind; and all would be happy, if all would practise it." [47] Further, the "outward forms of *worshipping* the Deity wanted a reformation," in the interest of sincere, inward, spiritual worship as contrasted with the externalities of magnificent temples and ceremonies. Again, Christ brought great encouragement to virtue and piety, amid difficulties and obstacles, pains and hardships, suffering for conscience' sake—encouragement through

---

46. John Locke, *The Reasonableness of Christianity, as Delivered in the Scriptures* (Boston, 1811) , pp. 217–223.

47. *Ibid.*, pp. 224 ff., 238.

assurance of a future state of reward and punishment, only dimly discernible by reason, but now divinely attested to reinforce men's natural understanding of the goodness of virtue. "Upon this foundation, and *upon this only,* morality stands firm," said Locke. Lastly, Christ promised assistance to support and carry a man through in his effort to live virtuously and practice true religion despite the "difficulties of his nature, beset with temptations, and hedged in with prevailing custom. . . ." [48] In sum, the Christian revelation added to natural religion a surer knowledge of God and of moral duties, made worship sincere and spiritual, and gave not only a sanction to virtue in terms of future reward and punishment, but also assurance of present help in living the good life.

Samuel Clarke was in virtual agreement with Locke on the necessity of revelation as supplement to reason in religion, but as against Locke's empiricism he began with innate ideas and a priori reasoning.[49] His 1705 Boyle Lectures, a decade after Locke's *Reasonableness,* were *A Discourse concerning the Unchangeable Obligations of Natural Religion, and the Truth and Certainty of the Christian Revelation.* As Leslie Stephen says, Clarke "starts by insisting upon the clearness, immutability, and universality of the law of nature. Morality, like mathematics, is founded upon 'the eternal and necessary differences of things'. . . . A rational being can no more forbear giving his assent to the eternal rule of right and equity, than 'one who is instructed in mathematics can forbear giving his assent to every geometrical demonstration of which he understands the terms.' " [50] Yet even a demonstrable natural religion—belief

48. *Ibid.,* pp. 238–245.

49. M'Giffert, *op. cit.,* p. 207. J. M. Robertson, in *A History of Freethought, Ancient and Modern to the Period of the French Revolution* (4th ed.; London, 1936), II, 664, comments that "The German historian Tennemann sums up that Clarke wrote his apologetic works because 'the consequences of the empiricism of Locke had become so decidedly favourable to the cause of atheism, skepticism, materialism, and irreligion' (*Manual of the Hist. of Philos.* Engl. tr. Bohn ed. #349) ."

50. Stephen, *op. cit.,* I, 123 f. Ralph Cudworth's treatise on *Eternal and Immutable Morality* (published posthumously, 1731), and William Wollaston's *The Religion of Nature Delineated* (1722) represent similarly the relation of realist epistemology and ethical absolutes. See John Tulloch, *Rational Theology*

in God and irrefutable moral obligation as divine will—required the moral sanctions of reward and punishment, and future life for redress of inequities.[51] Thus Clarke went beyond Locke in his rational demonstration of that required enforcement of virtue, immortality. Why, then, is revelation necessary? "Why is an inspired system of morality more needed than an inspired system of mathematics?" might well be asked.[52]

For Clarke, as for Locke, revelation was needed to reinforce reason and secure morality. In spite of rational demonstration, men persistently doubt a future life and retribution; their carelessness, prejudice, and worldly involvement, their vice and debauchery, have obscured necessary truths. But revelation is needed also to know whatever the Sovereign of the universe may do out of his goodness over and above what reason can ascertain of the fundamental laws and constitution of the universe. Reason can presume, but cannot positively prove " 'from any of God's attributes, that he is absolutely obliged to pardon all creatures all their sins at all times . . . barely and immediately upon their repenting' "; here reason's "strong presumption" requires the check or confirmation of direct revelation.[53] Hence, with somewhat less ground than Locke, Clarke found a particular revelation necessary; and like Locke, he believed that Christianity offered the necessary "evidences" of its divine authenticity and necessity.[54]

Jonathan Mayhew read and quoted these representative English Christian rationalists; but he read others besides, and all went through the crucible of his fiery spirit and were forged into a new American Christian rationalism. Locke and Clarke came to Boston in Mayhew, but it was to Boston they came, and to a Boston Mayhew knew and could speak to, with problems and concerns differing from the English scene and calling forth Mayhew's own distinctive presentation.

---

and Christian Philosophy in England in the Seventeenth Century (2nd ed.; Edinburgh and London, 1874) , II, especially 283 f., on Cudworth; and Stephen, *op. cit.,* I, 130 f., on Wollaston, as follower of Clarke.

51. M'Giffert, *op. cit.,* p. 207.
52. Stephen, *op. cit.,* I, 125.
53. *Ibid.,* pp. 126 f.
54. M'Giffert, *op. cit.,* pp. 209 f.

Mayhew's Views of Reason and Revelation

Mayhew's views of reason and revelation are presented in his *Seven Sermons upon the Following Subjects; viz. The Difference betwixt Truth and Falshood, Right and Wrong. The Natural Abilities of Men for Discerning These Differences. The Right and Duty of Private Judgment. Objections Considered. The Love of God. The Love of Our Neighbour. The First and Great Commandment, &c.* The first four sermons comprise a unit dealing primarily with the problem of reason and revelation. Because of their admirable logical organization and development, they may be followed in order as the argument unfolds, before comments are added on their implications. The second and related unit of three sermons deals with the essential content of natural and revealed religion, and will be treated topically in the closing part of this paper.

Mayhew begins with a text from Luke 12:54–57, the last two verses of which read: ". . . ye can discern the face of the sky and of the earth; but how is it that ye do not discern this time? Yea, and why even of yourselves judge ye not what is right?" After a paraphrase footnoted to "Dr. Clarke," he lays down "several universal truths" as theses of the sermons to follow:

  I. That there is a natural difference betwixt truth and falshood, right and wrong.

 II. That men are naturally endowed with faculties proper for the discerning of these differences.

III. *and lastly,* That men are under obligation to exert these faculties, and to judge for themselves in things of a religious concern.[55]

The first sermon undertakes the task Hobbes had bequeathed most moralists since his day; namely, of refuting his ethical relativism.[56] Mayhew begins with what was then the

---

55. *Seven Sermons*, p. 5. That Samuel Clarke is due credit for much more than this paraphrase will become evident in the course of the discussion which follows.

56. See Robertson, *op. cit.*, II, 618, 638 ff.; and his note on p. 618: " 'For two generations the effort to construct morality on a philosophical basis takes more or less the form of answers to Hobbes' " (Sidwick [Sidgwick], *Outlines of the*

simpler tactic of first setting epistemological skepticism at naught; he tilts with the ancient Skeptics, the Pyrrhonists, in what seems a gratuitous effort or even a fight with a straw man until later there appear the implications for Hobbes and even for the real opponents, the Calvinists.[57] He is concerned about the "notion which strikes at the root of all religion, and everything wherein the happiness of mankind consists . . . the notion of an absolute indifference in nature with relation to truth and falshood, right and wrong." For such skepticism, there is "no invariable rule of life and conduct"; one man's acts or thoughts are as right as any other's; and short work is made of "all questions and debates concerning truth, religion, and the rule of human conduct." [58] Using the classical arguments against relativism as old as Socrates' against the views of Protagoras, in Plato's *Theatetus,* Mayhew shows the self-contradictions of radical relativism. If anything exists, Mayhew argues, there must be truth—"the real nature and properties of things existing"—and existence "in some certain determinate manner" unalterable by our opinions. Hence truth is determinate in itself and independent of our notions of it. "Truth, as it exists in the *mind,* is nothing but the perception or knowledge of that independent truth . . . or a knowledge of things as they really exist." [59] The possibility of such knowledge Mayhew will take up more fully in his next lecture; here he is concerned primarily to establish its objective basis.

From the certainty of truth he now argues the certainties of ethics, with the thesis, "That as *truth* has a real existence in nature, so the distinction betwixt *right* and *wrong* necessarily takes place in consequence thereof." [60] He has laid the basis earlier for such an inference; in explaining his text, he said there is an inseparable connection between *truth in theory* and *right in practice:* "If certain things are *true* in speculation,

---

History of Ethics, 3rd ed. p. 169) . Cf. Stephen, *op. cit.,* I, 120 f., and II, 5 f. (on Clarke against Hobbes especially) ; and Tulloch, *loc. cit.* (on Cudworth) ; and Bradford, *op. cit.,* p. 46 n.

57. *Seven Sermons,* pp. 5–13.
58. *Ibid.,* p. 6.
59. *Ibid.,* p. 7.
60. *Ibid.,* p. 17.

there must be some correspondent *fitness* of actions resulting therefrom. And, on the other hand, if any thing be allowed *fit* in a practical sense, that fitness or rightness must be founded in certain *truths* and *relations* before subsisting." [61] Here Mayhew's indebtedness to Clarke is obvious.

The reality of our obligation to virtue is shown first of all in its tendency to happiness, which, with others of his day, Mayhew regards as axiomatically a good in itself; in its rendering us like to God, the standard of perfection; in its injunction by the positive will and command of God, whether by reason or revelation—not *how* we know his commands but whether we know them *in fact* to be his commands is what matters; and in its law written in our hearts, an internal consciousness of the moral excellency of virtue and the odiousness of its contrary, so that we cannot violate the rules of justice without violating our own minds at the same time. [62] After this not uncommon combination of moral intuitionism, utilitarianism, and deontological ethics, a combination defensible on certain rationalist assumptions about God and his purpose to make men happy, Mayhew turns to mark out one distinction from his master Dr. Clarke, who attributed men's confusion of right and wrong to their difficulty in discernment. Such confusion, Mayhew says, is "not so much from men's originally wanting clear ideas of the difference in general betwixt right and wrong, as from their having *made* these things indifferent, as far as their own *practice* could affect it." For those whose minds are blinded and calloused by vice, it is natural to get rid of distinctions by attributing them to civil and ecclesiastical tyrants. But men are never so blind as to lose the sense of difference between right and wrong; such a sense is inseparable from our rational nature. [63]

If truth and right are objective, then—he proceeds in application of his sermon to the New England theological situation —not custom, nor orthodoxy, nor antiquity, nor numbers can

61. *Ibid.*, p. 5.
62. *Ibid.*, p. 13.
63. *Ibid.*, p. 14.

be our guides to truth, else "we must even turn *Heathens* at once, *Paganism* being the most universal *Orthodoxy* in our world." [64] In short, expect no conformity from me, Mayhew is saying, in this first Thursday lecture of his own!

The implications of the position established in the first sermon become apparent when Mayhew begins the second by showing that skepticism as to man's capacity to know good and evil, truth and error, has the same practical implications as a denial of their objectivity. Those who question man's abilities to discover truth and right, he argues again in the Socratic vein, cannot consistently claim to investigate truth, or even boast of discovering that men cannot discover truth; nor can they upbraid their opponents with ignorance, vindicate their own conduct as right, or censure that of others.[65] With Locke,[66] Mayhew argues that we know for certain some things, by immediate and intuitive certainty; other truths we know by reason, by deduction from intuitive knowledge, such as the demonstration of God and our obligation to obey him. Still other things we know only probably but adequately—including nature, history, causation. The proofs in religion are stronger: we know God and duties more easily.[67] But not all have equal abilities for judging the true and the right. We must learn; we have a natural weakness, ineptitude, and awkwardness of reason before its cultivation. What the skeptics take as grounds for relativism is accounted for by alteration and variation. We can moreover learn from books and from learned men. Some are superior. Human knowledge, then, is finite, limited, but adequate.[68]

Nevertheless, there is need for a supernatural revelation to supply our natural defects of reason and knowledge. It is the office of reason here to determine whether what is proposed as revelation is really attended with suitable evidence of coming from God. Otherwise, rational men cannot receive it as such.

---

64. *Ibid.*, pp. 19 f.
65. *Ibid.*, pp. 25 ff.
66. John Locke, *(An Abridgment of Mr. Locke's) Essay concerning Human Understanding* (Boston, 1794), Bk. IV, chap. ii, pp. 147 ff.; chap. x, pp. 188 ff.
67. *Seven Sermons*, pp. 27 ff.
68. *Ibid.*, pp. 31 f.

A second office of reason is to determine the meaning of an authenticated revelation: "If God gives men a revelation, he gives it to them to be understood." [69] Hence it is actually we who do ourselves judge what is right. We cannot, to be sure, have equal certainty in all things: "Although truth does not admit of degrees, yet the evidence of it does"; the degrees of certainty, or probability, which suffice in secular affairs, must also in religion. A long quotation from Locke on the certainty and sufficiency of human knowledge is added in support.[70]

The issue of all this, to which Mayhew has been leading, and for which the first sermon was simply a basis, is a sally against Calvinism. Not only are men "naturally endowed with faculties for distinguishing betwixt truth and error, right and wrong"; but it follows, furthermore, "that the doctrine of a total ignorance, and incapacity to judge of moral and religious truths, brought upon mankind by the apostacy of our *First Parents,* is without foundation." However brighter the picture may have been for Adam, he leaves for others to conjecture; enough for him the present, in which it is evident that men retain a natural power to judge what is true and right, with the qualifications and restrictions already pointed out.[71]

From this vantage point he thrusts at the "vain *Enthusiasts*" of the Awakening, who, confronted with this point of view, denounce their opponents as in a *"carnal state, blind,* and unable to judge," while they are *"spiritually illuminated."* These "enlightened Ideots" assert the "grossest absurdities" as "divine truths and holy mysteries," thus making "inspiration, and the Spirit of truth and wisdom, the vehicle of nonsense and contradictions. Whatever is reasonable, is, with them carnal; and nothing is worthy of belief, but what is impossible and absurd in the eye of human reason." [72]

Jesus, on the contrary, supposed no such "total eclipse" or complete darkening of men's minds; he assumed that his hearers (in the text) had proper faculties for judging of religion,

69. *Ibid.,* p. 36.
70. *Ibid.,* pp. 37 f.
71. *Ibid.,* p. 38.
72. *Loc. cit.*

and blamed them for not exerting them. We therefore should "retain a suitable sense of the dignity of our nature in this respect." In reason, which distinguishes man from the beasts, allies him to the angels, and enables him to resemble God himself, is the justification for our being said to be created in the image of God. However weak our intellectual faculties, let us not speak reproachfully of reason in general, for that would be a little less than blasphemy against God.[73] It is important, however, to know our own ignorance and have the humility which leads to grateful and diligent improvement of all the means of knowledge we are favored with, especially that revelation which God has given us by his Son. While we are in this imperfect state, "we ought not to think strange that our understandings are baffled; or that many things remain mysterious and unaccountable to us, both in the natural and moral government of God." [74]

In the third sermon, "The Right and Duty of Private Judgment Asserted," Mayhew continues and climaxes his preceding arguments. This is the heart of his contribution—his application of Clarke and Locke to Boston.

First he asks what is meant by judging for oneself or by freedom of thought and action in religious matters. Four things are involved: suspended judgment, unbiased effort to examine evidence rationally; exertion of reason in active inquiry and weighing arguments ("for truth is coy, and must be courted") ; embracing the truth when it is found, whether we like it or not, without "superstitious veneration for great names"; and finally, assent proportional to evidence.[75]

Next, having made it clear what he means by private judgment, he proceeds to the duty, the obligation of private judgment, proved directly by reason and revelation, as he says. First, the duty of private judgment is supported by *reason*. Two main considerations are advanced. (1) "A regard to our own interest ought to put us upon examining and judging for our-

73. *Ibid.*, p. 39.
74. *Ibid.*, p. 40.
75. *Ibid.*, pp. 42 ff.

selves in religious concerns." [76] Every reasonable and accountable being, says Mayhew, taking the hedonistic axiom of his age, should inquire:

What is my chief good? Where is the road which will convey me to my happiness? . . . Is there any being who created, and who governs the world? . . . If there be a God, what is his character? Is he powerful, wise, righteous and good; or is he not? Does my happiness depend on pleasing and obeying him, and conforming myself to his will? If it does, what is his will? What are his laws? What does he expect of me? What kind of government is it I am under? What is the particular and certain way in which I may obtain the goodwill of this great Parent of the world . . . ? [77]

These questions are too interesting and important to be determined by a second person. But even if they are left to another, who shall be the judges? Which of the various claims to authority is true? Indians, Turks, Christians differ; and with them all, atheists. "Now shall we submit to Theists, or to the Atheists?" If the former, which sect—those who deny, or those who believe in a revelation? If a revelation, which—Jews, Mohammedans, or Christians? It is not *reasonable* to follow one, in preference to the others, *without a reason*. If convinced of the truth of Christianity, which of its many sects, most of them claiming the only truth and salvation, and anathematizing all others? "Now, amidst these differences and altercations, what is the part of a reasonable man, but to sit down, and exercise his intellectual powers, and so to *judge even of himself what is right*? What system of doctrine—what mode of worship—what form of church-government and discipline—is most agreeable to scripture and reason—what sect of Christians he shall unite with . . . ?" Instructions vary: Some say join the *true, primitive, catholic church*. Which is that? All claim to be; which has the best claims? Some say follow a living, *infallible* guide on earth—but where is he? Many deny there is such. Others are not agreed who he is, or whether one or many. "The heads of all sects usually decide disputable matters with full as much assurance and lordliness as it would become infallibility itself

76. *Ibid.*, p. 49.
77. *Ibid.*, pp. 46 ff.

to do, although they do . . . not pretend to be exempted from a possibility of erring." The King of England heads one church, the Pope another, both claiming authority. Whose claim is to be admitted? "How shall we act a rational and intelligent part, without judging of ourselves which is right?—or, whether either of them is so?" [78] Possibly, Mayhew archly suggests, there are these two churches, and still another of which Jesus Christ is head. In all of this, there are decisions which require examination. Thus our own interest—in being right, in obeying God, in being happy—implies the duty of private religious judgment.

(2) That duty may be "argued from the faculty of reason itself, which is common to all." [79] All our bodily organs have their apparent final causes or purposes. Similarly our understandings were given us for use in seeking and embracing truth. "Truth is the natural object of reason," says Mayhew:

Our obligation, therefore, to inquire after truth, and to judge what is right, may be found within us, in our own frame and constitution. This obligation is as universal as reason itself; for every one that is endowed with this faculty, is, by the very nature of it, obliged to exercise it in the pursuit of knowledge; especially of moral and religious knowledge.[80]

Mayhew next appeals to *revelation* in support of the right and duty of private judgment in religion. (It is characteristic with him to establish his point by reason, then confirm it by revelation; though he accords revelation another sort of priority by beginning with a text.) The Christian religion, says Mayhew, is not enemy to inquiry in religion, but enjoins it as a duty. Christ, its authority, appealed to men's senses and reason as proper judges of his miracles, divine commission, and doctrine.[81]

He did not demand of men an implicit and blind belief in himself, without offering matter of conviction to their understandings; but put them upon examining in a sober rational way, whether he were authorized from heaven, or were an impostor; and so, whether

78. *Ibid.*, pp. 47 f.
79. *Ibid.*, p. 49.
80. *Ibid.*, p. 50.
81. *Ibid.*, p. 51.

his doctrines were *of God, or whether he spake of himself*. He reasons with the *Jews* in my text; he blames them for their blind attachment to the *Scribes* and *Pharisees,* their spiritual guides; and for not judging for themselves in religious matters.[82]

In disputing with the Jews, Christ appealed to their ancient prophecies, and to the miracles he wrought, to convince them that he was the Messiah. The real purpose of the miracles was to beget in their beholders a rational faith. The evangelists committed the story to writing to affect similarly those who were not eyewitnesses. "These things are written," Mayhew cites in proof, "that ye might believe that Jesus is the true Messiah, the Son of God; and that believing, ye might have life in his name" (John 20:31). The apostles also "incouraged" inquiry and examination, "as is natural for honest and undesigning men to do." Some who desire submission to their dictates may wish to discourage this and keep people muffled in darkness and ignorance.

But he that has nothing in view but the interest of truth and virtue, desires nothing more, than that persons would give themselves the trouble of a free and impartial examination. Now the apostles knowing the goodness of their cause, and following the example of their divine Master, made it their practice to incourage liberty and freedom of thought; never intimating, as most of their *pretended successors* have done, that this is hazardous to men's souls.[83]

In the apostolic age, men were urged to "try" all. *Contra* "some grave divines" whose "pleasant advice is 'Determine first; and then examine,'" Mayhew urges the early Christian appeal to reason.[84] Both reason and scripture, then, show "the duty of Christians to assert their right of private judgment in religious matters, in opposition to all who are usurping authority over them." [85]

But not only are Christians commanded to assert their own natural liberty in religious concerns; they are not to assume authority over others. Again Mayhew has established a point from which to assail orthodoxy and its guardians. Those who

82. *Loc. cit.*
83. *Ibid.,* p. 52.
84. *Ibid.,* p. 53.
85. *Ibid.,* p. 57.

discourage freedom of inquiry and judgment in religion, he declares, are guilty of encroaching on the natural rights of man to make the best of his own intellectual faculties; they assert their authority against God's, and are enemies to truth and the gospel. Especially guilty are those who fine or imprison dissenters and non-subscribers or deny them their just civil privileges and honors.[86] Creed-making also hinders private judgment—"setting up human tests of orthodoxy, instead of the infallible word of God," or other terms of Christian communion than explicitly prescribed in the gospel. Those who arrogate to themselves the right to judge for their neighbors may not be so criminal as murderers and persecutors of men for their religious views, but by consigning disbelievers to the devil, they intimidate the weak. Despite pretense of pious and godly design, of reclaiming the unsound of faith and preserving the purity of Christian truth, the dictatorial, unchristian spirit of some "holy murderers, robbers, and faith-imposers" gainsays any real concern for Christianity or men's salvation. Whatever their views, their practices are unjustifiable, injurious, tyrannical, contrary to the gospel, infringing sacred rights of conscience, preventing improvements in religious knowledge, and entailing "ignorance, error, and superstition upon future generations." [87]

What if such authoritarian restraints were imposed upon the sciences? Mayhew asks. "We cannot think of supporting and propagating the sciences, by dint of *authority,* without smiling. And it is equally ridiculous to attempt to propagate religious knowledge and the doctrines of the gospel, by authority." [88]

Error, as well as *iniquity,* may be *established by a law:* And when it is so, a man must either subscribe to it, contrary to his sentiments; or seriously embrace it for truth: A sad dilemma! when a man is thus forced to be a knave or a fool! Mankind in general seem to be quite indolent enough, backward enough to examine into moral and religious subjects, without those unnatural restraints which are put upon them by the setting up of authority in matters of faith.[89]

86. *Ibid.,* pp. 57–59.
87. *Ibid.,* pp. 59–61.
88. *Ibid.,* p. 62.
89. *Loc. cit.*

Such compulsive measures are not those by which the truth as it is in Jesus was first propagated and defended, nor are they of present service to the cause of truth and religion. "To attempt to *dragoon* men into sound orthodox christians, is as unnatural and fruitless as to attempt to *dragoon* them into poets, physicians or mathematicians. A blow with a club," he continues, with the revivalists in mind,

may fracture a man's skull; but I suppose he will not think and reason the more clearly for that; though he may possibly believe the more orthodoxly, according to the opinions of some. And upon this account it must be confessed that they who make use of these methods to propagate their sentiments, act very prudently: for their doctrines are generally such as are more readily embraced by a man after his brains are knocked out, than while he continues in his senses, and of a sound mind.[90]

Mayhew's fourth sermon, "Objections Considered," anticipates and refutes possible arguments against the positions already established. He is firmly convinced that the objectivity of truth and right and the ability of human reason supplemented by revelation will yield the truth. This makes all compulsion not only superfluous but wicked. Whence comes the doctrine, he asks, that true orthodox Christians have a right to persecute heretics and unbelievers—to be more wicked and immoral than their victims? "Faith and repentance are the work of *reason* and of the *spirit* of God; and cannot be wrought in a man by a *cudgel*, a *sword*, or a *gallows*." [91]

Some might object that liberty of judgment would lead many into pernicious errors. But such liberty is not liberty to choose or judge wrongly. Men are obliged to judge truly and wisely, and to reject only what is wrong:

The right of private judgment does not imply, that it is indifferent whether a man judges truly, or not, any more than a man's right of disposing of his own property, implies that he may as innocently squander it away in rioting and drunkenness, as pay his debts with it, or appropriate it to charitable uses. . . . He is under a moral

90. *Ibid.*, p. 63. Perry Miller (*op. cit.*, p. 321) says that this is directed at Jonathan Edwards.
91. *Seven Sermons,* p. 69.

obligation to reject error, and to embrace the truth, as far as he is able to reject the former, and to discern the latter.[92]

It is error and superstition that suffer from examination; true religion flourishes the more, the more people exercise their right of private judgment. But even if the cause of truth and religion suffer thereby, such liberty cannot justly be denied:

This right is given them by God and nature, and by the gospel of Christ! And no man has a right to deprive another of it, under a notion that he will make ill use of it, and fall into erroneous opinions. We may as well pick our neighbour's pocket, for fear he should spend his money in debauchery, as take from him his right of judging for himself, and chusing his religion, for fear he should judge amiss, and abuse his liberty.[93]

One further quotation, in the vein of the "Philalethes" who had written just four years earlier, and of their common master Locke, sums up Mayhew's position: [94]

Did I say, we have a *right* to judge and act for ourselves? I now add—it is our *indispensible* [*sic*] *duty* to do it. This is a right we cannot relinquish or neglect to exercise if we would, without being highly culpable; for it is absolutely unalienable in its own nature. We may dispose of our temporal substance if we please; but God and nature and the gospel of Christ injoin upon us a duty to maintain the right of private judgment, and to worship God according to our consciences, as much as they injoin us to give an alms to the poor, to love God and our neighbour, and to practice universal righteousness. . . . They are all *duties,* and not *rights* simply. . . .[95]

From this digest of Mayhew's views of reason and revelation we are in a position to inquire: In what respects did he prove a disciple of the moderate evangelical rationalists, especially of Locke and Clarke? What characteristic assumptions, arguments, and emphases does he share with one or both of these? Without attempting to identify in every case their respective contributions to his thought, or implying in each case a necessary connection, we may briefly indicate the following shared views:

92. *Ibid.,* pp. 70 f.
93. *Ibid.,* p. 74.
94. *Supra,* p. 298; also see Baldwin, *op. cit.,* pp. 65 ff., for an extended quotation from Philalethes' pseudonymous pamphlet.
95. *Seven Sermons,* p. 86.

(1) In general Mayhew followed the ethical intuitionists—Cudworth, Clarke, and others—in defending epistemological and ethical objectivity against the relativism of Hobbes, though his interest was not so much in countering relativism (probably not a live issue in Boston then) as in laying a basis for opposing the theistic, Calvinistic counterpart of the Hobbesian atheistic pessimism about human nature.

(2) He shared with this school of thought, Clarke and Wollaston in particular, the characteristic inference from objectivity in knowledge to objectivity in morals and therefore in religion as essentially morality. The pragmatists were later to retain the mutual implication of truth and fitness without rooting either objectively; but for Mayhew, truth and right, knowledge and ethics, were firmly rooted in nature, a nature to which reason was key.

(3) With these thinkers and the various "moral sense" ethicists, he believed in a moral sense or faculty inseparable from man's rational nature. Further comment on this may await the next section of this paper, where his concept of such a faculty is seen in more detail. It is worth noting here, however, that this and the preceding points distinguish Mayhew's thought somewhat from the empiricism of Locke.

(4) When Mayhew turned from the question of the natural status of truth and right to the problem of man's knowledge of these objective realities, he shifted from Clarke's a priorism toward Locke's empiricism. Where Clarke reasoned deductively and with greater show of certainty, in the manner of his friend Newton, Locke, with Mayhew after him, thought in terms of learning, of inquiry, of assent proportional to evidence, of degrees of certainty and probability.

(5) With both Locke and Clarke, and against deism on the one hand and orthodoxy on the other, Mayhew found reason generally adequate but revelation also necessary. He seemed to be closer to Locke in tone—in emphasizing, for instance, the authoritarian and priestly submergence of reason, and the disvalue of creeds and speculative subtleties. With Locke rather than Clarke, he attributed men's moral confusion also to their

having made moral distinctions indifferent through practice. But with the rationalists in general, Mayhew made reason the final test even of revelation, which requires both authentication and explanation by reason.

(6) For Mayhew, as for most of the Christian rationalists, the Christian revelation authenticated itself by miracle and prophecy. Some emphasized miracle, some prophecy; Mayhew mentioned both but dwelt most on the former. As for Locke and the others, the purpose of Christ's miracles was primarily evidential. Once his Messiahship was thus established, his teachings were to be accepted as from God. His teachings were of course reasonable, and essentially moral, with the added assurance of immortality as sanction.

(7) With Locke, Mayhew placed strong emphasis on natural rights, which are unalienable, and which therefore render all ecclesiastical, theological, and political authoritarianism criminal. Much of Mayhew's ministry was given to a vigorous opposition to such authoritarianisms, as he denounced Calvinism, fought Episcopacy and the threat of Establishment, and advocated revolution against England, all for the natural rights of religious and political liberty.

(8) Finally, with rationalism in general, and against Calvinism, Mayhew assumed that man's happiness was his natural and supreme goal, and God's goal for man as well. Where a theocentric Calvinism said man's chief end was to glorify God and enjoy him forever, anthropocentric rationalism tended to see God, nature, and society as willing contributors to the glory and enjoyment of man. Where Calvinism saw the social order, the state, for instance, as directed ultimately to man's salvation and God's glory, rationalistic natural-rights theory dwelt on man's unalienable rights to life, liberty, property, and happiness. While conceiving these as God-given rights, Mayhew belonged essentially to the rationalist tradition. He was a faithful disciple of moderate, evangelical, Christian rationalism, but withal a distinctly American disciple, speaking to the American situation.

Mayhew's Natural and Revealed Religion: Theology and Ethics

The meaning of Mayhew's views of reason and revelation for the positive content of his natural and revealed religion— what his "truth and right" are in terms of theology and ethics— may be discovered especially in the last three of the *Seven Sermons*. Their text is, "Thou shalt love the Lord thy God with all thy heart, and with all thy soul, and with all thy mind. This is the first and great commandment. And the second is like unto it, Thou shalt love thy neighbour as thyself. On these two commandments hang all the law and the prophets" (Matthew 22:37–40). The three sermons deal with the nature and obligation of the two duties of love of God and love of neighbor, and with the centrality of the first commandment in particular.

We shall find at least six representative Christian rationalist emphases: (1) A reduction of Christian teaching to the simplest ethical and universal principles. (2) A consequent internalization of the first commandment. (3) The belief in a moral faculty or sense for which the love of a perfect God is natural. (4) The assumption of a rational harmony of interests uniting rational self-love with the love of God and neighbor. (5) The consequent natural self-evidence of the central obligations of piety and benevolence. (6) And finally, a clear delineation, lacking in the first sermons, of the way in which revelation supplements natural religion. These six themes may be illustrated with passages from the three closing sermons.

(1) Mayhew's fundamental ethical interest is underscored in the opening sentences of the fifth sermon, linking the latter with what has gone before:

That which renders it a matter of the highest importance to examine with freedom into moral and religious subjects, is not so much the advantage simply of knowing what is *true* and *right,* as the necessity of this in order to true and right *action.* It is scarce of any importance to us to gain a speculative knowledge of true religion, but as this has relation to practice. . . .[96]

Otherwise we confuse the end with the means. Knowledge in religion is like theory for "marriners," who must use it or be shipwrecked; man must avoid spiritual and moral shipwreck too. "Religious knowledge applyed to its true ends and purposes, is the only knowledge that can be finally profitable and gainful. . . ." [97] Mayhew finds Christianity eminently practical. Its main design, he asserts in the closing sermon, is to bring men to "that moral purity of heart and life, which is comprised in the love of God and of our neighbour." [98] These two commands are the sum of religious duty in natural religion, Judaism, and Christianity. This is confirmed in revelation; Christ and his apostles so taught: "What is his sermon on the mount, but a moral discourse wherein the excellency and necessity of internal piety, and holiness of life, is declared in the strongest terms?" Indeed, "the whole tenor of our Lord's preaching was *moral:* he seldom inculcated any thing upon his hearers besides piety towards God, and righteousness and charity towards man: and all his discourses were just as contrary to the *solifidian doctrines,* which too many" (of the Great Awakeners in particular) "have given in to since, as *light* is to *darkness,* or *Christ* to *Belial.*" [99]

The rational vindication of Christianity in fact requires such simplification to universal ethical principles. With the rationalist extension of the *"quod semper, quod ubique, quod ab omnibus,"* Mayhew lays down this test of true religion. It is "plain beyond dispute," he asserts,

that the substance of true religion must necessarily be the same, not only under the jewish and christian dispensations, but also, in all countries, to all rational creatures, in all parts of the universe, in all periods of time. Modes and ceremonies of religion may, indeed, be various as the circumstances and conditions of men; and God may afford different degrees of light and knowledge in different times and places: *But the sum of our duty results from the nature*

96. *Ibid.,* p. 89.
97. *Ibid.,* p. 90.
98. *Ibid.,* p. 145.
99. *Ibid.,* pp. 147 f.

of God, and our relation to him; and one another. And this must
therefore be as immutable as God himself. . . .[100]

Moreover, "that religion which must remain invariably the
same, under every change of curcumstance, through all ages,
in all places, and to all rational beings, consists in the love and
veneration of the Supreme Father and Lord of the universe,
and in the practice of righteousness and charity." [101] This
amounts to a sort of negative or permissive justification of the
Christian revelation: it is essentially ethical, and it is at one
with universal religion. The positive contribution of Christianity will appear later.

(2) The religion that is necessarily universal and essentially
ethical is also predominantly internal in its Godward reference.
With Locke, Mayhew finds Christianity a deliverance from the
externalities of worship in favor of sincere, unfeigned, uncon-
strained, rational, inward devotion. The first commandment
relates wholly to the mind; it "is distinguished not only from
all the duties of the *second table* but likewise from many of
the *first;* particularly, from all external acts of devotion; from
all rites and ceremonies and legal institutions; and in short
from all duties whatever, besides those internal ones of the
heart and *affections;* and of which God is the *only* and the *immediate object.*" [102] Here Mayhew must distinguish himself
from formalism on the one hand and from "enthusiasm" on the
other, and yet maintain a vital, warm religion. In thus emphasizing religion and devotion of the heart, he does not want his
hearers to think he is inculcating "enthusiasm," the bane of
the revival: "I propose to speak of nothing but what has its
foundation in scripture, and the nature of things: Nor will any
enthusiasm be incouraged, besides that which sober reason requires." [103] He does not mean "those flashy and rapturous sallies
of the heart toward God, which may proceed only from a fond
conceit, that we are singled out to be the peculiar favourites of
heaven. We may easily fall into an extasy, and run mad in reli-

100. *Ibid.*, p. 150. Italics mine.
101. *Ibid.*, p. 151.
102. *Ibid.*, p. 94.
103. *Loc. cit.*

gious contemplation, without having any thing of that divine love which is due to the perfections of our Creator." [104] But there is a justifiable and rational piety which goes beyond formalism and speculative aridity alike, without going to the revivalists' extremes:

The love of God is a steady, sober, calm and rational thing, the result of thought, and consideration—It is indeed a *passion,* but a passion excited by reason presenting the proper object of it to the mind. Nor ought we to be so solicitous about avoiding one extreme, as to fall into the contrary. We ought not to run so far from *enthusiasm,* as to lose sight of real devotion; we ought not to be so fond of a *rational religion,* as to suppose that it consists wholly in cold, dry speculation, without having any concern with the *affections.* Real piety necessarily supposes, that the heart is touched, affected, warmed, inflamed; and not barely that we have right speculative notions concerning God. A religion consisting in nothing but a knowledge of God's attributes, and an external conduct agreeable to his laws, would be a lifeless insipid thing: It would be neither a source of happiness to ourselves nor recommend us to the approbation of him, who requires us to give *him our heart.*[105]

(3) The subjective basis for such rational devotion is in the natural constitution of our minds. Our Creator has given us not only reason to distinguish between moral good and evil, but "has moreover given us another faculty, which is sometimes called *a moral sense;* and which St. *Paul* speaks of under the titles of the *law written in the heart,* and the *law of the mind.*" [106] When moral good is an object to our minds, it gives us pleasure; moral evil gives pain and uneasiness:

And this, as unavoidably as the eye is differently affected with regular and irregular figures in the body; or the ear, with the most grateful harmony, and the most harsh and grating discord: I say *as unavoidably;* but neither of them are absolutely unavoidable. There are some who have no *ear* for *musick,* and others who have no *eye* for *architecture, painting* or *statuary.* And so there are some, perhaps, who have little or no *taste* in *morals.*[107]

Here Mayhew must meet the problem posed for all ethical intuitionism, without surrendering either the objectivity of truth

104. *Ibid.,* p. 95.
105. *Ibid.,* pp. 95 f.
106. *Ibid.,* p. 97.
107. *Ibid.,* pp. 97 f.

and right or the natural competence of rational man: Why should some have little or no taste in morals, if they are created with a moral sense? It is not the natural state of their minds, says Mayhew, "but proceeds from their abusing and perverting *nature*. And all our animal senses may be viciated [*sic*] also."

> But take a man who has not violated frequently the *natural law of his mind;* and he can no more approve what is commonly called *malevolence, cruelty* and *injustice,* than a *skilful architect* can approve of the most *irregular* and *awkward* pile of building: And on the other hand, he can no more hate and nauseate what appears to be *honest, generous* and *benevolent,* than the other can be displeased at the sight of an edifice, all the parts of which are *adjusted* by the exactest *rules* of *proportion,* and the whole brought to the greatest *perfection of art.*[108]

The objective basis for our love to God is in his infinite perfection, to which our moral sense must respond. Both reason and revelation teach us "that God is perfect in all those moral qualities and excellences which we esteem amiable in mankind." Justice, integrity, and benevolence in our fellow men excite our esteem and love, unless we are irrational and debased in mind. God's goodness infinitely transcends that of his creatures; our Saviour said there was none good but God. "And can it be reasonable to love and admire the mere portrait of moral excellence" (in man) "and to let the substance, the source and standard of it, remain unregarded?"

> If goodness in a limited degree, be worthy the esteem of all rational beings, shall not that goodness that is without bounds, and absolutely perfect, be thought worthy to excite in all a real inward esteem also? an hearty and sincere complacency? an ardent, inextinguishable love? . . . For undoubtedly those qualities which being found in a limited degree, are really amiable, do not cease to be so, when they become infinite; but, instead of this, become *infinitely* amiable.[109]

Even apart from our self-interest, therefore, apart from our dependence on his providential care, God's moral perfection rationally, naturally deserves our love. When we go on to think

108. *Ibid.,* p. 98.
109. *Ibid.,* pp. 98 f.

of God as *"our* Creator, *our* moral Governour, *our* Father, *our* Friend, *our* Patron," we are all the more moved to love him. God evokes our gratitude; we desire his approbation and delight in it above the approval of men; we trust in him, depend upon him, need him in our weakness. He is the great end above all false ways to happiness; we can do our duty and trust him and his providence. In troubles and sufferings we can resign ourselves to his will, knowing he has ordered the best possible world. Resting our wills in God's will as our end is at bottom nothing but faith, honesty, and fairness of mind. We have joy and triumph of heart in God who governs the universe morally for his creatures' happiness.[110] Thus the first commandment of revelation is also the first commandment of reason and of self-interest.

(4) Such an identification of the requirements of self, reason, and God rests upon the assumption of a rational harmony of interests uniting man with God and his neighbors. This rationalist postulate was especially important in the thought of Joseph Butler, whose influence on Mayhew in these closing sermons might have been conjectured even without Mayhew's acknowledgment of indebtedness to the "Bishop of Bristol's" sermons on the love of God and the love of neighbor.[111] We have seen that God rules the world for his creatures' happiness; and that they love him in gratitude for his providence and because he is the source of true happiness. The self and the neighbor and all mankind are likewise cemented together in harmony and order through rational self-love.[112] Love is benevolence, good will, or charity, a disposition to do good and communicate happiness. Benevolence is directed by reason in the choice of effective means to its ends. Happiness is the only good end; therefore actions are good insofar as they produce it. From this general rule, subordinate rules follow as immediate regula-

110. *Ibid.*, pp. 100–105.
111. *Ibid.*, pp. 105 ff., 122 ff., where Mayhew quotes these sermons by the "Bishop of Bristol." It is quite likely that he read *The Analogy of Religion* as well; but Mayhew was more sanguinely rationalist than Butler. See Stephen, *op. cit.*, I, 292 ff., on Butler's ideas of the moral faculty, harmony of interests, and the nature of rational self-love.
112. *Seven Sermons,* p. 126.

tors of action, that is, as effective means: rules such as those of adhering to truth and justice, doing good to a benefactor, providing for our families first. It is the order of God and nature to see first to the good and happiness of kindred, then of friends and benefactors, then in ever larger concentric circles around the self, of neighborhood, country, nation, all mankind. But such neighbor love begins with our rational self-love: "Both our nature and condition require that each particular man should make particular provision for himself." This does not mean (as for Hobbes) that selfish men are set in mortal conflict; rather their harmony of interests correlates private and universal good. "That which tends to publick good, tends to private good also." "For *publick* happiness is increased no farther than the happiness of individuals is so." [113] Self-interest thus supports the revealed command to love our neighbor as ourself.

(5) There is moreover a support in the self-evident character of the obligation to love our neighbor. Reason and the moral faculty unite us with our fellows as they unite us with God. As the infinite perfection of God evokes the responding love of the man whose moral sense is normally exercised, so also love of neighbor is implied by the self-evident obligation to be morally good. If rational beings know what is right, they are obligated to it. That love of neighbor is right can be seen in the nature of mutual obligation; we expect good from others; we must therefore render good. Furthermore, God requires it, and "the will or law of a perfect Being, a Being who is in all respects fit to be obeyed, is what constitutes obligation in the primary and most formal notion of obligation." [114] The nearer we conform to the law of benevolence, the nearer we conform to the perfections of Deity, though we fall far short of his infinite perfection. In one final crowning expression of optimistic rationalism, Mayhew envisages rational man as realizing his place in the whole harmonious order of creation, the ever-widening circles of neighborhood, and being so ashamed of party spirit that benevolence springs up in him

113. *Ibid.,* pp. 115–127. Quotations from pp. 123, 126 f.
114. *Ibid.,* pp. 124 f.

and spreads to all.[115] Reason, self-interest, and revelation all converge in the second commandment to love our neighbor as our self.

(6) If reason so clearly teaches the natural duties of piety and charity, of love to God and love to neighbor, what need is there for revelation? This crucial question for Locke and Clarke and the other Christian rationalists was only partly answered in the earlier sermons. Three quotations from the final sermon will clarify Mayhew's basic assumptions as to the relationship of revelation to reason. The first will show once more how seriously he took the Scriptures as authority. When he says that all religion hangs on these two commandments, Mayhew explains, he takes it for granted "that Christianity is believed; that Christ is received as *a teacher sent from God;* as the *promised Messiah;* and that the doctrines of his *incarnation, death, resurrection* and *ascension* into heaven . . . and all the doctrines, delivered either by himself, or by his inspired apostles, are firmly believed." [116] Christianity not only adds doctrinal enrichment and divine authority to natural religion; it also imparts new motivation in a new relationship: The natural duties of piety and charity which comprise the substance of Christian duty "should be performed upon *evangelical* principles. The duties in themselves are really duties of *natural religion;* but being adopted into *christianity,* they are to be performed on *christian principles,* and from *gospel motives;* with a proper *regard to,* and *dependence upon* the *Mediator of this new covenant,* who gave himself for us." [117] Lest this seeming particularism be taken as a denial of his faith in universal reason, Mayhew finally reaffirms the rationalism of his Christianity:

Upon the whole, then, the case seems to stand thus—Although the christian revelation brings us acquainted with many truths besides those which the light of nature suggests, or Judaism plainly taught; although it injoins us to do several things which would not have been obligatory without an explicit command; although it furnishes us with a great variety of new and excellent motives to excite us to the practice of our duty in all its branches; and al-

115. *Ibid.,* p. 129.
116. *Ibid.,* p. 143.
117. *Ibid.,* p. 144.

though christianity cannot, for these reasons, with any sense or propriety, be said to be the same with natural religion, or only a re-publication of the law of nature; yet the principal, the most important and fundamental duties required by christianity are, nevertheless, the same which were injoined as such under the legal dispensation; and the same which are dictated by the light of nature. They are natural moral duties, inforced with revealed and supernatural motives; and to be performed from principles peculiar to the gospel.

And indeed, it is plain beyond dispute, that the substance of true religion must necessarily be the same, not only under the jewish and christian dispensations, but also, in all countries, to all rational creatures, in all parts of the universe, in all periods of time. Modes and ceremonies of religion may indeed be various as the circumstances and conditions of men; and God may afford different degrees of light and knowledge in different times and places: But the sum of our duty results from the nature of God, our relation to him; and one another. And this must therefore be as immutable as God himself.[118]

So imbued was Mayhew with the "first fine careless rapture" of American Christian rationalism. In Jonathan Mayhew and others of his day, but in Mayhew with especial freshness, vigor, and audacity, the Age of Reason came to America.

118. *Ibid.*, p. 150.

Solomon Stoddard and the
Theology of the Revival

THOMAS A. SCHAFER

There were other famous preachers and defenders of the eighteenth-century revival in America, but it is generally agreed that Jonathan Edwards was not only an important factor in the occurrence of the Great Awakening in New England but was also its most learned and discriminating exponent. For most people, his *Sinners in the Hands of an Angry God* [1] is still the symbol of revival preaching, and students continue to peruse the pamphlets Edwards exchanged with Chauncy and the "opposers" of the revival in order to understand what the real issues were in the controversy over the significance of that religious upheaval. [2] Furthermore, the only writings of permanent interest and value which emerged from the American awakenings were both written by Edwards: his description of conversion experiences in the *Faithful Narrative* [3] and his masterly delineation of true religion in his *Treatise Concerning Religious Affections.* [4]

What has not been so universally recognized is the fact that behind Edwards and his fellow revivalists in New England stands the figure of his predecessor and grandfather, Solomon Stoddard. In the *Faithful Narrative,* Edwards gave Stoddard credit for having made Northampton a place of recurring re-

---

1. Boston, 1741.
2. For a recent sympathetic but critical account, see Edwin S. Gaustad, *The Great Awakening in New England* (New York, 1957).
3. *A Faithful Narrative of the Surprizing Work of God* (London, 1737). After the first reference, titles will ordinarily be cited in much shortened form.
4. Boston, 1746.

vival, and he stressed the continuity of the 1734–1735 awakening with those that had gone before:

> The work that has now been wrought on souls, is evidently the same that was wrought in my venerable predecessor's days; as I have had abundant opportunity to know, having been in the ministry here two years with him, and so conversed with a considerable number that my grandfather thought to be savingly converted in that time; and having been particularly acquainted with the experiences of many that were converted under his ministry before. And I know no one of them that in the least doubts of its being the same spirit, and the same work.[5]

This was the revival which in many respects helped set the pattern for the Great Awakening of 1740–1742 and its successors; and it is noteworthy that it occurred in (and was mostly limited to) the Connecticut River Valley, where Stoddard's influence had been strongest.[6] Not only had Stoddard done much to teach Edwards the techniques of evangelism,[7] his works provided criteria of genuine conversion to which Edwards later appealed in the *Religious Affections*, as he sought to purify revival religion and curb its extravagances. And finally, when Edwards reversed his grandfather's policy of admitting the unconverted to the Lord's Supper, it was the town's memory of the great Stoddard, combined with tensions arising in part from the revival, which brought about Edwards' dismissal from Northampton in 1750.

Until recently, however, Stoddard seldom received more than honorable mention in treatments of Edwards or the revival. The situation is now changing. In 1941 Perry Miller first published his valuable account of Stoddard's career and theology.[8]

5. *The Works of President Edwards in Four Volumes, a Reprint of the Worcester Edition* (New York, 1843) , III, 259–260.

6. Gaustad, *op. cit.*, pp. 23–24.

7. During most of the two and a half years preceding Stoddard's death, Edwards shared with Stoddard the burden of Sunday preaching. In 1727 he even had the opportunity of participating with his grandfather in a mild revival, of which he later remarked, "I have reason to bless God for the great advantage I had by it" (*Works*, III, 232) . His sermons and theological notes from this period testify to Stoddard's influence on his thinking, especially on the subject of conversion.

8. "Solomon Stoddard, 1643–1729," *Harvard Theological Review*, XXXIV (Oct., 1941) , 277–320. This material is incorporated, with a larger context, in Miller's *New England Mind: From Colony to Province* (Cambridge, Mass., 1953) , chaps. xv-xvi.

And in his studies of Edwards, notably the intellectual biography,[9] he calls attention to similarities between the preaching of the two men (their emphasis on hell fire and divine sovereignty, for example) and shows at how many points Edwards' career was determined by the political and ecclesiastical achievements of his predecessor. Miller does not hesitate to call Stoddard "the first great 'revivalist' in New England," who "inaugurated the era of revivalism on the American frontier."[10] John E. Smith, in his introduction to the *Religious Affections,* reminds us that next to Thomas Shepard, Stoddard is cited most of the seventeen authors to whom Edwards appealed in that work.[11] Smith has opportunity for little more than a mention of certain differences between Edwards and Stoddard concerning the source of assurance and the nature of the steps preparatory to conversion, but he at least raises the question as to the precise relationship between the theologies of the two men.

This paper was begun as an effort to examine the influence of Stoddard on Edwards from a study of the published works of both men and of Edwards' unpublished sermons and notebooks. The examination showed that Edwards did indeed follow the general outlines of Stoddard's evangelistic theology and practice. But it also revealed that Edwards found things in Stoddard to question and some even to reject, and that he modified in subtle ways what he took from (or at least found strongly supported by) Stoddard. It also became clear that the limits of this essay would not permit adequate reference to the writings of both men. Much of the pertinent material in Edwards is yet unpublished; furthermore, Stoddard's theology of conversion is practically unknown and requires somewhat detailed exposition, while his works are unavailable outside of microcard and rare book collections. This essay has therefore been limited mainly to a delineation of Stoddard's doctrine of conversion, but with one eye on the theology of Edwards and the phe-

9. *Jonathan Edwards* (New York, 1949) , *passim.*
10. *Harvard Theological Review*, XXXIV (Oct., 1941) , 316, 319.
11. *A Treatise Concerning Religious Affections* (New Haven, 1959) , pp. 57–60.

nomena of the Great Awakening. It is hoped that such an exposition will further open the theology of Stoddard to serious study and contribute to an understanding of the revival and Edwards' part in it.

Stoddard's Career and Writings

Only a brief sketch can be given here.[12] A Harvard graduate of 1662, Stoddard came to Northampton, his first and only pastorate, in 1669. The next year he married Esther, widow of his predecessor Eleazar Mather, and by her had twelve children, the eldest of whom was a daughter, Esther, who married Timothy Edwards, Jonathan's father. At the Reforming Synod of 1679 Stoddard dared to defend the admissibility of the unregenerate to the Lord's Supper in a debate with Increase Mather. Those orderly but unconverted children of covenanting parents had been allowed by the Half-way Covenant of 1662 the privilege of having their children baptized; during the 1670's the Northampton church began to receive both children and grandchildren into full membership upon profession of belief in the main articles of the faith and evidence of a moral life. Most of the churches in the Hampshire Association (which was organized by Stoddard) followed his practice, as well as several other churches in the Connecticut Valley. Boston and the East did not, however, and when in 1700 Stoddard finally broached the subject in print, he became involved in a ten-year controversy with Increase Mather.[13]

Stoddard's *Doctrine of Instituted Churches* not only inaugurated his exchange with Mather, it also set forth his views

12. For more detailed information the reader is referred to the studies by Miller already mentioned and to James R. Trumbull, *History of Northampton, Massachusetts* (2 vols.; Northampton, 1898–1902) .

13. The main writings in this debate were: Stoddard, *The Doctrine of Instituted Churches* (London, 1700) ; Mather, *The Order of the Gospel* (Boston, 1700) ; Stoddard, *The Inexcusableness of Neglecting the Worship of God, under a Pretence of Being in an Unconverted Condition* (Boston, 1708) ; Mather, *A Dissertation, wherein the Strange Doctrine Lately Published in a Sermon . . . [the Inexcusableness] is Examined and Confuted* (Boston, 1708) ; Stoddard, *An Appeal to the Learned* (Boston, 1709) . Both men wrote further of the matter elsewhere, and there were other participants in the controversy.

on church polity. In this work Stoddard blithely discarded a fundamental doctrine of the congregational way, that the particular church covenant is the form of the church.[14] In place of it he stressed the covenant made by God with the whole people, and he proposed that to ensure the keeping of that covenant the "national church" be governed by synods of elders after the manner of Scotland.[15] The "presbytery" of the local church is to contain teaching elders (ministers) and ruling elders; the duties and powers of the latter are left rather ambiguous except for the point strongly made that in admitting and excluding from membership the minister is supreme.[16] Stoddard's presbyterian scheme was not accepted in Massachusetts, but his ideas bore fruit in the Saybrook Platform of 1708, under which the Connecticut churches were governed in Edwards' day.

With this theological support, "Pope" Stoddard not only ruled his congregation with a firm hand but engaged effectively in the civil affairs of town and province. Several of his published sermons were delivered on lecture days and other public occasions, chiefly at Boston. Most of these were typical "jeremiads" which excoriated the sins of the province, especially those of Boston, and called on New England's backsliding children to return to the simple piety of their fathers and obedience to the national covenant.[17] So famous was Stoddard in this role that he was often referred to as a prophet.[18]

But Stoddard also preached the covenant of grace, and during his ministry there were five great seasons of revival (which Stoddard called his "harvests"), occurring about the years 1679,

14. *Doctrine*, pp. 7–8.
15. *Ibid.*, pp. 32–34.
16. *Ibid.*, p. 12. Cf. *An Examination of the Power of the Fraternity*, p. 3; this work is bound with *The Presence of Christ with the Ministers of the Gospel* (Boston, 1718) but is separately paged. Edwards' acceptance of this and other elements in Stoddard's polity contributed to his later difficulties at Northampton.
17. An excellent example is *The Danger of Speedy Degeneracy Held Forth in a Sermon Preached at the Lecture in Boston the 5th of July 1705* (Boston, 1705).
18. See William Williams' sermon at Stoddard's funeral, *The Death of a Prophet Lamented* (Boston, 1729), pp. 26–28, in which Stoddard is Elijah and Edwards, Elisha (as also in the obituary in the *Boston Weekly News-Letter* for February 20, 1729). Speaking of Mather's *Dissertation* Stoddard complains, "He seems to intimate as if I pretended to be a prophet" (*Appeal to the Learned*, preface).

1683, 1690, 1712, and 1718, during which souls were converted in numbers probably unmatched anywhere else in New England.[19] Stoddard could therefore claim to speak authoritatively about God's dealings with the sinner. He published three major treatments of conversion [20] besides several other sermons published separately or in groups. In *A Guide to Christ* [21] Stoddard gathered his experience into a manual to aid young ministers in preaching for conversions and counseling troubled souls. He even ventured to speak sharply to his fellow ministers about their failings in these and other matters.[22]

Stoddard trained several ministers in theology, and his works were doubtless on the shelves of many other young divines. Jonathan Edwards had probably read most of them by the time of his ordination.[23] The *Guide to Christ* appeared just as Edwards' ministerial generation was entering upon theological training, and it was reprinted in 1735, when the revival in the Connecticut Valley was at its height. The *Safety of Appearing*, in many respects Stoddard's finest work on conversion, was reprinted in 1729, when his death would put many in mind of his career, and again in 1742, at the height of the Great Awakening.

Stoddard's conception of the evangelist's task was therefore influential, as well as his theology of conversion. The minister, he admits, is only an instrument in the hands of Christ, without whose presence his efforts are totally ineffectual; [24] never-

19. Edwards' "Faithful Narrative," *Works*, III, 232.
20. *The Safety of Appearing at the Day of Judgement, in the Righteousness of Christ* (Boston, 1687) ; *The Efficacy of the Fear of Hell, to Restrain Men from Sin . . . together with The Benefit of the Gospel, to Those That Are Wounded in Spirit* (Boston, 1713) ; and *A Treatise Concerning Conversion* (Boston, 1719) .
21. Boston, 1714.
22. See *The Defects of Preachers Reproved* (New London, Conn., 1724) . Stoddard also used ordination sermons for the same purpose.
23. The *Safety of Appearing* and the *Appeal to the Learned* are entered at the very beginning of Edwards' MS "Catalogue" of books to be read or purchased, and in his MS "Miscellanies" he treats with evident approval various of Stoddard's ideas on polity and conversion. Edwards' use of the *Guide to Christ* in his own *Religious Affections* is such as to indicate his thorough knowledge of its contents (see Smith's introduction, *op. cit.*, pp. 59–60) . Evidence now exists (in an account book of Timothy Edwards recently deposited in the Yale University Library) that by about 1720, and probably earlier, the family library contained at least the following works of Stoddard: *Appeal to the Learned, Doctrine of Instituted Churches, Guide to Christ,* and *The Inexcusableness of Neglecting the Worship of God.*
24. *Presence of Christ,* p. 20.

theless, he is obligated to acquire the best possible education in the Bible, divinity, and human nature. He must be able not only to preach but to deal with "cases of conscience" and guide souls through all the devious ways in which God may choose to lead them toward salvation.[25] Above all, the minister himself must be converted. He needs "experimental knowledge" as well as book learning; [26] for if he himself has only common grace, how can he lead others to faith? This objection to an unconverted ministry was later to be heard in more strident tones.

Stoddard frequently insisted on the necessity for what we would call "emotional" preaching. Most of the people are asleep in a perishing condition, and "whispering will not awaken them":

> . . . they are so hardnd, that talking moderately to them . . . takes no more impression on them, than on the Seats of the Meeting house. . . . Gods way is to bless suitable Means. . . . Some Ministers affect Rhetorical strains of Speech, as if they were making an Oration in the Schools; this may tickle the Fancies of Men, and scratch Itching Ears; but we have Mens Consciences to deal with: . . . . We are not sent into the Pulpit to shew our Wit and Eloquence, but to set the Consciences of Men on fire; not to nourish the vain humours of People, but to lance and wound the Consciences of Men.[27]

Such preaching will be "plain" in more ways than one. Stoddard objected to the use of notes in the pulpit for the same reason:

> Sermons when Read are not delivered with Authority and in an affecting way. . . . When Sermons are delivered without Notes, the looks and gesture of the Minister, is a great means to command Attention & stir up Affection. . . . It may be Argued, that it is harder to remember Rhetorical Sermons, than meer Rational Discourses; but it may be Answered, that it is far more Profitable to Preach in the Demonstration of the Spirit, than with the enticing Words of mans wisdom.[28]

---

25. *Ibid.*, pp. 5–6; *Guide*, pp. 7–9 (Stoddard's preface) ; *The Duty of Gospel-Ministers to Preserve a People from Corruption* (Boston, 1718) , pp. 8–12.

26. *Guide*, p. 9 (Stoddard's preface) .

27. *Presence*, pp. 27–28. All quotations in text or notes will retain the grammar, capitalization, and spelling of the original without further comment, except in cases otherwise confusing. Italics will occasionally be omitted in short quotations from topic sentences.

28. *Defects of Preachers Reproved*, pp. 24–25.

Nor did Stoddard neglect the social and psychological aspects of evangelism. Edwards' practice of gathering various age groups together for sermons and religious conversation was likely an inheritance from Stoddard. Stoddard himself encouraged the people to talk freely to one another on religious subjects and thought it a sign of degeneracy when men "seldom talk any thing of Religion" and "don't quicken one another by their discourse." [29] He also saw the special opportunities for conversion that came when numbers of people were being affected at the same time. A sermon of 1713 has the doctrine, "There are some special Seasons wherein God doth in a remarkable Manner revive Religion among his People." [30] In it he stirs up the congregation to pray for a new season of revival and addresses himself to the awakening of those left unconverted in previous outpourings.

Evangelism was the heart and soul of Stoddard's ministry. His views on church polity and the terms of communion caused much more stir in his own day; but it was his books on conversion, his evangelistic sermons, and his example as a soul-winner that were in the long run most powerfully to influence American religion.

Preparation for Conversion

The very cornerstone of Stoddard's doctrine of conversion is the idea that the sinner can and must do something to prepare himself for conversion. Stoddard summarizes the two main steps of this preparation as follows:

There are two degrees of this preparation: the first is a work of awakening, whereby the sinner is convinced of a present necessity of peace and reconciliation with God; whereby he is put upon a diligent use of all means in order to his salvation: the other is Humiliation, whereby the sinner is brought out of himself, and off

29. *Danger of Speedy Degeneracy*, p. 16. In 1737 Edwards referred to "a great deal of talk of conversion, and spiritual experiences" as a long-standing custom in Northampton (*Works*, III, 249) and later passed judgment on its evil tendencies. Sereno E. Dwight, *The Life of President Edwards* (New York, 1829), p. 465.

30. Printed in *Efficacy of the Fear of Hell*, pp. 184–208.

from all his carnal confidences, to yield himself a Prisoner to God: until the soul be thus humbled he is not capable of Faith.[31]

Awakening (or "conviction") and humiliation must be accomplished before faith is bestowed, and therefore with the aid of only such common grace as is available to every man. But, we may ask, is this not crypto-Arminianism, an unduly optimistic view of fallen man's moral ability?

Not at all, answers Stoddard, who holds uncompromisingly with Calvin that man is morally depraved and utterly impotent. Man as created possessed a regard to his own welfare, a natural self-love which as such was good; it was kept in its proper place by the higher principles of righteousness and love to God. But the latter were lost in the fall, and now an exorbitant self-love, out of all control, dominates man completely:

> When Man lost the image of God, there was nothing positive put into him. The condition of man by nature is, that he is destitute of Love, and Faith, and Humility; and thence he runs into evil, and is disposed to love the world, and set himself above God.[32]

So complete has been the degeneration that now even the best of unconverted men are sworn enemies to God's wisdom, power, and justice, "yea, to the very *being of God*." [33] All natural men

> have a preparedness to all the wickedness that is perpetrated in the world, if God did not restrain them . . . . That original sin that reigns in every natural man is the fountain of every abomination. Every natural man is over-run with the leprosy of sin from head to foot; has not one spark of goodness in him; all his faculties are corrupted utterly. . . . His whole Soul is like a dead carcass, like a heap of carrion, lothsom and noisom, and God may justly abhor him; which evidently shews a great necessity for his conversion.[34]

No salvation can be hoped for by the gradual improvement of any human faculties or abilities. There is an utter discontinuity between the highest goodness of the natural man and

31. *Safety of Appearing*, p. 205.
32. *Treatise Concerning Conversion*, pp. 27–28. Cf. *Guide*, p. 77, and the sermon, "That Natural Men Are under the Government of Self-Love," in *Three Sermons Lately Preach'd at Boston* (Boston, 1717) , pp. 34–64.
33. *Treatise*, p. 95.
34. *Ibid.*, pp. 95–96.

the grace which at conversion is instantaneously infused; for "the difference between saving and common Grace don't lie in the *degree,* but in the *nature* of them." [35] Therefore Stoddard takes the position, and frequently affirms it, that *"Preparatory Work* is no part of Conversion," though it precedes it; for, he continues,

Men under the work of Preparation are under the dominion and government of Sin . . . and whatever shew they make, they are destitute of Holiness, in all their affections there is no love to God, in all their lamentations for Sin there is no Godly sorrow; their religion proceeds only from Natural Conscience and Self-love . . . . When they have gone thro' *Preparation* Work, Conversion remains wholly to be wrought.[36]

The most thorough preparation does not make it any easier for God to infuse grace, nor does the lack of it hinder God in conferring it; [37] even so, Stoddard insists, "there is an absolute necessity in nature, that men be *prepared* before the *Exercise of Faith;* men cannot exercise Faith, till the heart be prepared by a *sense of danger,* and the *insufficiency* of other things." [38] As the Jews needed the ministry of John the Baptist to prepare them to receive the Messiah, "so particular Souls need a Work of Preparation to make way for their accepting of Christ." [39]

Stoddard could speak with authority and freedom about preparatory work not only because of his own success as an evangelist but because he was conscious of standing in a distinguished tradition. In his preface to the *Guide to Christ* he listed eleven Puritan divines who supported his contention as to the necessity of preparation. The eight Englishmen include Perkins, Sibbes, and Preston; the three colonial witnesses are Thomas Hooker, Thomas Shepard, and John Norton. It was the special glory of the English Calvinists to have studied with

35. *Ibid.,* p. 7.
36. *Ibid.,* pp. 3–4.
37. *Guide* (Stoddard's preface) , p. 7.
38. *Ibid.*
39. *Efficacy,* p. 64. "It is to be lamented that many men are grown ignorant of the doctrine of Regeneration. Some take Baptism for Regeneration, some think that men may be Regenerate, without any antecedent Preparation." *The Way for a People to Live Long in the Land That God Hath Given Them* (Boston, 1703) , p. 17. For Stoddard, one error was as bad as the other.

scientific thoroughness the preliminary steps of the *ordo salutis,* and of all their brethren the New England divines were the most accomplished. "Indeed," Stoddard boasts, "the World has had but little distinct understanding about the work of Conversion, until some latter Divines at *Boston: Norton, Hooker, Shephard,* & some others have held forth light; there was great darkness about the way of Conversion." [40]

Hooker, like Stoddard, divided preparation into two parts, contrition (comparable to Stoddard's first stage) and humiliation, which he defined in much the same way. Both "are of necessity required, that the heart may be fitted for the impression of Faith." [41] Shepard distinguished three steps before faith: conviction, compunction, and humiliation or self-abasement; "all which," he insisted, "are distinctly put forth . . . in the day of Christs power; and who ever looke for actual salvation and redemption from Christ, let them seek for mercy and deliverance in this way, out of which they shall never find it." [42] Norton showed how subtle the analysis might become; he listed no fewer than twelve "Parts of Preparatory Work," six wrought by the law and six by the gospel.[43] Like Stoddard, the older divines exhorted men to strive to prepare their hearts for grace, notwithstanding the fact that through it all their souls would really be passive, the preparation being accomplished "by the impression and motion of the Spirit, [rather] than performed by any inward principle, and habitual power of Grace received." [44] Hooker gave short shrift to the plea of inability—he called it unwillingness.[45]

Since the cultivation of the moral life, at least in the negative sense of forsaking sinful acts and habits, was of the essence of preparation, the New England divines had found the doctrine of inestimable value in two particular respects.[46] It enabled

40. *Appeal,* p. 36.
41. *The Application of Redemption* (London, 1657) , p. 15.
42. *The Sound Beleever* (London, 1649) , pp. 4–5.
43. *The Orthodox Evangelist* (London, 1657) , pp. 142, 152. Only the "principal parts thereof," however, require a "distinct Experience" (p. 160) .
44. Hooker, *Application of Redemption,* p. 16; cf. pp. 43–52.
45. *Ibid.,* p. 143.
46. See Perry Miller, " 'Preparation for Salvation' in Seventeenth-Century New England," *Journal of the History of Ideas,* IV (June, 1943) , 253–286.

them to combat the antinomianism of Anne Hutchinson, and later it provided a weapon against the moral degeneration of society. Hooker, Shepard, Bulkeley, and Norton had had the former problem in mind; but by the turn of the century men like Samuel Willard and the Mathers (Increase, Cotton, and Samuel) were preaching the doctrine not only to bring about conversion but to encourage obedience to the terms of God's "external" covenant with the nation, so that New England might be rewarded with prosperity and spared from divine judgment. Men's *"Natural Power"* to comply with the external covenant came to be stressed; if sinners would but do what they now were able to do, God might well grant them the power "to Exert those Acts of Religion, which are Internal." [47]

Stoddard's notion of preparation was essentially that of Hooker and the earlier Puritans, and his conception of its place in the total scheme of things was in harmony with that of his own contemporaries. Like them he stressed moral preaching and preparatory work with an eye to both the national covenant and the conversion of sinners:

> There are many licentious Liberties that are taken by Men, in their Apparel, in their Drinking, in their Dancing and other Recreations, and in their Discourses upon the Sabbath, and in their Dealings with one another . . . . Men should be solemnly Warned against all evil Carriages; and if this be omitted, it gives great increase of Sin in the Land. . . . Faithful Preaching would be beneficial two ways; one way as it would cut off occasions of anger, and prevent those sins, that bring down the Wrath of God on the Land; we should enjoy much more Publick Prosperity: The other is, that it would deliver men from those Vicious Practises that are a great hindrance to Conversion.[48]

Such duties as an outwardly moral life and attendance on the means of grace, especially public worship and the sacraments, are all part of the external covenant, and even the unregenerate among God's covenant people are bound to perform them and have the ability to do so:

> The Covenant that God makes with his Visible People ought to be attended, the Visible People of God have a natural power to attend

47. Cotton Mather, quoted by Miller, *ibid.*, p. 285.
48. *Defects*, pp. 20–21.

those duties, & they have a legal power to attend them . . . . There is no part of the external Covenant, but it may be kept by the Visible Church . . . but if Sanctifying Grace were necessary in order to the lawful attending of them, than [*sic*] it would be out of their power.[49]

At this point Stoddard went beyond his Boston contemporaries; he made the Lord's Supper also a part of preparation. The unregenerate ought to be admitted to communion not only because New England's scandalous neglect of the Supper is "a visible denying of the Gospel" and thus "one great cause of Gods Judgments," [50] but because the Supper itself is a "converting ordinance":

This Ordinance hath a proper tendency to draw sinners to Christ; in this Ordinance there is a particular Invitation to sinners, to come to Christ for Pardon, here is an affecting Representation of the Virtue of Christs sufferings, here is a Seal whereby the Truth of the Gospel is confirmed, all which are very proper to draw sinners to Christ.[51]

Besides calling men to faith, the Supper is powerful to beget conviction and humiliation.[52] If then it is such a valuable part of preparatory work, it must be made available to sinners as well as to saints. Unworthily attended, the Supper is dangerous to the soul, Stoddard concedes, but no more so than other parts of preparation for conversion: "to partake of it without Faith is a sin, and so deserves damnation, and so it does to pray or hear without faith." [53]

Conviction and Humiliation

Having seen the centrality of "preparation" in the Puritan tradition which Stoddard inherited and its relation to other of his distinctive ideas, let us look more closely at the steps to conversion as Stoddard taught and preached them. First of all, the careless sinner must enter into conviction by the awakening of

49. *Inexcusableness,* pp. 17–18.
50. *Ibid.,* pp. 26, 27.
51. *Doctrine of Instituted Churches,* p. 22. Cf. *Appeal,* p. 25.
52. *Appeal,* p. 71.
53. *Safety,* pp. 338–339.

his conscience. This is accomplished, so far as the minister can have a hand, by preaching moral duties, denouncing particular sins, and proclaiming the sanctions of the law. Men "need to be brought to Mount Sinai, and to hear the Thundrings, and see the Lightnings . . . men that are not sensible of the Terrours of the Law, will not regard the Invitations of the Gospel." [54]

This is, of course, traditional Puritan doctrine; but Stoddard is outstanding in the place that he gives to the dread of damnation as a motive. Fear of temporal judgments, the sense of shame, gratitude for mercies—all go for naught compared with the fear of hell, to make men reform.[55] It is not enough for men to acknowledge their liability to eternal punishment; they need to be made "sensible" of their danger:

> *When men don't preach much about the danger of Damnation, there is want of good preaching.* . . . if Sinners don't hear often of Judgment and Damnation, few will be converted. . . . They need to be told of the Terrors of the Lord . . . . A little matter will not scare men . . . Ministers must give them no rest in such a condition . . . . Reason will govern men in other things; but it is Fear that must make them diligently to seek Salvation: If they be but thoroughly convinced of their danger, that will make them go to God and take pains.[56]

Stoddard followed his own advice. In the applications of his sermons he frequently reminds his hearers of the danger of sudden death, the incredible length of eternity, the inconceivable misery of having to bear an unbearable torment of soul and body. For example:

> Will it not be dreadful to be filled brim full with the fiery wrath of God: to have every limb of thy body, and faculty of thy soul as full as it can hold of the indignation of the Almighty . . . men would shrink into nothing if it were possible, terrors will take hold upon them as waters . . . how will you draw back . . . what will you think of it when the Devil shall lay hold of you to drag you down to hell? how will you cry out when tumbling into the lake that burns with fire and brimstone? what can comfort you in that condition? men take great delight here in their worldly enjoyments and pleas-

54. *Efficacy*, p. 67.
55. *Ibid.*, pp. 9–14; *Guide*, p. 3.
56. *Defects*, pp. 13–14.

ures, but what comfort will it be to have [had] good things when they are tormented in this flame?[57]

What Shepard called compunction is achieved when through fear of hell men are brought to forsake their sins and use the means of grace diligently; this Stoddard calls "reformation."[58] To men who, quaking with terror, ask what they must do to be saved, Stoddard answers, *"Strive to enter in at the strait gate . . . press into the kingdom of God, and be violent* that you may obtain it. . . . Avoid every thing that has a tendency to hinder Success . . . . Spare no cost, no pains, so you may be converted."[59] Suppose you *are* passive in receiving grace and God is a free agent, you still have power to do much more than you have done:

you are able to reform your selves more thoroughly: You may abstain from Sins of Omission, as well as Sins of Commission: You may ponder a great deal more upon your misery, than you do. . . . You may cry mightily to God. . . . If men were seeking more earnestly, they would have more success, Matth. 11. 12. *The Kingdom of Heaven suffereth violence, and the violent take it by force.*[60]

A large part of the *Guide to Christ* is devoted to the problems of souls under conviction. For example, men who have passed through a period of guilt and concern for their sins frequently try short cuts to grace: they discern in themselves a desire for grace, they have comforting verses of Scripture suddenly come to them, they have strong feelings of affection toward God and think they really believe in Christ and love him. The wise pastor will help them see how full of hypocrisy, self-love, and carnal confidence their hearts still are—such people are not yet ready for saving impressions and experiences. On the other hand, some fall into discouragement or despair: they lack comforting scriptures, they complain of their spiritual dulness, they are obsessed with the thought that their day of grace is past or that they have committed the unpardonable sin. For

57. *Safety*, pp. 272–273. Cf. *Efficacy*, pp. 24–25, where Stoddard makes use of some "doleful Comparisons."
58. *Guide*, p. 7.
59. *Treatise*, pp. 93–94.
60. *Those Taught by God the Father, to Know God the Son; Are Blessed* (Boston, 1712) , pp. 31–33.

each of these a specific remedy is prescribed; their guilt is not to be glossed over, he counsels, but they should be given all manner of encouragement to persevere in striving, short of any hope that God considers them sufficiently prepared for faith. Sometimes periods of confidence and discouragement alternate, for "God commonly intermingles *smiles* and *frowns*." [61] The minister must be ready with appropriate counterbalances: "God leads men through the whole work of *preparation* partly by *fear,* and partly by *hope.* If they run into either extream . . . they are like a Ship that goes beside the Channel, and is in danger to be broken to pieces; a mixture of fear and hope makes men diligent." [62]

And what about those wretches who are apparently concerned about their danger of damnation but who hang onto pet sins and are not striving vigorously? Stoddard answers that their terrors, however great, need to be made greater, "so much terror as to bring them to a separation from sin"; if their danger is painted in a sufficiently lively and dreadul manner, their hearts may be pierced, and "if they be but thorowly scared, they will be brought to an universal Reformation." [63]

In any case, Stoddard believes that men must achieve a rather high level of personal morality if the work of conversion is to proceed further. This is not because the unregenerate can perform any good act or claim any divine promise, but precisely because they cannot; they must be brought to do their utmost in order to learn by "experience of the failing of all means" that their utmost is not good enough.[64] Once thoroughly acquainted with "the plague of their hearts" (a favorite Stoddardean phrase) they will accept the fact that God may justly damn them even after their most sincere and earnest efforts to do his will. Only then will they reach the plateau of humiliation:

They are to be urged to *Reformation* . . . . For the neglect of Reformation will put a stop to the work, & they will not get forward in the work of *Humiliation,* till they are Reformed; as the first Con-

---

61. *Guide,* p. 10.
62. *Ibid.,* p. 2.
63. *Ibid.,* p. 7.
64. *Safety,* p. 212.

coction prepares for the second, so Reformation does for Humiliation . . . he that will not part with sinful practices, will not yield himself into the hands of Justice.[65]

Humiliation, we are repeatedly told, is a state of mind in which the subject is finally convinced that there is absolutely nothing of goodness or righteousness in him, and no strength to strive for any; that even his present submission was not brought about by his past struggles. He is quiescent, neither confident nor despairing, receptive but not demanding.

No wonder Stoddard's parishioners sometimes found it difficult to tell when they had arrived. And at this stage there begins another round of problems and difficulties, now in somewhat different forms.[66] One man is afraid to do good works lest he trust in them; another insists that he is so blind that he *cannot* see how bad his heart is! The work in another is at a stop because he can never convince himself that he is yet humble enough—a sure mark of spiritual pride. Another complains that he has been brought to humiliation many a time but nothing further happened—nonsense, says Stoddard: humiliation happens only once; if it is genuine, conversion always follows soon after. And the man who reports that he thinks himself humbled must be carefully questioned to see whether his attitude is of the right kind. Especially difficult are those eager *humiliati* who proclaim that they are now willing to be damned for the glory of God. Nothing of the sort, Stoddard retorts bluntly.[67]

65. *Guide*, p. 7.
66. For Stoddard's handling of these, see especially the *Guide*, pp. 61 ff.

67. Stoddard's answer to this "case" occurs more than once in his writings, but always to the same effect. His words in the *Guide* (p. 77) are worth quoting, in view of the common notion that the Puritans generally required such a willingness:

"1. *No man acting understandingly is willing to be Damned*. All Ungodly men do interpretatively love Damnation. *Pro*. 8.36. but no man that understands himself, is willing to be damned; it is against Nature; Nature teaches every man to desire Happiness. Damnation is a dreadful terror to them that know what it is, *Isa*. 33. 14.

"2. *No such thing is required of men*. For God has put a spirit of self-love into men, & binds them to love themselves; and commands men to be seeking of Salvation, *Joh*. 6. 27. *Luke* 13. 24.

"*Such willingness is either only pretended; or if real, it must arise either from desperate rage and passion, or from some violent pang of false affection to God*. The Spirit of God don't stir up such workings in the hearts of men."

The greatest bar to humiliation, however, is seen in the man who *"finds a dreadful murmuring spirit; he is dreadful apt to quarrel with God,* and can't tell how to justifie him."[68] He comes up with all manner of objections against God's right to punish him for Adam's sin, or even for his own sins which he cannot help committing, and against the fairness of God's arbitrary election of some and damnation of others.[69] These the minister must patiently clear up, says Stoddard, for it is absolutely necessary that the sinner come to see "that God has great cause to find fault with him, but he has no cause to find fault with God."[70]

Stoddard's voluntarism becomes most apparent in his answers to these objections. He reminds the fault-finder that God's decree does not take away human freedom, for every man does as he pleases: "Though the *Decrees* brings [*sic*] a necessity, yet men act as freely, as if there were no Decrees. The Decree of God offers no violence to the will of man; men *chuse the ways of sin.*"[71] Ultimately, however, Stoddard will not try to defend God's ways. In damning the sinner, *"God does but use his Sovereign Liberty"*:

If God will make a multitude of *Men* and *Angels,* must he be bound to bring them all to *Eternal Life?* Who shall lay a prohibition upon God, that he shall not make use of some of them for the *Glory of his Justice?* If it be injurious for God to Decree that men shall sin, and then punish them for their sin, then he is utterly cut off from all opportunity for the glorifying of his Justice; but it is worth the while for Men and Angels to suffer for the manifestation of Gods *Vindictive Justice.*[72]

Sinners may cavil at the justice of God in their damnation, "but the Law shews that their Damnation is just. Rom. 3. 19. . . . *That every Mouth may be stopped.*"[73]

The step of humiliation is fulfilled when those who have been brought to lie low before God catch the glimmer of a hope that God may be merciful to them without infringing his free-

68. *Ibid.,* p. 61.
69. There is a concise list of such objections in *Efficacy,* p. 71.
70. *Guide,* p. 62. Cf. *Safety,* p. 215.
71. *Ibid.*
72. *Ibid.,* p. 63.
73. *Efficacy,* p. 72.

dom and sovereignty. "The merciful nature of God," as Stoddard defines it, "is a divine perfection, whereby he can find it in his heart to shew mercy if he pleases." [74] Note the words "if he pleases." In us a merciful nature is a real inclination or bent, which on occasion necessitates us to perform acts of mercy; but there is no such necessity in God. If God had such an inclination by nature,

> he could not have forborn to shew mercy without going contrary to the inclination of his own heart: the exercise of mercy does not flow necessarily from the merciful nature of God: but he exercises grace freely from His Sovereign Will and Pleasure . . . . God had been infinite in mercy if it had pleased him never to exercise any.[75]

Stoddard carries this conception of God's absolute freedom even into the domain of justice. The covenant of works with Adam and his seed was no mutual agreement; Adam did not consent to it but was created under it. Rather, it was only "a righteous rule" which God made "for himself to walk in" in dealing with man; he might have made a quite different rule: "he was at liberty, might if he had pleased have forborn to exact punishment for sin, might have annihilated man after a course of perfect obedience . . . might have bestowed blessedness on him as an absolute free gift without any condition at all." [76] And this in spite of the fact that Stoddard is said to have maintained for his A.M. thesis the *affirmative* of the question, "Utrum Deus puniat peccata necessitate naturae"! [77]

Illumination, Calling, and Faith

Humiliation is not humility: "There is nothing of Piety or love to God, or godly Sorrow in it. It is a meer forced thing." [78] Nevertheless, the way to eternal life leads through the valley of humiliation. *"If any be taught that Humiliation is not neces-*

---

74. *Safety,* p. 14.
75. *Ibid.*
76. *Safety,* pp. 30–31; this applies also to the necessity for the satisfaction of Christ (*ibid.,* pp. 79–82).
77. *Sibley's Harvard Graduates* (Cambridge, Mass., 1873—), II, 101.
78. *Efficacy,* p. 63.

sary before Faith, that is not good Preaching." [79] For the humbled man is the prepared man: "It is probable that God may give Grace to all those that have this Poverty of Spirit," though God cannot make promises without compromising his liberty; "but the reason is, Because such Men are *prepared* to receive the Gospel." [80] Then my work of preparation is finally completed, the humbled sinner asks? Well, not quite, Stoddard answers:

There needs another Work of God, further to prepare Men before they will come to Christ. If a Man were Poor in Spirit seven Year together, that will not prevail with him to come to Christ; but further to prepare him, his Eyes must be opened to see the Divine Authority of the Gospel.[81]

This further work of preparation is not, however, one to which the subject of it can make any contribution; it is solely an operation of the Spirit, who gives the first saving grace "by *letting spiritual light into the Soul;* by irradiating the mind, letting in beams of light into the heart." [82] This opening of the eyes by spiritual light Stoddard also calls spiritual conviction, spiritual sight, and spiritual knowledge. He considered this doctrine so important that he devoted a great part of the *Treatise Concerning Conversion* to its exposition, and he spoke of it often to his people. For it is by the gift of spiritual light that the last work of preparation becomes the first act of true grace.

Spiritual light must be carefully distinguished from that "common illumination" which the reason and affections of the natural man may receive.[83] Yet it, too, is wrought on the minds of natural men; it precedes the habitual change in their understandings which takes place at the first act of faith. Depraved man has a power in his understanding to know God, for no new faculty is added by spiritual light; he is "capable to behold the glory of the Lord before the habitual change. God discovers his Glory, and that inclines him to assent"—the dead

79. *Defects,* p. 11.
80. *Efficacy,* p. 64.
81. *Ibid.,* p. 65.
82. *Treatise,* p. 30.
83. See especially *ibid.,* pp. 69 ff.

hear the voice of the Son of God before they are made alive
(John 5:25).[84] Men must have a first experience that honey is
sweet before they can habitually judge its sweetness; it is the
"actual light" given the natural understanding, which begets
the "habitual light" of the godly mind.[85]

Spiritual light acts first upon the intellect, which in turn
moves the will:

> The Nature of Man is such, that the Will always follows the last dic-
> tates of the Understanding; the Will it self is a blind faculty, and it
> follows the direction of the Understanding. When once Men have a
> Spiritual Sight of the glory of God, they can do no other but serve
> him.[86]

In spite of man's corruption, the will retains its connatural
disposition to follow the intellect,

> so that when God makes this change in the *Understanding,* there is
> always a proportionable change made in the *Will.* When God . . .
> renews the Understanding, he renews the Will: They are not two
> things, but one and the same soul, diversely denominated accord-
> ing to *two* several *ways* of *working,* which are inseparably con-
> joined. When the soul has this spiritual light, it necessarily acts ac-
> cordingly.[87]

Because of this essential unity of the soul (and also with reference to external means) Stoddard can also say that "spiritual
light prevails immediately upon the heart." [88] But the light
prevails on the heart by illuminating the object in the behold-
ing mind.

What is seen by the soul thus enlightened? It is, says Stoddard, the glory and excellency of God, especially as these are
revealed in the gospel.[89] Only this will change the soul: "God

84. *Ibid.,* p. 36.
85. *Ibid.,* p. 38.
86. *Three Sermons,* pp. 71–72. Cf. *Treatise,* pp. 13, 35.
87. *Treatise,* pp. 57–58.
88. *Ibid.,* p. 31. Stoddard seems to have followed those Reformed divines who,
according to Mastricht, taught that God's operation on the will in regeneration
is mediated through the understanding, by so enlightening and convincing it
that the will cannot but follow its last practical judgment. The majority, along
with Dort, held that regeneration acts immediately on the will, conferring on it
"a new propensity toward spiritual good." Mastricht preferred the latter view,
and Edwards followed him rather than Stoddard at this point. See Petrus van
Mastricht, *Theoretico-Practica Theologia,* Editio Nova (Trajecti ad Rhenum,
1699) , VI, iii, 26 (p. 666 in the 1715 ed.) .
89. *Treatise,* pp. 39 ff.

is so glorious, that if he be known, the heart will be drawn to him . . . . The excellency of God draws the heart irresistibly to him, when it is known." [90] Something is accomplished which no common illuminations, no fear of hell, no heightened affections could bring about: faith, love, and holiness—and the more knowledge of God, the more holiness.[91] The mind now sees the true foundation for "spiritual carriages"; its love for God is drawn forth by the sight of God's glory and the excellence of his attributes.[92] Once convinced of God's gloriousness, a man now "sees" how free is God's grace, how sufficient is Christ's righteousness, how faithful are God's offers in the gospel.[93] So illumined is the mind that the heart is irresistibly drawn: "There is such a light let into the Soul of the Sinner, that he cannot but come to Christ." [94] Stoddard has little place for any doctrine of "indifferency" in the will.[95] Two of his favorite texts are: "Thy people shall be willing in the day of thy power" (Ps. 110:3), and "Every man therefore that hath heard, and hath learned of the Father, cometh unto me" (John 6:45).

Stoddard understood John 6:45 to teach, in their proper order, the specifically converting experiences: the external call, the internal or effectual call, and faith. The outward call, though not by itself effectual, is indispensable, for

The External call is our warrant to believe. The Gospel is the word of God, and offers of God recorded in the Scripture make it our duty to believe, and are our security in a way of believing. In the External call there is Gods command and Gods promise, and we must be judged by what is written.[96]

Hence Stoddard repeatedly tells us that *"the Gospel is the means of Conversion."* [97] Conversion is not so much an event

90. *Ibid.,* pp. 31–32.
91. *Ibid.,* pp. 31–35; *Efficacy,* pp. 147–152.
92. *Treatise,* pp. 58–61.
93. *Ibid.,* pp. 43–47.
94. *Safety,* p. 227. See also *Treatise,* p. 14.
95. "Liberty does not consist in an indifferency unto contrary Acts or Objects: sometimes indeed men have such a liberty, but that is peculiar to some cases: liberty is not opposed to necessity but to force: the will cannot be force[d] by any external violence, but it may be necessitated by reason and conviction: natural men sin voluntarily yet necessarily . . . . Saints in heaven love and serve God necessarily yet freely" (*Safety,* p. 230).
96. *Three Sermons,* pp. 31–32.
97. *Treatise,* p. 18.

in the subliminal depths of the soul as it is a personal encounter with the redeeming God who comes to us in the Scripture:

> In the first closure of the soul with Christ, the Soul comes to him, meerly upon the incouragement of the call of God in the Gospel: God invites sinners in the Gospel, to come to Christ, and many ways urgeth them so to do: and from thence the soul takes its encouragement.[98]

Hitherto the preacher's message has been based primarily on God's justice and man's condemnation. But now the evangelist must appeal to the humbled sinner with the most winsome representations of God's love and mercy. Here Stoddard's preaching becomes christocentric. The greatest evidence of God's love is his sending his Son to die for us, this being "the meer fruit of electing grace."[99] The "extremity" of Christ's sufferings is a measure of the greatness of God's love. Not only did Christ suffer terrible physical pain and cruel death, but he had to endure temptation, disgrace, contempt, and the sense of God's wrath.[100] It was his suffering of soul rather than of body, his inner experience of alienation and wrath, which "was the principal part of the punishment of Sin; this made Christ sweat drops of blood."[101] And if it is asked how the brief and finite sufferings of Christ can satisfy for sins deserving the eternal torment of many men, Stoddard answers that Christ did not suffer the exact punishment due the sins of the elect but one which was "equivalent" to it: "The infinite dignity of his person, made his short sufferings equivalent to the everlasting punishments of the damned: for an infinite person to suffer a temporal punishment, is as much as for a finite person to suffer an eternal punishment."[102]

Since Christ suffered as our "surety," both his active and passive obedience are laid to our account; and because he has been exalted by God to his right hand, he is mighty to save. Stoddard's first published book is one long effort to convince the

98. *Safety*, p. 222.
99. *Ibid.*, p. 80.
100. *Ibid.*, pp. 71–77.
101. *Three Sermons*, p. 11.
102. *Safety*, p. 52. Cf. *Three Sermons*, pp. 12–13; *Those Taught by God, p.* 14.

sinner that it is "safe" to trust in Christ's blood and so to appear in his righteousness at the day of judgment, no matter how great his own sins have been. The *Safety of Appearing* piles argument upon argument; every part of the Bible is shown to afford testimonies to the faithfulness of God's invitations; the sacraments of the new covenant are witnesses and seals to the truth of the gospel call.[103]

But the humbled sinner may have heard Christ's call many times, and he has progressed thus far in his preparation only because he now has experiential knowledge that he is indeed blind to the truth of the message and deaf to its appeals. He ordinarily continues in this "thorough discovery" of his natural blindness for a short but memorable period before conversion.[104] The call of the gospel has been "heard," but it remains only empty words until it is "learned" by the internal and effectual operation of spiritual light: "The inward call is no distinct call, but only the opening of the eyes to see the External call to be true." [105]

Spiritual light does not reveal any new truths that the soul did not know before; the intellectual content of saving faith is the same as that of a "historical" faith derived only from the Christian tradition and its rational corroboration. The difference is that "they are convinced of these things after a *better manner* than they are under the work of preparation." [106] Having once seen the glory and excellency of God and Christ, sinners believe the gospel solely on God's authority; "they are convinced of the Divinity of Gospel Invitations." [107] The illumined and sanctified reason no longer has to be content with mere probability; it does not suppose but *knows* that Christ is the Son of God, that he is a willing and sufficient Savior from sin and death, and all other gospel truths. On the other hand,

103. *Safety*, pp. 141–155; thus early appears the notion (though not expressed in so many words) that the Lord's Supper is a converting ordinance. This is the book for which Increase Mather refused to write a preface.
104. *Those Taught by God*, p. 24. Stoddard, however, does not think the time will be so long as "a Twelve month" (*ibid.*).
105. *Three Sermons*, p. 31.
106. *Treatise*, p. 56.
107. *Those Taught by God*, p. 15.

men who possess only carnal reason may give some description of God's perfections, but they lack "a right Idea of divine things. . . . they have not a right *Idea* of his glorious nature, are not sensible what reverence and glory is due to him." [108] Common illuminations are "affecting, but not convincing"; therefore, they do not draw forth the heart in faith, love, and other "gracious exercises," as spiritual light does.[109]

Faith, which is the condition of the covenant of grace and of justification, contains implicit within itself the "spirit" of all the other virtues; [110] nevertheless, saving faith in its first exercise is an explicit act of acceptance directed toward the gospel:

This Faith in Christ can be wrought only by the Gospel. Faith in Christ is an accepting the offer of the Gospel . . . there can be no act of Faith without the knowledge of the object of Faith, there can be no act of Faith without the knowledge of the incouragements to believe. Faith is a rational understanding action: In order to the act of faith, there must be a knowledge of the Gospel, and the actual consideration of it, at the very time.[111]

The last words are very important. There must be a decisive moment in which the call confronts the sinner, internalizes itself as spiritual conviction, and receives its response in the act of faith. This "call" may come to the soul as God's call, as Christ's call, or as a general invitation; it may come during a sermon, the reading of Scripture, or prayerful meditation; it may come "by any Gospel Precept, promise, declaration: God by any such word may let in a light to shew the soul the truth of the Gospel Call" [112]—but come it must.

Stoddard cannot allow that there is a scintilla of grace in any part of preparatory work, because it is a fundamental principle with him that the act of accepting Christ in the gospel is the *first* gracious act of the soul:

In *this respect* Conversion is wrought after the same manner in all that are converted: After the first act of Grace there is no certain order in the exercise of Graces, but this act of believing in Christ

108. *Treatise*, p. 74.
109. *Ibid.*, pp. 75–77.
110. *Ibid.*, p. 19. All of chap. v (pp. 19–24) is devoted to the proof of this thesis.
111. *Three Sermons*, pp. 79–80.
112. *Safety*, p. 225.

has the preceeding in all. Some men don't make a beginning in Godliness in loving God, and others in sorrow for Sin, and others in patience, and others in humility; but they all begin by *receiving Christ as offered in the Gospel* . . . . There is no sure sign of Election before this.[113]

No acts of love or repentance can precede the act of faith, for these are the fruits of faith: "If there be appearances of Repentance and Love to God's Glory, they are but delusions." [114] There is no need for any kind of sanctification before faith either to encourage or to enable men to believe; the gospel that God justifies the *ungodly* ought to provide enough encouragement, and "when God discovers Christ, that inclines the heart to come unto him." [115] Stoddard even denies that there is any infused habit of faith antecedent to the act. He rejects the argument that holy principles and inclinations must precede holy actions; it is true that the faculty must precede its act, but the holiness of the act does not need to be anticipated by any antecedent holiness in the faculty. Being must precede operation, "but it doth not follow from thence, that there must be a gracious habit before there be any gracious action: There is no necessity that there be an *antecedent habit,* it is sufficient if there be a *concomitant habit* and inclination." [116] Here again we find Stoddard exalting the category of act over that of substance, and a personal decision for the gospel over an *ex opere operato* infusion of the Spirit.

Assurance

In the application of almost every sermon Stoddard exhorts the sinner to strive after conversion; not to cultivate true repentance and love of God, for these he cannot do,[117] but to embark on preparation and labor that he may pass through each stage in proper manner and order. One of the chief signs by

---

113. *Treatise,* p. 15.
114. *Ibid.,* p. 17. Cf. *Guide,* pp. 26, 87.
115. *Ibid.,* p. 16.
116. *Ibid.,* p. 11. Adam and Eve, adds Stoddard, needed no habitual inclination to sin before they actually did sin (*ibid.*) . See above, n. 88.
117. *Guide,* pp. 4–6.

which Stoddard tests the genuineness of alleged conversions is the question "whether they have passed thorow the several steps of the work of Conversion." [118] Biblical converts may have progressed more swiftly, but modern sinners experience so many pitfalls, wrong turnings, and failures "that commonly several months are spent, and sometimes some years, before they get through the work of Preparation." [119] When authentic humiliation has been reached, conversion is to be expected soon after; and once men are truly converted, even their most provoking sins will not keep them from eternal life: "There is no falling from a state of Adoption, or Justification." [120] For that reason they must not rest content with "probable signs" of their conversion, for "twenty Probabilities will not make a thing certain." [121]

But what are the signs of grace? There are many things that are not trustworthy signs, and "many Professors build their Hopes of Salvation upon a sandy Foundation." [122] A man cannot argue from special acts of benevolent providence toward himself, nor can he reason from an exemplary "moral and religious conversation"; such things as "savoury Discourse, Zeal against Sin, strong religious Affections, sorrow for Sin, quietness under Afflictions, delight in Ordinances, suffering for Religion, &c" cannot be certain signs, for they "may flow from Common Principles, as natural Temper, natural Conscience, fear of Hell, false Imaginations." [123] There is just too great a resemblance between common and saving grace: "Common Grace is the picture of Sanctifying Grace, and common affections are sometimes stronger than saving." [124] Assurance is not to be obtained by believing that we are godly (for this is not an object of faith), nor by revelations in the Word (for the Scripture says only that the believer will be saved, not who the believers are), nor by any

---

118. *Ibid.,* p. 94. See also Stoddard's preface, in which he deals with the experience and teachings of ministers.
119. *Treatise,* p. 2. Cf. *Defects,* p. 10; *Efficacy,* p. 64.
120. *Ibid.,* p. 102; see also pp. 137–138.
121. *Efficacy,* p. 30. Cf. *Treatise,* pp. 140–141.
122. The doctrine of a sermon preached in Boston in 1708.
123. *Defects,* p. 17.
124. *Guide,* p. 25.

"inward testimony" of the Spirit (for the Spirit communicates no "new truths not revealed in the word") .[125] Even the effectual call is only a call to faith, not a revelation that God loves the person called: "Gods particular love is not the foundation of Faith, but the call of the Gospel"; [126] it is an inversion of God's order to seek a faith of assurance before exercising a faith of dependence.

But if morality and emotional states are not signs of grace, inner piety or "holiness" may be, for this is only grace exercising itself in faith and the gospel virtues. These, however, must be viewed directly, not inferred from conduct:

> It is *by Intuition or seeing of grace in their own hearts.* It is by consciousness; as *Peter* knew his love to Christ. . . . There is a reflective power in man: As he can look out and see external objects, so he can *look* in, and see his *own actions.* In this manner saints know the *corrupt workings* of their own hearts . . . so they know their grace. . . . they know that they think . . . they know the acts of their Wills . . . and the acts of their Affections . . . . So they may have the knowledge by intuition, that they know God and Christ; that they receive the gospel; that they love God and the saints; that they are sorry for their sins.[127]

This intuition is to be distinguished from that inward testimony of the Spirit which Stoddard opposed. The Spirit does not by some suggestion directly assure a man of his good estate but "draws forth special actings of faith and love, which," when intuitively perceived, "are evidential." [128] Hence his dictum: "There is no infallible Sign of Grace, but Grace. Grace is known only by intuition." [129]

Grace, Stoddard admits, is not quite so easily observed in the heart as are corruption and worldliness, for grace is often weak and may be counterfeited. "But sometimes grace works so

---

125. *Treatise,* p. 84. Commenting on this passage in his *Religious Affections* (ed. John E. Smith, p. 230 n. 1), Edwards says, "The late venerable Stoddard in his younger time, falling in with the opinion of some others, received this notion of the witness of the Spirit, by way of immediate suggestion; but in the latter part of his life, when he had more thoroughly weighed things, and had more experience, he entirely rejected it." Little trace of that phase of Stoddard's thought can be found in any of his published works.

126. *Safety,* p. 226.
127. *Treatise,* pp. 85–86.
128. *Ibid.,* p. 84; see above, n. 125.
129. *Defects,* p. 17.

powerfully, that it is *very visible;* and men are able to distinguish between grace and the resemblance of it, and be satisfyed
understandingly." [130] Let them therefore examine their most
soul-shaking experiences to see if they can find at least one act
of a gracious quality: "If a man do's not certainly know, that he
has performed one act of Saving Grace, he cannot be certain of
his Sincerity from his Walk." [131] But if he can recall one such
act, he has a firm ground of assurance: "When the Soul has performed *one holy Action* it is *converted.* . . . If he performs
one act of Faith, he is a Believer; if he perform[s] one act of
humility, he is a humble man . . . . Men become morally tem-
perate and chaste by degrees, but they are not made converts
by degrees." [132]

In the doctrine of a sermon on "The Way to Know Sincerity
and Hypocrisy," Stoddard formulated his test in a slightly
different way: "Men may know their Hypocrisy only by their
Course of life; but their Sincerity only by particular Acts." [133]
If the saint can remember one indubitable act of grace, his
assurance need not be threatened by the discovery of corruption and particular acts of sin, no matter how grievous. Sinful
habits persisted in, however, are quite another matter, for if
grace is present it will have the predominance: "A *Course of
sin* is an evidence of hypocrisy. . . . If Men live in the neglect
of known duties, or in the practice of known evils, that will be
their condemnation." [134] Signs of godliness derived from the
moral life are therefore of most value not for infallibly discovering grace by their presence but for discovering graceless-
ness by the habitual presence of their opposites. Even the most
"certain" intuitions of gracious activity must be re-examined if
the moral life does not correspond.

"Any act of grace is a sure token of regeneration," [135] and

---

130. *Treatise,* pp. 86–87.
131. The doctrine of *The Tryal of Assurance* (Boston, 1698) , p. 3.
132. *Treatise,* p. 5. Note the title of another sermon, *The Sufficiency of One
Good Sign to Prove a Man to Be in a State of Life* (Boston, 1703) .
133. *Treatise,* p. 119. The sermon is bound at the end of the *Treatise* as pp.
117–143.
134. *Ibid.,* pp. 122–123.
135. *Ibid.,* p. 136.

this is pre-eminently true of the first act of faith. Hence men ought to be taught that they can know the time of their conversion:

If any be taught that frequently men are ignorant of the Time of their Conversion, that is not good Preaching. Some are of that Opinion, and its like they may drink it in from their Ministers. This is a delusion, and it may do them a great deal of hurt; it hardens men in their Natural Condition. . . . but surely men that are Converted must take some notice of the Time when God made a Change in them . . . . Conversion is the greatest change that men undergo in this world, surely it falls under Observation.[136]

Apparently Stoddard's own conversion not only followed distinctly the several steps prescribed by his theological teachers but was of a vivid and memorable character. It came, says William Williams, "upon his Entrance into the ministry; which Work was so *clearly carried on,* and made so *deep* an impression upon his Spirit, that he always remembr'd it, and often spake of it." [137] But if the first act of grace cannot be remembered, all is not lost. This is a bad sign; but Stoddard considers it one of those *"bad signs,* that are *not demonstrative"* of a false conversion,[138] provided later exercises of grace are visible. Even the saint who remembers his conversion ought to strengthen his assurance by cultivating gracious acts throughout life, for "the more these visible exercises of grace are renewed, the more certain you will be. . . . If a man sees a thing once, that makes him sure; but if afterwards he fear he was deceived, when he comes to see it again he is more sure he is not mistaken." [139]

A man can know his own conversion, but his knowledge of the conversion or godliness of another person always lacks cer-

---

136. *Defects,* pp. 10–11.
137. *Death of a Prophet,* p. 25. These were the features of Stoddard's conversion which influenced his theology, not, as in the tradition, its having occurred during a celebration of the Lord's Supper. (For the tradition, see I. N. Tarbox, "Jonathan Edwards as a Man," *New Englander,* XLIII [June, 1884], 615–631.) Increase Mather, who in his preface to the *Guide* slyly taxed Stoddard with forcing others' conversion experiences into his own mold, correctly appraised the effect of Stoddard's conversion on his views of the Supper: it set him a standard for conversion so high that he must admit many he thought unconverted or not have enough members to make a church. See Miller, *Harvard Theological Review,* XXXIV (Oct., 1941), 317.
138. *Guide,* p. 94.
139. *Treatise,* p. 142.

tainty. "It is difficult for some good men to know it concerning themselves, but much more difficult to know it concerning others. We may have grounds of strong perswasion concerning some; but we must not pretend to an infallible knowledge respecting any other men." [140] Since others must judge by external and thus only probable signs, "men may have Foundation enough for a *judgment of Charity,* but they have no Foundation for *a judgment of Certainty.*" [141] The church must of course proceed on the basis of a judgment of "rational Charity" in admitting members,[142] and the minister especially may on occasion express his opinion of a man's good estate, if he uses common sense and caution.[143] Stoddard's skepticism as to the possibility of knowing another person's conversion undoubtedly influenced his stand on the terms of communion,[144] though it was probably subordinate to his concern for the external covenant and the conversion of sinners.

Some Conclusions

Stoddard's doctrine of conversion, if it did not actually furnish the bridge from Puritan piety to revival religion, at least illustrates the process by which the transition came about. Stoddard took over the conception of conversion taught by the earlier New England divines and developed a teaching and a method which anticipated the New England revivalists at several points. Such as the following have been noted: a concentration of religious interest on the experiences from awakening to the first moment of assurance; the "preaching of terror"; the requirement of "holy violence," that the sinner must reform

140. *Those Taught by God,* p. 17.
141. *Efficacy,* p. 30.
142. *Appeal,* p. 3.
143. Some indication as to Stoddard's own practice may be found in the *Guide,* pp. 91–95.
144. "Indeed by the rule that God has given for admissions, if it be carefully attended, more Unconverted persons will be admitted than Converted" (*Appeal,* p. 16). The precise significance of so extreme a statement (which stands almost alone in his writings and occurs in a polemical context) is difficult to assess. It probably tells us more about Stoddard's standards than about his opinion of the visibility of the saints; see above, n. 137.

his life and pass through the successive emotional states of preparation; the final quiescence of humiliation before divine sovereignty; faith as the response to a "call" received from a word of the "gospel" and wrought by spiritual "light"; the first act of faith as a climactic, unforgettable experience which could be dated and upon which an assurance of salvation could be built. Besides these should be mentioned Stoddard's insistence upon the preacher's own conversion; his manuals to guide the minister in pulpit and conference room; his use of such devices as group meetings and special prayer for revival; and his encouragement of "religious conversation" and the telling of experiences.

Though it would require a separate study to demonstrate it in detail, it seems clear that the preachers of the Great Awakening could at least have found most of their teachings and techniques already in Stoddard and his preaching tradition. Primarily concerned as they were with preconversion experiences, they too preached hell fire and the somewhat negative morality of reformation; they alternately stirred up and sifted the "raised affections" of their people. The main difference seems to be that as the pressure on the sinner was intensified by the later evangelists, so the time allowed for the preparatory processes was correspondingly shortened. Also, unfortunately, many of the revivalists lacked the control of themselves and their congregations exercised by Stoddard (and even by Edwards), and they often failed to make use of Stoddard's common-sense guidance in such matters as the unpardonable sin, the willingness to be damned, and the judging of other people's conversion.

Criticism of Stoddard's rigid programming of conversion had not been lacking in his own day, though it was more gently administered than that given the Awakening by the "opposers" of the 1740's. In his preface to Stoddard's *Guide to Christ*, Increase Mather objected (though without pointing directly at Stoddard) to the notion "that men must be so many years or months under a spirit of bondage, before they can believe on Christ." And he almost certainly had Stoddard in mind when he quoted Goodwin's observation concerning Hooker, *"That a man may be held too long under* John Baptist's *Water,* and that some have urged too far, and insisted too much on that, *as preparatory,* which includes the beginning of true Faith."

It is significant that even as an understudy of Stoddard, Jonathan Edwards had become uneasy about his grandfather's teaching at both these points.[145] No doubt Stoddard's main influence on the theology of the Great Awakening was exercised through Edwards; for Edwards may be taken as typical of the revival at many points where he is also in harmony with Stoddard,[146] and there is general agreement that Edwards' example and writings were enormously influential on the whole evangelical movement. Nevertheless, Edwards' attitude to both his grandfather and the revival was one of independence and critical appraisal. His own conversion did not fit anywhere in Stoddard's case book, and he witnessed others which could be said to agree with the pattern only in a general way. Besides, while Edwards distinguished between the sinner and the saint as sharply, and announced the divine sovereignty as uncompromisingly as did Stoddard before him, much of Edwards' theology was actually devoted to building bridges from preparation to conversion. His doctrine of grace as divine love, of excellence as harmony of being, of spiritual light as changing the sense of the heart, of true virtue as consent to being in general —these and other elements in his thought were efforts to overcome in one respect or another the dichotomies which constantly beset the Puritan who preached preparation by man and conversion by God.

Hence an adequate study of Stoddard's relation to the Great Awakening would have to take account of the ways in which

145. In the MS "Miscellanies" of the late 1720's there are several entries in which Edwards tried to find a rationale for the "preparatory work" which would relate it more integrally to conversion itself, and he specifically took issue with Stoddard's refusal to allow that grace was operative in any of the traditionally "preparatory" experiences.

146. The degree to which the preparation scheme of Stoddard and his predecessors underlies Edwards' preaching is shown by the recent study of John H. Gerstner, *Steps to Salvation: the Evangelistic Message of Jonathan Edwards* (Philadelphia, 1960). Of Edwards' own writings (besides the sermons themselves) the most revealing is his *Faithful Narrative* of the 1734–1735 revival.

Edwards, the main channel of his influence, criticized and modified the evangelistic tradition which he inherited. On the other hand, as this paper has suggested, Stoddard's theology of evangelism was such as to be an important influence on the revival in its own right—and there were points at which Northampton, the revivalists, and even Edwards' own disciples understood Stoddard better than they did Edwards.

Theology and Architecture in America: A Study of Three Leaders

JAMES F. WHITE

The architectural movement known as the Gothic Revival can now safely be called a matter of the past, but it cannot be said that all of the ideas of its exponents have vanished. It may well be that some of the concepts developed in conjunction with this particular period in the history of taste have found a permanent place in the life and thought of American Christianity.

This essay does not pretend to be a history of the Gothic Revival, but rather an outline of the lives and theological concepts of three important figures whose work in one way or another influenced the course of American church architecture. These men can hardly be called typical or representative, but it would be difficult to deny that the work of John Henry Hopkins, Ralph Adams Cram, and Von Ogden Vogt mark prominent episodes in the history of American church building and worship.

I

Bishop John Henry Hopkins (1792–1868), a native of Ireland, came to this country in 1800. Largely self-educated, while still a young man he found a position supervising an ironworks near Pittsburgh. The decline of business after the War of 1812 led him to seek a career as a lawyer. In the midst of a successful practice in Pittsburgh, he was asked to play the organ at Trinity

Episcopal Church, although he was at the time a Presbyterian. Shortly he became a communicant at Trinity, and, in the absence of a rector, the parish persuaded him to accept the vacant position. Ordained by Bishop William White in 1823, Hopkins gave up an income of five thousand dollars a year and as rector accepted a stipend of eight hundred dollars, a sum which was three hundred dollars in excess of his future salary as Bishop of Vermont.

As he was the only Episcopal minister west of the mountains, Hopkins busied himself organizing seven new parishes and guiding the destiny of his growing parish in Pittsburgh. His versatility was soon tested: here was a demand for a larger building to replace the existing structure—a brick audience room of octagonal shape. His sole architectural training consisted of copying by hand the plates of some of the "works of Britton." [1] According to his son, John Henry Hopkins, Jr.: "In this manner he became more thoroughly a master of that noble style [Gothic] than any professional architect who had as yet appeared in America." [2] This pre-eminence was by default, as very few Gothic churches had been built in America at the time. Hopkins put his amateur training to work and designed the new Trinity Church, a building erected in 1823 which seated a thousand people. By later standards, it was a terribly crude effort at Gothic. Galleries surrounded three sides of the building, the fourth being occupied by a central pulpit with a prayer desk, altar, and font all directly in front of it and each progressively lower. The slight recess for the pulpit was flanked by two chairs. A "perfectly flat" ceiling was painted in imitation of fan vaulting. [3]

Whatever the defects of this building, it was a token of the future, more remarkably so because of its location beyond the

1. Presumably John Britton's series on the *Beauties of England, Architectural Antiquities of Great Britain,* and *Cathedral Antiquities,* well-illustrated volumes which caused quite a publishing sensation in England 1800–1835.

2. *The Life of the Late Right Reverend John Henry Hopkins, First Bishop of Vermont, and Seventh Presiding Bishop.* (New York, 1873), p. 71. Cited hereinafter as *Life.*

3. John Henry Hopkins, *Essay on Gothic Architecture, with Various Plans and Drawings for Churches: Designed Chiefly for the Use of the Clergy.* (Burlington, Vt., 1836), Plate VI.

Appalachians. Few, if any, professional architects of the time cared to design in Gothic, preferring the more popular Classical style. Applications for church plans came to Hopkins from various parts of the country, and the demands soon exceeded the time he could expend in answering them. Nor was architecture his only interest: church music also received his attention, and he began to compose. Before he left Pittsburgh, the rector had composed much of the music used at Trinity Church. More or less for recreation, he also took up the painting of religious scenes. At the same time he began a careful study of Patristics, a pursuit which he kept up throughout his lifetime.

In 1831 Hopkins left Pittsburgh to become assistant rector at Trinity Episcopal Church, Boston, Massachusetts, and to accept a teaching position in a new theological school in Cambridge. These activities were cut short in 1832 by his election as the first Bishop of Vermont, a position which he occupied for thirty-six years. During much of this time he was also rector of St. Paul's Church in Burlington.

Though elected with the favor of the Low Church party in Massachusetts, Bishop Hopkins was always somewhat suspect of being a High Churchman. While laying the cornerstone of his church in Pittsburgh, he had vindicated "the use of a gorgeous ceremonial in the worship of God." [4] This tendency toward the ceremonial manifested itself in his crusade of thirty years for the wearing of the surplice during the daily offices and sacraments. Hopkins championed the wearing of the surplice because of his conviction that it was the garment used by the priests in the Old Testament and that its use was retained by the Apostles.[5] He found it no more Roman Catholic than the black gowns commonly worn during services by ministers of the Episcopal Church at the time. Vestments were reintroduced much later.

4. *Life*, p. 72.
5. *The Primitive Church, Compared with the Protestant Episcopal Church, of the Present Day: Being an Examination of the Ordinary Objections Against the Church, in Doctrine, Worship, and Government, Designed for Popular Use; with a Dissertation on Sundry Points of Theology and Practice, Connected with the Subject of Episcopacy, &c.* (2nd ed., Burlington, Vt., 1836), p. 160.

Although he felt it necessary to apologize for such a diversion from his "more strictly spiritual duties," Hopkins in 1836 issued his *Essay on Gothic Architecture*. It was a response to the continuing requests for church plans. In subsequent years, a reviewer lauded it for being "the earliest work, (so far as our inquiries extend,) issued from the American Press for the furtherance distinctly of Ecclesiastical Pointed Architecture; and . . . [for] laying down Ecclesiological principles with a clearness and firmness then new among us." [6] There seems to be no reason to doubt the priority of Hopkins' book. The lithography of the thirteen plates was done by the Bishop himself.

Avowing the work as that of an amateur, Hopkins concluded:

Well knowing the want of some plain and simple directory of the kind, I lay it upon the altar of utility with the hope that it may be found acceptable to some of my brethern, and save them from many of those perplexities which commonly attend an attempt to erect the earthly sanctuary of God.[7]

Much of his information on Gothic had obviously been gained from the works of John Britton and from Augustus Charles Pugin, author of the *Specimens of Gothic Architecture* (1821–1823). Architectural history was still in its infancy. Hopkins found a remarkable affinity between Gothic and Solomon's temple and considered the Gothic style "the most ancient in the world which has been applied to sacred purposes." [8] Fourteen years later, the better informed writers of the *New-York Ecclesiologist* found Hopkins' work

not now a safe guide. . . . In other words, the *historic* as well as the artistic claims of the Parish Church of England, to be received and acknowledged as the Christian 'Type,' for us Americans at least, was either not perceived or not recognized, and thence the grievous want in our author's plans of *settled* proportions; of *distinct* chancels; of definite ritual arrangements. . . . Now, we doubt not, on most if not all these points, the views of our author, as of all of us, have since that time greatly matured; that we all see many things in a very different light than we did; and are now willing in all these

6. "Review," *New-York Ecclesiologist,* II (Sept., 1850), 161. The term "Ecclesiology" is here used (with its original English connotation) in the sense of "the science of the building and decoration of churches." *Oxford Dictionary of the Christian Church,* ed. F. L. Cross (London, 1957), p. 436.

7. *Gothic Architecture,* p. 46.

8. *Ibid.,* p. 9.

matters to acknowledge a *Law* having reasonable authority over Churchmen, as well as *Principles* of Taste having intrinsic truth and beauty.[9]

The very reasons which in only fourteen years made the *Essay on Gothic Architecture* "not . . . a safe" guide are those which make it most interesting today. Hopkins' thirteen plates illustrate many details taken from genuine medieval examples (via Britton and Pugin), but these details have been used to garnish simple rectangular structures. Chancels do not appear because Hopkins saw no need for them. The most common liturgical arrangement is typified in a plate representing the "interior of a plain village Church." It is described in these terms:

Below the pulpit, is seen the desk; on each side of which are the doors of the screen. Below the desk appears the communion table, and at each end of the chancel is a gothic chair. In front is the chancel railing, in the center of which is placed the font for baptism.[10]

A similar arrangement was used in his own church, St. Paul's Episcopal, Burlington, Vermont. In an alternative scheme which appears in Plate VI, "the pulpit and the desk are at each side, and the altar in the middle." [11] Several of the plates locate a vestry where one would expect a chancel.

The chief adornments in these buildings are sentences from Scripture, a decoration beloved of the Puritans. One example includes the letters "IHS" with a cross rising out of the "H." Hopkins hastens to advise us: "Many pious people are afraid of this figure of the cross, because it is used so extensively by the Church of Rome; but this is a weak and unworthy argument for laying aside any thing, which, in itself, possesses an edifying and wholesome character." [12] He had already cautioned against the use of pictures since in the early church they "led the way to a species of idolatry, at least among the ignorant and superstitious," and he suggested "adorning the walls of Churches only with the appropriate architectural enrichments,

9. "Review," *New-York Ecclesiologist,* II (Sept., 1850), 166.
10. *Gothic Architecture,* p. 36.
11. *Ibid.,* p. 39.
12. *Ibid.,* p. 36.

and with judicious and edifying selections from the word of God." [13] Hopkins later changed his mind and painted some pictures for churches; but it is noteworthy that in 1836 an Episcopalian bishop with a reputation for High Churchmanship could entertain doubt regarding the propriety of a cross as ornament, or consider pictures so used actually dangerous.

Hopkins makes it quite clear that Gothic gives "an impression of sublimity more exalted than any other sort of architecture can produce." [14] He prefers dimly lit interiors, suggestive of "solemnity and repose." His attachment to the style seems to have been primarily because of its subjective conditioning on "devotion." He chooses Gothic not because of any liturgical requirements, but rather for its effect on individual worshipers. Emotive factors dominate. In short, his preference seems to be based largely on Gothic's ability to condition the individual rather than on any role in corporate worship.

In 1838 Hopkins traveled to England. While he was there he went up to Oxford and met John Henry Newman and E. B. Pusey. He also visited Newman's chapel in Littlemore and sketched it carefully, noting the chancel arrangements. Although he found himself in almost complete accord with the theology of the Tractarians, he was, in the years and conflicts ahead, to maintain "his sensitive and conscientious determination not to be identified with either party in the Church." [15] Indeed, his faith in the Oxonians was shaken by the secessions to Rome. After Newman embraced Roman Catholicism, Hopkins wrote that "the meaning of the Church must be gathered, not from the *bare letter of her written law* but from *that and her practice together.*" [16] On this ground he discouraged the recovery of vestments, altar candles, monastic vows, and other practices associated with the Catholic Revival, though on some of these points he later changed his mind.

By 1840 Hopkins had become certain that "the modern cus-

13. *Ibid.*, p. 15.
14. *Ibid.*, p. 1.
15. *Life*, p. 198.
16. *Ibid.*, p. 271. His son noted: "My Father grew wiser as he grew older" (p. 272).

tom of making the pulpit the principal object in the Church, instead of the Altar, is altogether unsupported by any authority in Scripture, in antiquity, or in the Mother Church of England." [17] Meanwhile, American interest in Gothic architecture was growing steadily. The completion in 1846 of both Trinity Church and Grace Church in New York, almost a generation after Hopkins' first efforts at Pittsburgh, marks the coming of age of the Gothic Revival. There were also many less pretentious structures, such as the Chapel of the Cross, Chapel Hill, North Carolina, which were being erected. The movement was aided and directed by the New York Ecclesiological Society founded in 1848 in conscious imitation of the Ecclesiological Society then flourishing in England. The New York group promulgated explicit laws as to correct church building and campaigned for "the adoption of the old Parish Church of England as our fixed type—with its lengthened Nave and ample Chancel." [18] On several occasions Hopkins was invited to become a patron of the group. "This, however, he thought it wise to decline, though expressing 'the most friendly feeling towards its objects and its labors.' " [19] His son was an active member of the company.

Perhaps because of the influence of this society, perhaps for his own reasons, Hopkins in 1851 undertook the rebuilding of St. Paul's Episcopal Church in Burlington. Previously there had been no chancel in the building. Now one was added in accordance with the mandates of "correct" ecclesiology. It was divided into choir and sanctuary by a communion rail, and provided with a wooden altar, prothesis, altar chairs, and a pulpit and lectern west of the choir stalls. Purists deplored the fact that the church still had no central aisle, and lamented the galleries that remained.[20] But the finished structure was in remarkable conformity to the laws and principles of the New York Ecclesiological Society.

17. *Ibid.*, p. 215. Quoted from the 1840 Convention *Journal* of his diocese.
18. "Address," *New-York Ecclesiologist*, II (May, 1850), 135.
19. *Life*, p. 269.
20. "St. Paul's Church, Burlington, Vermont," *New-York Ecclesiologist*, IV (Nov., 1852), 192.

Bishop Hopkins subsequently designed two other stone Gothic churches: St. Thomas' in Brandon, Vermont, and Trinity in Rutland, both of which still stand. He painted tablets and religious scenes for several churches. The University of the South at Sewanee, Tennessee, employed him to make "plans for buildings." By this time Bishop Hopkins was no longer a pioneer. In fact, his son reported with condescension: "My Father's means for keeping up with the progress of the revival of Pointed architecture were, however, very slight; and his preference for the four-centre arch remained during his whole life." [21] This was not correct dogma, as his son knew, for "the stronger and purer style of an earlier age" had become the orthodoxy of the New York Ecclesiologists.

Similar traits of heterodoxy appeared in the bishop's rebuilding of St. Paul's Episcopal Church, Burlington, in the last years of his life. In 1866 he provided plans for a new enlargement incorporating transepts. A basilican arrangement of the chancel was introduced into the new cruciform structure. The altar stood on the chord of the apse with the bishop's throne and a semicircle of priests' seats behind it. Evidently, Hopkins had not become convinced that English medieval arrangements were mandatory, though he liked the more emotive aspects of Gothic. "No one," his biographer writes, "was more conscious than its architect of the points in which the building is open to professional criticism," but one wonders whether the more orthodox son might not have been an exception to this statement. [22]

By virtue of seniority of consecration, Hopkins became Presiding Bishop of the Episcopal Church in 1865, and his great popularity helped to reconcile Northern and Southern bishops after the Civil War. Nevertheless, Hopkins' publication of *The Law of Ritualism* in 1866 was the cause of considerable consternation among the bishops. The book appeared at a time when some suspected that ritualists were exploiting architecture and the arts in the interest of Roman Catholicism.

21. *Life,* p. 72.
22. *Ibid.,* p. 365.

Bishop Coxe of Western New York was perturbed since he felt it was " 'a serious thing, as it opens the door for experiments which are not unlikely to be made in respectable Churches, if not in some of the most important seats of the Church's dignity and strength.' " [23] Today it is difficult to understand the vehemence of the controversy, but by 1866 Ritualism had become a burning issue on both sides of the Atlantic. Hopkins had begun his book with a statement that he would "propose nothing which is not derived from the Bible." [24] Accordingly he affirmed that the Christian church of the apostles followed the ritual of Moses. His chief concern, a passion with him for thirty years, was the use of the surplice rather than the black gown in preaching. He felt the Ritualists were on a safe legal position in their new practices. *"Personally,"* he remarked, "I prefer the more simple ceremonial to which I have been accustomed all my life, and men can hardly be expected to adopt new tastes and habits at the age of seventy-five." [25] Nevertheless, he did try a few experiments himself beyond the use of the surplice. On Christmas day, 1866, he wrote his son that he had placed

two lights on the Altar [at St. Paul's]. Quite an advance for Ritualism! But St. Paul's is so dark that I really could not see to read with the wall lamps lighted by gas as usual. Thus I have had a very good *practical* argument for the remedy, which I intend shall be a permanent improvement in the right direction.[26]

The Law of Ritualism concludes with a prediction "that this Ritualism will grow into favor, by degrees, until it becomes the prevailing system." [27]

Actually the Ritualism of which Hopkins spoke would be considered normative Low Church today. In 1867 he went as a delegate to the Lambeth Conference. On this journey, while attending St. Michael's, Brighton, Hopkins "for the first and

23. *Ibid.,* p. 380.
24. *The Law of Ritualism, Examined in Its Relation to the Word of God, to the Primitive Church, to the Church of England, and to the Protestant Episcopal Church in the United States.* (New York, 1867) , p. 4.
25. *Ibid.,* p. 76.
26. *Life,* p. 386.
27. *Law of Ritualism,* p. 94.

only time in his life, saw a really high ritualistic service of the Anglican rite." [28] Evidently he approved of it, but never had an opportunity to imitate the advanced practices. He died shortly thereafter while on a winter visitation of his diocese in 1868.

Bishop Hopkins' lifetime spanned the period of the introduction of Gothic architecture and medieval ceremony in American churches. By the time of his death, Gothic had become widely accepted among Episcopalians as the correct style for a church. Very explicit regulations had been worked out to create the standard Episcopal church arrangement of the nineteenth century. Characterized by a deep chancel, impressive altar, and with separate pulpit and lectern at the west end of the chancel, it has since become common in every part of the country.

II

The budding of the Gothic Revival which appears in Bishop Hopkins' work comes to full flower in the career of Ralph Adams Cram. Born the son of a Unitarian minister in 1863, Cram lived as a child in various New Hampshire parsonages. His formal education never went beyond that provided by Exeter High School, but his father's library opened other doors. It was here he discovered and read "everything that Ruskin had written." [29] Ruskin, Wagner, and William Morris were Cram's heroes when he was a young man, though in later years he found Ruskin "quite the most unreliable critic and exponent of architecture that ever lived." [30]

At the age of seventeen Cram sought his fortune in Boston, working at various positions, including, for a period, the post of art critic for the *Boston Evening Transcript*. During the 1880's he spent five years working in the office of an architectural firm, his "only professional education." In reflection, Cram judged that the time had hardly been propitious for good

---

28. *Life*, p. 439.
29. Ralph Adams Cram, *My Life in Architecture* (Boston, 1936), p. 9. Cited hereinafter as *My Life*.
30. Ralph Adams Cram, *The Gothic Quest* (New York, 1907), p. 149.

architecture. He compared his arrival in Boston with "being plunged in the infusion of false principles, horrid methods, and shocking bad taste that marked American architecture and architectural practice in the year 1881." [31] American architecture, he felt, had fallen "to a lower level than history had ever recorded." What had happened was that the earlier Gothic Revival had been swallowed up in a morass of stylistic revivals, especially imitations of H. H. Richardson's Romanesque or Charles F. McKim's Renaissance. The earlier Gothic Revival of Richard Upjohn and James Renwick seemed forgotten.

Cram burned with desire to "get to Europe to see the old work Ruskin had taught me was so supremely good." [32] His wish was granted, and the next few years brought two opportunities to visit Europe. He made a pilgrimage to the sites Ruskin had taught him to revere, particularly Venice. In 1890 Cram established his own architectural firm in Boston in collaboration with Charles Francis Wentworth. The talented Bertram Grosvenor Goodhue soon joined the firm, remaining until 1913. At Wentworth's death in 1899 he was replaced by Frank Ferguson, who died in 1926. Artistic problems were left to Cram and Goodhue; the other partners dealt with engineers and contractors. As Cram expressed it, Ferguson's task "was to keep the buildings Bertram and I designed from falling down." [33]

Far more important for Cram than the buildings which he saw in Europe was his conversion. Before his trips overseas, he considered himself devoid "of all religious superstitions of every sort." But on his second trip, his friendship with Henry Randall, a layman of the Episcopal Church, brought a transformation. Cram was persuaded to attend a Christmas Eve mass in Rome, and of this experience he confessed, *"I understood."* On his return to the United States, he was baptized in the Church of St. John the Evangelist on Beacon Hill, and continued a devout Anglo-Catholic for the remainder of his life.

---

31. *My Life,* p. 27.
32. *Ibid.,* p. 47.
33. *Ibid.,* p. 83.

He remained closely associated with the Society of St. John the Evangelist. His partner, Bertram Goodhue, on the other hand, showed "no particular interest" in religious matters.

The thirty or more books which came from Cram's pen show how closely associated his theology and architectural practice became. He was convinced that only a man "in loving sympathy" with Catholicism could build a good church. Catholicism, as he saw it, had been the fountainhead of the best art of the West. Cram took for his motto the phrase: " 'Art is a result, not a product.' " [34] As he surveyed the great art of the past, he concluded that Catholicism had been the source of all that was great in every art form. Protestantism, on the other hand, brought a deadly blight. It could destroy or imitate, but only Catholicism possessed true "creative force." The ethos of Catholicism was friendly to the arts; that of Protestantism, however, enjoyed no such rapport. Much of this difference was, in Cram's opinion, due to Sacramentalism. According to him, "sacramentalism is . . . the essential element, of the very *esse* of Catholic faith and Catholic philosophy." [35] The absence of this principle in Protestantism had caused irreparable harm in the destruction of genuine art and in the creation of an abundance of ugliness.

In order to explain the excellence of art at various periods, Cram developed a theory of history. He found that periods of crisis had occurred at intervals of about every five hundred years since the time of Christ. Culture flowered in the intervals between these moments of regression. In everything Cram wrote "mediaevalism" was the greatest of these ages, the one to which modern man must return. "Back to mediaevalism we must go, and begin again." [36] No great religious art had developed since the fall of Constantinople. "The civilization of Mediaevalism," he found, "was more nearly perfect than that of Athens, far nobler than that of Rome, and separated by the entire diameter of being from the repulsive barbarism of the

34. *Ibid.,* p. 284.
35. *Gold, Frankincense, and Myrrh* (Boston, 1919) , p. 34.
36. *The Ministry of Art* (Boston, 1914) , p. 240.

High, or Pagan Renaissance." [37] Cram did much to promote the study of this golden age of mediaevalism. He helped found the Medieval Academy of America, and he persuaded Henry Adams to publish *Mont-Saint-Michel and Chartres*.

As one might expect, the spirit of the Middle Ages found expression in its art, particularly in Gothic architecture. Cram was not content simply to recover the forms of this art, but felt that "if we would have back the old art (in its essence and its relation to life, not in its forms), we must have back the old life in its unity, in its joyfulness, and in its human scale." [38] One might fairly say that Cram, to borrow Chesterton's phrase, saw the Middle Ages "by moonlight." This romantic glow of the "great thousand years" ended with the fifteenth century, followed by the threefold catastrophe of "Renaissance, Reformation, and Revolution." The Renaissance, to Cram, was nothing more than "a brazen affectation of all the vices and evils of paganism; to express this new spirit in the world recourse was had quite properly to the very forms of pagan art." [39] Renaissance architecture was only "neo-pagan," and though perhaps appropriate for Protestants, completely wrong for any branch of Catholicism. As one might expect, Protestantism appeared to Cram as a culprit of history, being incapable, in his eyes, of producing "vital art of any kind."

Not until the nineteenth century did there seem to be hope of an end to the "artistic dark ages" of Protestantism. The new hope broke out in the Oxford Movement, but its prophet was a Roman Catholic architect, "the immortal Pugin" (Augustus W. N. Pugin), whose ideas Cram's duplicated constantly. The Gothic Revival had flourished in England ever since the Oxford Movement. Its first practitioners, Cram pointed out, "saw at first only archaeological possibilities, . . . copying with scrupulous exactness." [40] But the late nineteenth century had produced such leaders as John Sedding, whose principle was not imitation but "development." Gilbert Scott's Liverpool

37. *The Gothic Quest,* p. 40.
38. *My Life,* p. 306.
39. *The Gothic Quest,* p. 42.
40. *Ibid.,* p. 130.

cathedral was perhaps the best expression of this new approach. America had not been so fortunate as England in this respect, for the movement had bogged down in eclecticism. By the turn of the century, however, there was hope, and the restoration of Gothic was proceeding rapidly. An epoch was ending, but Cram wondered "whether the next step is into five centuries of Dark Ages or into a new era of five centuries of a restored Christian commonwealth." [41]

This was the exciting period in which Cram and Wentworth began their architectural practice in 1890. The new "cathedral age" was still in its infancy, the Episcopal cathedral in Albany, New York, having marked the new beginning during the previous decade. Gothic, though used occasionally, had vigorous competitors in the Richardsonian Romanesque and in other styles. There was none of this uncertainty in Cram's mind. In words reminiscent of Pugin, he declared: "There is one style, and only one, that we have a right to; and that is Gothic as it was when all art was destroyed at the time of the Reformation." [42] It must be remembered that Gothic was far more to Cram than simply a superior architectural style; it was "less a method of construction than . . . a mental attitude, the visualizing of a spiritual impulse." [43] Classical architecture lacked these spiritual qualities, hence it was to be avoided as a "visible expression" of Christianity. He illustrated his creed in his first church, All Saints', Dorchester, Massachusetts—a stone Gothic structure—and in many similar buildings which followed.

Cram made it quite clear that he had a definite principle in his work:

The obvious inference was that the thing for me was to take up English Gothic at the point where it was cut off during the reign of Henry VIII and go on from that point, developing the style England had made her own, and along what might be assumed to be logical lines, with due regard to the changing conditions of contemporary culture. This of course meant using English Perpendicu-

---

41. *The Substance of Gothic: Six Lectures on the Development of Architecture from Charlemagne to Henry VIII* (Boston, 1925) , p. 200.
42. *Church Building, A Study of the Principles of Architecture in Their Relation to the Church* (2nd ed.; Boston, 1914) , p. 43.
43. *The Gothic Quest*, p. 57.

lar Gothic . . . as the basis of what we hoped to do. As for its development, the course was laid down and the precedent established
by John D. Sedding, at that time the most vital and inspiring of
contemporary English ecclesiastical architects.[44]

The principle of "development," thus conceived, was later
modified in some details. As Cram admitted: "I was so anxious
to demonstrate the continuity of tradition (theologically as
well as artistically) in Christian culture . . . that I tended
naturally, at first, to reproduce rather than to recreate." [45] As
his work matured, Cram's interest in the different phases of
Gothic broadened and he showed increased influence from
Continental varieties rather than just the sixteenth-century
English "of our earliest amatory experience."

The struggle to secure enthusiastic acceptance of Gothic was
not an easy one. Few contemporary architects accepted Cram's
conviction of the absolute superiority of Gothic, and even fewer
were persuaded that the Middle Ages had been a better period
in culture. The Columbian Exposition of 1893 in Chicago had
caught the imagination of the American people with its impressive classical buildings. The École Des Beaux Arts in Paris,
where many American architects were trained at the time,
vigorously promoted classical architecture. All of this was based
on wrong principles, Cram felt, for it ignored the far superior
work of the Christian civilization of medieval Europe. It was a
conflict between paganism and Christianity, and there was no
doubt on which side Cram himself stood.

Hardly less disastrous in Cram's opinion was the "débâcle
of contemporary modernistic art." Though all of it was not
entirely bad, most of it disgusted him. German churches built
in the contemporary fashion before World War II he found
revolting. The style might be appropriate for garages and
movie theaters, but for Catholic churches it "must absolutely
be eschewed." Cram did not live to see widespread use of contemporary architecture by American churches, a development
which hardly began until after World War II.

44. *My Life*, p. 73.
45. *Ibid.*, p. 78.

The Church had a particular right and obligation to Gothic, Cram felt, because Christian art (which could be only Gothic) would serve the Church "as a language and as a mighty missionary influence, winning back the world from heathenism." [46] Christian art was to be one of the mighty tools in restoring Christian civilization, and the work of Gothic architects was all part—an important part—of beginning a "new Reformation, the second Renaissance, the Restoration."

Cram stressed the subjective elements of Gothic: "We must realize that the first desideratum of a church is . . . [that the occupant] shall be filled with the righteous sense of awe and mystery and devotion." [47] But he had very definite ideas about the arrangement of the building. This for Catholics, Anglican or Roman, was to be the neo-medieval arrangement with deep chancel, remote altar, and the various *instrumenta ecclesiastica* of the medieval church. Cram scoffed at Roman Catholic churches built without this design. All of this was necessary for "the Fine Art of religious ceremonial." As might be imagined, Cram preferred elaborate ceremonial, the proper settings for which are illustrated in *Church Building*. One cannot escape the impression that much of worship for Cram was largely a subjective matter of individual devotion. This had also been true to a marked degree among the gothicists of the nineteenth century. A modern liturgical scholar criticizes their architecture:

Such edification as it communicates is always individualistic, rarely corporate. For it does not aim to call attention to the action of the liturgy—indeed it frequently obscures or obstructs the action—but rather to stimulate the contemplation of personal prayer by evocative symbols that surround and adorn, but do not necessarily inhere in the action of the liturgy.[48]

The charges made against those churches which Cram built for Catholic worship could as easily be laid against Gothic churches built for Protestants.

46. *The Gothic Quest*, p. 49.
47. *Ibid.*, p. 101.
48. Massey Hamilton Shepherd, Jr., *The Reform of Liturgical Worship: Perspectives and Prospects* (New York, 1961) , p. 25.

There can be no doubt as to the powerful emotive factors involved in Cram's buildings. There is hardly space here to go into a detailed analysis of any particular building. We are concerned, of course, only with his religious work, not with such major landmarks of the later Gothic Revival as buildings at the Military Academy at West Point, Princeton University, and other schools.

Some of the most outstanding examples of the later Gothic Revival are the great school and university chapels erected in the 1920's and 1930's. Cram designed one of the largest for Princeton (1928), as well as school chapels for St. George's School (1928) and Mercersburg Academy (1926), and worked with Goodhue on the chapel at West Point (1910). Other universities soon raised magnificent Gothic chapels under the direction of different architects, Duke (Trumbauer, 1932) and Chicago (Goodhue, 1928) being the most remarkable.

The same period saw the full flower of the cathedral movement. For Roman Catholics this had begun early in the nineteenth century. Among Episcopalians, the work of the New York Ecclesiological Society finally bore fruit in the last decades of the nineteenth century. Albany was begun in the 1880's but never finished. More ambitious projects were soon under way in New York, Washington, and San Francisco, with smaller buildings projected in Cleveland, Detroit, Baltimore, Spokane, and many other cities. The Cathedral of St. John the Divine in New York was begun by Heins and LaFarge in a Byzantine-Romanesque style; Cram was appealed to in 1911. He rebuilt a portion of the apse, added one chapel, the baptistry, and constructed the largest nave in the world in a manner reminiscent of French Gothic yet with many original features. Cram designed the Episcopal cathedral in Detroit himself. He was also briefly involved in the design of the Swedenborgian cathedral in Bryn Athyn, Pennsylvania, perhaps the most exquisite product of the twentieth-century Gothic Revival.

Cram shuddered at the suggestion that the National Cathedral might be built in Renaissance or French Gothic. The former was a threat to the Church for Cram insisted on "the necessity of preserving the continuity of architectural idea, in order that we may adequately show forth the perfect continuity of the Church." [49] In this case, French Gothic was forbidden "from ethnic and historic reasons." After all, the Episcopal Church was English in its succession and traditions. Fortunately, both Renaissance and French Gothic were rejected in favor of fourteenth-century Gothic, the style in which the National Cathedral is now being built. Cram announced with pleasure that of the architects who eventually took over this work, Robb and Little, "had been largely educated in our offices, while Frohman had previously declared himself as a follower of our leading." [50] The three most ambitious structures begun in the cathedral movement, New York, Washington, and San Francisco, remain unfinished, although the completion of the San Francisco cathedral is now assured. Whether this is a sign that the cathedral movement has vanished like a romantic dream, that Gothic is no longer considered appropriate, or simply the consequence of the income tax is an open question.

Far more important, in many respects, were the numerous parish churches which Cram and his partners built all over America. St. Thomas' in New York and Calvary in Pittsburgh are perhaps the best known, but they had many companions. Most interesting of all was the demand of such denominations as the Congregationalist, Presbyterian, Baptist, and Methodist for Gothic of the same quality as that represented by Cram's work.

Cram's comments on this new development are interesting. Concerning the beginning of his career, he wrote:

We began to experiment in Colonial work, both for Protestant churches and for schools. . . . We held, or I did then, that there was something incongruous in using Catholic Gothic to express the ethos of that Protestantism which had revolted against all things Catholic and had done its best to destroy its architectural and other artistic manifestations, so we did our best to induce our 'Nonconformist' clients to let us do Colonial structures for them.[51]

49. *Church Building*, p. 207.
50. *My Life*, p. 250.
51. *Ibid.*, p. 96.

Without any doubt, he was sincerely convinced that while Georgian might be adequate for a Congregational church, medieval art was altogether inappropriate. But it was another matter to convince clients of this:

> Protestant congregations declined pretty generally to admit our Colonial premises, and increasingly demanded good Catholic art, refusing to accept any substitute, so we had very promptly to abandon our original position and do just as good Gothic as we possibly could for Presbyterians, Congregationalists, Baptists and even Unitarians.[52]

The result was that Cram decided that even here art might have a missionary force as it had in the spread of Catholicism among pagans in medieval Europe. He concluded that his firm was justified in "being as Gothic (and as Catholic) as we liked" even when building for Protestants. Numerous other firms soon began building Gothic churches for Protestant clients, frequently with full medieval arrangements.

Throughout the 1920's and 1930's Cram observed with increasing delight the progress of the Gothic movement. Strangely enough, the Roman Catholic Church, though certainly as Catholic as Cram desired, stood "chained hand and foot by utter artistic depravity, ignorance, and self-satisfaction." [53] Its barbarism was matched only by that of the Baptists and the Methodists. Even these benighted groups began eventually to improve. In the 1900 edition of *Church Building* Cram confessed that he saw little good Gothic architecture outside of the Episcopal Church. In ten years' time, he discovered that Congregationalists and Unitarians "were beginning, quite clearly, to see the light." And before another decade had passed, he found that "Roman Catholics and Presbyterians . . . demanded, and obtained, the best architecture and the best arts of every kind." [54] Soon Methodists and Baptists were repenting of their ugliness. Cram was delighted that his East Liberty Presbyterian Church in Pittsburgh "could be prepared for a pontifical High Mass" in a few minutes simply by adding

52. *Ibid.*, pp. 96–97.
53. *Church Building*, p. 269.
54. *My Life*, p. 133.

a crucifix and six candles. There was sweet satisfaction in this: "It would have surprised and even horrified Doctors Calvin and Knox in their day, but we are permitted to believe they are better informed now!" [55]

It is possible to overestimate the role of Ralph Adams Cram as a writer and architect in bringing Protestants to a deeper desire for beauty in their churches. The 1920's in this country were a period of developing sophistication and prosperity, with correspondingly greater support of secular art as well as religious. But one cannot deny that Cram's contribution was large. He wrote in 1936: "Fifty years ago none of this beauty would have been imaginable in any branch of Protestantism." [56] Certainly a major reorientation had occurred in the half century of his architectural career. With Cram's death in 1942 and the wartime cessation of church building, the Gothic Revival came to an end, but the demand for good art and architecture on the part of all sections of American Christianity has continued.

III

Von Ogden Vogt, the third leader here considered, links the Gothic Revival to the present day. At first glance, his work seems less directly involved in the Gothic Revival, but his writings combine both an advocacy of historic architecture and an attempt to develop a theology relevant to the concerns of modern man. His earlier writings exhibit the Gothic Revival becoming domesticated among liberal Protestants; his later writings reflect the subsequent rejection of Gothic and the search for a contemporary style with few historic roots.

Vogt, who is now living in retirement in Florida, was born in 1879. Most of his lifetime has been spent in the Midwest, though, after graduating from Beloit College, Vogt attended Yale, where he earned a Master of Arts and also a Bachelor of Divinity degree. He spent five years in Connecticut as minister of a Congregational church and then went to Chicago to be-

55. Ibid., p. 255.
56. Ibid., p. 256.

come pastor of the Wellington Avenue Congregational Church. After nine years at Wellington Avenue he was invited to become pastor of the First Unitarian Church, Chicago. As pastor of this congregation he was responsible for building the magnificent Gothic structure on the edge of the campus of the University of Chicago. During his pastorate there (1925–1944) Vogt was intimately associated with Chicago Theological Seminary, as lecturer in Liturgics, and in Christian Art and Architecture.

In examining Vogt's work, it is well to note his place in the development of Protestant worship and theology. The 1920's were a period of a great deal of church building. Hundreds of congregations erected impressive Gothic or Georgian buildings. In these dignified structures, spontaneous prayers and unstructured services seemed out of place. Numerous books appeared giving the needed instruction in worship. Naturally, few Protestants could accept the Catholic forms of worship which Cram advocated. Much of the new Protestant literature on worship was avowedly liberal in its forms as well as in its theology. One of the products of this interest was the psychological approach to worship, a field explored by such individuals as George A. Coe. Henry Sloan Coffin remarked of this school: "Most of the psychologists were pragmatists in philosophy, and regarded worship as a means of achieving results in those who worshipped." [57] Naturally, others sought to redress this utilitarian tendency and Dean Willard L. Sperry of Harvard Divinity School published his *Reality in Worship: A Study of Public Worship and Private Religion.*[58] This work together with Vogt's *Art & Religion* (1921) and *Modern Worship* (1927) have had as much influence on Protestant worship as any published between 1900 and 1945. The ideas of both books remain current today. Indeed it would be quite difficult to understand the contemporary situation in the worship of American Protestantism without a knowledge of these works. For

57. "Public Worship," *The Church Through Half a Century: Essays in Honor of William Adams Brown,* ed. Samuel McCrea Cavert and Henry Pitney Van Dusen (New York, 1936), p. 191.
58. New York, 1925. Sperry had not read Vogt's *Art & Religion* before writing this book.

present purposes, however, we will limit our attention to Vogt's writings.

Vogt's *Art & Religion* was first published in 1921. Subsequent reprintings in 1929, 1948, and 1960 attest to the continuing popularity of the book. It was followed by *Modern Worship* in 1927, a work both theological and practical. The more theoretical *Cult and Culture,* which appeared in 1952, attempted to find a unifying factor in culture. Vogt's most recent book, *The Primacy of Worship* (1958) opposes worship to dogmatism.

Without exception, Vogt's writings contain a vigorous polemic for liberal theology. On page after page one discovers the hallmark of liberalism, especially in the continuing effort to make religion relevant to modern man. Consequently, there is a rejection of any form of ecclesiastical or theological authority. "We cannot enter the new age," he writes, "until the old churches give up their concepts of an authoritative faith 'once delivered to the saints' and freely accept the spirit of modernism." [59] Vogt's outlook on man's nature is optimistic, the natural man being in his opinion "great in capacity and in natural endowments." Moreover, Vogt believes that "Jesus was so wholly absorbed in his great task of the imitation of God and sonship to God by loving ministry that he put nothing higher. . . . This is the highest conception he held of himself and the highest conception that may be held about him." [60]

For Vogt this belief implies the end of dogmatism. The *Primacy of Worship* contains a vehement chapter on "The Damages of Dogmatism" which Vogt considers guilty of obscurantism, aggression, and duplicity, and repugnant alike to genuine education and to devoted seekers. He concludes that "the way out is to abandon creedalism altogether and undertake the practice of immediate religious experience and action." [61] Theology, Vogt argues, has usurped the place of experience. "The essence of religion," as he sees it, "is a form or pattern of religious experience and action rather than a specific content of

---

59. *Art & Religion* (New Haven, 1921), p. 3. Unless otherwise noted, references are to this edition.
60. *Primacy of Worship* (Boston, 1958), p. 144.
61. *Ibid.,* p. 69.

ideas and usages." [62] From first to last he has contended that "the primary effort of all religion is communion with the Final Powers." [63]

With religion so interpreted, it is not strange that worship is much more important to Vogt than theology. Worship for Vogt becomes the inclusive category. *Modern Worship* begins with the statement: "For the sake of simplicity and clearness I am proposing abruptly to consider worship as the celebration of life." [64] Some idea as to how inclusive the element of celebration (with its overtones of Schleiermacher) becomes is seen in a subsequent statement: "Religion celebrates nothing less than the whole of man's existence and all his faiths about its source, nature, duties, and destiny." [65] Worship is primarily celebration, but Vogt hesitates to try to analyze too precisely the events or ideas which it celebrates. Being very sensitive to the modern man's difficulty in seeking religious belief, he is most reluctant to confuse the "celebration of life" with any specific theological definitions about "the Object of our devotions."

It is not surprising, then, that Vogt advocates the use of modern materials in worship, even a "substitute scripture reading taken from modern sources." The deliberate attempt to make worship relevant to modern life in all its complexities is an outgrowth of his concepts. This appears most strikingly in the series of vocational services which Vogt conducted at the First Unitarian Church, Chicago, during the course of his ministry there. Typical examples include services in honor of teachers, bakers, railroaders, and lawyers. The various orders of worship composed by Vogt featured symbols of the trades or professions involved, a Psalm of Labor, and addresses concerning the group honored.

At the same time, Vogt made constant use of historic materials. He found that it was desirable for ministers to select

62. *Cult and Culture: A Study of Religion and American Culture* (New York, 1951) , p. 223.
63. *Art & Religion* (Boston, 1960) , p. 245.
64. (New Haven, 1927) , p. 3.
65. *Ibid.*, p. 12.

"from the materials of the past those treasures which are least burdened with abandoned concepts." [66] It is noteworthy that the chapter in *Art & Religion* concerning "The Order of the Liturgy" is closer than one might expect to the traditional sequence of Christian worship. The single "Order of Worship" appended to the first edition includes an Introit, a Prayer of Confession, an Anthem of Praise, a Scripture Reading, a Confession of Faith, and a Sermon, as well as hymns and prayers. In Vogt's terms, the normal pattern of worship includes "Vision, Humility, Exaltation, Illumination, Dedication." [67] Of course, many of these elements have undergone a metamorphosis, particularly the confessions of faith. These vary from service to service, sometimes making no mention of God, though stressing a belief "in man, and the worth of all persons."

One sees in Vogt's services and in the patterns which he advocated in *Art & Religion* an openness to historic materials, but a determination to avoid anything offensive to modern man. In the 1948 edition of *Art & Religion* he mentioned that "some of the best new liturgical composition is now being done by the more radical bodies, including several so-called humanist churches." [68] These were not the only ones to share Vogt's ideas. Similar principles soon pervaded the worship of the Methodist Church and many of the larger Protestant bodies which had no fixed liturgical forms.

Perhaps even more influential were Vogt's ideas concerning the architectural setting of worship as advocated in *Art & Religion*. Indeed, no other American book on these subjects rivals this volume in importance. The first edition was introduced with a declaration that "beauty is desirable and good" and that "the religion of Protestantism stands profoundly in need of realizing it." [69] Chapter III, on "The Unity of Religion and Art," points out the similarities between "the experience of Beauty" and "the experience of religion in its essential assumptions or demands in the realms of thinking, feeling, and will-

66. *Modern Worship*, p. 39.
67. *Art & Religion*, p. 152.
68. (Rev. ed.; Boston, 1948) , p. viii.
69. P. ix.

ing." [70] The two were united by "Origin, Subject Matter, and Inner Experience." A further common element was the desire for "a composition that will harmonize all things." As Vogt saw it, art had a need for religion "to universalize its background of concepts" and to improve its "moral content." Religion, on the other hand, needed art in order "to be impressive, to get a hearing." As he expressed it: "The assistance of various arts can be brought to bear upon the worshiper in church in such a way as to help him to be reverent and to display to him the larger cause of religion over against which his own life may be seen to be unsatisfactory." [71]

With such hospitality to the arts, it is interesting to see the forms which art took under Vogt's direction. One of the conditions for his call to the pastorate of the First Unitarian Church of Chicago, several years after the first publication of *Art & Religion,* was that he undertake the erection of a new building. The result was the present impressive edifice, a masonry structure of Gothic design. The building was the gift of Morton Denison Hull. Denison B. Hull was the architect and shared with Vogt the determination of the iconography. It remains an excellent example of the very best of the later Gothic Revival buildings erected by Protestants.

In his writings of the 1920's Vogt indicates the features of Gothic which he found attractive. His interesting article on "The Art of Ralph Adams Cram" raises questions as to how the Gothic Revival could be justified in twentieth-century America. Vogt attempted to answer his questions: "I venture to suggest three lines of consideration along which lie the justifications of this movement: the cultural contribution of Gothic, the plasticity of work on the Gothic base, and the intimation of new catholicity in Mr. Cram's own most recent work." [72] In 1929 he was more outspoken:

Work in the Gothic mode has become predominant. It has two important justifications. As a people, we are aware of our inheritance

70. *Ibid.,* p. 23.
71. *Ibid.,* p. 53.
72. Originally published in *Arts and Decoration,* June, 1926. Quotation from typescript copy furnished by Vogt.

from the Greco-Roman world through the classical character of the most of our civil buildings. But we have not yet so appropriated our proper share in the thousand years of western culture from the fall of Rome to the Italian Renaissance. Gothic buildings enable us to incorporate this also. The other reason is that a Gothic structure emphasizes primarily religion itself rather than ideas about it or ethics that flow from it. There is ample evidence in the most recent developments of the pictorial and plastic arts in churches, that they may intimate new theologies and new ethics caught up into and enlivened by the abiding psychological forms of the religious experience realized in a great building of the Gothic lineage.[73]

As originally written, *Art & Religion* had expressed some reservations about the adaptability of Gothic design. The use of Gothic by those churches which refused to "revive also at least some important elements of mediaeval worship" Vogt considered unfortunate, and on the other hand he saw that Gothic suffered from its too close association with the Episcopal Church a "sectarian lineage . . . inadequate for the new age." [74] If these faults could be overcome, Gothic would be most appropriate; otherwise Colonial would be more suitable. The buildings which illustrate the early editions of *Art & Religion* are both Gothic and Colonial. At the same time Vogt looks forward to the development of a "new architecture."

One of the most interesting developments of the later Gothic Revival in the various Protestant churches was the conscious attempt to use a historic style and yet to make it relevant to the conditions of modern life. In Vogt's church in Chicago, a row of symbols around the nave represents various occupations in industry, commerce, and agriculture. Representations of nature, the state, and the church appear about the chancel. The various emblems representing "man's vocations are to teach the ethics of productivity, the mutuality of human toil, the social point of view for every man's labor, and to recognize the social worth of every man's daily work." [75] Vogt felt that such recognition was doubly needed in an age of mass production in industry.

73. *Art & Religion* (New Haven, 1929), pp. x–xi.
74. P. 200 (1921).
75. *Ibid.*, p. ix (1948).

Despite the introduction of novel subjects into religious symbolism, Vogt pointed out that "culture is a continuum" and that the churches must guard against being "cut adrift from the inestimable treasures of devotion that are our Christian inheritance." [76] One sees in a large number of churches built during the 1920's and 1930's a deliberate effort to develop a symbolism which was both relevant to modern man and yet reflected "our Christian inheritance." At the University of Chicago Chapel (1928) the traditional Christian saints were joined by symbolic figures representing the Artist, Philosopher, Statesman, Scientist, Merchant, Craftsman, and others. A Committee on Iconography at Riverside Church (1930) carried this concept of vocation even further in sculpture and stained glass. Chancel screen, portals, and windows unite Charles Darwin, Albert Einstein, Matthew Arnold, John Ruskin, Booker T. Washington, and countless others whose influence on modern life has been great. They are accompanied by biblical figures, Greek philosophers, and figures as varied as Mohammed, St. Thomas Aquinas, and John Calvin. Less impressive buildings introduced equally varied figures, particularly those representing different occupations. It was a gesture at once appreciative of the past and eager to relate the life of the Church to contemporary man.

It might seem that a medieval style such as Gothic would appear totally irrelevant to twentieth-century American Protestantism. But this was not the case. Indeed, Vogt's favor for the medieval arrangement with full chancel was apparent in 1927 when he wrote: "The possibilities of helpful worship are much increased by the adoption of the traditional chancel plan of building, where also the choir can be disposed about the altar." [77] His fondness for the chancel rests as much upon its success in creating "an atmosphere of worship" as upon its liturgical function. The neo-medieval or divided chancel arrangement has since become the most common one in many large denominations.

76. *Ibid.*, p. 127 (1921).
77. *Modern Worship*, p. 116.

A major reason for the appeal of Gothic seemed to be its emotive powers. Gothic attracted Vogt because of its subjective elements much more than its operation in the actions of liturgy. Vogt cherished Gothic for its mystical intimations which, he felt, elevated unchanging processes of worship above less stable structures of belief. He wrote: "The intimations of Gothic building, then, are not chiefly intellectual . . . but emotional and mystical. . . . The high vaulted aisles . . . lead the imagination to find some communion with the infinite unknown." [78] Such interpretations of Gothic made it acceptable to Protestants of every denomination.

The domestication of Gothic architecture among Protestants occasioned some harsh criticisms. Cram, the acknowledged high priest of the later Gothic Revival, wrote Vogt a long letter after reading *Art & Religion*. He found much to praise in the book, but Cram could not help reflecting upon a basic difference between his theology and Vogt's:

What you are trying to do, I think, is just this, i.e. get back all the richness and beauty and symbolic content of a Gothic church with nothing of the informing force that made it live. That is to say, you would get back the richness of ceremonial, the opulence of the old liturgies and the poignant devotions but without the very things they were developed to expound, express and enforce, i.e. the Real Presence of God in the Blessed Sacrament, the Sacrifice of the Mass and the intercession and communion of saints with the Mother of God as chiefest of these, and veritably, Queen of Heaven.

. . . .

A book like yours will do . . . good, and every step along the way you have indicated is so much clear gain, but the end is the Catholic Faith, not the plenitude of Catholic worship without the Faith.[79]

Here are two distinct theological positions. For Cram "Catholic plenitude" includes particular beliefs; for Vogt it simply means full devotion to the ultimate reality, however defined. Architectually, though, both parties sponsored buildings remarkably similar.

Cram and the Gothic Revival both died in the 1940's. Vogt had long ago predicted the advent of a "new architecture." In

78. *Art & Religion*, p. 189.
79. Letter from R. A. Cram to Von Ogden Vogt, from Seville, April 3, 1922.

the 1920's he felt it would be connected with the past but would be "freshly saying what we newly experience and feel about life." [80] In 1948 Vogt noticed that the central pulpit had become almost a thing of the past in new churches. The illustrations of the 1948 edition of *Art & Religion* recognize the new architecture with several examples. Full recognition of the modern movement in architecture appears in the long Epilogue added to the 1960 edition of *Art & Religion*. Vogt finds himself inclined to agree with the current criticism of the "recent revival period" but points out in its defense that "it came before the means of new design were available; it rescued us from the dreadful chaos which just preceded it; and it affords us a visible connection with the best of the past not otherwise realized." [81] Nevertheless, he enthusiastically accepts the modern movement, listing some outstanding examples and illustrating others.

Though the Gothic Revival may be a thing of the past, much more of it lives on in contemporary Christianity than may be apparent at first glance. With few exceptions, most contemporary churches have adopted the neo-medieval arrangement of the chancel containing altar and choir stalls, divided from the nave where the congregation worships.

Much more significant is the persistent tendency to evaluate buildings on a subjective basis whatever the style. This is reflected in the constant concern for emotive effect, so frequently referred to as creating a "worshipful atmosphere." Worship, in this sense, is largely an individualistic and subjective matter conducted within the privacy of one's soul. Unfortunately, this viewpoint often overlooks the more fundamental actions of the Christian community in common worship.

The Gothic Revival is a thing of the past. And yet the same subjective approach to church architecture which it expressed so successfully is very much present. Only the future can tell how permanently established this attitude will become as a part of American Christianity.

80. *Art & Religion,* p. 201.
81. P. 243.